Women Encounter Technology

This collection of essays explores the effects of information technology on women's employment and the nature of women's work in the third world. Contributors discuss the challenges faced by women, along with their responses and organizing strategies, as they adjust to new technologies in less affluent communities. Also outlined are the roles that family, ideology, state policies and trade union structures can play in distributing information technology-related employment among women and men. Particular chapters highlight differences in the interests and needs of different groups of women, challenging the concept of a monolithic, specifically feminine vision of technology and science. The book provides a critique of postmodernism and ecofeminism and suggests ways in which modern technologies could promote gender equality in the developing world.

In looking at the impact of information technology on the working lives of women in the third world, this volume begins to redress the imbalance in the literature, which has so far tended to focus mainly on the experiences of first world countries. Presenting fresh research from leading academics around the world, *Women Encounter Technology* lays a vital foundation for further debate and research in this important area.

Swasti Mitter is the Deputy Director of the United Nations University Institute for New Technologies (UNU/INTECH), Maastricht, the Netherlands, and holds the Chair of Gender and Technology Studies at the University of Brighton, UK. **Sheila Rowbotham** has written extensively on women in history and the contemporary position of women. She is a Research Fellow in the Department of Sociology, University of Manchester and an Honorary Fellow in Women's Studies at the University of North London.

UNU/INTECH Studies in New Technology and Development

Series editors: Charles Cooper and Swasti Mitter

The books in this series reflect the research initiatives at the United Nations University Institute for New Technologies (UNU/INTECH) based in Maastricht, the Netherlands. This institute is primarily a research centre within the UN system, and evaluates the social, political and economic environment in which new technologies are adopted and adapted in the developing world. The books in the series explore the role that technology policies can play in bridging the economic gaps between nations, as well as between groups within nations. The authors and contributors are leading scholars in the field of technology and development; their work focuses on:

- the social and economic implications of new technologies;
- processes of diffusion of such technologies to the developing world;
- the impact of such technologies on income, employment and environment;
- the political dynamics of technology transfer.

The series is a pioneering attempt at placing technology policies at the heart of national and international strategies for development. This is likely to prove crucial in the globalized market, for the competitiveness and sustainable growth of poorer nations.

1 Women Encounter Technology
Changing Patterns of Employment in the Third World
Edited by Swasti Mitter and Sheila Rowbotham

2 In Pursuit of Science and Technology in Sub-Saharan Africa
J.L. Enos

3 Politics of Technology in Latin America
Edited by Maria Inês Bastos and Charles M. Cooper

4 Exporting Africa
Technology, Trade and Industrialization in Sub-Saharan Africa
Edited by Samuel M. Wangwe

Women Encounter Technology

Changing Patterns of Employment in the Third World

Edited by Swasti Mitter and
Sheila Rowbotham

London and New York

Published in association with the UNU Press

First published 1995
by Routledge
11 New Fetter Lane, London EC4P 4EE

Simultaneously published in the USA and Canada
by Routledge
29 West 35th Street, New York, NY 10001

First published in paperback 1997

Typeset in Times by LaserScript, Mitcham, Surrey
Printed and bound in Great Britain by
Mackays of Chatham PLC, Chatham, Kent

British Library Cataloguing in Publication Data
A catalogue record for this book is available from the British Library

Library of Congress Cataloging in Publication Data
Women encounter technology: changing patterns of employment
   in the third world/edited by Swasti Mitter and Sheila Rowbotham.
   p. cm. – (UNU/INTECH)
   Includes bibliographical references.
   ISBN 0–415–12687–8
   1. Women – Employment – Effect of technological innovations on
   – Developing countries. 2. Information technology – Developing
   countries. I. Mitter, Swasti, 1939–   . II. Rowbotham, Sheila.
   III. Series: UNU/INTECH studies in new technology and development.
   HD6223.W654   1995
   331.4′09172′4 – dc20   95-7345

ISSN 1359–7922
ISBN 0–415–12687–8 (hbk)
ISBN 0–415–14118–4 (pbk)

To Will, Rana, Pamina and Partha, with love.

Contents

Figures

Tables

Contributors

Liliana Acero (Ph.D. Sussex, UK, 1982), is Director of CIS (Centro de Investigaciones Sociales) in Argentina. The CIS studies the role of women and gender in various social spheres. She has edited or written several articles and books in women's studies. Her current research examines the social effects of environmental changes in the aluminium industry in Brazil. Her contribution to this anthology was prepared while serving as an Associate Professor and Tinker-Lampadia research fellow in the Sociology Departments of the University of Massachusetts and Brown University, USA.

Fatma Alloo is an activist and journalist who has worked with a number of newspapers and radio stations in England, Tanzania, and Uganda, as well as being associated with the Women's Global Network on Reproductive Rights and coordinating the Aiding Villages in Development programme in Zanzibar. She was a founder member of the South-South forum in Geneva and has served on the production teams of several international magazines. She is at present Chairperson of the Tanzania Media Women's Association, as well as serving on a number of development bodies.

Nirmala Banerjee is Professor of Economics at the Centre for Studies in Social Sciences, Calcutta. Previously, she worked as an urban planner, and she retains an interest in the urban economy and industrialization. Her research focuses on the analysis of women's issues, particularly women's work experience. She is deeply involved in the women's movement in India.

Maja Bučar graduated from the Faculty of Economics in Ljubljana in 1980. Her Master's dissertation on 'Women's employment in the restructuring of global industry' was completed in 1985. The following year she was visiting Research Fellow at Boston University. She is currently Senior

Research Fellow and Director at the Centre for International Cooperation and Development in Ljubljana. She has published a number of articles on international economics and new technologies.

Fatima Gaio is a Senior Lecturer in production engineering and development economics at the Federal University of Rio de Janeiro. Her recent research interests include: the development of software activities and export opportunities in newly industrializing economies; the diffusion of emerging organizational and information technologies, and their social impact; and the gender structure of employment.

Charlene Gannagé is an Associate Professor in the Department of Sociology and Anthropology at the University of Windsor, Ontario, Canada. She received her Ph.D. from the University of Toronto in 1984. She is author of *Double Day, Double Bind: Women Garment Workers* (Women's Press, 1986), and co-editor of *Working People and Hard Times: Canadian Perspectives* (Garamond Press, 1987). She teaches in the areas of labour studies and women's studies.

Sujata Gothoskar is currently attached to the Workers' Solidarity Centre in Bombay, India. She has also worked with women's campaign groups on diverse issues, and has been involved in research for unions and training for non-governmental organizations. She writes regularly for newspapers and journals in India, the Women's Feature Service, and the *Asian Labour Update*.

Ursula Huws divides her time between lecturing in the School of Policy Studies, Politics and Social Research at the University of North London, freelance writing and lecturing, and managing Analytica, the economic and social research consultancy of which she is the director. She has published numerous reports and articles on various aspects of work, technology and gender relations and has acted as a consultant to the European Commission, the International Labour Organization, the World Health Organization and a variety of national and local government departments, NGOs, companies and trade unions.

Pavla Jezkova is an economist with a working experience in developing countries in Africa and Asia. At the time of writing she was a staff member of UNIDO, working in the area of integrating human resources issues in general, and gender issues in particular, into industry-related policy analysis and research. She is presently working as a freelance consultant in Southern Africa.

Swasti Mitter was born in West Bengal, India, and educated at Calcutta University, the London School of Economics and Cambridge University. She is the Deputy Director of the United Nations University Institute for New Technologies (UNU\INTECH) in Maastricht, the Netherlands. At UNU\INTECH she coordinates the research programme on gender, technology and development. She simultaneously holds the chair of gender and technology studies at Brighton University, UK. She has written on the areas of women and industrialization as a consultant for a wide range of international agencies, including the European Commission, ESCAP, ILO, UNDP, UNIFEM, and UNIDO. Her books include *Common Fate, Common Bond: Women in the Global Economy* (1986), *Computer-aided Manu- facturing and Women's Employment* (1992) and, with Sheila Rowbotham, *Dignity and Daily Bread: New Forms of Economic Organisation Among Poor Women in the Third World and the First* (1994, Routledge).

Cecilia Ng Choon Sim teaches Gender and Development Studies at Universiti Pertanian Malaysia, where she is an Associate Professor. Her present research and writings focus on technological change and gender relations in the service and industrial sectors. She is currently seconded as a Research Fellow to the United Nations University Institute for New Technologies in the Netherlands. Cecilia is also active in the women's movement in Malaysia.

Mayuri Odedra-Straub completed her Ph.D. at the London School of Economics on 'The Transfer of IT to Developing Countries' in 1990. Since then she has worked as a consultant with the Commonwealth Secretariat in London, as editor of *PC World Africa*, and as a lecturer in Information Systems at the National University of Singapore. She is currently working as an independent consultant in Germany.

Ruth Pearson is Senior Lecturer in Economics at the School of Development Studies, University of East Anglia, Norwich, UK. She has researched and written widely on industrialisation and women's employment, particularly in Latin America, the Caribbean and Europe. Her recent work has focused on new information technology and the internationalization of service sector employment. She is also director of a graduate teaching programme in Gender Analysis and Development, and is engaged in research and consultancy on reproductive technologies, macroeconomic change and household responses.

Sheila Rowbotham has a background in economic and labour history and is the author of several books, including *Women, Resistance and*

Revolution (1972), *Woman's Consciousness, Man's World* (1973) and *Women in Movement: Feminism and Social Action* (1993, Routledge). She has been active in labour organizing and the women's movement for many years. Her interest in economic development and global labour links grew out of her work at the Economic Policy Unit of the Greater London Council, 1983–6. She has worked as a consultant research adviser to the Women's Programme at the World Institute for Development Economics Research (WIDER UNU), and has held research fellowships at Birkbeck College, London University, and Manchester University, UK. She is Research Fellow in the Department of Sociology of the University of Manchester.

Carol Yong is a freelance researcher, and has worked on a range of issues concerning women and rural indigenous communities. She now works in Sarawak with the Institute for Community Education.

Acknowledgements

We should like to acknowledge a number of debts. First of all to Judy Wajcman whose book *Feminism Confronts Technology* (1991) inspired the title of our own. We wanted to pay homage to her contribution and, at the same time, wished to highlight our differences. The essays in this book bear testimony to the fact that the relationship between women and technology is not always, or necessarily, confrontational.

We are immensely grateful to our contributors who, in the midst of their many other professional commitments, produced on time the papers for the workshop 'Information Technology and Women's Employment'. The papers submitted for the workshop, which took place on 26–29 April 1993, were subsequently edited to provide the material for this book.

Professor Peter Dronke of Cambridge University generously spared his time to go through most of the papers and gave suggestions as to how to avoid making too many alterations to the writing of the non-English-speaking contributors, in order to retain their individual style as well as clarity.

Jane Williams, of UNU/INTECH, has made a significant contribution to the book by liaising with the contributors on the one hand and with the publisher on the other. Without her shared excitement, we could not have completed the editing work so swiftly.

We also take this opportunity to thank Sen McGlinn for his superb copy-editing. His commitment to perfection, in the case of language as well as in the citation of references and tables, has made it possible for the publisher to meet the deadline without agony.

Professor Charles Cooper, Director of UNU/INTECH, has been a pillar of strength in lending us all possible encouragement and financial support for reducing the labour involved in preparing the manuscript. It was heartening to know that he shared our conviction that a gender focus was essential for formulating appropriate technology policies.

Some of my other colleagues, inside and outside the Institute, likewise deserve a special mention. Dr Renée Pittin, of the Institute of Social Studies at the Hague, gave valuable comments on the papers as a discussant at the workshop. Rohini Banaji offered useful reflections on the Slovenian paper. The paper was read by Miriam Pandel in the absence of Maja Bučar, who could not travel to Maastricht at the last stage of her pregnancy. We are grateful to Anneke van Luijken of IRENE (International Restructuring Education Network Europe), who provided a critique of the paper by Cecilia Ng and Carol Yong. Irene Santiago, from UNIFEM, New York, provided her expertise and advice in shaping the book. As a discussant, Hedva Sarfati, from the International Labour Organisation, Geneva, lent ILO's own perspective on women's opportunities in new white collar employment in less developed countries. Dr Ludovico Alcorta and Dr Maria-Ines Bastos of UNU/INTECH commented on some of the papers. Professor Gu Shulin of UNU/INTECH suggested ways of taking the work forward in China.

Finally, Swasti is grateful to Rana, Pamina and Partha for providing her with a home environment where the limits of postmodernism in the study of technology are discussed with just as much gusto as the next evening meal; Sheila is more evasively relieved that the case for or against 'pomoism' has not yet crossed her threshold.

1 Beyond the politics of difference
An introduction

Swasti Mitter

It is not that there is a lack of thinking and writing about the impact of information technology on women's working lives. Indeed, there has been a plethora of literature in this field, especially since the mid-1980s. The literature, however, reflected a certain class and regional bias, as it focused mainly on office work and almost exclusively on the experiences of first world countries.[1] In the last decade, in my professional capacity, I have attended and contributed to a large number of workshops and seminars, in Europe and in the United States, on the subject of women and IT. In the discussion and formulation of areas of concern, I invariably felt dismayed at the lack of voice of third world women, and at the lack of an authentically international perspective. I noted a shift in the mood of academic gatherings in the 1980s – reflecting contemporary obsessions with nationhood, and with tradition and identity. In the climate of identity politics, there was, understandably, little chance for recognizing and comparing workers' experiences across cultural boundaries – in spite of the pervasiveness of the information revolution and the globalization of the market economy.

I often thought of taking up the challenge of redressing the balance, of documenting, however roughly, the changing position of women of the third world. In such a venture, I knew I could rely on the research and documentation assembled by some of my friends – friends whom I have collected, like precious pearls, in different phases of my working life. I was, of course, aware of the limitations of such an initiative and the difficulty of encapsulating, in one short-term project, the wide-ranging experiences of the whole third world. Yet I was convinced that only such a bold, and perhaps foolhardy, initiative, would lead to a more systematic and integrated investigation and analysis.

My vision became a reality in 1991, with the support and enthusiasm of two leading feminist scholars: Sheila Rowbotham and Fatima Mernissi. Well known for their work in recovering women from the oblivion of history (Rowbotham, 1992; Mernissi, 1994), it is not surprising that they encouraged my plan to document women's role in, and response to, IT in our time. It is because of their initiative that I received an opportunity to place my project, for consideration, in the research programme of the United Nations University. To my great elation, Lal Jayawardena, who was then the Director of WIDER (World Institute for Development Economics Research), liked my project proposal and passed it on to Professor Charles Cooper, who had just taken up the Directorship of INTECH (Institute for New Technologies) at Maastricht. From 1992, INTECH as an institute, and Charles Cooper as my colleague, gave me unstinting support: in commissioning the papers, in organizing the workshop, and in helping to bear the human and financial cost of editing.

The essays in this anthology, thus, are contributions towards filling a major lacuna in the literature of women's studies and of development economics. They document the impact of information technology on the working lives of women in third world countries. The writings are by thirteen committed academics, and convey more than just empirical observations. They raise questions of women's autonomy and agency and try to articulate women's needs and demands. Challenges that women face in adjusting to the demands of information technology are the focal points of the essays; yet women's responses and organizing strategies when confronted with such challenges equally permeate the arguments and analyses. They alert us to the roles that family, ideology, state policies, and trade union structures play in distributing IT-related employment between women and men.

WHO ARE THE WOMEN OF THE THIRD WORLD?

The essays focus mainly, but by no means exclusively, on the third world. Indeed, over the years, the definition of 'different' worlds itself has become somehow elusive and contentious. With the rising economic power of countries such as Japan, it becomes difficult to include all affluent countries even under the oft-used blanket category of western nations. Likewise, the entry of the east European countries into the category of developing nations poses definitional problems. Whether these countries of eastern Europe, previously described as the second world, would now like to be seen as parts of the third is far from clear. Terms such as 'economies in transition' are makeshift jargon, to designate precisely those countries which are uncertain about their status and alliances. In any case, given the hybrid nature of the cultural identity and consciousness of peoples in most societies (Bhaba, 1994), it is prudent to stay clear of an exclusive and binary categorization. The effects of postcolonial migration, and the rise of underprivileged migrant communities in the so-called 'first world', give yet another reason to remember the interconnections between different national economies and regional blocs. In this anthology, the term 'third world' refers simply, and admittedly roughly, to non-affluent communities and nations. In this extended sense it includes the ex-socialist countries of eastern Europe, as well as immigrant groups residing in technologically and economically developed nations.

The anthology does not exclude consideration of the experiences of women from richer countries on strategic grounds. The success and failure of women in having their voices heard in rich countries provide a valuable point of reference for women of the third world. Gender – or the social construction of the role of women – is only one of many factors which determine the impact of information technology on a worker's life; ethnicity, religion, age and class, in some cases, play even greater roles in defining one's position in the world of work.

By highlighting the differences in the interests and needs of different groups of women, the anthology challenges the validity of any monolithic, specifically feminine vision of technology and science. The contributions in this volume, independently of one another, affirm the view that, instead of demanding an essentialist, ahistoric, universal, woman-friendly technology, it will be more rewarding to study, in the context of the current technological revolution, the needs and experiences of groups of women in different societies. Women, even in a single society, do not form a homogeneous group. In their dual role as mothers and workers, however, the majority of women do face certain common difficulties. Women's access to and control over childcare and reproductive technology, understandably, determines their ability to share the benefits of IT. Women's entry into the world of new tech urban employment in turn augments, as the essays highlight, their social power and control over their fertility.

ACCOUNTING FOR WOMEN'S POSITION IN INFORMATION TECHNOLOGY

It is precisely in the context of women's autonomy and choice in poorer countries and in less affluent communities that it is now pertinent to focus on the impact of information technology on employment opportunities. In doing so, it is important to bear in mind the distinctive features of the current revolution in the mode of production, which is primarily knowledge-intensive. IT comprises a set of technologies that actively process information rather than merely storing or transmitting it. Computers, the key hardware, and non-material software systems form its essential core.

The convergence of computing, telecommunication and satellite technology in recent years alters the structure of work not only in the economies that are at the centre of Research and Development in this field, but also in countries that primarily adapt and adopt these technologies for market orientation. Even in nations which are in economic terms relatively poor, IT substantially changes the traditional production process as well as the marketable goods and services produced. The demand for components of IT-related hardware – such as microchips – or for information-processing activities – such as data entry or software programming – creates new areas for employment in developing countries. In addition, the telecommunication revolution, which allows companies to shift parts of their manufacturing and service production to geographically distant locations, makes it possible for low-wage countries to receive some amount of labour-intensive relocated work from the first world countries. The evolving international division of labour now encompasses a vast range: from the production of semiconductors or telecommunications equipment to service-related software programming and data entry.

In this scenario, it has not been easy to ascertain whether women, in aggregate terms, have benefited from the information revolution or lost out. In some spheres, women, especially older women, are now threatened with imminent technological redundancies, especially in manufacturing. The skills needed for traditional labour-intensive assembly-line work have given way to new requirements for polyvalent, cognitive skills. The spread of information processing work, especially in banking, finance or telecommunication, by contrast, has opened up new opportunities for women who are computer-literate and young enough to learn newer skills. In the sphere of self-employment, information technology, as the contributions in the volume show, heralds new possibilities for women and men; yet women, more than men, fail to achieve their potential because of their lack of access to business and marketing skills.

Against this background of contradictory trends, it is futile to formulate a generalized strategy for giving women access to education and training. The opportunities and barriers that women face in gaining appropriate skills depend too much on the historical specificity of the situation and on their class backgrounds for this to be possible. As it is important to have a clear vision of the commonality and differences in the interests of different groups of women, it is equally strategic to move beyond an ahistoric, and thus simplistic notion of an unchanging women's response to technology. The empirical work in the anthology, in order to avoid such an approach, is deliberately presented in a historical perspective: of women's entry into and exit from the invention, application and management of technology in different periods.

By charting the contributions of women who have been obliterated from history, Sheila Rowbotham argues in her paper that:

> Rather than viewing history in terms of an undifferentiated structure of patriarchy, it is possible to see women emerging intellectually in some periods and forced into retreat in others . . . examination(s) of both the barriers which have prevented women from gaining access and the circumstances which have made it possible for women to . . . contribute to technology . . . have a significant and direct relevance to the contemporary position of women.

Indeed, it is not that women did not play any role in the development of information technology. But their contributions have been forgotten or obliterated from history because women, as a group, have remained invisible in the public domain of commercial decisions and vocational training. The marginalization of Rosalind Franklin's role in the discovery of DNA, the key concept of biotechnology, highlights the difficulty even extremely privileged women face in gaining recognition, even in recent times (Rose, 1994: 150-153). The picture that emerges out of the papers in this anthology is clear. Women's role in the formulation and construction of technology is best understood not in terms of their essential differences from men but in terms of material conditions that include them in the market and institutions, or preclude them from these. As I claim in my own paper in this anthology:

> The technological innovations become commercially successful if and when the creator of the innovation could make use of political, economic and legal networks. Thus the dominant group in a society determines the shape and direction of a society's techno-economic order – and the image of an inventor has almost always been male.

IT AND THE WORLD OF WORK: MANUFACTURING AND SERVICES SECTORS

The employment implications of IT assume a special importance in the context of an uneven distribution of economic and political power. In the past, women's limited access to paid employment and corporate networks has led to a bias in the adoption of technology and to a differential impact on women and men.

It is important at this point to explore why the subject of women and IT has received so little attention in recent research and literature. The reason can hardly be the lack of relevance of computers to women of the developing world. In urban areas of the majority of countries, the use of computers is no longer a novel phenomenon, even among less privileged women of poorer nations.

The case study of TAMWA (Tanzania Media Women's Association), as documented by Fatma Alloo in this anthology, demonstrates how IT could enhance the power of journalists and media people to disseminate news and views for educating and for mobilizing a wide range of non-elite women. The effective use of desktop publishing and printing work augments TAMWA's income generating activities. TAMWA does not have to be at the cutting edge of technology. Reasonably cheap, and by western standards old, computers allow TAMWA to be effective in networking and to remain sustainable in the long run. As Fatma Alloo so passionately asserts:

> The fact that we can produce so-called 'first world' quality in spite of being a so-called 'third world' group has been an empowering process. . . . [It has led to] the demystification of information technology for that class which needs it the most in order to have their voices heard. . . . For example, we produce brochures on the laws which affect women's lives, written in a simplified Kiswahili, with visuals and big letters for the new literates in Tanzania. Information technology can be used to destroy [Africa's] 'poor and powerless' myth, and to mobilize a community for empowerment and social change.

The current research and documentation are not extensive enough to make possible a quantitative estimate of the impact of IT on women's manufacturing employment in the developing world. The sectoral and country studies, as documented here, merely give a 'bird's-eye view' of the fundamental transformation that IT is generating in the production process of some developing countries.

Argentina and Brazil – two major Latin American countries – have been in the forefront of the adoption of new technologies in sectors such as textiles, which provided a major source of employment to women. On the basis of extensive interviews and published data, Liliana Acero constructs the way in which women are responding to a new industrial culture – where companies are automating not just to save labour costs, but also to obtain higher efficiency and flexibility in order to meet international quality standards. Her paper delineates the demands women themselves are making in relation to the formal and informal training system that companies and the state are providing for workers.

Acero highlights the complex way in which technological changes affect the quality and quantity of women's work. In some ways, she agrees with Braverman's 'degradation of work' hypothesis, which postulates that advances in technology essentially lead to deskilling and feminization of work. Yet her paper points also to a contradictory trend: the new production process increasingly demands technical and managerial expertise and poly-valent skills for core occupations. Acero's work highlights the factors, social and educational, that bar women from the opportunities to upgrade their skills, so as to have access to these core jobs. Her observations on women's status and role at work and at home stress the need to have a deeper insight into the links between private and public domains in workers' lives. New technology, in reducing the skill components of assembly-line jobs, makes these more accessible to women. Increased job opportunities, however, bring new tensions in workers' domestic lives. Acero documents the life of a typical woman textile worker in Argentina: 'My marriage started to break down when I started work. . . . I had more chances than he did. So things started going wrong.' The evolving situation in the household poses special challenges to women who take time off in order to organize around their workplace demands, or who take initiatives in family planning. The relative shift of power, nonetheless, as Acero shows, has contributed to some autonomy for women and extended work and training possibilities.

Pavla Jezkova's paper in this anthology complements Liliana Acero's documentation of Latin America. The adoption of computer technology in textiles, in countries such as Thailand, Indonesia and Bangladesh, has been less extensive and more recent than in Brazil and Argentina. The dis-placement of women in response to new technology has thus been less marked than in Latin America. In fact, large numbers of women have entered the garments sector of the textiles industry, where the use of new technology is becoming more extensive. Export-oriented industrialization and foreign direct investment – vehicles of technology transfer – have opened up new opportunities to women. Women, however, are rarely represented in the decision-making areas and are predominant only in blue-collar jobs. In the next phase of technological change these are pre-cisely the jobs that will be vulnerable. Jezkova, in the context of shifts in the world trading order, thus gives reasons and methods for more effective state policies in order to ensure and to improve women's position in industrial employment.

Upgrading women's skills through a continuous learning process bene-fits women and the countries involved. Jezkova confirms observations that I have made in my own paper, that highly-skilled women workers are a good selling point for countries to attract direct foreign investment. In an economic environment where achieving international competitiveness through foreign collaboration is considered a high priority, women's education and training for new technology production jobs assume special importance. In the training programme, as Jezkova points out, it is crucial to give women access to 'soft' and transferable business skills that allow them to cope with the dictates of the market and of technology.

The nature and direction of IT is shaped essentially by a country's geopolitical environment, which includes its alliance to specific trading blocs. But, even within a country, the impact of technology is never uniform. The response and the speed of adjustment to IT depend much on a worker's group identity and her social position.

Charlene Gannagé's paper in this anthology elucidates this point. Gannagé's analytical categories go beyond the usual Marxist feminist categories of class and of gender. She stresses instead the need to combine class, gender and ethnicity simultaneously in understanding the changing labour process in our postcolonial time. The paper elucidates the way information technology, in tandem with trading alliances and new corporate strategies, alters the job opportunities and career structure of immigrant women in a society such as Canada. The technology has not simply replaced labour, it has also led to a polarization in skills and to decentralization of work to home-based workers. Charlene Gannagé's observations thus call for a government policy and union strategies towards education and training programmes that are anti-racist and feminist, and that take account explicitly of the specific needs of immigrant workers.

In a discussion of identity and difference – personal or national – the access to and control of IT have a special meaning. The degrees of exclusion that arise from the information revolution sharply differentiate individuals, regions and communities. Women of the east European countries provide a striking illustration of this. With the phasing out of socialism and moves towards a market economy, the economies of these countries are going through a period of restructuring and reorientation. The inflow of foreign direct investment in this new scenario is viewed as the main vehicle of technology transfer. The state-owned manufacturing companies rationalize their politics in terms of success in wooing international investment. In the context of Slovenia, Maja Bučar elucidates the impact of such a process on the gender structure of employment.

Overall, in the transitional phase of Slovenia, the adoption of IT has been relatively small and the preparatory rationalization process has not affected women's share of employment, at least in manufacturing jobs. This could be the result of generous employment protection legislation in

Slovenia, a legacy of socialism. It could also, as she reflects, be because women are more willing than men to accept lower wages and greater loss of autonomy: these are now, increasingly, features of the economic restructuring. At this historical juncture, she points out, women's organizations in Slovenia need to be in close contact with their counterparts in the non-European world in order to counteract the negative aspects of the coming technological revolution. In Slovenia there are no vigorous unions or popular movements to monitor the effects of technology on the structure and conditions of work.

In developing countries, information technology alters the pattern of production even in the non-formal sector, characterized by unregistered firms that do not disclose their production and income. The subterranean or 'do-it-yourself' economy contributes significantly to the total product in certain sectors, and it recruits women in large numbers, especially in assembly-line work. Nirmala Banerjee, in her paper, unravels a fascinating picture of this hitherto undocumented side of computer-related production. In Calcutta, a city with an exceedingly high rate of unemployment, poor infrastructure and an exorbitant state-government levy on consumer electronic goods, illicit units are enjoying a boom, producing black and white television sets or cassette players – lookalikes for famous brands – for the 'dowry' of the clients' daughters. Most of the components are imported, and local women from specific communities are hired on a temporary basis, mainly to do the simple, repetitive, assembling operation. Such women come from poor families, often not even with primary education, but on the job, in a crowded space, women 'become familiar with the men's skills and feel confident they too could mend a television set or even assemble a full one'. The tacit skill potentially presents them with an opportunity for upward mobility, for setting themselves up as entrepreneurs. Yet, as the paper shows, for women, and not for men, 'it is important to have some formal qualification, which they do not possess', in order to be able to convince customers of their expertise in this area.

Banerjee's documentation of pluralism in the process of technology diffusion fits well with the postmodernist vision of everything in constant flux. Hybridity and 'in-betweenness' permeate the industrial culture of the problem-ridden city of Calcutta. Thus, in a Japanese joint venture producing micro-motors outside Calcutta, young girls, aged around 19 or 20, from conservative backgrounds, practise Japanese Ikebana (early morning physical exercise) on Bengali soil. Women find it embarrassing, and yet they are willing to undergo any discipline in order to keep a job. As Banerjee observes: 'The only thing they were worried about was the possibility of the plant closing down, and whether the skills that they had acquired would be adequate to get another job.' In the midst of such diverse modes of production of electronic goods and services, it is class bias in education and training, as Banerjee points out, that presents a real bottleneck in the expansion of production and employment. Given the institutional rigidities and the expense, it is difficult for women of modest backgrounds to have access to relevant training in electronics and software. In a city beset with unemployment and shortages of skills, to waste the opportunities for growth and employment, she asserts, would be criminal. Radical thinking about training, that takes into account the obstacles that gender and class pose to a trainee, will be essential for utilizing human potential to the full.

The importance of taking a strategic view of women's education is likewise stressed in Mayuri Odedra-Straub's paper. In Sub-Saharan Africa, computer equipment is often not used when it would be advantageous to do so, because of a lack of skilled personnel, poor buying plans and the scarcity of foreign exchange for importing expertise and the necessary software. In this situation, to train women for the IT sector jobs may alleviate some of the problems. But as Odedra-Straub points out, given the social environment and cultural norms, it is extremely difficult for most women in Africa to have access even to primary and secondary education. In her paper, she makes a case for extending general literacy and basic technical education to women before formulating computer literacy programmes. She draws attention to cultural factors that explain why even the most privileged women decide to drop out of the field in Africa, in spite of the fact that 'final year female students perform better than their male counterparts in both the computer hardware and software disciplines.' The question she poses is 'whether "women and information technology in Africa" should be a topic of discussion or not, whether we should first examine other issues concerning women in Africa, or whether Africa needs IT at all'.

The picture that emerges from the service-sector of other developing countries is less pessimistic, albeit uncertain. It neither confirms nor refutes the 'degradation of work' or 'deskilling' hypothesis. In terms of sheer numbers, as the papers by Sujata Gothoskar, and by Cecilia Ng and Carol Yong show, women have made startling gains. Between 1975 and 1988, in the financial sector of India, women's employment increased by more than 300 per cent. This continues a trend which began in the 1950s, in both public sector companies and private foreign-controlled banks.

The situation is similar in Malaysia: the case study of a major tele-communications company by Ng and Yong in this anthology indicates that women have been the major beneficiaries of new computer-related white-collar jobs. Employment opportunities grew at a rapid rate in the eighties in Malaysia, as the government pledged to use science and technology for transforming the country into a 'scientific and progressive' nation. The largest number of jobs have been created in the low-skilled areas – such as data processing, where women predominate numerically. Women's visibility is relatively less pronounced in the area of programming and systems analysis. Significantly, few women who have made it to these higher echelons belong to the indigenous Malay population. Ng and Yong urge us to shift away from an exclusive focus on gender, since that leads to a simplified analysis of the true picture:

> ethnic and class differentials are as important (and sometimes more important) than gender differentials. . . . Feminist theories of work have to consider the complex inter-relationship of the forces contributing to segmentation in employment . . . rather than just focusing on gender *per se.*

Sujata Gothoskar's observations corroborate those of Cecilia Ng and Carol Yong. In the context of her own study of the banking sector in Bombay, she finds that class position bears just as much relevance as gender in determining an employee's opportunities in information processing sectors. A growing polarization by skills, gender, class and ethnicity now characterizes the structure of information processing jobs in the services sector. It is in this context that women need to formulate their demands *vis-à-vis* technological changes, inside and outside the unions. As Gothoskar's paper shows, the changing forms of employment entail a reduction in the 'non-bargainable' staff – those who are not allowed or encouraged to join unions. As white-collar employees, women, even in low paid areas, find their multiple identity difficult to cope with in a challenging and often insecure employment environment:

> In the union workshops and meetings, we are addressed as union members; in the management training programmes we are bank employees. But all of us are much more than that. We are employees, we are women, we are home-makers, we are thinking and feeling human beings, we are ambitious and much more.

The multi-dimensionality in the identity of a woman worker is the focal point of new organizations which are lobbying around issues such as VDU hazards, flexible contracts, intensification of workloads and discrimination in training and education. Women employees are focusing attention on newer demands. In Malaysia, as Ng and Yong narrate, the hazards of the use of VDUs, especially to women's reproductive health, have not been matters of concern for the male-oriented trade unions. In response, women's groups have taken their own initiatives to bring these issues to public attention and to make them relevant to collective bargaining.

Women's sharing of experiences has proved rewarding at the community and at the national level, but it has also extended beyond the boundaries of nation states. The examples, given by Ng and Yong, in the Malaysian context make Gothoskar's observation in India pertinent:

> In the wake of liberalization and globalization and the changes in Indian banking, they want to know what is happening in the banking and finance sectors in other countries in terms of women's employment and organizing, what the experiences of women in those countries have been and what strategies they have used.

DISEMBODIED TECHNOLOGY: SOFTWARE AND DATA ENTRY WORK

It is not only the application of IT that gives rise to new challenges and opportunities, it is also the production of the core of IT – software programming – that shows novel, and often contradictory, potential. In processing and retrieving information, one needs to get involved in a wide range of activities: from the inputting of primary data (data entry work) to conceptualizing and modelling the software that instructs the processing. This operational side of information technology is often described as 'disembodied' technology, in order to distinguish it from that of machines or 'hardware'.

In her essay in this anthology, Fatima Gaio explores the potential of women's success in the field of software, which is free of a historic gendered division of labour. Using published statistics as well as material from her structured interviews, she highlights women's entry and career progression in the information processing sector of Brazil. The sector encompasses a vast range of activities, from simple data processing to complex tasks related to software. In Brazil, women account for nearly half of the information processing employees, but, significantly, the largest number are found near the base of the employment pyramid. While the majority of the data entry and data processing workers are women, women lag behind men in software development work. Nonetheless, as her figures show, women in this sector have fared far better than in the traditional professional jobs, such as engineering. Women of the third world, in the right circumstances, as she asserts, could look forward in the future to an equitable distribution of jobs in this area. But women's gains are not cost-free. Women who survive in these highly paid jobs, as one of her interviewees remarked, become somewhat 'phallic', 'they compete aggressively like men'.

Fatima Gaio's work challenges the traditional labour process theory as well as some socialist feminist's evaluation of technology, in the context of software development work. The labour process theory, she argues, gives too much attention to the 'hard' side of technical knowledge, which is amenable to deskilling through Taylorism and automation. The approach fails to note the growing importance of the 'soft' side of technical knowledge, such as communication and user-producer interaction, which enables women to achieve economic advancement and greater social power. The declining importance of mainframe computers, she argues, gives a reason also for revising a certain strand of the radical feminist vision of technology, that thinks primarily in terms of 'hard' machines, embodying male dominance and power (Cockburn, 1985). Gaio ends on an optimistic note:

> [Men tend] to be clustered closer to the machinery, where technical expertise associated with mainframes has been assigned a high social prestige. Small processor platforms . . . and activities involving close interaction with users, seem to offer more conducive environments for women. Since the epoch of the powerful centralized mainframes is passing . . . women may well become core agents in the technical and social changes necessary for the further diffusion of information technologies.

Ruth Pearson's paper is less optimistic about the prospects that the disembodied technology presents to women. She is particularly concerned about the working conditions – such as the contractual terms, wages, training, health and safety – of new technology white-collar workers. Data-entry workers are the most vulnerable. This is especially so when women are employed as offshore data processing workers by European or American multinationals. Admittedly such jobs give a measure of economic power and autonomy to women of the third world; but Pearson declines to share the current view, either of the radical economists or of the World Bank, that these jobs create a cost-free, 'win-win' situation.

Her paper particularly draws attention to emerging issues, such as the health hazards which these 'clean' technologies bring to women. Her paper records the difficulties that women and men have faced and are still facing, even in rich countries, in establishing the reality of computer-related diseases, such as Repetitive Strain Injury (RSI), as genuine industrial hazards. Such an injury has few external symptoms, and the attitude, in the medical as well as the official world, is 'if we cannot find it in the body, it must be in the mind'.

The paper stresses the need for an international exchange of experience in organizing around some of the new issues, in order to ensure that women's employment benefits from new technologies are not outweighed by the associated health and environmental costs. The idea is not that all risk-bearing employment for women should be prohibited, but that the health and safety issues should not be totally subordinated to wider concerns of economic growth, employment creation and foreign exchange generation.

POSTMODERNISM: A SHIFT FROM COLLECTIVE TO INDIVIDUAL

Despite the ever-increasing relevance of IT, both to women and to their countries, there has been a conspicuous silence about it in academic literature, mainly, I suspect, on theoretical and ideological grounds. The ascendancy of postmodernism in the discourse of women's studies has led to an unease in the developed world about taking up research that seems to promote internationalism in matters of women's economic empowerment. In our current intellectual climate, women of the third world have become the subject of research in connection with the study of the 'other'; it is the 'difference' rather than the issue of economic liberation that has assumed a central position in academic analysis. Disillusionment with the legacy of the Enlightenment – modernization, modernity and promises of historical progress – has led to a serious questioning by some western academics of the claimed objectivity and rationality of western technology and science. It is not too uncommon in the west now to acknowledge that the assumed 'universal' visions of the Enlightenment – such as progress propelled by modernity and technology – merely reflected the values of interest groups in power, and did not include the voices of marginal groups such as those of non-Europeans and of women. Feminist critiques of Eurocentric 'grand narratives' of the Enlightenment – such as the promises of capitalism, liberalism or rationality – have made a potent contribution to a slow, but gradual, acceptance of plurality in the location of culture and of knowledge systems. Yet, it has not led easily to a modified position for western feminists. The universalizing feminist critique of Enlightenment value has, consciously or unconsciously, overlooked the different needs and experiences of women of non-European origins. Linda J. Nicholson, in *Feminism/Postmodernism*, reflects on this impasse:

> feminist scholars replicated the problematic universalizing tendencies of [general] academic scholarship. . . . Like many other Western scholars,

feminists were not used to acknowledging that the premises from which they were working possessed a specific location.

(Nicholson, 1990: p. 2)

Fear of an inevitable Eurocentric bias in their work has prompted many women academics to hold back from research that deals with the life and work of women with a different heritage.

Responses of women from the 'other' world itself have contributed further to the schism. Gayatri Chakravorty Spivak, in her book *Outside in the Teaching Machine*, voices the anguish and dilemma that postcolonial feminist scholars face in establishing a straightforward alliance. How, she asks:

> does the postcolonial feminist (like myself) negotiate with the metropolitan feminist? I imagine a sympathy with (the Algerian writer) Marie-Aimée Hélie-Lucas's subject position . . . she too is revising her earlier position. As she does so she speaks of solidarity with Islamic women around the world. . . . And I, a non-Islamic Indian postcolonial, use her (the Algerian writer) to revise my reading of French (Western) feminism.

(Spivak 1993: p. 145)

In the developed world, postmodernism and associated cultural theories furnished reasons for not studying the changing material conditions of third world women in response, for example, to information technology and to globalization of finance and production. The trend coincided with the ascendant philosophies of the 1990s, which uphold the market mechanism, self-help and individual entrepreneurship. There is a trend now to shun collective responsibility for vulnerable or marginal groups, even within the boundaries of a nation. The end result has been, as Ursula Huws recounts in her paper:

> it now seems to me that of all the changes which have taken place over the last two decades, perhaps the most important has been the erosion of any belief in the power of collective action, and the slow dawning in each of us of the depressing realization that if we don't do it for ourselves, the chances are that nobody else will do it for us. . . . It wasn't that [interest in] feminist publishing had declined. Far from it. There were shelves and shelves of poetry and fiction, books about sexuality, about race, about health, about housing, about violence, about psychology. It was just that the attention had shifted away from those previously central concerns of economic independence and the study of work, whether paid or unpaid. I tried looking under 'technology' and

found a few collections of essays about women's relationship with technology, but these were heavily outnumbered by 'how to' books about computing. What seemed to have happened was a radical shift of emphasis from the collective to the individual.

ECOFEMINISM AND THE POLITICS OF IDENTITY IN THE DEVELOPING WORLD

There has been some reluctance to discuss the effects of modern technologies on the working lives of women, even among activists and scholars in the developing world. The discussion to them seems irrelevant and unproductive, as the technologies themselves are seen as incorporating values and moulding a future that are harmful to poor nations. The inappropriateness of modern western technologies for the third world is powerfully argued by eco-feminists, such as Vandana Shiva. She challenges the claims of the universality of western *epistémé*: 'Emerging from a dominating and colonizing culture, modern knowledge systems are themselves colonizing' (Shiva, 1993: p. 9). While asserting plurality in the knowledge system, ecofeminists do see the possibility for some common action, shared by women and men of different heritages and backgrounds, but only in drawing up an alternative, community-based economy in opposition to global capitalism. Maria Mies, from Germany, in the same spirit as Vandana Shiva, gives us a vision of this alternative framework, where technology is conceptualized from a perspective of subsistence. This perspective means not only a change in the various accepted social and economic divisions of labour, but also a process of substituting money or commodity relationships by principles such as reciprocity, sharing and caring, and respect for the individual. This subsistence perspective can be realized only within a network of reliable, stable human relations; it is incompatible with the philosophy of the atomized, self-centred individuality of the market economy (Mies and Shiva, 1993: p. 319).

A subsistence perspective demands a shift away from the prevailing instrumentalist, reductionist mode of technology, which, according to eco-feminists, has given rise to and maintained man's domination over nature, women and other peoples. In its place, an ecologically sound, feminist, subsistence science and technology could be developed in participatory action with the people. Such science and technology will not reinforce unequal social relationships and will lead to greater social justice.

As an activist, I admire the inspiring vision of such an ideal society. Yet, as a business economist, I find it difficult to be convinced of its feasibility. For strategic management, I believe, it is incorrect and unsound to set a goal that will lead inevitably to disillusionment. In the visionary ideal of ecofeminism, we are never told how to attain such a utopia without altering the power structure nationally or internationally. For women, for the third world, and for women of the third world, it would be even more difficult to shift the balance of power if they were urged to retreat to indigenous social and knowledge systems, in open opposition to modernization and modern technologies.

As the papers in the anthology demonstrate, women in the third world welcome modernization, as long as they can have some say in the manner in which the technology which is affecting the quality of their working and family lives is adopted. Women usually have insignificant power over decision-making when they are confined by traditions and constrained by the norms of behaviour in their communities. In this anthology, women, understandably, extol the liberating aspect of the information revolution, which, in the right circumstances, has begun to give them economic power, autonomy and the chance to escape the tyrannies of traditional societies. They make concrete demands, such as knowledge of and access to technical know-how and business skills; they welcome an international exchange of experience of organizing, inside and outside trade unions, to counteract the hazards of new technologies.

The critics of modernization, significantly, are themselves products of Enlightenment education and philosophy. Some caution is thus necessary, so that their voice does not muffle the appeals and aspirations of many millions of less privileged women and men, who are 'hungry' for the information revolution and advanced technologies. The word defines the world, and the term 'alternative', which the critics of modernization have so often used to describe their own position or vision, perpetuates, rather than questions, the notion of their own marginality. As Suniti Namjoshi's allegory, 'Dusty Distance' (1990, pp. 196-197), brilliantly suggests, the language of 'difference' and antimodernity, ironically, gives the politics of exclusion and Eurocentrism a new lease of life:

> There were landscaped gardens, immaculate woods, and in one of these woods there was a Beautiful Lady [the first world woman] reclining gracefully against a convenient tree trunk. She was reading a book. As the Blue Donkey [the third world woman] approached, the Lady looked up and smiled at her. 'Hello,' said the Blue Donkey. 'What are you reading?' 'Poetry,' sighed the Lady. 'I think poetry is so beautiful. I feel I could live on poetry and fresh air for ever.' The Blue Donkey edged closer. 'Well, as it happens,' she ventured diffidently, 'I am a poet. Perhaps you would like me to recite some of my verse?' 'Oh. Oh no,' the

Lady replied hastily, then she recovered herself. 'The fact is,' she explained, 'that though I have studied many languages and my French and German are both excellent, I have never mastered Blue Donkese. And though I have no doubt whatsoever that your poems are excellent, I fear they would fall on untutored ears.' 'But please, I speak English.' The Blue Donkey could hear herself sounding plaintive. 'Oh,' murmured the Lady. 'But surely as a Blue Donkey, integrity requires that you paint the world as it appears to you. And consider: what have a lady and a donkey in common?'

NOTES

1 See, for example, International Federation of Information Processing, 1985, 1989, 1991.

REFERENCES

Bhaba, Homi K. (1994), *The Location of Culture*, London and New York, Routledge

Cockburn, Cynthia (1985), *Machinery of Dominance: Women, Men and Technical Know-how*, London, Pluto Press

International Federation of Information Processing (1985, 1989, 1991), *Women, Work and Computerization*, conference proceedings, Amsterdam, London and New York, North-Holland

Mernissi, Fatima (1994), *The Forgotten Queens of Islam*, trans. Mary Jo Lakeland, Oxford, Polity Press

Mies, Maria and Vandana Shiva (1993), *Ecofeminism*, London and New Jersey, Zed Books

Namjoshi, Suniti (1990), 'Dusty Distance', in Lakshmi Holmström (ed.), *The Inner Courtyard: Stories by Indian Women*, London, Virago Press

Nicholson, Linda J. (ed.) (1990), *Feminism/Postmodernism*, New York and London, Routledge

Rose, Hilary (1994), *Love, Power and Knowledge: Towards a Feminist Transformation of the Sciences*, Oxford, Polity Press

Rowbotham, Sheila (1992), *Women in Movement: Feminism and Social Action*, New York and London, Routledge

Shiva, Vandana (1993), *Monocultures of the Mind: Perspectives on Biodiversity and Biotechnology*, London and New Jersey, Zed Books, and Third World Network, Penang, Malaysia

Spivak, Gayatri Chakravorty (1993), *Outside in the Teaching Machine*, New York and London, Routledge

2 Information technology and working women's demands

Swasti Mitter

It is not obvious whether women should make demands different from those of men of technologies, old or new. The caring and childbearing role that women play assigns them a special function in most societies. The juggling act that the majority of working women perform, in balancing home and a job, gives rise to a set of priorities that are generally quite distinct from those of working men. Yet, even these almost essential or universal experiences of women do not give an unquestionable legitimacy to claims for woman-specific orientations of technological change. As our identities get constantly defined and redefined in terms of ethnicity, religion and class, gender does not always seem the primary basis for forming alliances. There are understandable misgivings, even among some concerned philosophers, about an emphasis on gender, as it distracts attention from other elements that determine vulnerability in the world of paid work. Rajni Kothari of India is not atypical in his belief that:

> it is not just a question of women. It is a much larger issue of a new technological basis of economic and cultural exploitation which is urging for a new spirit of democratic resistance against what is undoubtedly a considerably changed (transnationalized, corporate, computerized, militarized and televised) model of capitalist growth and integration.
>
> (Kothari, 1989: p. xii)

Only a broad-based alliance is seen to have the potential of distributing the benefits of technology to the unprivileged of all kinds, men as well as women.

An attempt to evaluate the effects of new technologies on women's employment needs some justification against the background of such current thoughts. This is especially important at a time when the commonality in women's needs and experiences is being questioned by the women of the developing world. The women's movement, which includes organized working women, is now being celebrated in the non-European world in terms of the heritages of the countries concerned. Fatima Mernissi, a leading feminist author of Africa and a Professor at the Technical University of Agdal Rabat, Morocco, for example, puts forward a case for such a culturally-rooted basis for action:

> We Muslim women can walk into the modern world with pride, know- ing that the quest for dignity, democracy, for full participation in the political and social affairs of our country stems from no imported values, but it is a part of a Muslim Tradition . . . its prophet spoke of matters dangerous to the establishment: of human dignity and equal rights.
>
> (Mernissi, 1991: pp. viii and ix)

The 'universal' needs of women are also being questioned in the developed world. This questioning is part of the current debate around the legitimacy of a 'modernity' that projects science and technology as rational and value-free, transcending the perspective and experiences of a group or of an individual.[1] The disadvantaged groups view this concept of a universal method of scientific enquiry with understandable suspicion. To start with, some of the metaphors and assumptions used in the description of scientific methods have hardly been value-neutral. Feminist historians, for example, have evoked the language used by Sir Francis Bacon (1561–1626), and other fathers of science, to stress the misogynist context of the epistemology of science. The severe testing of hypotheses through controlled manipulation of nature, and the necessity of such manipulations, if experiments were to be repeated, were formulated by them in sexist metaphors of rape and torture (Anderson, 1960: p. 25). In the post-Enlightenment period of the eighteenth and nineteenth century, biomedical science deployed similar symbolisms whereby nature was viewed as a woman to be unveiled, unclothed and penetrated by masculine science (Jordonova, 1980: p. 45).

The objectivity of scientific knowledge has also been questioned on the ground that the method of knowledge is not invariant, but is shaped by its social context. The recognition of diversity in the method of knowing – for example by women, or by the third world or by working class people – became known as 'standpoint epistemology' (Harding, 1991: p. 119). The concept subsequently merged with the language of post-modernism, that either celebrated or denounced the end of all 'grand narratives' (Jameson, 1991: pp. ix–xxii), including that of universal canons of rational science. It became increasingly acceptable to argue that the scientists revise the criteria of rationality as they move along and enter new domains of research (Feyerabend, 1978: p. 10).

For disadvantaged groups, including women, the stress on social specificity has been particularly refreshing in the context of technology, a branch of applied science. A focus on social and cultural factors has been useful in revealing the marginal role that women have been assigned, for example, in the history of technology and science. The formulation and implementation of technologies, in the public domain, have always affected relationships of economic power. The technological innovations become commercially successful if and when the creator of the innovation could make use of political, economic and legal networks.[2] Thus the dominant group in a society determines the shape and direction of a society's techno-economic order – and the image of an inventor has almost always been male.

Lack of access to relevant networks in the public domain explains the historical marginalization of women's contribution to technological innovations. It is not that women did not advance the technological frontiers, but their role was obliterated from mainstream documentation. It is a worthwhile task to reclaim their contributions, but it is equally important to highlight the factors that led to their oblivion.

The uneven distribution of economic power explains the differing control over technologies by diverse social groups. Distributive justice, thus, becomes the key issue in a programme for the democratization of technology's beneficial productive power. The question of distributive justice is particularly relevant in our 'postmodernist' decade, when it has become acceptable to recognize heterogeneity in the needs and aspirations of different groups in a population. Respect for diversity is empty unless the disadvantaged groups have access to political and economic networks. In the absence of such access, a celebration of plurality may simply give the dominant groups an excuse for non-action.

If not placed in the context of the question of distribution, the search for a culture-specific technology can be alarmingly anti-progressive, as is often the case with the eco-feminists of India, Germany and elsewhere. The destruction and depletion of the environment and of community life, which western-style development had caused in many parts of the world, has been a reason for despondency among concerned scholars. Vandana Shiva, for example, in *Staying Alive*, passionately calls for the rejection of a technology that supports and is supported by the socio-political-economic system of western capital patriarchy, which dominates and exploits nature, women and the poor (Shiva, 1989: p. 25; Shiva and Mies, 1993). In contrast, she argues, women of the third world have the holistic and ecological knowledge of what the foundation and protection of life is all about:

They retain the ability to see nature's life as a precondition for human survival and the integrity of interconnectedness in nature as a precondition for life . . . ecology and feminism [thus] can combine in the recovery of the feminine principle and through this recovery, can transform maldevelopment.

(Shiva, 1989: pp. 48–49)

The feminine principle, I fear, is an extremely vague concept. Also, the eco-feminists do not tell us how women of the third world can have the power to shift the pattern of development in the absence of increased economic power. A return to a mythical tradition and indigenous technology is not necessarily liberating; the majority of women will be reluctant to give up opportunities of work that advanced technologies bring them in modern urban sectors. It is the economic empowerment through paid work that allows women, and other disadvantaged groups, to voice their aspirations, priorities and demands.

It is crucial that the appropriateness of new technologies should be assessed in the cultural, political and economic context of a community or of a nation. But it becomes alarming when the quest for such cultural specificity urges us to go back to an unchanging tradition, complete with its indigenous technology and social norms. Recent work by two American scholars is an example of such a seductive but disturbing persuasion. Frédérique Apffel Marglin and Stephen A. Marglin, in *Dominating Knowledge*, put forward a case for technē, a mode of knowing in the non-western world that combines the use of 'one's hands, eyes and heart as well as one's head' (Marglin and Marglin, 1990: p. 234). In sharp contrast to the western reductionist and cerebral mode of enquiry – defined as epistémé – the secrets of technē can be learned only in a network of relationship: 'the parent–child, master–apprentice, guru–shisha [relationships] are intensely personal' (ibid.: p. 235).

I have two objections to arguments of this kind. To start with, the Marglins ignore the significant role that the concept of 'tacit knowledge' plays in the current design and implementation of computer-integrated manufacturing systems. A second and more serious objection is that this approach condones, if not justifies, a social order that has been highly oppressive to groups that are disadvantaged and marginal:

tradition of course grants the Brahman superiority over other castes and grants their knowledge superiority over the technē of other castes . . . but just as each caste is accorded its distinct and necessary role in a well-ordered cosmos, so must the technē of each caste be recognized as distinct and necessary.

(ibid.: p. 276)

The Marglins, in their celebration of diversity, urge us to accept, un-questioningly, the cultural norms and beliefs that support technē.

> It may be readily agreed that the sacrifice of a young woman on an altar in a traditional society is barbaric . . . but such practices must be under-stood in context, as a part of a cultural whole . . . female circumcision should not be a pretext for labelling African culture as backward, or suttee a pretext for proclaiming the inferiority of traditional Hindu culture.
>
> (ibid.: p. 12)

A search for contextuality and an abandonment of absolute values soon leads to the absence of all moral imperatives.[3]

THE CHANGING REQUIREMENTS IN SKILLS

Against these rather uncertain moral and economic principles of our time, it becomes important to pay attention to women's own voices if we are to ascertain their fears and aspirations with respect to information technology and patterns of industrialization.

The perspective of garment workers in Bangladesh, as documented by UBINIG[4] (the Centre for Policy Research for Development Alternatives in Bangladesh), is representative of many women in the developing countries who, for the first time, found employment in the formal sector, thanks to export-oriented industrialization. In a traditional Muslim country like Bangladesh, the export-oriented garment industry was a ground-breaker in creating a new workforce of nearly 500,000 young women industrial workers. Jobs in the factories are not perfect: the pay is low, there are health hazards, and the security of employment is not great. Yet the conditions of em-ployment are superior to alternatives that women are likely to find as domestic workers, prostitutes, or as workers in the informal sector. The introduction of digital automation and robotic technology in the western world makes the future of these jobs increasingly uncertain. Faced with such prospects, they are willing to learn any new technique and adjust to changed working conditions (UBINIG, 1991: p. 67). As one worker said, 'We will not go back to villages, we will not become dependent on others.'

Employment in the modern sector has given these women a certain amount of freedom from tradition and social oppression. As the UBINIG report so assiduously documents, women do not relish the idea of going back to villages that they left precisely in order to search for employment in the urban sector.

The impact of information technology on women's manufacturing employment in the developing world, until now, has been positive in terms of quantities of jobs. In the seventies and eighties, the improved telecommunication system and transport facilities encouraged transnational companies to relocate a considerable amount of manufacturing jobs, especially in textiles, clothing and electronics, to countries where the wages were low and where there was a plentiful supply of young women workers (Mitter, 1986: chapter 2). Within a decade or so, several million women workers were employed in manufacturing for export. This new form of employment gave women of the developing world a visibility as an important industrial workforce, a visibility they did not receive while working in small-scale or home-based units, broadly and vaguely defined as the informal sector. The future of these feminized manufacturing jobs appears less certain in the coming phase of technological changes, which make wage bills less significant in the total production costs of transnational corporations. As a result of a steady decline in the price of computer-aided technologies, manufacturing companies, even in a labour surplus country, now adopt some labour-replacing manufacturing methods to achieve speed, flexibility and quality control. Among the diverse patterns and directions of manufacturing employment in different parts of the world, one can identify certain trends in the corporate sector, in that

- the cost of capital is rising;
- the input of labour is declining;
- the demand for multi-skilled operators is increasing;
- new skills required in hardware and software development are becoming important;
- expertise in material resources planning and total quality management is proving crucial;
- marketing skills are becoming significant;
- skills in the management of organizations as well as of technologies are becoming essential.

Even in the affluent parts of the world, women do not easily find access to the scarce marketing, technical and management skills that they will need in order to be equipped for jobs in the future.

The quality of women's employment has been affected by recent organizational changes, in preparation for the effective use of computer technologies. The just-in-time system (JIT) and total quality management (TQM) are examples of such emerging practices that aim to ensure continuous workflow and zero defects in a highly capital-intensive process of production. The implementation of such work practices demands managerial, technical and marketing skills among workers. It also requires training in teamwork. The skills that women traditionally learn in assembly-line jobs do not equip them for these new tasks. Yet it is not impossible, and indeed could be managerially beneficial, to train women in the tools and philosophies of JIT and TQM. In the pursuit of people-oriented total quality management, the manager of Toyota stresses:

It is only human beings that can have the ability for innovation; hence, once the number of human beings decreases, as a result of automation or computerization, the built-in self-innovation ability of the workplace declines, no matter how effectively the automation is implemented.[5]

In Bangladesh the women workers in textile mills express similar views: 'We possess the skills; machines cannot take away our skills. A machine can increase our skill. The management should bring these machines; then we will survive and the mill will survive' (UBINIG, 1991).

MISMATCH BETWEEN DEMAND AND SUPPLY OF COGNITIVE SKILLS: IMPLICATIONS FOR WOMEN

The case for complying with such demands for upgrading women's skills arises from the projected estimates of a mismatch between demand and supply of certain types of cognitive skills in all parts of the world.

As Figure 2.1 shows, the importance of labour-intensive work is declining in the planning horizon of the industrialized world, with the introduction of computer-aided systems of production. Corporate organizations mainly need an assured supply of the requisite management and technical skills in order to meet the challenges of information-intensive methods of production. Even in the midst of world-wide recession, companies of the western world and of Japan face shortages of workers who possess such technical qualifications. Hence, those developing countries which can offer a supply of scarce skills become the favoured destinations for relocated manufacturing work from the developed part of the world.

The demographic trend in the western world accentuates this process. It indicates an impending shortage of skilled young workers in the developed world. From 1985 to 2000, the world's workforce is expected to grow by some 600 million people; 570 million of them will join the workforce in the developing world. In countries such as Pakistan and Mexico the workforce will grow at about 3 per cent a year. In contrast, growth rates in the United States, Canada and Spain will be closer to 1 per cent a year. Japan's workforce will grow by just 0.5 per cent a year and Germany's workforce will actually decline. The resultant shortages of skilled (and unskilled) workers are unlikely to be relieved by greater female participation in the

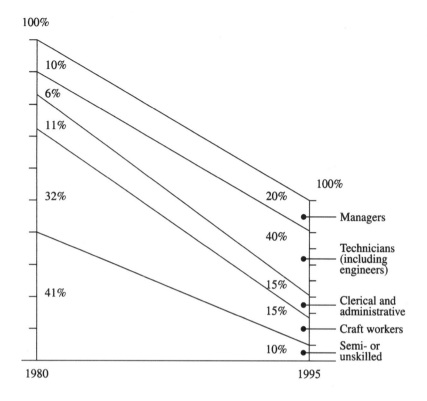

Figure 2.1 Expected changes in the volume and occupational structure of employment in the UK manufacturing industry

Source: Derived from figures supplied by the FAST Commission of the European Union (1984)

developed world; this is because the developed nations have already absorbed a much higher percentage of women into the labour force than the developing world.

The ageing population of the developed world, compared with the youthful workforce of the developing nations, is likely to be less flexible and hence less amenable to the challenges of information-intensive jobs. Companies and countries in the richer parts of the world will increase their dependence on international sourcing for the requisite expertise; the trend will become more pronounced as the developing nations will produce an ever-increasing share of the world's graduates in science, mathematics and engineering. Between 1970 and 1985, the proportion of the world's college students from the United States, Canada, Europe, the Soviet Union and Japan dropped from 77 per cent to 51 per cent, and by the year 2000, students from developing nations will make up three-fifths of all students in higher education.[6]

For some countries and some companies, measures to attract scarce human capital have become an important strategic policy, even in the face of the political explosiveness of the immigration issue. According to experts in INSEE (Institut National de la Statistique et des Etudes Economiques), between now and the year 2010 it will be necessary for France to admit 100,000 immigrants per annum – perhaps through yearly quotas by profession – if it is to avoid economic 'anaemia' arising out of shortages of skilled labour.[7]

Alternatively, the companies of the developed world will have to relocate the information and knowledge-intensive jobs to countries where the youthful population is well-equipped to take up the challenges of the new tasks.

The extent and direction of foreign direct investment (FDI) from the developed to the developing world is already influenced by this trend. A small number of Asian countries, mostly located in East Asia, have experienced an upsurge in the inflow of foreign direct investment (Table 2.1).[8] Significantly, these are the countries, such as China and the Republic of Korea, which have a relatively highly trained female workforce and possess adequate industrial infrastructures.

In the pioneer days of electronics, employers needed the nimble fingers of women workers for connecting tiny wires to a semi-conductor. The same task is now being done by a machine, with as many as ten machines under the charge of just one woman. It is not only the labour content that is decreasing; the quality of labour that is being demanded of electronic workers by the global companies is rising at the same time.[9]

The need for skilled workers also arises from the changing nature of marketing strategies adopted by corporate organizations. In semi-conductors, for example, the global trend is away from mass-produced 'jelly-bean' chips to high-value-added, application-specific, integrated circuits (ASICs).[10] The production of ASICs, unlike that of standardized semi-conductors, involves a far greater input of circuit design and of software programming. The limited supply of design engineers thus poses an obstacle for moving up in the product cycle.

In other words, a country can entice investments from global companies by offering cheap skilled labour. It is, of course, not possible for all countries to produce these cognitive skills in the right quantities to attract adequate FDI. It is unlikely that the majority of women in any country will

Table 2.1 Foreign direct investment in selected South East Asian countries
(US$ million)

	1986	1987	1988	1989	1990	1991	1992
ASEAN Countries							
Malaysia	489	423	719	1,668	2,332	3,998	4,469
Thailand	263	352	1,105	1,775	2,444	2,014	2,116
Indonesia	258	385	576	682	1,093	1,482	1,774
Philippines	127	307	936	563	530	544	228
Singapore	1,710	2,836	3,655	2,773	5,263	4,395	5,635
Total ASEAN (a)	2,847	4,303	6,991	7,461	11,662	12,433	14,222
Total as percentage of global inflow into developing countries	20.0	25.1	25.1	27.3	37.3	31.8	27.6
China	1,875	2,314	3,194	3,393	3,487	4,366	11,156
Korea	435	601	871	758	715	1,116	550

Sources: UNCTAD, 1992 and 1994
(a) excluding Brunei, which has small negative flows, reaching US$4 million in 1992

have access to the relevant training and education. A handful of elite
women can be trained for new openings in management, technical or
software programming jobs, but it will be difficult for a vast number of
blue-collar workers to be trained, in a short period, in the multiple skills that
computer technology and the global companies demand. For them, it will
be important to explore alternative avenues of employment – perhaps in the
small and medium-scale sectors.

The general mode of training in large companies could also be incompatible with the needs of blue-collar workers. Women's ability to make use
of formal training schemes depends much on their position in the society
and in the family. A woman worker often has to cope with violence and
abuse in the family, along with the responsibilities of childcare. These
factors affect her ability to pursue education and career progression. Informal training – such as is often gained by women in the small and medium-scale
sector – could be of greater relevance for blue-collar workers.

For blue-collar workers, employment prospects in the high-tech era
remain uncertain. Computer-aided technology improves productivity and
wages, but it also reduces the need for unskilled labour. In some situations,
when the market expands continuously to absorb the surplus labour, the
volume of employment of blue-collar workers widens or remains unchanged in spite of new technology. In Bangladesh, for example, a worker

displaced by new technology could easily find another job with the same employer or have an option in employment with another enterprise (UNIDO, 1993). The possibilities are not always so optimistic, particularly when the technology is coupled with radical organizational innovations. The innovations demand not only less labour on the factory floor but different and complex skills to which blue-collar workers, who are women, rarely have access. In Malaysia, for instance, the introduction of the JIT system in the semi-conductor sector increased the demand for expertise in material control systems such as Materials Requirement Planning (MRP), and Materials Resource Planning (MRPII).[11] The result of introducing JIT has been impressive. In one firm, the use of JIT and automation has, since 1984, halved the labour and the factory space needed and resulted in a reduction in the working week to four days (Narayan and Rajah, 1990). Most firms in Penang have reduced machine set-up time and manufacturing lead time.

The increased overall productivity, however, has meant a reduction in the share of female employment in the electronics industry of Malaysia. Whereas in the first phase of the industry up to 80 per cent of the workers were women, a 1986 survey showed that female representation had fallen to 67 per cent. Retrenchment, automation and the decentralization of work have mainly affected female assembly-line workers. When automation did create new opportunities, they were largely in the male-dominated professional, technical and maintenance categories.

The experience of the pharmaceutical and other chemical industries in India has been similar. Increased sub-contracting in the 1980s has entailed huge job losses for women assembly-line workers (Gothoskar, 1990; Gothoskar *et al.* 1991: pp. 100-102). Most new recruitment, in contrast, has been in the 'core', executive and managerial categories where women have negligible representation (Gothoskar *et al.*, 1991: p. 101).

Retrenched women, and by definition older women, find it difficult to gain access either to in-service training or to academic training institutions that equip them for jobs in the formal sector. It is the small-scale satellite companies that often absorb retrenched workers in the labour-intensive assembly operations.

COMPUTER TECHNOLOGY AND THE SMALL SCALE SECTOR

Computer technology itself has been instrumental in promoting the growth of the small and medium-scale sector in both rich and poor countries (Pineda-Ofreneo, 1987). Changes in technology have broadened the possibilities of decentralization through:

- miniaturization of machines, as in printing and publishing;
- modularization of products, as in television;
- fragmentation of the production process, as in garments and pharmaceuticals.

This process of decentralization has been enhanced also by:

- government policies which encourage the small-scale sector as a cost-effective way of creating employment;
- the increased role of new forms of investment (NFI) by multinationals in the shape of joint ventures with smaller firms, which are less encumbered by intellectual property rights.

The effects of decentralization have been complex, and in some ways contradictory, for women's employment. In the small-scale units, women more readily find jobs. Such units also offer the possibility of combining a job with the commitments of childcare. The conditions of work, however, are generally worse than those in the large-scale factories, where employees enjoy the protection of employment and labour legislation. There is hardly any monitoring of the health hazards in small scale enterprises, and the incidences of sexual harassment in community-based small-scale businesses are higher, in both high-tech and low-tech sectors (see e.g., Franzinetti, 1994). It is extremely difficult to organize workers of the small-scale units for collective action, within or outside trade unions (Mitter, 1994).

On the positive side, the growth of the small-scale sector offers new openings for women. In all societies, it is rare to find a woman industrialist, but it is not difficult to locate a succesful businesswoman. With the use of cheap computers in the designing stage, women in some countries have managed to carve out a niche in the fashion market, by offering diversity and flexibility in fashion and design. In the garment industry in Italy, for example, retailing companies rely heavily on local subcontractors for supplies of goods in small batches with high and varied design contents, to cope adequately with everchanging instant fashion (*Pronta Moda*). A sizeable number of these subcontractors are young women (Gaeta *et al.* 1992). Such possibilities are rarer for women in the poorer parts of the world, as the cost of acquiring computers and computer literacy is high. Also the world of business demands strategic skills that blue-collar and women workers find difficult and expensive to acquire (see Table 2.2). A progression from worker to entrepreneur thus depends on the availability of broad-based training in marketing, business and negotiation skills. It is also important for women to learn what to demand.

Even in terms of production skills, women workers of the small and medium-scale sector are often at a disadvantage. Even when women learn

Table 2.2 Management skills in the era of new technology

Conditions of success	Strategic issues
Offer consistently low defect rates	Quality
Offer dependable delivery promises	Delivery
Provide reliable/durable products	Design
Provide high performance products	Design
Offer fast deliveries	Delivery
Customize products and services to user needs	Customization/Flexibility
Profit in price-competitive markets	Price
Introduce new products quickly	Product innovation
Effective after-sales service	Service
Offer a broad product line	Variety/Flexibility

the key skills of the trade, their experience and expertise are often under-valued by the customers. To set up as entrepreneur, women, more than men, need to convince customers of their skills.[12]

WOMEN IN NEW-TECH SERVICE INDUSTRIES

Women's employment position alters with the increased inputs of information-intensive work even in traditional manufacturing. In the clothing industry, for example, computer-aided designing and cutting methods give rise to labour processes that are akin to those in the services sector (Cockburn, 1985: chapter 2; Rosen, 1992). The use of information-intensive methods of production demands computer-literacy and some knowledge of pro-gramming. Access to relevant training in a given type of employment, in this situation, gives women and men skills that are transferable between industries and sectors.

In the developed world, it is the services sector, particularly office work, that has been the focus of debates and enquiries around the impact of new technology on women's work. In the seventies, the feminist discussions were influenced by what is known as the 'labour process perspective' or the 'deskilling' debate, as formulated initially by Harry Braverman (1974). Labour process analysis characterizes the office as a white-collar mirror of an assembly line, with office work fragmented into many sub-tasks, each performed by a specialized worker, who loses both contact with the total product and variety in the tasks performed.

The 'proletarization' of white-collar workers, however, has not followed the predicted, uniform pattern. In some cases, the new technology has deskilled workers or automated certain functions of female workers. In other areas, it has upgraded the labour, by integrating fragmented production processes and by demanding complex skills from workers. The effects of new technologies, in other words, created a polarization in the workforce in terms of quality of work. One study, by Juliet Webster (1989), of office workers in Britain highlights the way computer technology contributes to polarization by accentuating inequalities in a given occupation. As she showed, the rationalization and fragmentation of clerical work had long predated the advent of computer technology; its introduction only reinforced a tendency for typists to perform repetitive, standardized tasks. At the same time, word processors reduced the burden of routine work for secretaries, enabling them to continue to do a variety of relatively responsible tasks. Thus the introduction of word processors exacerbated preexisting divisions between two groups of women office workers, enhancing the position of some secretaries but not that of typists.

In the service industries, the use of computers has been generally women-friendly. The QWERTY-keyboard[13] of the computers allows women to use the typist's skills in many jobs in the services sector. In the banking, insurance, and telecommunications industries, the rate of entry of women has been impressive in both the rich and poorer parts of the world. Despite the current quantitative gains, however, women's career progression in these new fields has been less spectacular: their presence in managerial and technical posts has been minimal (Tremblay, 1991: p. 140).[14]

Women's numerical predominance is visible also in the Information Technology (IT) industry. In the major European telecommunications companies, delivering either equipment or services, there has been a growth in the demand for employees with computer literacy and knowledge of software. Women have gained a fair share of the new employment, but are characteristically congregated at the level of the lower cadres, in assembly-line data-entry or low-level office work (see Figure 2.2). In the next phase of automation, these feminized, repetitive, new-tech jobs are the ones that are likely to disappear (Mitter *et al.*, 1993, p. 22). The picture in the poorer parts of the world is the same.

In certain occupations, such as in software, companies are keen to recruit highly-trained women at managerial level. In spite of the demand, women are less visible in these jobs, as they find it difficult to combine the challenges of a demanding career with domestic peace and social norms. The experiences of high-powered women in new-tech jobs are similar all over the world. One of the ex-directors of F-International, UK, recounts:

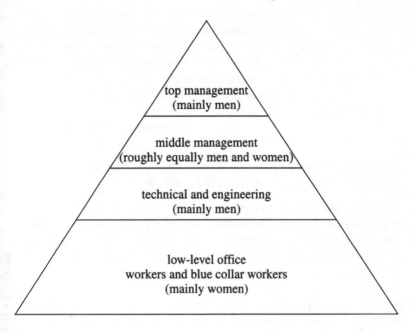

Figure 2.2 Summary of the employee profiles of European telecommunications companies, by gender, 1993

Source: Mitter, *et al.* (1993)

As I became successful, my husband felt depressed. I don't blame him, he wanted a wife and not a director of a company to live with. At the end, I had to make a choice, between my marriage and my career. I opted for my career. I think I made the right choice – but it was lonely and painful to have to make the choice.[15]

Similarly, in Nigeria, as Bimbo Soriyan and Bisi Aina explain,

it is believed that once you are married, you must have children. A computer scientist who has no child, therefore, would either not be dedicated to the profession for fear of her husband marrying another wife or be so involved to forget the problems at home. The computer scientist who is a wife and a mother is treated better than the unmarried or those without children, but at a price. More responsibility is placed on her to fulfil the three-in-one role. Not many Nigerian women are in the middle and top management positions, because these jobs make numerous demands on women which they might not easily be able to meet. With the alarming rate of divorce in Nigeria, many women strongly desire lucrative, executive positions, like those occupied by computer scientists, with stable homes. This brings a dilemma to the average woman: should she pursue her ambition at the expense of her home or sacrifice her job for her marriage?

(Soriyan and Aina, 1991: p. 206)

CHANGING LOCATION OF WORK AND THE NEW INTERNATIONAL DIVISION OF LABOUR

Both class and gender structure the patterns of access to, and choice for, new-tech jobs; they also determine the emerging international division of labour around information-intensive work. The key element in this division consists of shifts in the location of work. Computer technology facilitates the fragmentation of information-intensive work as effectively as it does manufacturing work. Certain parts of such work can be transferred to people and regions where wages are lower. In the developed part of the world, the changing location of information-intensive work is discussed mostly in the context of 'electronic cottages' and telework. The combination of computer and telecommunication technology makes it technically possible for large numbers of workers, whose jobs involve information processing, to work at terminals from home. A vision of an 'electronic cottage' features in all scenarios of the future of work in such societies. Although the number of people involved in telework is still small, its potential is quite large for professionals as well as data-entry and clerical employees (Huws, 1991; 1993). From research carried out in industrialized countries, one can identify the important differences that are already emerging between professional and clerical teleworkers. While men predominate among managerial staff, computer programmers and systems analysts, women are the majority among clerical workers (Wajcman and Probert, 1988).

A very large proportion of women teleworkers are married women with young children; this form of work is especially attractive to them because of their household responsibilities and the lack of adequate childcare. Judy Wajcman's observations in Australia in this field are similar to those by Ursula Huws in Britain. Electronic homework, for women, is an extension of traditional homework with all its disadvantages. Like traditional homeworkers, electronic homeworkers are typically paid at piece rates and earn substantially less than comparably skilled employees working in offices.

They are not entitled to benefits such as sickness pay and have no security of employment. The experience of male computer and software professionals is quite different. Male professionals work from home rather than at home, and earn far more that way, by lowering the overhead costs of running a business from an office. As Judy Wajcman concludes from her experience in Australia, Europe and America:

> It is only for male professionals who possess skills which are in short supply that new technology homework presents an unambiguous attractive choice. Overall . . . computer-based homework appears to reinforce sexual division in relation to paid work and unpaid domestic work, as well as to the technical division of labour.
>
> (Wajcman and Probert, 1988: p. 42)

Software production itself, however, is not a homogeneous process and can be broken down into various stages, from the first specification of requirements and prototyping through the design and encoding stages to testing and maintenance (Brady, 1989). The earlier stages require higher levels of skill and experience, whereas coding and testing are less skill-intensive. Given the sexual division of labour at home, it is understandable why women, either as teleworkers or as office employees, predominate in the stages that involve fewer challenges and risks.

The possibility of fragmenting the production process allows the global companies to relocate coding and testing jobs to low wage countries (Mitter *et al.*, 1992). Alternatively, the companies recruit programmers from such countries on a 'contract' basis to work on site. Married women, with young families, find it difficult if not impossible to undertake such contract work. Social norms in non-European countries also stand in the way of unmarried young women working abroad.

Exports of programmes and of programmers have become a major source of earning for a number of developing countries. India, for example, has experienced spectacular success. In the 1980s the annual average rate of growth in the programming area was 35 per cent, but between 1991 and 1992 Indian software exports rose by 67 per cent to US$144 million. Export earnings are likely to reach US$350 million by 1995. This is a major development for the country, because software is steadily replacing traditional agriculture and manufacturing exports in importance. One of the keys to India's success lies in the low cost of its computer programmers. It costs 40 to 50 per cent less to develop a programme in India than in the US. A substantial proportion of the contracts that India receives, however, are not for the offshore development of programmes; American and other companies often prefer to have programmes developed on-site, near the hardware. The result has been a steady export of software programmers, working on a contract basis in OECD countries.

The software field offers new employment opportunities for women with adequate training. India's example may not be too atypical for women of other developing countries. There is a general consensus that women stand a better chance of receiving a position of seniority in this area than in other fields of science and technology. Yet women constitute less than 10 per cent of the employees in this field and rarely hold management posts (Mitter *et al.*, 1992: pp. 23–24). The factors inhibiting women's career progression arise mainly from

- lack of international mobility on account of family commitments;
- regulations against night work which prevent companies from hiring women for contracts that need round-the-clock work;
- clients' reluctance to use women consultants, especially in the Middle East.

In addition, the training courses are expensive: families are often reluctant to spend too much money on a daughter's education, as she is primarily groomed to get married and have a family.

Women who enter software programming generally come from a relatively privileged background. The choice of education and career is by definition more limited for poorer women. Their integration in the international division of information-intensive labour has taken a different route. Ruth Pearson's recent work, and some of my own, has focused on the transfer of low-skill data-entry jobs to 'digiports' or 'teleports' in the Caribbean, where women type into computers for long hours at low pay, with insecure employment contracts. In many ways the data-entry work in teleports mirrors clerical telework in developed countries (Mitter *et al.*, 1992: p. 46). Offshore data-entry typically consists of high-volume activities such as airline ticketing, data processing, company data storage, credit card transactions and company databases.

Given the current developments in office automation, such as voice recognition, offshore office services are likely to be a short-term phenomenon. Just as the development of advanced automation systems has reduced the need for offshore assembly work, the next phase of technology may bring this new avenue of employment for women in the developing world to an end. Computer literacy learnt on the job, on the other hand, could be a stepping-stone towards alternative employment, so long as women are given chances to demand adequate and appropriate training.

HEALTH HAZARDS OF NEW TECHNOLOGY

Offshore data-entry work may turn out to be short-lived, but research around it has raised new awareness of health-related issues with regard to new technologies. The hazards affect women and men, but as women congregate at the low-skill end of new technology white-collar occupations, where bargaining power is less, these issues, along with wage demands, have a particular urgency for them.[16] There is an acute need for exchanges of information and learning between women of developed and developing countries. The health hazards of new technology are a concern common to both blue-collar and white-collar employees.

The use of computers has also led to a steady expansion of the microelectronics manufacturing industry. The expansion has given women new employment opportunities, but it has also exposed women assembly-line workers to harmful substances and fumes. The long-term effects may not yet be known, but this could prove to have been one of the more hazardous industries of the last quarter century. While there is growing evidence that occupational hazards within the industry cause health problems, it is still very difficult for workers to prove a direct link and to gain adequate protection, treatment or compensation. Headaches, muscle strain, skin allergies and eye damage are all too common, but national governments and company managers, and frequently trade unions too, write these off as minor complaints.[17]

AT THE MARGIN OF NEW TECHNOLOGY: GROUPS AND COUNTRIES

Women's experiences of the effects of new technology depend also on their position in the international economy. Decisions regarding formulation, implementation and transfer of technologies are predominantly taken by transnational companies, mostly located in the West. Access to networks of power related to global technical transformations eludes some groups and economies.

In contrast with the seventies and eighties, it has now become less common to describe the world economy in terms of a 'core' and 'periphery'. In the context of information technology, perhaps, it makes sense to revive the dichotomy, especially for understanding the specificities in the needs and demands of certain groups of women. The dichotomy is no longer spatial. There are groups, even within the western economies, who have extremely limited access to relevant political and economic networks. Migrant workers, especially from the developing world, are such an excluded group. With the political upheavals in Africa, eastern Europe and parts of Asia, it is difficult to estimate how many million migrant workers are looking for employment in the official and the clandestine economy of the West. It is not possible to assess the effects of new technologies on their job prospects. The impact of new technology is, however, already visible among those groups of immigrants who came to Europe and the United States in the postwar period to meet the demands of labour-intensive industries. In the fields of clothing, textiles and electronics, where migrant women workers provided the required cheap labour, labour-replacing robotic technology now makes much of their skill redundant. They demand and need access to relevant training for sustained employment.

Just as certain groups face special challenges, so do certain countries in the new economic world order. For most of the ex-communist countries of central and eastern Europe, a linkage to the international economy is a new experience. Transitional phases to a market economy have not been easy: as the countries grapple with the difficulties of operating in a new way, the 'woman' question, as well as forming assessments of new technology, receives less importance among policy-making bodies.[18] Yet women in that part of the world feel a need for international networking for the exchange of information. Such an exchange is relevant for the women as well as for the region.

Whereas economic and political changes have lead to the linking of central and eastern Europe to the world economy, the debt crisis, war, and structural adjustments have resulted in uncoupling Sub-Saharan Africa from the global economy. This makes it perhaps the most problematic of all regions for realizing the potential advances that IT can offer to women workers.[19]

TRANSCENDING THE POLITICS OF GENDER

There is scope for discussing the appropriateness of new technology in the context of a number of countries. Yet it seems to me that the flexibility and speed of communication which computer technology offers could become instruments of change for disadvantaged groups, even in poor countries. The facilities provided by computerized data-bases and e-mail are increasingly being used in developing countries for effective communication among grassroots women's organizations.[20] Desktop publishing helps such groups to produce relevant literature and materials at a low cost and to attain professionalism.

For women and for countries, the question is not whether to accept or to reject the new technology: rather it is to demand the appropriate use of new technology for the benefit of the majority. Such a demand is linked with the challenges of distributive justice – between genders as well as among races, classes and regions.

It will be difficult, if not impossible, to attain the goal if we give up the ideals of collective action in the name of relativism, contextuality or post-modernism. There is of course some truth in the claim that for the disadvantaged 'partiality and not universality is the condition of being heard' by the dominant group (Collins, 1991: p. 236). Yet, in the field of technology as in other spheres of life, there is scope for negotiation and international understanding. It will be important to transcend the politics of gender to include the dimensions of race, class and other disadvantages in discussions of the employment implications of new technologies. To be aware of other factors is not to belittle the role of gender. Women in all societies, irrespective of their race or class, have to adjust to a pattern of work that, to a greater or lesser extent, is incompatible with their needs and aspirations. The new technology itself offers some possibilities towards redressing the past gender imbalance in the quantity and quality of work; but for these possibilities to become realities certain changes will be required in the division of labour in domestic life. There too, the solution lies not in confrontation, but in achieving greater cooperation and understanding. Man's consciousness, at home and at work, has been formed by his tradition and heritage. The hope lies in freeing him from the myth of an unchanging tradition. 'The image of his woman', to quote Fatima Mernissi (1991: p. 195), 'will change, when he feels the pressing need to root his future in a liberating memory. Perhaps the women should help him to do this through daily pressure for equality' – with or without new technology.

NOTES

1 For an overview of the current critique of modern science see, for instance, Harding, 1991 and Rose, 1994. For a summary of such a critique in the context of technology, see Wajcman, 1991 and Haraway, 1990. Marshall, 1994 provides a critique of postmodernism and critical theory in social sciences.
2 For example, it was a combination of technical genius and entrepreneurial ability to manipulate such networks that led to Thomas Edison's success with a viable electrical bulb (Law, 1991: p. 9).
3 For a cogent criticism of Marglin's papers see Nussbaum, 1992: pp. 202–244.
4 UBINIG is a research organization in Dhaka, Bangladesh, which conducts research on development issues from the people's perspective.
5 Takao Nuki, 'Quality circles and just-in-time system under development of computerization' SEAKE Centre, Brighton Polytechnic, UK (mimeo), quoted in Mitter, 1992.
6 Figures compiled from relevant UN agencies in Johnston, 1991.

7 For a summary of the report see Lebaube, 1991.

8 For a detailed breakdown of FDI inflow and outflow in Asia, see Khan, 1992 and UNCTAD, 1994.

9 *Financial Times*, Survey of Thailand, 5 December, 1990.

10 See Hobday, 1991. In contrast to standard components, ASICs are customized or semi-customized integrated circuits which allow the user to closely specify the design of the IC. ASICs have been given various names including tailored circuits, custom chips, semicustom devices and CSICs (customer-specific integrated circuits). Since 1985, the term ASIC has been widely adopted as a generic term to describe the various segments of the custom and semicustom IC market.

11 Materials Requirement Planning (MRP) refers to a technique which takes a forecast of anticipated sales over time and produces a breakdown of the total materials requirements – raw materials, components, and sub-assemblies – for meeting those targets. From such information a series of activities – purchase orders, sub-contract orders, in-house production of components orders – can be initiated. Materials Resources Planning (MRPII) extends the concept of materials requirements planning by introducing the idea of a master production schedule which is a mixture of forecasting of sales demand and actual customer orders. From this master schedule a materials requirement plan and a capacity requirement plan are generated. MRPII differs from materials requirement planning in its strategic nature, taking into account the entire operational resource base of the company.

12 See Nirmala Bannerjee in this anthology.

13 Q-W-E-R-T-Y are the characters on the second row, left-hand side, of a conventional typewriter, and now of computers, in the English-speaking world.

14 See also the contributions from Ng and Yong, and Gothoskar, in this anthology.

15 From the discussion at the Women and Management Workshop at the IFIP Conference on Women, Work and Computerization, Helsinki, Finland, 30 June–2 July 1991.

16 See Ursula Huws (1987). The original and pirated versions of her book, the *VDU Hazards Handbook*, have been used extensively in Europe and in non-European countries to generate awareness of VDU-related health hazards. See also Mitter *et al.*, (1992).

17 For documentation of women workers' struggle to increase the visibility of health issues see Women Working Worldwide (eds), 1991, pp. 60–62, pp. 105–108 and pp. 148–150.

18 This was the response from Maria Lado, who works at the Ministry of Labour, Hungary, to my letter asking her to contribute to the workshop in 1991.

19 See Odedra-Straub, in this anthology.

20 ISIS in Asia, and TAMWA in Africa, are examples.

REFERENCES

Anderson F.H. (ed.) (1960), *Francis Bacon: The New Organon and Related Writings*, Indianapolis, Bobbs Merrill

Brady, T. (1989), *Software Users as Producers: Silent Majority*, working paper No. 3, Science Policy Research Unit, Sussex University, UK

Braverman, Harry (1974), *Labour and Monopoly Capital: the Degradation of Work in the Twentieth Century*, New York, Monthly Review Press

Cockburn, Cynthia (1985), *Machinery of Dominance: Women, Men and Technological Know-how*, London, Pluto Press

Collins, Patricia Hills (1991), *Black Feminist Thoughts: Knowledge, Consciousness and the Politics of Empowerment*, New York and London, Routledge

Feyerabend, Paul (1978), *Science in a Free Society*, London, New Left Books

Franzinetti, Vicky (1994), 'The Informal Sector in an Industrialized Country: Textile and Garment Workers in Northern Italy', in M. H. Martens and S. Mitter (eds) *Women in Trade Unions*, Geneva, ILO.

Gaeta, Raffaele, Fiorenza Belussi and Swasti Mitter (1992), 'Pronta moda: the new business venture for women in Italy', in Swasti Mitter (ed.), *Computer-aided Manufacturing and Women's Employment*, London, Springer Verlag

Gothoskar, Sujata (1990), *Automation and the Challenge before Unions*, New Delhi, Society for Participating Research in Asia (PRIA), December

Gothoskar, Sujata *et al.* (1991), *Job Losses and Closures: Management Strategies and Union Counter-Strategies*, report of a study sponsored by Asia Partnership in Human Development

Harding, Sandra (1991), *Whose Science? Whose Knowledge: Thinking from Women's Lives*, Milton Keynes, UK, Open University Press

Haraway, Donna (1990), 'A Manifesto for Cyborgs: Science, Technology, and Socialist Feminism in the 1980s', in Nicholson, Linda J. (ed.) (1990), *Feminism/ Postmodernism*, New York and London, Routledge

Hobday, Michael (1991), 'Semiconductor technology and the newly industrializing countries: the diffusion of Application Specific Integrated Circuits', *World Development*, Vol. 19, No. 4: pp. 375–397

Huws, Ursula (1987), *VDU Hazards Handbook*, London Hazards Centre

Huws, Ursula (1991), 'Telework: projections', *Futures*, January–February

Huws, Ursula (1993), *Teleworking in Britain*, report to the Employment Department, UK

Jameson, Fredric (1991), *Postmodernism or The Cultural Logic of Late Capitalism*, London, Verso

Johnston, William B. (1991), 'Global workforce 2000, The New World Labour Market', *Harvard Business Review*, April: p. 119

Jordonova, L.J. (1980), 'Natural Facts: A Historical Perspective on Science and Sexuality', in C. MacCormack and M. Strathern (eds), *Nature, Culture and Gender*, Cambridge University Press, UK

Khan, Zafar Sha (1992), *Patterns of Direct Foreign Investment in China*, World Bank Discussion Papers, China and Mongolia Department Series, No. 130

Kothari, Rajni (1989), Foreword to Vandana Shiva, *Staying Alive: Women, Ecology and Development*, London, Zed Books

Law, John (1991), 'Introduction: monsters, machines and socio-technical relations', in John Law (ed.) *A Sociology of Monsters: Essays on Power, Technology and Domination*, London, Routledge

Lebaube (1991), 'Immigration au futur', *Le Monde*, 30 July

Marglin, Frédérique Apffel, and Stephen A. Marglin (eds) (1990), *Dominating Knowledge: Development, Culture and Resistance*, Oxford, Clarendon Press

Marshall, Barbara L. (1994), *Engendering Modernity: Feminism, Social Theory and Social Change*, Oxford, Polity Press

Mernissi, Fatima (1991), *Women and Islam: An Historical and Theological Enquiry*, Oxford and Cambridge, Mass., Blackwell

Mitter, Swasti (1986), *Common Fate, Common Bond: Women in the Global Economy*, London, Pluto Press

Mitter, Swasti (1992), 'Computer-aided manufacturing and women's employment: A Global Critique of Post-Fordism', in I.V. Eriksson (ed.) *Women, Work and Computerization: Understanding and Overcoming Bias in Work and Education*, Amsterdam, North Holland

Mitter, Swasti, and Ruth Pearson (in collaboration with Cecilia Ng) (1992), *Global Information Processing: The Emergence of Software Services and Data Entry Jobs*, Geneva, ILO

Mitter, Swasti (with Gillian Shapiro and Paul Levy) (1993), *Equality and Total Quality Management: A New Approach to Positive Action in the European Telecommunications Sector*, report prepared for the Equal Opportunities Unit of DG V, Brussels

Mitter, Swasti (1994), 'On organising women in casualised work: a global overview', in Sheila Rowbotham and Swasti Mitter (eds), *Dignity and Daily Bread: New Forms of Economic Organising among Poor Women in the Third World and the First*, London, Routledge

Narayan, Suresh and Raiah Rajah (1990), *Malaysian electronics: the dimming prospects of employment generation and restructuring*, (mimeo)

Nussbaum, Martha C. (1992), 'Human Functioning and Social Justice: In Defense of Aristotelian Essentialism', *Political Theory*, May

Pineda-Ofreneo, Rosalinda (1987), *Industrial Homework in the Philippines*, monograph prepared for the International Labour Organization, Geneva, mimeo

Rosen, Ellen (1987), *Bitter Choices: Blue Collar Women In and Out of Work*, Chicago, Chicago University Press

Rose, Hilary (1994), *Love, Power and Knowledge: Towards a Feminist Transformation of the Sciences*, Oxford, Polity Press

Soriyan, Bimbo, and Bisi Aina (1991), 'Women's Work and Challenges of Computerisation: the Nigerian Case: Understanding and Overcoming Bias in Work and Education', in I.V. Eriksson *et al.* (eds), *Women, Work and Computerization*, Amsterdam, North Holland

Shiva, Vandana (1989), *Staying Alive: Women, Ecology and Development*, London, Zed Books

Shiva, Vandana, and Maria Mies (1993), *Ecofeminism*, London, Zed Press

Tremblay, Diane-Gabrielle (1991), 'Computerization, Human Resources Management and Redirection of Women's Skills', in I.V. Eriksson *et al.* (eds), *Women, Work and Computerization*, Amsterdam, North Holland

UBINIG (1991), *Bangladesh's Textile and Clothing Industry: The Role of Women*, working paper prepared by UBINIG for UNIDO and presented at a seminar in Dhaka on 7 October

UNCTAD (1994), *World Investment Report*, New York and Geneva, United Nations

UNIDO (1993), *Changing Techno-Economic Environment in the Textile and Clothing Industry; Implication for the Role of Women in Asian Developing Countries*, Vienna, February

Wajcman, Judy (1991), *Feminism Confronts Technology*, Oxford, Polity Press

Wajcman, J. and B. Probert (1988), 'New Technology Outwork', in E. Wills (ed.) *Technology and the Labour Process: Australian Case Studies*, Allen and Unwin, Sydney, Australia

Webster, Juliet (1985), *Office Automation: The Labour Process and Women's Work in Britain*, London, Wheatsheaf

Women Working Worldwide (eds) (1991), *Common Interests: Women Organizing in Global Electronics*, obtainable from Box 92, 190 Upper Street, London N1 1RQ, UK

3 Feminist approaches to technology

Women's values or a gender lens?

Sheila Rowbotham

INTRODUCTION

Confronted by the lack of women technologists and scientists, feminists in Europe and North America in the 1970s were inclined to focus on the impediments of a male-dominated capitalism; male prejudice, attitudes and relations within families, schools or work, lack of places in higher education, job segregation and the sexual division of labour. Like an earlier generation of feminists, they were preoccupied with the obstacles preventing women's access. The campaign for abortion and a growing awareness of reproductive rights brought an added incentive to break down the male bastion of science and technology. Women's entry was seen not only as a matter of individual advance but as a means of gaining control for women collectively. Opposition to arguments that women were essentially unscientific or untechnological initially engaged with the wider social relations which constrained women's choices and opportunities.

Feminist ideas develop partly within their own area of debate, acquiring their own momentum. They also, however, interact with other intellectual currents. The changing paradigms in scientific thought are sites for just such a crossover. Indeed sometimes it can be difficult to distinguish social critiques of science from strands of feminism which assume that 'feminism' by definition is to be equated with a rejection of science, technology and indeed reason.

The recognition that values are embedded within the social processes of scientific study and technological innovation has challenged the assumption that these are neutral forces. This has an obvious relevance for understanding the peculiar difficulty women have confronted in gaining access to the theoretical and practical scientific and technological worlds. Feminist writers on science and technology, in the words of Evelyn Fox Keller, have detected the presence of gender markings in the root categories of the natural sciences and their use in the hierarchical ordering of such categories for example, mind and nature; reason and feeling; objective and subjective (Keller, 1992: pp. 18-19). This awareness of gender has contributed to new insights into the history of science and technology in western thought and society. Instead of wondering what is wrong with women, with capitalism, or with 'patriarchy', feminist enquiry has shifted during the last decade to what is wrong with the tradition of modern western science. This approach has converged with a broader questioning of the automatic benefits which western science has brought. The view that technological discoveries and their application inevitably represent incontestable progress has been extensively critiqued, and the social reasons for certain kinds of technologies being developed rather than others have been explored.

Of course wariness about the powers of science, technology and reason is not entirely new within western culture. Intense faith in reason, progress and objectivity generated its opposites. The Enlightenment has various and contradictory currents, one being the elevation of nature. Mary Shelley's *Frankenstein* evoked a fear common within romanticism of an unbridled human scientific intellect. Throughout the nineteenth century, thinkers in the West sought alternatives to industry and modernity in several versions of nature, ranging from idealizations of the folk, the working class, black people, the Orient or women. In our own times, anxiety about science, technology and indeed reason, has become especially acute as the grim consequences of both capitalism's and state socialism's visions of progress have become apparent. For better or worse, the *zeitgeist* of the late twentieth century appears to be a profound scepticism about the possibility of applying reason for social progress and a tendency to dismiss the value of western science and technology.

This has made the feminist claim for entry in order to gain control somewhat problematic. For how can we demand access to forms of knowledge which we are defining as inherently flawed?

The hidden perils of alternatives amidst the critique of existing male dominated science

Some strands of feminism have taken hope from the view that women will necessarily 'do' science differently and will develop alternative forms of technology. Among eco-feminists in particular, this conviction has stimulated a literature of opposition which ranges from a claim that women are essentially different to a proposal that women might bring a socially-based experience of alternative values: caring and reciprocity versus control and objective detachment. The advantage of this utopianism is that it opens the possibility for a culture of science and technology which is different to the perspective which has prevailed in the West from the seventeenth century.

There are however some unforeseen consequences of positing a distinct set of existing women's values which are in opposition to the existing forms of science and technology. For a start, there is the question, where have they come from? Essentially female values are formed in cultures in which gender inequality prevails. They are not apart from social relations. An obvious danger is that we enclose ourselves within definitions which are just as much part of a 'male' culture and which confine rather than emancipate. For example, identifying with nature is problematical: it has, after all, also been used to justify the subordination of women, as Janet Sayers shows (1982). Moreover, how nature is regarded is itself historical and cultural and has changed over time (Thomas, 1984). It is hardly firm ground for resistance to masculine hegemony.

In challenging a narrow technological determinism and false optimism about the inherently 'progressive' aspects of technology, feminists who have sought to argue that existing cultural stereotypes of feminine identity should be embraced as an alternative to male definitions of technology ignore the fact that many of these social interpretations of 'nature' are as restrictive as mechanical versions of reason. The argument for women's closeness to nature:

> has involved confinement to activities such as reproduction and denial to them of capacities for reason, intelligence and control of life conditions, that is, of their exclusion from the valued features of human life and culture.
>
> (Plumwood, 1990: p. 232)

These exclusions are of particular significance for women in third world countries where the question of access to modern technology or the creation of alternatives is far from abstract. By embracing a position of absolute opposition to the practical achievements of western science, some strands of eco-feminism have begun to display a strategic weakness in their incapacity to grapple with the actual impact of existing science and technology. The utopian desire for an alternative can close up and become a denial of the contradictory possibilities present within the realities facing women.

The feminist critique of the tradition of western science has come from several perspectives, anti-utopian as well as utopian. Scepticism about essential female values, utopias and grand plans has combined in 'postmodernism' to undermine the very possibility of objectivity. This too has had an unforeseen effect in paralysing any effort at strategic resistance.

Postmodernism, as Kate Soper observes, is the obverse of liberal and Marxist teleologies of inevitable progress. It has now shifted from a challenge to the 'technical-fix' approach to human happiness into a collapse of any hope in gaining even approximate understanding of the world (Soper, 1992: p. 45). This 'postmodernist "over-drive"' has, in Kate Soper's words, 'pushed on to question the very possibility of objectivity or of making reference in language to what itself is not the effect of discourse' (ibid.).

Consequently it fails to engage with the actual work of scientists and technologists, for it occludes the tangible results of particular modes of enquiry. Scepticism about scientific objectivity, as Evelyn Fox Keller points out, has to reckon with degrees of approximation to reality – 'not all metaphors are equally effective for the production of further knowledge' (Keller, 1992: p. 33). The dilemma really is how far the questioning of reason and objectivity is to be pushed. When taken to extremes this line of thought, which originally had the intention of emancipation, ends by actually disempowering those who are already vulnerable by making exploration, analysis and comparison impossible. As Kate Soper says, the momentum of postmodernism

> now invites us to disown the very aspiration to truth as something unattainable in principle, no longer even a regulative idea; and in doing so, it has also disallowed us any reference to a common sensibility or consensus about what is wrong with our times and hence any reference to the idea of collective political endeavour.
>
> (Soper, 1992: p. 45)

Curiously the impulse to reject a technocratic certainty can actually turn into its opposite, through the denial of the possibility of conscious human agents acting in specific social relations and circumstance upon the world and one another to improve their lives together (Varikas). Applying a gender lens[1] then is a more risky business than many feminists envisaged. In the words of Barbara Drygulski Wright: 'the ideological problem women face in gaining full access to science and technology is perhaps more complex than we have heretofore acknowledged' (Wright, 1987: p. 17).

REFRAMING THE QUESTION

Claiming reason

A useful counter to the utopian desire for women to incarnate an absolute alternative, or the complete rejection of any reality outside of discourse, has been a philosophical and historical endeavour to dig beneath dichotomies of mind and nature, reason and feeling, objective and subjective. Evelyn Fox Keller summarizes this extensive process of reframing the questions about Western science.

> How is it that the scientific mind can be *seen* at one and the same time as both male and disembodied? How is it that thinking 'objectively', that is thinking that is defined as self-detached, impersonal, and transcendent, is also understood as 'thinking like a man'?
>
> (Keller, 1992; p. 19)

A growing body of feminist historical work has taken off from this set of conundrums, overturning *en route* not only the view that invention has been exclusively male but also over-simple feminist propositions. For example, one line of enquiry has begun to question the idea that women's alienation from modern Western science can be explained simply in terms of exclusion through the development of a rationalism which emphasized objectivity. The impact of rationalism has to be regarded more dialectically. Londa Schiebinger reminds us of the historical context not only of what came after but of what came before. It is misleading to project our contemporary disenchantment uncritically upon the past, for this obscures how access to reason through education was seen as the key to emancipation by many advocates of women's rights in the seventeenth and eighteenth century. She shows that the dictum 'the mind has no sex', was popularly regarded as a defence of female aspirations (Schiebinger, 1989a: pp. 172–175; see also Harth, 1992).

It is important to recognize that while women grounded their critiques of male bias within the existing structures of knowledge, they also subverted these in the process. For example, Elisabeth of Bohemia, the Princess Palatine, who influenced Descartes, was a sceptical disciple from the 1640s through the 1660s. She and other Cartesian women embraced and used Cartesian dualism, 'the radical disassociation of mind from body', critically.[2] So the argument that the masculinist characteristics of modern western science are traceable to the mechanistic methodologies of the seventeenth century is an over-simplification (Merchant, 1980). These ingenious Cartesian women used rational objectivity as a means of insinuating themselves into the intellectual space it opened. The epistemological claim to transcend difference provided a social context for women of rank to enter the world of science. As Londa Schiebinger observes:

> Elisabeth of Bohemia insisted that the thinking subject be grounded in the materiality of the body. Catherine Descartes reinfused her uncle's vision of mechanical 'dead' nature with soul and moral value.

Madeleine de Scudery pointed to the necessity of incorporating ethics into science.

(Schiebinger, 1992: p. 9)

The advantage of several hundred years hindsight of course is that we can now remark on the disadvantages of being disembodied on male terms.[3] Nonetheless the traces of this ambiguous route to freedom reveal that the aspiration to reason had several propensities. The Cartesian women were not the first upper class women to make sallies against masculine cultural hegemony. Renaissance humanism, which, from the fifteenth century, had, as Londa Schiebinger says, 'chipped away at the oppressive Aristotelian dictate about the nature of women' (Schiebinger, 1989a: p. 165), had already presented women with a mixed legacy well before Descartes. Though inclined, like the scholastic clergy they criticized, to dwell in male fraternal networks, humanist academics were in some cases beholden to women patrons. Juan Luis Vives and Thomas More advocated female education and were influenced by Catherine of Aragon. However, More believed instruction was necessary because women were by nature inferior intellectually (Noble, 1992: pp. 171-174).

Humanism thus argued for only a limited admission of women into the institutions of learning. Yet it nonetheless made the demand for women's entrance into the academy possible. Similarly the Enlightenment was to open a corridor into culture while making sure that its route was restricted. So when women in aristocratic intellectual circles through the seventeenth and eighteenth centuries sought admission not on the basis of a suppressed experiential understanding but as equals in rational learning, they encountered an ironic acceptance which disassociated them from their gender. Voltaire wrote of his friend, collaborator and lover, the Marquise Emilie du Châtelet, a leading advocate of Newtonian physics, 'Never was a woman so learned as she. She was a great man whose only fault was in being the woman' (cited in Noble, 1992: p. 199). However, women have not necessarily accepted cultural definitions which excluded and denied their knowledge and experience. Du Châtelet wrote to Frederick of Prussia, 'Do not look upon me as a mere appendage. I am in my own right a whole person, responsible to myself alone for all that I am, all that I say, all that I do' (ibid.). So the very notions of individual control over nature which imposed restrictive concepts of women's essential character were also used by women to question custom and prejudice. No body of thought, then, can be regarded as containing a single inclination. Very different theoretical approaches to science can be seen as containing women's potential while also presenting certain possibilities which women have manipulated to the best of their abilities.

Science and heterodoxy

The recognition that 'science is not a cumulative enterprise', and that consequently 'the history of science is as much about the loss of traditions as it is about the creation of new ones' (Schiebinger, 1992: p. 2), has been influential in bringing into focus opposing intellectual currents. For instance, the mind-body split was contested but not overcome in the sixteenth and seventeenth centuries when neo-Platonists, cabalists and alchemists emphasized the union of male and female principles as the basis of creativity. In the case of alchemy the iconoclastic character of its adherents in the sixteenth and seventeenth centuries led some of its exponents to defy clerical misogyny. Cornelius Agrippa even argued the superiority of women. While dependence on learned women patrons might have made such advocacy opportune, their intellectual and social defiance could also reach out beyond women of the upper classes to present a democratic approach to learning (Noble, 1992: pp. 175–183). Paracelsus declared:

> The universities do not teach all things so a doctor must seek out old wives, gypsies, sorcerers, wandering tribes, old robbers, and such outlaws and take lessons from them. A doctor must be a traveller because he must enquire of the world. Experiment is not sufficient. Experience must verify what can be accepted or not accepted.
>
> (cited in Noble, 1992: p. 181)

Paracelsus also revived ancient ideas within alchemy about oneness; instead of regarding the existing form of masculinity as a perfect model for humanity, he saw masculinity as an incompleteness seeking union with its opposite.

> Man having become separated from the woman in him, lost his true light. He now seeks for the woman outside of his true self, and wanders about among shadows, being misled by the will of the wisps of external illusions.
>
> (cited in Noble, 1992: p. 177)

There was an ambiguity within this subordinated approach towards knowledge in relation to gender and power. The space for the woman as other was still marked out on male terms. The alchemist's desire for androgynous union, 'entailed less a primordial reunification of the sexes than an appropriation of the one by the other' (Noble, 1992: p. 178). Moreover the alchemists were safeguarding an occult tradition in the manner of a sect, even while legitimating practical understandings against scolasticism. Their challenge to the existing intellectual hierarchy was driven by two impulses; the elitism of a knowledge apart from the mainstream and the democratic potential of experience.

Other histories

The significance of submerged heterodoxies is not simply how they regarded women but how they saw the aims and constitution of science. A gender lens can bring into view not only women's relation to men but wider questions about an extended terrain. Buried within alchemical tradition was a vision of social purpose. It was not simply about the dream of wealth but the quest for the elixir of life. For Paracelsus this meant that 'the business of alchemy is not to make gold, but to prepare remedies for human ills' (cited in Needham, 1981: p. 6).

Such a view placed him in a direct line of descent, according to Joseph Needham, with the Chinese alchemy of disinterested Taoists which pre-dates the pre-Christian era. The idea of the elixir and the social value of its pursuit reached Europe through Arab culture. So alchemy provides us with a clue about the loss of tradition not simply as a subordinated culture within western science but of other histories of science. It opens another window of remembering.

Joseph Needham quotes an Arab scholar from the ninth century musing upon the migration of learning.

> I, Muhammad ibn Ishag, have lastly only to add that the books on this subject of alchemy are too numerous and extensive to be recorded in full, and besides the authors keep repeating themselves. The Egyptians especially have many alchemical writers and scholars, and some say that that was the country where the science was born. The temples with their laboratories were there, and that was where Mary the Jewess worked. But others say that the discussion on the art originated with the Persians, while according to others the Greeks were the first who dealt with it.
>
> (cited in Needham, 1981: p. 70)

Alchemy probably reached Egypt from ancient Mesopotamia. It flourished in Alexandria when the Greco-Roman world was in decline, AD 85-165. It drew, as Margaret Alic tells us in her account of women in science, *Hypatia's Heritage*, upon several sources: the formulation and manufacture of cosmetics, perfumes and imitation jewellery – major Egyptian industries; the artistic tradition – the mixing of dyes and the theories of colour; and gnosticism, an esoteric mixture of Jewish, Chaldean and Egyptian mysticism, neo-Platonism, and Christianity, centred in Alexandria. In the gnostic tradition, as in ancient Taoism, the male and female were equal – a precept which became the cornerstone of alchemical theory.

(Alic, 1986: pp. 20–22)

The gnostic belief in the transcendence of all divisions, including that between the sexes, as a sign of redemption meant that they strove to make the two one. This could be an absorption and reduction of the female to the male or it could be a symbolic reunification of male and female. Small study circles provided 'a close spiritual companionship between men and women in which sexual identity had all but lost its significance' (Noble, 1991: p. 16). By claiming to have overcome sexual desire, the gnostics were able to accept women as equals.

Diverse strands of scientific heterodoxy can be found exercising their influence long before the emergence of modern western scientific paradigms. Not only does western science have its opposing heterodoxies, there are all the other scientific traditions with their various histories. If Evelyn Fox Keller's 'lens of feminist inquiry' (Keller, 1992: p. 18) were to be applied to this wider spectrum, it would undoubtedly reveal a more complex picture of the scientific mind than the present western feminist history of science has yet uncovered.

Space to manoeuvre

Instead of conceiving masculine-oriented science as an unchanging block, it is apparent that there have been significant shifts and considerable variations. This recognition has enabled historians to re-examine the argument that women have been completely absent. Women as historical actors have begun to be restored to the history of western science, they have come into view, in Londa Schiebinger's phrase 'manoeuvring within the gender boundaries prescribed by society' (1989a: p. 7). Such manoeuvring surely also existed outside western science, for even in very ancient times women can be found studying science in many cultures. Margaret Alic describes women doctors in Egypt before 3000 BC, while ancient Babylonian women perfumers developed the chemical techniques used among alchemists in Alexandria in the first century AD (Alic, 1986: pp. 20–22). She observes that the Dark Ages, were not as bleak a time for women as one might expect. In the Byzantine Empire a succession of women rulers pursued scientific interests. In China women engineers and Taoist adepts pushed science and technology forward at a steady rate. With the rise of Islam and the subsequent conquest and unification of the Arab regions, translations and elaborations of ancient Greek works formed the basis of Arab science. A diverse and tolerant culture, the early Moslem empire preserved and expanded upon the knowledge of antiquity. Women studied at the medical school in Baghdad and female alchemists followed the teachings of Maria the Jewess. If Moslem women scholars are not recorded in the historical text, their existence is at least testified to by stories from the Arabian Nights.

(ibid.: p. 47)

She goes on to tell the legend of the Arab slave girl Tawaddud, who outwitted readers of the Koran, doctors of law and medicine, scientists and philosophers with her wisdom and learning.

Rather than viewing history in terms of an undifferentiated structure of patriarchy, it is possible to see women emerging intellectually in some periods and forced into retreat in others. Historians have begun to examine what David Noble has described as differences within the 'recurring fact' of female subordination. As he says, 'There have been significant variations of experience, variations that have shaped particular cultures and lives' (Noble, 1992: p. 4).

This nuanced view of history makes it possible to enquire into the actual social circumstances which have enabled women to enter the world of science and technology, for it has not simply been an ideological struggle but a practical one. Several broad features can be outlined. Firstly it has certainly been an advantage to be a member of the upper classes. Class has created a certain space for gender manoeuvring. For example, one of the most celebrated Byzantine women scholars, Anna Comnena (1083-1148), was the daughter of Emperor Alexius. Her father's many wars provided her with material for her favourite subject, military technology, and her book *The Alexiad*, contains 'detailed descriptions of weapons and military tactics' (Alic, 1986: p. 48). In medieval Europe the 'ladies of Salerno' contributed to the eleventh-century revival based on translating ancient Greek medical writing from Arabic into Latin. They were a group of noble Italian women who were able to enter the universities in this period.

According to legend an upper class scholar called Trotula wrote on medicine, dealing with subjects such as skin diseases and cosmetics, birth control, gynaecology, lice, toothache, and even slimming. In a work attributed to her this advice was given: 'The obese person was to be smeared with cow dung and wine and placed in a steam cabinet or in heated sand four times per week' (Alic, 1986: p. 53).

The patronage of royal and aristocratic women, which played a significant part in scientific innovation in early modern Western science, can be observed elsewhere. An early example is to be found in Japan, where the Empress Shotoku-Tenno ordered the printing of one million charms in 767. These were distributed in 770, the earliest printed documents produced in any country (Sarton, 1927: p. 529).

Science and daily life

There were, however, other ways of entering science for women from less privileged backgrounds. An important influence upon science has been the tradition of practical experiments associated with craft skills, and women have contributed both through the workshop and through the household. Way back in the second millennium BC, cuneiform tablets name two women chemists Tappūti-Bēlatēkallim and Ninu. Although women had a low status in ancient Sumerian culture, they could engage in business. Margaret Alic writes:

> The perfume industry was very important in ancient Babylon since aromatic substances were used in medicine and religion as well as for cosmetics. The apparatus and recipes of perfumery were similar to those used in cooking. Women perfumers developed the chemical techniques of distillation, extraction and sublimation.
>
> (Alic, 1986: p. 21)

The textile crafts, where women are to be found in many cultures spinning wool, silk and linen, are also female trades closely linked to household duties. Irfan Habib describes how, in 1301–2, Amir Khusrau advised his daughter in Delhi to be content with the needle and spindle which he compared to her spear and arrow, a source of wealth and a means of hiding one's body (Habib, 1992: p. 12).[4] Nearly fifty years later another poet, 'Isami, was grumbling at Raziyya's presumption on becoming Sultan though a woman, and urging women to sit with the charka rather than assuming sovereignty (ibid.: p. 13). Irfan Habib comments,

> To these two poets one feels truly grateful in spite of their unacceptably reactionary views on the place of woman: their admonitions have enabled us to fix the generalization of the spinning wheel at least in India in the first half of the 14th century.
>
> (ibid.)

Unfortunately the poets were not concerned with a gendered account of technological innovation or implementation.

In China the memory has survived of Huang Tao P'o, a famous woman textile technologist of the thirteenth century who brought knowledge of cotton growing, spinning and weaving from Hainan to the Yangtze (Needham, 1981: p. 111). In Hainan she is remembered still as the inventor of the loom.[5]

Who is remembered and revered is not a matter of chance but bound up with how science is defined and what model of the relationship between science and technology is adopted; it indeed depends on how knowledge is constituted. The recognition that 'technology' means much more than applied science, that it is itself a creative area of culture which involves the tacit know-how based on doing, has opened up a much broader approach to the history and sociology of science and technology, which has enabled feminists to redefine the parameters of women's contribution to technology. This understanding is by no means new: the fifteenth-century French writer and defender of women, Christine de Pisan, located women's technological creativity in precisely these areas of human culture. The rediscovery of how the domestic sphere has interacted historically with certain kinds of technological and scientific know-how has recently begun to blur the boundaries between formal and informal knowledge. Women's cultural traditions have been passed on orally or through household manuals rather than through the academy. Medicine is an obvious example. Long before the invention of penicillin, Elizabeth Stone, in nineteenth-century Wisconsin, specialized in treating lumberjacks' wounds with poultices of mouldy bread in warm milk or water (Stanley, 1983: p. 14).

In medieval Europe women were active in many areas of craft production, but from the sixteenth century they were to be excluded from many trades. Still, Maria Winkelmann, the daughter of a Lutheran minister, born near Leipzig in 1670, was able to receive an advanced training in astronomy by serving as an unofficial apprentice in the house of the self-taught Christopher Arnold. Astronomy in late seventeenth-century Germany was organized partly along guild lines and partly through study at the university. The practical observation work occurred, however, largely outside the university. Maria Winkelmann was able to pursue her work by marrying Germany's leading astronomer, Gottfried Kirch. This enabled her to continue as an assistant to Kirch in Berlin. She became celebrated for her scientific work, which included the discovery of a previously unknown comet in 1702. Together she and her husband worked on astronomy which contributed to the production of an astronomically accurate calendar (Schiebinger, 1989b: pp. 21-38).

Family connections have been important to women entering scientific study from early times. Hypatia of Alexandria, born AD 370 when the city was in turmoil as the Roman Empire was converting to Christianity, was the daughter of the mathematician and astronomer Theon. As well as theoretical writing, Hypatia was interested in mechanics and practical technology. She designed a plane astrolabe for measuring the positions of stars, planets and the sun to calculate time and the ascendant sign of the zodiac, and a graduated brass hydrometer for determining the density of a liquid. She was murdered by fanatical and jealous Christian monks hostile to her learning (Alic, 1986: p. 44).

The persistent appearance of women as practitioners of alchemy was not only because of ideological affinities. Alchemy presents an example of a craft form through which women could be technologically creative. Maria the Jewess was a prominent early alchemist. She invented a water bath in the first century AD which resembled a double boiler and was used to heat a substance slowly or maintain it at a constant temperature. The French still call a double boiler a *bain-marie*. She also invented distilling apparatus. Maria compared the thickness of the metal in part of the still to a 'pastrycook's copper frying pan' and recommended flour paste for sealing joints (Alic, 1986: p. 37). It is possible to see here the connection between domestic craft and technology, present in much of women's inventiveness, which the hierarchical model of technology as applied science or a narrow definition of technology as physical objects would obliterate. Another creative link has been to the reproduction of life. Cleopatra, a later Alexandrian alchemist, brought imagery of conception and birth into her writing and studied weights and measures in an attempt to quantify experiments. However, in the third century the Roman emperor Diocletian persecuted Alexandrian alchemists. Consequently alchemy was to be culturally rerouted. As Margaret Alic says, 'The Arabs rescued the science and ancient alchemy reached Europe during the Middle Ages, but by that time it had degenerated into mystical mumbo-jumbo' (Alic, 1986: p. 41).

Interest in alchemy was to appear again during the thirteenth-century scientific revival. In fourteenth-century Paris, Perrenelle Lethas married the well-to-do scribe Nicholas Flamnel. Together they discovered an ancient alchemical manuscript. They laboured together experimenting with mercury and silver trying to create gold.

Separate communities

Women can be found studying science and making practical contributions through medicine or technological innovation within the separate space of intellectual or religious communities. An early example was the famous mathematician Pythagoras of Samos, c. 582–500 BC, who formed a community in the Greek colony of Croton in southern Italy between 540 and 520 BC, in which there were at least twenty-eight women teachers and students. The most famous of these was Theano, who married Pythagoras when he was an old man. She and her daughters were renowned as healers and believed that the human body in microcosm reflected the macro universe. When the community was forcibly dispersed she took Pythagoras's philosophical and mathematical ideas with her through Greece into Egypt (Alic, 1986: pp. 22–24).

Some medieval European convents provided women with education in medicine, sanitation and nutrition. Hildegard, born 1098, was a learned abbess in Germany who studied scientific ideas and developed ideas of links between the body and the universe. Hildegard lived in a period when the influence of the ancient Greeks was being translated from Arabic into Latin and her writing indirectly expressed these influences which were to continue to affect scientific thought into the Renaissance (ibid.: pp. 62–67).

The Shakers also provided a communal situation in which women were able to contribute to technological inventions. Catherine Greene's contribution to devising the cotton gin is uncertain, though, according to a Shaker writer, Whitney once publicly admitted her help (Shaker Manifesto, 1890: p. 10). One certain breakthrough is the invention of the circular saw, c. 1810, by Sister Tabitha Babbitt of the Harvard Massachusetts Shakers.

> After watching the brothers sawing, she concluded that their back and forth motion wasted half their effort, and mounted a notched metal disc on her spinning wheel to demonstrate her proposed improvements. . . . Sister Tabitha intended the blade to be turned by water power.
>
> (ibid.: p. 19, footnote)

The entry points for women into the world of science and technology in cultures which have been hostile to their participation have thus been through the power of aristocratic wealth and patronage; through learning within a practical craft situation or housewifery; through their family networks; and through groups and communities set apart from society. These social and material circumstances have entwined with ideological factors. Cultures which have respected experience have enabled women to practice skills gained through doing rather than academic knowledge. Oppositional ideologies have also contained a critique of elitist knowledge, which has sometimes been sympathetic to the claims of women, even though these have been subordinated in relation to a hegemonic academy. Nonetheless, given conducive social conditions, women have contributed to invention and drawn on aspects of their experience as well as upon formal learning.

Access and exclusion

It is misleading to present a unified or steady progress for women as a homogenous group even within Western science, for as cultural gates opened through education and the upper-class women's salons, which were to become spaces for exchanging ideas from the seventeenth century, they were also closing. The formal academies created in the late seventeenth century tended to be exclusively male. The Académie Royale des Sciences was founded in 1666 and closed the intellectual paths opened by Cartesian women like Elisabeth of Bohemia, Catherine Descartes, Madeleine de Scudery (Schiebinger, 1992: p. 9). The Berlin Academy of Sciences did admit Maria Winkelmann, but she was denied a post in the observatory. She wrote: 'Now I go through a severe desert, and because . . . water is scarce . . . the taste is bitter' (cited in Schiebinger, 1989b).

The professionalization of science made it harder for women who were practitioners through craft and family connections. However, the popularity of science also inspired upper class European women to take up the study. Many of these gained a reputation for eccentricity, like Mad Madge, the Duchess of Newcastle, who broke into the Royal Society of London in 1667, or Lady Mary Montagu who brought the knowledge of inoculation to Britain from Turkey in the eighteenth century and was described as having 'a tongue like a viper and a pen like a razor' (Alic, 1986: p. 90). Later examples come from an enlightened and radical milieu. Dr James Miranda Stuart Barry, a protégé of James Barry who was a follower of Mary Wollstonecraft, dressed as a man to become a doctor at Edinburgh in 1812 and pursued a successful career as an army surgeon (ibid.: p. 105). Ada Byron Lovelace developed a concept for an analytical engine and studied cybernetics in the 1840s, reviving old ideas of microcosm and macrocosm. Unfortunately this early pioneer of the computer imagined that she had found an infallible system for winning at the horse races, and with Charles Babbage lost a great deal of money (ibid.: pp. 157–163).

Professionalization meant that education became of crucial importance. Access to colleges in the nineteenth century was an important demand among women who sought entry into the public sphere of scientific debate. In the early nineteenth century in America, educational ideas which emphasized science with a practical application for industry included women. For example Amos Eaton, founder of RPI, was a proponent of women's education and opposed to 'the monkish policy' of the universities

(Noble, 1992: p. 266). Vassar College, Smith College and Wellesley College were established to educate women scientifically as well as in other subjects. Oberlin was the first coeducational school. It modelled itself on manual labour schools, in particular the Oneida Academy which grew out of a community and combined religious instruction with science and practical training in agriculture and mechanical arts. In the 1850s the People's College movement in upstate New York also took a practical approach to education, while Wesleyan University, a Methodist institution, was initially coeducational with an orientation to industrial scientific education. MIT was also coeducational (ibid.: pp 267–270). Women moved into higher education in the United States in the late nineteenth and early twentieth century in large numbers. However, a reaction became evident in the latter part of the nineteenth century, when arguments about 'women's nature', in terms of physical and psychological difference, were used as reasons to exclude them. Wesleyan College eliminated coeducation, and women's enrolment at MIT fell off. From the institutes of technology a concerted male opposition consolidated akin to that of the academies of the earlier era.

Recent research has then effected a remarkable recovery of women excluded from conventional histories of Western science which has in turn brought about a deeper exploration of the relationship between gender and science. This work can lead us to an examination of both the barriers which have prevented women from gaining access and the circumstances which have made it possible for women to learn about scientific ideas and contribute to technology themselves; questions which have a significant and direct relevance to the contemporary position of women. However such an assessment of the possibility of women gaining power to shape the design and purpose of technology would need to refer not only to the internal tensions within scientific thought but also to the wider social context. This necessary connection has tended to fall into the background in the focus upon the scientific milieu itself which has characterized much of the new gender-sensitive history of science and technology.

THE IMPACT OF TECHNOLOGY

It is not only how women do science which matters but what science does to women; not simply women's lack of power to shape technologies but also the effect of existing technologies upon women's lives. Though there is a growing literature on both production and consumption, our focus here is on production. Feminism has had an impact on several relevant disciplines, bringing scholars to ask questions which had been generally ignored. Industrial sociologists, development economists and labour historians have all contributed; engendering their accounts of the effect of technology.

The initial consensus was one of general gloom. Many socialist feminists were influenced by Harry Braverman's *Labour and Monopoly Capital* (1974) which argued that technology tended to intensify the labour process and deskill workers. Feminists writing on the organization of production observed women's lack of power to determine how technology was designed and applied. In development literature too, Ester Boserup's influential *Women's Role in Economic Development* (1970), was to be the basis for a socialist feminist literature demonstrating how technology and capitalist industrialization was displacing women from production.[6]

Pessimism has also marked the work of feminists who have prioritized gender as the crucial determinant of the context in which technologies were imposed. For example, Rosemary Pringle in *Secretaries Talk* (1989) said that new technology enhanced men's power, 'If men are represented as the masters of technology, women are its servants. Technology does not empower them but reinforces their powerlessness and dependence on men'.[7]

There have been, however, some dissenting voices. In *Labour Pains*, for example, Pat Armstrong modified the prevailing pessimistic attitude towards new technology with the view that while it did imply increased productivity and control over workers, it also presented new possibilities for women workers (Armstrong, 1984: p. 139).

By the late 1980s and early 1990s, absolute positions, whether optimistic or pessimistic, about the impact of the development process upon women's employment patterns came to be questioned (Acevedo, 1992: pp. 223-225). With this came an awareness that 'a new theoretical perspective on the relationship between women and technology' (Bhaskar, 1987: p. 14) was needed. This does not mean an unquestioning acceptance of the extreme anti-modernist critique of science and technology. For as B.N. Bhaskar observes, 'the Achilles heel of this perspective is in translating its ideas into concrete reality' (ibid.). On the other hand it does not return us to viewing technology as a neutral force completely apart from culture. A valuable starting point is the growth of concrete studies of technology and gender in recent feminist historiography, particularly in the United States.

Historical work

Contemporary debates have generated historical enquiry into the actual consequences of the impact of technology. These question the original hypothesis of a uniform debasement of labour and skill. Feminist work has revealed many examples of the introduction of technology which is accompanied by the exclusion of women from the new skills required, and the displacement of their labour and reclassification of their jobs as low-skilled. However, evidence has also been found of benefits because of a general expansion of employment. Sometimes a mixed situation of loss and benefit has occurred. For instance, the typewriter helped to establish secretarial work as a female domain, which saw a loss of status for secretaries from the 1880s. However, Carole Scrole argues that it did not *instigate* women's entry into offices but accelerated their numerical domination (Scrole, 1987: p. 96). Frieda S. Rozen (1987) describes how the increasing size of airplanes contributed to the organization of women flight attendants in the period 1974 to 1978.

Moreover, recent historical work is demonstrating that women are not all affected by technology in the same way. Mary H. Blewett (1988), for example found that in the New England shoe industry, mechanics tried to train women homeworkers to use the new sewing machines introduced to factories in the middle of the century, but the women resisted the transition from hand to machine work. Interestingly, it was not until sewing machines were made for home use and a new generation of young women were familiar with them that women began displacing men in factories as sewing machine operators.

Not only differences between generations but ethnic, racial and class segregation are being shown to have interacted with gender to produce hierarchies among women. Gender cannot be regarded as a distinct unchanging category. Examining the American printing industry's response to technology between 1850 and 1930, Ava Baron has argued that 'we need to scrutinize how class and gender are constructed simultaneously' (Baron, 1987: p. 62). Gender itself is shaped by circumstances of class, race, and ethnicity. She also cautions against an undifferentiated concept of 'patriarchy' as an unchanging structure.

> The view that men shape work to protect their gender interests assumes that gender is monolithic, rather than multidimensional and internally inconsistent. It also assumes that men are omnipotent, that they know what their gender interests are and have power to construct the world the way they want. Feminist research needs both to question male power rather than assume its existence, and to examine what its limitations are.
>
> (ibid.)

This recent historical examination of gender and technology has been mainly concerned with the first world, not the third. However, there has been a growing awareness of the need to extend the boundaries of women's labour history through exploring the social histories of work and community in the third world. A picture is beginning to emerge of a gendered class experience in, for example, Japan, India and China from the late nineteenth century (see, for example, Hershatter, 1986; Kumar, 1993). The specific structures of the family, the dynamics of class struggle and ideas in the workplace or in communities, as well as state policies have all affected the impact of technology upon third world women. For example, in Japan women's work in the coal mines was affected by recession after World War I, when more women became redundant than men. Protective legislation introduced after World War I left women working above ground. However, in 1939 these labour laws were set aside because of the intense demand for labour and women again worked underground. The prohibition of women's work in the mines was restored in 1947 but they continued to sift the coal until mechanization of this process in the 1960s. In this example the interplay of political, economic and cultural factors can be seen – technology has an effect but within a specific social context (Mathias, 1993: pp. 101-105; Saso, 1990: pp. 25-26). An exclusive focus on gender and technology could run the risk of artificially abstracting the impact of technology from the wider circumstances of work and life and ignore how state policy affects women's position, so this more comprehensive approach is particularly valuable.

Theorists of industrial relations and welfare

Technology is developed and applied within wider social relationships, which involve assumptions about how people should live and work. Women have certainly had much less influence upon shaping their social contexts and intellectual frameworks than men. However, even here they have not been entirely absent. For instance, several notable figures are to be found developing the theory and practice of modern technological environments.

Lillian Gilbreth was a theorist of industrial engineering in the 1920s. She analysed the effect of Taylor's standardizing of managerial practices in the United States, including improved lighting, reduced pollution, rest intervals and breaks, incentives for workers, greater control by workers over their own speed and tasks. She studied the chairs and positions in which women worked in order to prevent fatigue and backache. Rationalization of production was extended into housework by several women impressed by Taylorism, an approach which profoundly influenced the construction of the welfare state (Trescott, 1983: pp. 29–32). One advocate of efficient house management was the American Christine Frederick who promoted Taylorism. Along with Emmy Wolder in the early 1920s she pioneered works canteens which were adopted by supporters in Europe concerned about welfare (Tanner, 1992: pp. 67–70).[8]

These liberal proponents of the rationalization of production and reproduction were concerned to increase productivity. The maximization of profit which benefitted employers was assumed to accord with workers' interests. It was seen as the means of promoting industrial harmony. Women workers were likely to be less enthusiastic about the reason for the Tayloristic time and motion studies. However, by formalizing and reforming the organization and conditions of work they inadvertently provided possibilities for struggles for workers' control which would not have existed under completely informal and sweated working arrangements. Consequently it could be argued that instrumental reason in its Tayloristic form was not simply a coercive ploy to extract labour from workers. The regulation of wages, despite gender inequalities, marked a certain advance over the personal whim and sexual power of a coercive foreman or employer, which could decide pay in a small clothing shop for instance.

It would be a mistake to assume that all women theorists, simply because of their gender, have thought in the same way or that they have concurred over what kind of organization of production best serves workers' interests. Helen Marot, for example, opposed the reshaping of American industry in the early twentieth century, through wage incentives and rationalization. She accused the methodology of scientific management of plucking out some of [the worker's] faculties and discarding the rest of the man as valueless (Polanski, 1987: p. 253). Marot believed instead in 'the creative impulse . . . a strong emotional impulse, a real intellectual interest in the adventure of productive enterprise'. Unlike Gilbreth's emphasis on instinct, in which human beings were passive, she presents human character as dynamic and self-motivating. Against competition she argued for a cooperative emphasis upon giving.

Helen Marot also developed a vision of a transformed educative workplace in which technical skills were balanced with the humanities and social sciences. For example, in running a toyshop, students would deal not only with the technical problems or work, keeping financial accounts and estimating costs, maintaining the workplace and health of the workforce, but also study economics, aesthetics, literature and history. These were to be integrated into the industrial process, transforming the mechanical and the human. This approach to industrial education was to be important in influencing the work of Lewis Mumford later. Helen Marot refused to accept a technological cancellation of human beings by reducing them to passive objects, not because of her gender but because of her political and intellectual stance. She had spotted at a very early stage the fatal weakness of Taylorism – its inability to enhance human creativity (ibid.: pp. 254, 250).

Helen Marot's approach has obvious relevance for modern attempts to question authoritarian modes of management. The prevailing orthodoxies of management theory themselves have recently changed gear to emphasize participation as a means of incorporating workers' knowledge. An unintended consequence of this apparent appropriation of the ideas of their opponents could be the possibility of a renewed critique of the meaning of work, not only by theorists of industrial relations but by workers themselves (Binns, 1991: p. 54). It is within this potential for democratizing work and social existence that alternative feminist approaches to technology might lose an abstract and purely utopian quality and become an element in shaping a new reality.

CONCLUSION

The feminist movement has presented new questions about the relationship of women to technology. These have stimulated interest in the manner in which women have been excluded by the social construction of science and technology. Historical studies of the western scientific tradition have revealed how the process of exclusion has not simply been a matter of external obstacles but has been embedded within the cultural assumptions of mainstream science. These approaches within feminist scholarship have converged with a powerful current of disillusionment, not simply with the results of technology, but with science, reason and the claim that objective assessment is possible. There have been two strands to this wholesale rejection of science: the assertion that in women's alienation an alternative can be found and the denial of the value of applying reason.

While the resulting challenge to the hidden presumptions of western science, and the recognition of its gender bias, have provided important correctives to over-estimates of the virtues of objective scientific methods and neutral technology, it has nonetheless contained snags. It denies an important aspect of women's claim to emancipation through equal access to reason. Also the absolute dismissal of science and technology fails to engage with their application; the actuality which so manifestly affects people in their daily lives. Thus neither the postmodernist nor the eco-feminist rejection of modern science have much to offer women seeking to manoeuvre within gender boundaries or attempting to shift them to establish better terms. Studies of women's complex relation with science and technology in earlier times suggest that a more nuanced approach could indicate how certain groups of women made gains or contrived to turn technology to their advantage.

Recent historical work has shown that women have not been excluded completely from science and technology. It also questions the idea that technological transformations simply happen to women, showing them instead as struggling to shape and exercise some control over these. Rather than a monolithic interpretation of gender, male/female relationships have been, to use Ava Baron's phrase, 'multi-dimensional and internally inconsistent' (Baron, 1987). The historical evidence suggests that men are not omnipotent nor indeed completely concerted in their effort to exclude women from scientific and technological knowledge. Nor have women acted from a unity of interests or aims.

The theoretical engagement of women with western science moreover has been philosophically varied, ranging from gnosticism and alchemy through to Cartesianism and Newtonian theory. It has also been affected by their social position. Aristocrats and craftswomen have entered scientific worlds through differing entrances. Quite contrary philosophies and strategies have been employed. A history of gender and science which extended to include non-western traditions would make for an even more variegated picture.

Thus women have questioned the prevailing assumptions of science from very different vantage points, rather than presenting a single set of alternative values. They have not only claimed entry but sometimes critiqued and sought to reshape the ideas around science. Moreover, they can be seen not only reacting to scientific invention and the application of technology, but conceiving ways in which technology could be applied. Again, these have come from differing political and social perspectives. Values cannot be read off from gender. There has been a continuing tension between gaining a foothold in a social and cultural environment outside the mainstream and demanding access to the prevailing social organization of the scientific and technological world. It is within this contrary pull between heterodox oppositional strands in science such as alchemy, and the claim to enter the academy, that a gender lens leads to wider questions about the purposes of scientific and technological knowledge. At this point a gender lens alone becomes insufficient: other forms of social exclusions, other groups' subordinated experience, have to be considered. While the most obvious fact has been the marginalization of women, the historical entry-points through which, against the odds, women have still gained access to knowledge and invention provide pointers towards the forms of social organization which would enable women to participate in scientific and technological cultures. Examination of the wider social, material and intellectual conditions in which women have been able to overcome marginalization and the contradictory histories of the impact of technology upon them could then connect with some of the questions being raised by contemporary feminist writers about the purposes of production and the democratic uses of technology (e.g. Cockburn, 1985; Huws 1991; Biehl, 1991; Mellor, 1992). In Judy Wajcman's words: 'Feminist debates about political strategy concerning technology posit forms of action that break with conventional politics. They are about making interventions in every sphere of life' (Wajcman, 1991: p. 166). A new relationship between technology and gender cannot be devised only in the seminar, it has to be created, by users and workers internationally, from the experiences of daily life.

NOTES

1 I am grateful to Ruth Pearson for the phrase 'gender lens'.
2 They were reviving an early Christian theme: 'the mind has no sex' (Schiebinger, 1992).
3 I am grateful to Roy Bhaskar for discussion which helped to clarify this point.
4 I am grateful to Navsharan G. Singh for this reference.
5 I am grateful to Tongjiang Long for this information.
6 See Acevedo, 1992. On Harry Braverman see for example Baxandall *et al.*, 1976: p. 1 and Armstrong and Armstrong, 1990: pp. 88–96.
7 See also Cockburn, 1983 and 1985.
8 I am grateful to Eleni Varikas for this reference.

REFERENCES

Acevedo, Luiz del Alba (1992), 'Industrialisation and Employment', in Cheryl Johnson-Odim and Margaret Strobel (eds), *Expanding the Boundaries of Women's History*, Bloomington and Indianapolis, Indiana University Press

Alic, Margaret (1986), *Hypatia's Heritage: A History of Women in Science From Antiquity to the Late 19th Century*, London, The Women's Press

Armstrong, Pat (1984), *Labor Pains: Women's Work in Crisis*, Toronto, The Women's Press

Armstrong, Pat and Hugh Armstrong (1990), *Theorising Women's Work*, Networks Basics Series, Toronto, Garamond Press

Baron, Ava (1987), 'Contested Terrain Revisited: Technology and Gender Definitions of Work in the Printing Industry 1850–1920', in Barbara Drygulski Wright (ed.), *Women, Work, and Technology: Transformations*, Ann Arbor, The University of Michigan Press, 1st edition

Baxandall, Rosalyn, Elizabeth Ewen and Linda Gordon (1976), 'The Working

Class Has Two Sexes', *Technology, the Labour Process and the Working Class, Monthly Review*, July/August

Bhaskar, B.N. (1987) 'Technological Innovation and Rural Women: An Overview', in Cecilia Ng (ed.), *Technology and Gender, Women's Work in Asia*, Women's Studies Unit, Department of Extension Education, Universiti Pertanian Malaysia, Jerdang Selangor Malaysia and the Malaysian Social Science Association

Biehl, Janet (1991), *Rethinking Eco-Feminist Politics*, Boston, South End Press

Binns, David (1991), *Total Quality Management, Organisation Theory and the New Right: A Contribution to the Critique of Bureaucratic Totalitarianism*, London, University of East London

Blewett, Mary, H. (1988), *Men, Women and Work: Class, Gender and Protest in New England Shoe Industry 1780–1910*, Urbana, University of Illinois Press

Boserup, Ester (1970) *Women's Role in Economic Development*, London, George Allen and Unwin

Braverman, Harry (1974), *Labour and Monopoly Capital: the Degradation of Work in the Twentieth Century*, New York, Monthly Review Press

Cockburn, Cynthia (1983), *Brothers: Male Dominance and Technological Change*, London, Pluto Press

Cockburn, Cynthia (1985), *Machinery of Dominance: Women, Men and Technical Know-how*, London, Pluto Press

Habib, Irfan (1992), 'Pursuing the History of Indian Technology. Pre-modern Modes of Transmission of Power', *Social Scientist*, Vol. 20, Nos.2–3, March–April

Harth, Erica (1992), *Cartesian Women: Versions and Subversions of Rational Discourse in the Old Regime*, Ithaca, NY, Cornell University Press

Hershatter, Gail (1986), *The Workers of Tianjin, 1900–1949*, Stanford, California, Stanford University Press

Hunter, Janet (ed.) (1993), 'Japanese Women at Work, 1880–1920', *History Today*, May

Huws, Ursula (1991), 'What Is a Green Red Economist? The Future of Work', *Z Magazine*, September

Keller, Evelyn Fox (1992), 'Gender and Science: An Update', in Evelyn Fox Keller (ed.), *Secrets of Life, Secrets of Death, Essays on Language, Gender and Science*, New York and London, Routledge

Kumar, Radha (1992), 'City Lives: Women Workers in the Bombay Textile Industry 1911–1947', PhD thesis, Department of History, Jawaharlal Nehru University, Delhi

Mathias, Regina (1993), 'Female Labour in the Japanese Coal-mining Industry', in Janet Hunter (ed.), *Japanese Women Working*, London and New York, Routledge

Mellor, Mary (1992), *Breaking the Boundaries: Towards a Feminist Green Socialism*, London, Virago Press

Merchant, Carolyn (1980), *The Death of Nature: Women, Ecology and the Scientific Revolution*, San Francisco, Harper Row

Needham, Joseph (1981), *Science in Traditional China*, Cambridge, Massachusetts, Harvard University Press

Noble, David F. (1992), *A World Without Women, The Christian Clerical Culture of Western Science*, New York, Alfred A. Knopf

Plumwood, Val (1990), 'Women, Humanity and Nature', in Sean Sayers and Peter Osborne (eds), *Socialism, Feminism and Philosophy, The Radical Philosophy Reader*, London and New York, Routledge

Polanski, Janet (1987) 'Helen Marot: Mother of Democratic Technics', in Barbara Drygulski Wright (ed.), *Women, Work, and Technology: Transformations*, Ann Arbor, The University of Michigan Press, 1st edition

Pringle, Rosemary (1989), *Secretaries Talk*, London, Verso

Rozen, Frieda S. (1987), 'Technological Advances and Increasing Militance: Flight Attendant Unions in the Jet Age', in Barbara Drygulski Wright (ed.), *Women, Work, and Technology: Transformations*, Ann Arbor, The University of Michigan Press, 1st edition

Sarton, George (1927), *Introduction to the History of Science*, Vol.I, From Homer to Omar Khayyam, Baltimore, Carnegie Institution of Washington, The Williams and Wilkins Company

Saso, Mary (1990), *Women in the Japanese Workplace*, London, Hilary Shipman Ltd.

Sayers, Janet (1982), *Biological Politics: Feminist and Anti-feminist Perspectives*, London and New York, Tavistock Publications

Schiebinger, Londa (1989a), *The Mind Has No Sex? Women in the Origins of Modern Science*, Cambridge, Massachusetts, Harvard University Press

Schiebinger, Londa (1989b), 'Maria Winkelmann: The Clash Between Guild Traditions and Professional Science', in Arina Angermen, Geete Biinena, Annemieke Keunen, Vefte Poels and Jacqueline Zikzee (eds), *Current Issues in Women's History*, London, Routledge

Schiebinger, Londa (1992), Why Science is Sexist, *Women's Review of Books*, Vol. X, No.3, December

Scrole, Carole (1987), 'A Blessing to Mankind, and Especially to Womankind: The Typewriter and Feminisation of Clerical Work, Boston 1860–1920,' in Barbara Drygulski Wright (ed.), *Women, Work, and Technology: Transformations*, Ann Arbor, The University of Michigan Press, 1st edition

Shaker Manifesto (1890), cited by Autumn Stanley in 'Women Hold Up Two-thirds of the Sky: Notes for the revised history of technology', in Joan Rothschild (ed.), *Machina Ex Dea: Feminist Perspectives in Technology*, NY, Pergamon Press, 1983

Soper, Kate (1992), 'Postmodernism, critical theory and critical realism', in Roy Bhaskar (ed.), *A Meeting of Minds, Socialists Discuss Philosophy – Towards a New Symposium?*, London, The Socialist Society

Stanley, Autumn (1983), 'Women Hold Up Two-thirds of the Sky: Notes for a Revised History of Technology' in Joan Rothschild (ed.), *Machine Ex Dea, Feminist Perspectives on Technology*, New York, Pergamon Press

Tanner, Jakob (1992), 'Le Repas dans l'Usine, L'Association Suisse du Service du Peuple et les Cantines de Fabriques, 1917–1937', in *Histoire et Société Contemporaines Lieux de Femmes dans l'Espace Public 1880–1930*, (proceedings), Lausanne, Monique Pavillon and François Vallotton, Vol. 13

Thomas, Keith (1984), *Man and The Natural World: Changing Attitudes in England 1500–1800*, London, Penguin

Trescott, Martha Moore (1983), 'Lillian Moller Gilbreth and the Founding of

Modern Industrial Engineering', in Joan Rothschild (ed), *Machina Ex Dea*, NY, Pergamon Press

Varikas, Eleni (n.d.), Feminism, Modernité, Postmodernisme: Pour un Dialogue des Deux Côtés de l'Ocean, unpublished paper

Wajcman, Judy (1991), *Feminism Confronts Technology*, London, Polity Press

Wright, Barbara Drygulski (1987), Introduction, in Barbara Drygulski Wright (ed.), *Women, Work and Technology: Transformations*, University of Michigan

4 Conflicting demands of new technology and household work

Women's work in Brazilian and Argentinian textiles

Liliana Acero

It is not enough to rely on the development process itself to diminish male bias. The development process acts in multifarious ways on male bias: reinforcing some forms of the subordination of women, decomposing other forms and recomposing yet new forms.

Diane Elson (1991, p. 25)

THE CONTEXT

The introduction of information technology in the developing world is markedly changing the pattern of female employment even in a so-called 'traditional' industry such as textiles. This essay documents the way such changes have affected the working and domestic lives of blue collar women employees in the textiles industries of Argentina and Brazil since the early 1980s, when computer technology was first incorporated in the sector in these countries. I undertook most of the fieldwork between 1984 and 1986, and supplemented the original findings by further desk and field research in 1992. The initial empirical study was undertaken in collaboration with several colleagues in Argentina and Brazil. In evaluating the effects of technology I took into account the broader social and economic changes, especially those arising out of the opening up of the market to the international economy, and of structural adjustment in both countries.

The key questions relating to the workplace of women that I have addressed are:

- Where have women been, and where will they be, in the industry in the future?
- How is technology related to the flexibilization of working patterns?
- Are new opportunities, in which female labour is actually preferred, arising?
- What would these require in terms of skills and training patterns?
- What differences and similarities can be detected between the two countries?
- Are the new jobs and work environments safer and healthier for women?

In the context of technological changes, these issues assume a certain urgency. Most studies have explained the increased participation of women in the labour market of these two countries[1] in terms of survival strategies in the current economic crisis rather than as women workers' response to new skill requirements arising out of the industrial application of information technologies. Even those studies that focus on technological changes have, with some notable exceptions, largely disregarded the possibility of a differential impact on men and women (Humphrey, 1989; Hirata, 1988). But there is ample documentation of the ways these technologies are being incorporated in production and service occupations in both countries (Schmitz and Cassiolatto, 1992). As a rule, either digital automation or new management techniques, or both combined in 'a systemic strategy of modernization', to borrow a phrase from Fleury (1988), are increasingly being introduced at strategic points in the production process in varied economic sectors and branches. Companies are automating not only to save labour costs but also to obtain higher efficiency, speed, and flexibility in order to respond to fluctuating demand and to meet international quality standards.

There is now some agreement that new technologies affect labour use in textiles, as in other manufacturing sectors, by reducing the number of workers in each production unit. There is less consensus as to how they change the nature of work, of women and men employees. There are generally two contrasting theses about the current and future impact of new technology on the quality of work:

1 the 'postindustrial thesis', in which automation is seen as liberating workers from routine tasks and producing a skilled, stable, well-paid, committed and autonomous labour force (Touraine, 1962; Davis and Taylor, 1972);
2 the 'degradation of work thesis', in which innovation is seen as designed to reduce skill requirements and transform work activities into repetitive routines, so that labour becomes cheap and easy to substitute (Braverman, 1974).

More recent findings from the study of specific branches and occupations affected by digital automation (such as microelectronics-based equipment, numerically-controlled machine tools, computer-aided design and manufacturing, robotics, programmable controllers) in various Latin American countries show that digital automation tends to affect the nature of work in specific ways. These can be most effectively explained, I feel, by applying a variation of the 'degradation of work thesis' (Acero, 1990b). My own analysis of textile workers of both genders in Argentina and Brazil generally tends to confirm this.

My study, however, goes beyond a straightforward evaluation of technical changes on women's work at the factory level. It explicitly takes into consideration the effect that the changed nature of employment has on women's autonomy and control over household decisions. The new relationships of power within the household, in turn, affect productivity, wage levels and career progression in the workplace (Acero, 1991; Beneria and Roldan, 1987; Hirata and Humphrey, 1986). Academic studies, with the exception of some feminist scholars, have generally disregarded the interrelationships between workplace and household demands, and how these alter with the direct and indirect effects of changes in technology. I am trying to establish a link between women's positions, at home and at work, in the light of certain existing and emerging features in Latin American societies in the era of new technology. Some of the most important of these features are:

1   the increasing participation of women in both the tertiary and formal manufacturing sector;
2   the growth in casualized forms of work, in the formal sector as well as in the so-called 'informal' sector, with women being more exposed to casualization than men;
3   the increasing participation of young women in the industrial labour force, resulting in changed attitudes and practices as regards childbearing;
4   that the main burden of housework continues to be borne by women, even among those employed in industry;
5   new requirements and realities of childcare, for women entering the labour market earlier in their life-cycles;
6   the predominance of non-participatory authority within blue-collar households, which subjects working women to various forms of exploitation, violence, and abuse.

THE RESTRUCTURING OF THE TEXTILES INDUSTRY: TECHNOLOGY AND NEW ORGANIZATIONAL MODELS

Brazil

Until 1970, small textile firms (less than 500 workers) accounted for approximately 50 per cent of the textiles output in Brazil, while medium and large firms were responsible for 15 per cent and 35 per cent respectively (BNDE, 1977). But after the economic policy implemented during the Brazilian miracle (1968-1973), the sector became much more concentrated. Concentration and restructuring have continued in recent years, which have been characterized by:

1 the stagnation of internal demand for textiles due to economic recession and social impoverishment;
2 the gradual liberalization of domestic tariffs, and the relative opening of the economy to international competition;
3 an increased incentive to export, given the international increase in export quotas allowed by the weakening of the controls built into the Multifibre Agreement operating between 1974 and 1992;
4 the beginnings of the implementation of the Mercosur Agreement, a common market between Uruguay, Paraguay, Brazil and Argentina, which will create a market of 200 million consumers;
5 the need to recover lost productivity and competitiveness in the industry which, between 1990 and 1992, was operating at 50 per cent to 60 per cent of its installed capacity.

The push towards technological upgrading was reflected in increasing imports of textiles machinery over the years. In 1991, such machinery accounted for 17.2 per cent of total capital goods imports. Modernization with computer technology began in the 80s, with the incorporation of microelectronic devices into machinery in some phases of the production process and in other sub-branches of textiles (e.g. into the circular automatic looms used in knitting). Innovations were further developed in the finishing stages of production. Technologically, Brazil is considered to be at an intermediate level within the international economy; with the average age of its textile machines being 14–16 years (as opposed to 6–8 years in developed countries). Some 60 per cent of its installed equipment is locally produced, a pattern found among the ten most advanced countries in textile production (*Revista Textil*, various numbers).

Greater use of mixed fibres tends to facilitate the use of microelectronic control devices. These intensify managerial control of the manufacturing process by registering, storing and transmitting information at each stage of the production process. They also take over or modify tasks that previously required human intervention. For example, they crucially affect the jobs of quality controllers. The devices demand an upgrading of supervisory and technical skills, but also training in basic informatics techniques for many types of operators, many of whom are women. The use of microelectronic control devices has facilitated the adoption of new forms of management and work organization at the plant level, such as semi-autonomous groups, quality control circles (CCQs) and just-in-time production (Ferraz, 1992).

In general, industrial automation and new organizational techniques are seen by respondents in large textile firms as contributing to higher employment levels, but only among technical staff and mostly at the levels of project planning and maintenance. The knowledge relevant for industrial automation is thus expected to be in the fields of management, electronics, and the maintenance of machines. While the need for polyvalence and flexible work rhythms is increasing, the number of occupational categories and labour-intensive tasks is decreasing. With the introduction of new equipment, more weight is now being given to general education and to vocational training, rather than to workers' experiential and tacit skills.

Argentina

There is very little information available on the technical levels of the textile industry in Argentina. The best way of analysing the degree of modernization in the sector is to look at the latest trends in textile machinery imports. Since 1982 (with the exception of 1983, which was a year of turmoil, with the return to democracy and the switch to the economic liberalization model), imports of textile machinery have increased steadily. Since 1985 textile machines have been the main type of machinery imported, representing in most years more than two thirds of total machinery imports. The rapid modernization of the textile industry since 1985 has partly reflected the influence of the economic model underlying the economic readjustment policy, proposed by the IMF, which was intended to return Argentina to the world market. New technology was recognized as indispensable for international competitiveness and, in the case of textiles, the promotion of certain product-lines for exports urgently required technical renewal.

The effects of textiles modernization on new forms of work organization in Argentina have not been sufficiently researched. A case-study of one of the largest national textile firms (Novick and Lavigne, 1988), however, shows that the firm had introduced semi-autonomous groups and the just-in-time system to all its plants. This was done in order to be able to respond quickly to changing export market needs, to adapt production to higher quality products and to different types of customer orders. The authors estimated that such organizational innovations, being used in four or five of the leading textile firms, had led to job 'restructuring' for approximately 7,500 workers. Quality control had been brought down to the shop floor and relegated to blue collar workers, whom the firms now require to have new skills such as a higher disposition to group work and greater flexibility.

TECHNOLOGY-INDUCED JOB LOSSES

Brazil

There is no satisfactory empirical evidence on job losses, differentiated by type of task and gender. However for Brazil, Visao (1992) reports that employment levels in textiles for 1991 were the lowest in the last six years. While sales had fallen by 13.5 per cent, employment fell 16 per cent, with a consequent loss of 56,800 jobs. The spinning and weaving subsectors, which had modernized the most and adopted an export-oriented strategy, were responsible for a third of those dismissals, while the textile goods sub-branch, with smaller firms, had a modest employment growth of 0.3 per cent.

The Brazilian textiles sector, though a traditional employer of female labour, substantially reduced its female labour force between 1960 and 1975, with some recovery between 1975 and 1980. But in the latter period the female workforce rose by 14 per cent, and the male workforce by just 6 per cent. This reversal can be explained by the behaviour of modernizing firms towards female labour. They initially arranged for their new equipment to be tested by male workers, then they operated it with new young women recruits, with lower wages for jobs that had become unskilled. The subcontracting of work to women working in their homes or in small workshops also increased, improving women's job opportunities. Between 1980 and 1985, there was an overall decrease in employment in the sector of 4.3 per cent, but the remaining jobs became increasingly feminized. Yet data on textiles employment by gender in 1992, based on a reduced sample (337 workers), shows the ratio of women to men falling from 0.7 per cent in January to 0.65 per cent in October of that year (IBGE, Pesquisa têxtil, 1992). The picture is thus still unclear.

Argentina

In Argentina, as in Brazil, the textiles industry has always absorbed a significant proportion of female labour. In August 1982, 36.6 per cent of workers in the industry were women. This is a high rate, as overall female participation in manufacturing was only 24.1 per cent, increasing slightly to 26.1 per cent in 1990 (INDEC, Household Survey, various numbers).

FITA (1988) reported that in 1987, in the whole textile sector, there were only 82,000 employees, of which approximately 75 per cent were blue-collar workers. A third of this blue-collar employment was female. The greatest reduction in employment took place between 1973 and 1984 (from

122,697 to 88,352 employees), due to a general economic and political crisis. Job-losses due to technical change have occurred mostly since 1985, when the newest modern equipment was being imported on a large scale. Between 1985 and 1989, the number of workers employed in textiles decreased by 7.8 per cent, while the hours worked diminished by only 3.9 per cent, revealing an intensification of work, mostly to be attributed to technical change (INDEC, 1992). Only a minor part of that intensification was due to longer working hours among the self-employed: much more was due to the casualization of employees' contracts. Three-month contracts, without rights to social legislation, have become common in the last two years in the Argentine industry (Roldan, 1992).

TECHNICAL CHANGE AND LABOUR USE

In textiles, technology has done away with some tasks altogether by incorporating them into the machinery. Pirn-strippers and pirn-winders, for example, are no longer required. Technology has also changed the characteristics of other tasks, simplifying some and so reducing the number of specializations in some occupational categories, such as spinners and weavers. In some cases, jobs have vanished due to changes in work organization. The foreman's job, for example, could be done away with as workers themselves were left to supervise machines. Half the foreman's jobs which were lost were previously carried out by women. Few new jobs were created to compensate for these job-losses. Moreover, since the technology for both countries had been designed abroad, few new technical and engineering posts became available. Some job opportunities opened up later in the domestic equipment industry, principally in sales, but the numbers were insignificant. Furthermore, there was a continual reduction in overtime employment, at least part of which could be attributed to technical change.

The skills of workers who remained employed were also substantially altered, though not in uniform ways. Maintenance workers in new technology were required to make their skills more machine-specific, hence reducing their knowledge of more abstract principles that could be applied to a broader range of textile machinery. Their skills became both more sophisticated and less broad. From the point of view of individual crafts and experience, technical change did not produce a straightforward de-skilling of all categories of production and maintenance workers. In most cases, however, technological changes led to a downgrading of skills. The jobs that required long experience were done away with, for instance drawing-in hands, doffers and tying-in hands. These vanishing positions were previously all occupied by women. At the same time, some jobs that contained a higher level of formal skill were also downgraded. For instance, the skills required of foremen were changed completely, as the job was split into maintenance and supervision roles, and the latter became more important. One common feature among all categories of workers remaining in the modernized plants was that the intensity of their work increased substantially. Spinners, for example, were literally running around the machines for eight hours a day, and work intensity for weavers increased by 20 per cent. An ability to cope with high work rhythms was considered a preferred attribute, and was described by management as among the 'typically women's qualities.'

If the skills needed from the majority of blue-collar workers in the firms were reduced (mainly by the reduction of posts requiring higher skills), one would expect the overall training time to diminish. But in fact more resources were devoted to in-plant training in the new sections, especially in Brazilian plants. This was done primarily for economic gains: first, it guaranteed a tax deduction, and second, a payment was drawn from workers themselves during their training time. However, such in-plant training also fosters an acceptance among workers of the devaluation of experience-based knowledge and its replacement by technically-based knowledge. This shift helps to downgrade the jobs that use less technically-based knowledge, which are jobs performed by women.

In the textile factories studied, the management had established a clear distinction between men's work and women's work, built into the job descriptions used in recruitment procedures. Most of the pre-spinning sections were male. Both genders were employed at the spinning stage, but twisting and winding were considered female sections. The job descriptions were based on the assumption that women should be employed for safer jobs or for those that need less strength and more dedication and acceptance of routinization. Understandably, women received low wages, or wages lower than men. Wage differentials of between 25 per cent and 50 per cent were common. Women were never recruited for the top skilled jobs, such as maintenance work.

By reducing the skills component of many of these tasks, new technology allowed management to recruit workers with no previous experience in the industry, so reducing the constraints imposed by historical gender divisions in the workplace. New technology, by decreasing the skill content of jobs, brought about the 'feminization' of tasks that had been male and the 'masculinization' of tasks that had been female. The result, unfortunately, was that most jobs were paid less than previously.

Generally, women gained a larger share of the deskilled jobs. The new machines were initially operated by male workers, but once the production and organizational know-how needed to run the new sections had been built up, firms developed the policy of employing young female machine operators (up to 25 years old). Women were seen as 'naturally' more reliable, hard-working and disciplined than male machine operators.

Firms developed specific practices that made female workers more vulnerable to managerial control. First, it was less common to enter promotions in work records for women than for men. This gave women, indirectly, fewer rights to wage increases, as well as lowering their bargaining position when looking for jobs in other textile plants. Second, women were subject to a permanent threat of dismissal if they became pregnant. Pregnancy was periodically checked among the female labour force in the firms (in Brazil more than in Argentina).

Women's subordinate position in the factory was defined also by certain differences in their own responses and relationships. They tended to relate to supervisors as if they were family figures and to prefer men to women in these positions. At the same time they were more readily aware and active than men in denouncing faulty working conditions and high machine-pacing, as factors affecting their health. They were also keener than men to defend the principal of equal wages for equal work. Younger women in the new sections expressed support for other workers' movements. They blamed themselves, individually, for not taking a strong position within the workplace by demanding the registration of promotions in their work records; yet they took no group action. Their consciousness was contradictory, and was expressed differently from that of male workers. There was thus a recomposition of the forms of subordination of women after technical change.

VOCATIONAL TRAINING AND RETRAINING PATTERNS FOR TEXTILES: IMPLICATIONS FOR WOMEN

The most important centres of vocational training are SENAI in Brazil and CONET in Argentina.[2] However the textile industries in both countries mainly train their production and maintenance workers on the job. This is true not only of large and medium-size firms, but even of small firms. Large and medium-sized companies in Brazil usually set up their training centres at the plant in collaboration with SENAI. Maintenance staff tend to attend specific short formal courses, complementary to their on-the-job training, at SENAI or CONET.

Brazil

SENAI, in the State of Sao Paulo, where textiles are still concentrated, offers a wide range of courses: *direct action courses*, where the training takes place mainly in SENAI's professional training units (schools) or in technical training units of the Regional Departments; and *indirect action courses*, organized by the firms through their own training centres but under SENAI's supervision. The two types of courses differ significantly in the types of posts for which training is developed, their duration and costs per student (SENAI, 1987). In 1988 there were 4,805 registrations in all SENAI's textile courses, almost three quarters of them from students attending the direct action courses, with an average course duration of 216.5 hours per trainee. The *indirect action courses* offered only industrial training for blue-collar textile workers. Indirect action courses were shorter, involving on average one to two weeks' training, seventy hours per trainee. Understandably, many more women attended the second type of course. Some 70 per cent of the students are women, many of them 17 years old or younger, and many with little or no schooling.

SENAI's training model is developed mainly by studying, through occupational analysis in the industry, the work content for each post. Then it is transformed into teaching materials, which are largely delivered through 'directive teaching' (Caruso, 1990). However, 'problem-solving' training, which is seldom given, is what is required for some posts in the new technical paradigm, especially in relation to the transferable skills that workers need to move from one type of task to another. The new organizational techniques which are spreading through the industry also require this type of flexible skill. The extended application of task techniques to areas in which women concentrate further devalues jobs and skills.

Argentina

CONET's training scope is much smaller than that of SENAI. General industrial training agreements, of the type developed by SENAI in Brazil, are virtually non-existent between CONET and textile firms. The only courses that deal with the new requirements for microelectronics-based textile equipment at all are the course for technicians at CONET and the course for textile engineers at the National Technical University (UTN). These types of training are not accessible to most women.

Textile technicians do study programming, but subjects such as quality control and industrial reorganization, greatly needed in working with the new technologies, are not addressed in the syllabus. This failure to adapt to the demands of new technology production methods is not due to a need to keep training costs low, since these costs are quite moderate. At the firm level, training costs are very low for most categories of workers. The lack of training for many activities, such as those of foremen and supervisors, can also not be explained simply in economic terms. It costs, on average, only US $90 a month to train one worker for each post.

Recent research reveals the difficulties of the Argentine textile industry in finding specialized skilled workers (CONET, 1992). The discovery of what is termed the 'industrial illiteracy' of the Argentine worker in this phase of automation led to the creation of a Sub-secretariat of Vocational Training, within the Ministry of Labour, in 1992. All of CONET's educational units were transferred to it, in order to connect the productive sector with vocational training schemes. The impact of this change, at the national level and specifically for women workers, remains unclear.

THE WORK ENVIRONMENT IN TEXTILES

A textile mill in Brazil or Argentina is frequently a world of noise, dust, and sometimes humidity and heat. The production uses a vast quantity of water and a variety of chemicals. These generate liquid waste containing substantial pollutants, in the form of organic and suspended matter, such as fibres and grease (UNEP, 1991). Field-work has shown that, in both countries and most production stages, noise-levels well beyond the legal limit of 80 decibels are common. Floors are usually dirty, the pre-spinning stages extremely dusty and the finishing stages toxic, with highly concentrated odours. In Brazil, moreover, daily monitoring of safety issues by the CIPA (Commissions for the Prevention of Accidents) is largely nominal, with the exception of some general training campaigns in risk awareness. In both countries, work accident data is usually not made available, or is not even collected at the plant level.

More surprising still is that neither SENAI nor CONET, or the newly formed Secretariat for Vocational Training in Argentina, systematically tackle training on environmental issues in their programmes for the sector. SENAI has environmental awareness training courses for the younger generation, but these are not sector-specific. The Secretariat does not include environmental training in its programme. Greater awareness in this field in both countries, and particularly in Brazil, came from the trade unions, especially DIESSE (The Inter-Departmental Training and Research Trade Union Institute), which publishes several booklets to promulgate work and safety measures for selected industries (DIESSE, various numbers). Still, the real concern is very new, and hardly addresses the new types of work hazards that microelectronic technologies can bring about, such as: isolation and fatigue from reduced communication, higher machine pacing, and the embodiment of work control within the technological system; headaches and loss of sight from working with VDUs; miscarriages due to new chemicals related to semi-conductors and new materials previously almost unknown or untested, and other reproductive risks; and severe localized muscular tensions leading to possible atrophies or acute back pain and arthritis.

TEXTILE WORKERS' HOUSEHOLDS[3]

Nuclear families, of three or four people, are the norm in both countries. They are more common in Argentina (41.7 per cent vs. 38.1 per cent in Brazil). In Brazil, more extended households are more common. There are usually two wage earners. In Argentina, 35 per cent of the households in our sample had only one wage-earner, and only 15.8 per cent of the households in Brazil. In Argentina, 18.5 per cent of the households have women as sole providers, and only 9.7 per cent in Brazil. Labour conditions, employment stability and compensation for dismissal were better in Argentina at the time of our initial study in 1986. Argentina also had more stable and higher wages. This could partially explain why more Argentinian households have only one wage-earner.

Being the main breadwinner can make women workers much more vulnerable in the world of work. One woman interviewed in Argentina put it thus: 'while I feel calmer without a husband to look after, I have only myself to rely upon, the children are still too small . . . so I must under any circumstances keep my job, but I can't take any extra time off to do the training required. . . . It is a vicious circle because I lose the possibility of promotion and wages do not make ends meet. I sometimes wonder if this is autonomy.'

In a quarter of the households in Argentina and Brazil – slightly more in Argentina – couples make decisions about the managing of income jointly. The proportion was higher for younger couples. Control over key economic decisions very much depended upon whether the female interviewee was an income provider. Sole providers, whether they be men or women, are usually the sole managers of the household budgets. 'Now that I bring in money to the family, at least, my husband does not control so much what I buy for the kids or for myself,' said a woman worker. Offspring seldom have any role in the management of the household budget, whether they are providers or not: this was especially marked in Brazil.

The burden of housework was carried mostly by the female textile workers in these households. Paid work and travel sometimes take ten to twelve hours per day. Part of Sunday is spent doing extra housework. A very high proportion of men, particularly Brazilian men, do not participate in household chores.

The tasks that men claimed to perform varied markedly between the two countries. Argentinian men are involved in some cooking, tidying the house, and washing dishes, but they also participate in shopping and childcare. Brazilian men look after the children only on odd occasions and they engage in a limited way in cooking and shopping. But this participation is sporadic and discontinuous. Sharing of housework among married couples is not very common. The greatest cooperation was found among younger couples, with and without children, in Argentina. But even here, there is not necessarily an equal level of participation. Cooperation between family members substantially reduces the burden of household chores on the individual woman. But this is only found among women belonging to the same household. For example, our study shows that, in Brazil, chores that could take an individual woman an average six hours daily, can take only four hours when performed collaboratively with other women.

Workers marry early in their life in both countries, women even earlier than men, when they are teenagers. Men tend to marry younger women and women to marry older men. In Argentina, these unions are quite stable, second marriages being infrequent. Women initiate a separation more frequently than men, especially in Argentina. When they do so, they tend to remain single. Qualitative information shows that, in Argentina, married women who work outside the household have more autonomy, but also face new household conflicts in relation to housework and childcare. A woman who had recently become separated presented it thus: 'Everything was OK till I became a worker, then I would come back at six or seven o'clock at night to find nothing had been done and the children were unfed and dirty. I would tell him to help, but he became violent. Several times he "aimed" at me. The thing he most hated was that his shirts were not ironed. Also, he resented my handing him money because it was mine. So he could not go drinking when he pleased.'

Workers in both countries tend to have some work experience before marrying, which shows their need to secure an income before marriage and also reflects the early age at which they start work. Women have less work experience at the time of marriage than men. In a few cases women had married without having any experience of paid employment, but there are no such cases among males, who are brought up to become income-providers.

More than half the workers in the samples had children. However, more men than women were parents: as the women textile workers explained, paid work leaves little time for child-bearing. There were an average of three children per interviewee in Brazil and two in Argentina, low figures for developing countries. Women workers prefer to wait longer than men, after marriage or forming a stable union, to have their first child. Industrial work has undoubtedly influenced this. In Argentina, women are less likely to have children after beginning work in the textile industry. They see their work both as limiting their reproductive role and widening their social field. In Brazil, a significant number of women are dismissed from industrial work owing to pregnancy, which significantly affects the continuity of their work records. In the households which we studied, the childcare was usually carried out by the women, whether or not they were also working. Childcare facilities provided by firms or by local groups were rare in both countries, although the law in Brazil requires medium-size and large firms to provide facilities.

Most workers had permanent accommodation. Brazilian workers tended to live with their families of origin after marriage, until they obtain government funds to buy their own house, a facility offered to local workers. This living arrangement means that they receive help from mothers or mothers-in-law for childcare. In Argentina, on the other hand, the norm is the nuclear family, and it is common for workers to move back to parents' or parents-in-law's houses only when the first child is born, in order to secure childcare facilities. They revert to the nuclear family when the older children, particularly daughters, are able to help with childcare.

Broadly speaking, the relation between events in the life-cycles of female textile workers in the two countries followed a similar pattern. The workers have a first job, they then enter textiles, they marry a few years before or after that time, they move from their parental home, they have their first child and, around that time, they begin to use contraceptive methods. But significant differences by gender and age could be found between countries.

Among Brazilian women the events followed each other very rapidly, occurring in their teens and the early years of their mature life. The time span between their entrance into textiles and marriage, as well as between marriage and motherhood, is shorter than that of Argentinian women. They also show a strong work continuity and, although their reproductive role interferes with their working lives, they manage to limit this interference more effectively than Argentinian women. This can be explained largely by their living arrangements, with older women taking care of their children, and their more critical approach to social attitudes towards gender.

Discontinuity in an individual's work history is more common in Argentina, where gender stereotypes about marriage, birth control and, especially, childcare have a greater hold. They leave a longer time between marriage and childbearing, once they become industrial workers. This is not because they are more work-oriented, as management argues, but because they 'have a feeling' that, once married, part of their flexibility in handling their own lives will be lost.

Modernization in the textiles sector has had little direct effect on workers' behaviour as regards marriage, living with parents or in-laws, fertility and family planning. There was more information available on contraception, and the periodical checking of women for pregnancy was more common, in modernized firms and sections in Brazil. However, we could not identify any marked trend towards more reliable or continuous birth control practices among these women, nor any significant increase in their knowledge about contraceptive measures.

WOMEN WORKERS' PERCEPTIONS AND VOICES

The samples provided not only evidence of the objective behaviour of textile workers but also material on how they perceived their own distinct identities as workers. They highlighted the norms and expectations of each gender. It was, indeed, not easy to unravel the norms which resulted from various social practices from the norms which gave rise to them.

An amazing number of men in both countries believe that women should 'under no circumstances' work outside the home; this is especially marked in Argentina. The more the men contribute to household income, the less they are inclined to accept women's work in the labour market. It is more striking still that a small portion of the female textile workers themselves think likewise. When there are small children in the family, outside work for women is not valued highly by either gender, except among Brazilian women. 'Children need us', 'We have to be with them as mothers', and 'The factory life doesn't allow for motherhood and work' were frequently voiced statements. These opinions are based in part on the lack of childcare facilities, but also reflect social conceptions about gender. When women voiced a different opinion, they also spoke of the tensions that working placed upon their lives, in terms of time allocation and relationships with their partners, sometimes even leading to violent con- frontations about childcare. Men in both countries still feel more strongly about this than women. The agreement between the genders in this respect is greater in Argentina than in Brazil.

Women's work was considered acceptable when 'it is necessary to maintain the household.' A third of the men surveyed, but also many of the women, agreed with this view. Men felt threatened by women's contribution to income, even though survival in these households depended on the economic independence of all family members.

Yet, while the majority of women saw their wages as crucial for family subsistence, two thirds of the men regarded them as complementary, even in the many cases in which women were contributing more than two thirds of the household budget. The men were less realistic than the women. For example, few Brazilian men considered women's wages as essential for family subsistence, regarding themselves as the main household income providers, though this was not objectively the case. Argentine men were somewhat more realistic, as 31.3 per cent think of women's wages as essential for their household budget. Many women – half in Brazil and a quarter in Argentina – saw female wages mainly in terms of 'helping out', or 'supplementing' the wages of their husbands. Argentine women were generally more realistic than Brazilian about the role of their own wages in family subsistence, but they were less likely to question their autonomy in relation to their husbands:

> Without my salary it would be impossible to buy clothes and send our children to school. The problem is that my husband wants still more children, at least two more. I do not know how I am going to do everything, the cleaning, the shopping, etc., especially because he does not want me to work during pregnancy. I sometimes use pills without telling him, but if I happen to be pregnant, I will leave the job and then we shall see . . .

In both countries, only those women who pooled income more equitably with their husbands had a more positive perception of what wage-earning could give to women.

The woman's salary often became a subject for conflict within the family group, especially if men earned less or were unemployed. This is how this conflict was expressed by one of the women interviewed in Argentina:

> My marriage started to break down when I began working outside. I mean recently. I started being more independent and he saw that . . . My salary was higher than his. I could earn more than he; for example, I began dressing the girls, buying clothes for myself . . . and still there was enough for transport. His salary was not enough even for himself, because he was getting less than me. I think that made him mad . . . because I had more chances than he did. So things started going wrong. . . .

Such opinions were expressed by women workers in a context of progressive perceived impoverishment, and unemployment, particularly among Argentine male workers. Unemployed men do not find it easy to accept their wives as major bread-winners.

Such rigidities in the perception of gender roles within the household, in turn, affected women's behaviour in the world of work, and contributed to their fear of organizing around their work place demands. However, when these conflicts were discussed in groups, potential for change emerged. For instance, as a result of the research, some women in both countries formed their own awareness-raising groups. These retained semi-autonomy from the local trade unions, but still presented the union with women's specific demands, such as the establishment of childcare facilities and better health treatment for members. In collective bargaining negotiations,[4] they also persuaded male leaders to take into account the differential effects of new technologies on women workers.

Overall, it was mainly the younger generation that achieved a sense of autonomy through the extended possibilities of paid work. They appeared to be less affected by the conflicting demands of workplaces and households. This gave them greater flexibility in seeking jobs and in training. However, this was only partly the result of changes in the social acceptance of greater gender equality. Another important reason was the role played by older women in their households and neighbourhoods in releasing them from some of the tasks of housework and childcare. However, the trend towards nuclearization of the 'typical' working family, and the decrease in the overall numbers of extended families among these textile workers, could eventually diminish the relative advantage enjoyed by the younger generation, and even increase the conflicts between different generations of women, as well as between genders.

These findings for textiles in Brazil and Argentina can be related to similar ones for other industries or sectors in Latin America. Together, they contribute to a newly emerging picture of the use of female labour in 'traditional' and 'modern' industries and services in the region, where microelectronic technologies have become diffused. They indicate scenarios for women's employment in the future. Without extensive changes in training and education, women will remain locked into low-paid jobs. The employment possibilities of Latin American women (cf. Acero, 1994a) are also affected by the manner in which their household activities overlap with their employment. Both aspects need to be analysed when academics, planners and policy-makers look at women's work and training, if gender-awareness is to permeate future paths of development.

NOTES

1 In both Brazil and Argentina there was a substantial change in the female labour force during the 1970s and 1980s, when new technologies began to be gradually incorporated. In Brazil, the sustained growth of the economically active population could be partly explained by the increased participation of women in the labour market. The female activity rate rose from 33.6 per cent in 1979 to 38.7 per cent in 1989, while men's rates were unchanged. In the early 1980s, the growth in the participation of female labour in industry was 10.7 per cent a year (Humphrey, 1987). Not only young, unskilled females joined the market at the time, but also educated women from intermediate age-brackets (Saboia, 1991a and 1991b). A large proportion of them would have joined the tertiary sector (DAWN, 1985). However, only 55 per cent of wage-earning women were officially registered (Abreu, 1992), indicating a possible increase in the number of self-employed female workers. In Argentina, most female employment was traditionally concentrated in the tertiary sector. Between 1960 and 1980, 95 per cent of the growth in the female economically active population was due to the feminization of the tertiary sector (Cortes, 1988). While the participation of the total population in the labour market decreased between 1970 and 1980, the participation of women remained stable at 27 per cent, and male participation decreased from 81 per cent to 75 per cent (INDEC, Population Census, various numbers). There was also an increase in these years in the proportion of female workers of the intermediate age-cohort, between 35 and 44 years old (6 per cent), relative to younger cohorts (2 per cent for the 25-34 year olds) and a rise in the participation of 'spouses' as opposed to household heads (INDEC, Household Surveys, various numbers). Most unemployed males were skilled blue-collar workers. Self-employment was not a significant choice for female labour during those years, but it was for male labour. For both countries, the data cited is the last information published that is compatible for comparative purposes.

2 SENAI is the National Service of Industrial Training, and CONET is the National Council. The latter has, since 1993, been integrated into a new structure functioning within the Ministry of Labour.

3 Much of the data in this section is derived from fieldwork in 1986. The survey sample consisted of 520 textile workers from the two countries, and the 2,088 members of their households.

4 Women's sections in trade unions were set up to deal with specific demands in many countries in the region in past decades: in Argentina in the 1950s, and in Brazil in the late 1970s. However those issues did not systematically permeate the discussion of trade unions in wage negotiations, or they were not taken up seriously enough by the male leaders, especially in the textiles branch. For discussions of this issue see, especially, Alvarez, 1991, and other items in Jacquette, 1991.

REFERENCES

Abramo, Laís W. (1990) 'Novas Tecnologias, Difusao Emprego e Trabalho no Brasil', in *Boletim Informativo Bibliografico*, Rio de Janeiro, BIB, No. 30

Abreu de Paiva, Alice (1990), 'Dressmakers or Workers, Sex and Skill in the Garment Industry of Rio de Janeiro, Brazil', mimeo, XII World Congress of Sociology, Madrid

Abreu de Paiva, Alice (1992), 'The Gendering of Technological Change in Brazil', unpublished paper presented at LASA XVII International Congress, Sept. 24–27, Los Angeles

Acero, Liliana (1983), *Technical Change, Skills and the Labour Process in Brazilian Textiles*, unpublished doctoral dissertation, Sussex University, UK.

Acero, Liliana (1984), 'Technical Change in a Newly Industrializing Country: a Case-study of the Impacts on Employment and Skills in the Brazilian Textile Industry', Brighton, UK, *SPRU Occasional Papers*, No. 22

Acero, Liliana (1990a), 'Report on Vocational Training and Retraining in the Textile Industry', submitted to the 12th Session of the Textile Committee, *The Cases of Brazil and Argentina*, Geneva, unpublished report of the ILO Training Policies Branch, July

Acero, Liliana (1990b), 'Microelectronics: the Nature of Work, Skills and Training; an Analysis of Case-studies from Developed and Developing Countries', *Training Discussion Papers*, No. 51, Geneva, ILO Training Policies Branch, November

Acero, Liliana (1991), *Textile workers in Brazil and Argentina: a Study of the Interrelationships Between Work and Households*, Tokyo, United Nations University Press

Acero, Liliana (1994a) (ed.), *Women in Development*, Washington, IDB, forthcoming

Acero, Liliana (1994b), 'Environmental Management in the Mining Industry: the Case of Bauxite, Alumina and Aluminium in Brazil', Ottawa, IDRC, forthcoming

Aguiar, N. (ed.) (1984), *Mulheres na Força de Trabalho na America Latina: Analises Qualitativas*, Petrópolis, Ed. Vozes

Alvarez, S. (1991), 'Women's Movements and Gender Politics in the Brazilian Transition', in Jacquette, J. (ed.), (1991), *The Women's Movement in Latin America*, Boulder, Colorado, Westview Press

Anderson, J. and D. Dimon (1992), 'The Impact of Globalization of Production on Women's Labour Sector Participation: the Case of Mexico', unpublished paper presented at LASA XVII International Congress, Sept. 24–27, Los Angeles

Arruda, J. *et al.* (1986), 'Pesquisa Nacional Sobre Saúde Materno-infantil e Planejamento Familiar', Relatorio preliminar ao V Encontro Nac. de Est. Populacionais. São Paulo, BEMFAM

Balan, J. and S. Ramos (1989), *La Medicalización del Comportamiento Reproductivo: un Estudio Exploratorio Sobre la Demanda de Anticonceptivos en los Sectores Populares*, Documento CEDES/29, Buenos Aires, CEDES

Barroso, C. and T. Amado (1987), 'The Impact of the Crisis upon Poor Women's Health: The Case of Brazil', in UNICEF, *The Invisible Adjustment*, Santiago de Chile, UNICEF

Beneria, L., and S. Feldman (1992), *Unequal Burden: Economic Crises, Persistent Poverty and Women's Work*, Boulder, Westview Press

Beneria, L., and M. Roldan (1987), *The Crossroads of Class and Gender: Homework, Subcontracting and Household Dynamics in Mexico City*, Chicago, University of Chicago Press

BNDE, (1977), *Diagnóstico Sobre a Industria Têxtil*, (mimeo), Rio de Janeiro, BNDE, Area de Planejamento

Braverman, H. (1974), *Labour and Monopoly Capital: the Degradation of Work in the Twentieth Century*, New York, Monthly Review Press

Buvinic, M. (1990), *Women and Poverty in Latin America and the Caribbean: a Primer for Policy-makers*, Washington, ICRW and IDB

Caruso, L.A.C. (1990), *Difusão de technologia microelectrónica e modificações do trabalho. Implicações para a formação profissional*, master's thesis for the Instituto de Economia Industrial, Federal University of Rio de Janeiro

Centro de Tecnologia da Indústria Quimica e Textil (CETIQT) (1980), *Efeitos dos Avanços Tecnológicos Sobre o Emprego na Indústria Textil*, (mimeo), Rio de Janeiro, SENAI

Cockburn, Cynthia (1986), 'Women and Technology: Opportunity is Not Enough', in Kate Purcell, Stephen Wood, Alan Waton and Sheila Allen (eds), *The Changing Experience of Employment, Restructuring and Recession*, Basingstoke, Macmillan and the British Sociological Association, Explorations in Sociology series No. 22

Cockburn, Cynthia (1988), 'Maquinaria de Dominación: Mujeres, Hombres y Know-how Técnico', in *El trabajo a través de la mujer*, Madrid, Sociología del Trabajo 3, Siglo XXI ed

Cockburn, Cynthia (1990), 'Technical Competence, Gender Identity and Women's Autonomy', mimeo, World Congress of Sociology, 9–13 July

CONET (1988), *Información Estadistica Ciclo Básico y Ciclo Superior*, 1975–1988, Buenos Aires

CONET (1992), *Informe Evolutivo de las Neusidades de Calificacion en la Industria Textil*, mimeo, Buenos Aires

Cortes, R. (1988), *Informe Sobre el Mercado de Trabajo Femenino en la Argentina*, Buenos Aires, UNICEF, Subsecretaria de La Mujer de la Nacion Argentina

Davis, L.E. and J.C. Taylor (eds) (1972), *Design of Jobs*, Harmondsworth, Penguin

DAWN (Development Alternatives with Women for a New Era) (1985), *Development, Crisis and Alternative Visions: Third World Women's Perspectives*, Delhi, DAWN

DIESSE, *Indicadores Socioeconomicos*, Sao Paulo, various numbers

Division for the Advancement of Women (1990), *Social and Economic Policy Issues in Female-headship and Vulnerability*, paper prepared by the Division for an expert-group meeting on vulnerable women, with special emphasis on female-headed households, 26–30 November, Vienna

Doeringer, P. and M. Piore (1971), *Internal Labour Markets and Manpower Analysis*, Lexington, Massachusetts, Heath

ECLAC (1992), *Major Changes and Crisis: The Impact on Women in Latin America and the Caribbean*, Santiago

Elson, D. (1991), *Male Bias in the Development Process*, Contemporary Issues in Development Studies, Manchester, Manchester University Press

Elson, D. and R. Pearson (1981), 'The Subordination of Women and the Internationalization of Factory Production', in K. Young *et al.* (eds), *Of Marriage and the Market*, London, CSE Books

Ferraz, João C. (1992), *Modernização Industrial à Brasileira*, Série Documentos, No. 7, IEI, UFRJ

FITA (1988), *Estadisticas Recientes de la Industria Textil*, mimeo, Buenos Aires

Fleury, Afonso (1988), 'Análise a Nível de Empresa dos Impactos da Automação Dobre a Organização da Produção e do Trabalho', in Sales de Melo Soares Rosa Maria (ed.), (1988) Gestão da Empresa, Automâço e Competitividade. Novos Padrões de Organização e de Relações do Trabalho, Brasília, IPEA/IPLAN

Foxley, A. and O. Muñoz (1977), 'Politicas de Empleo en Economías Heterogéneas', *Revista Paraguaya de Sociología*, 1438

Garcia de Fanelli, M. Gogna, and E. Jelin (1990), 'El Empleo Femenino en el Sector Publico Nacional', Buenos Aires, CEDES Bulletin

Hirata, Helena (1988), 'Transferência de Tecnologias de Gestão: o Caso dos Sistemas Participativos', in Sales de Melo Soares, Rosa Maria (ed.), (1988), Gestão da Empresa, Automação e Competitividade. Novos Padrões de Organização e de Relações do Trabalho, Brasília, IPEA/IPLAN

Hirata, Helena and John Humphrey (1986), 'Division Sexuelle due Travail dans l'Industrie Brésilienne', in *Hommes, Femmes et Pouvoir dans les organizations*, Paris, Ed. EPI

Hirata, Helena and Chantal Rogerat (1988), 'Technologie, Qualification et Division Sexuelle due Travail', *Revue Française de Sociologie*, Vol. XXIX: pp. 171–192

Howden, S (1992), *Assessment from a Gender Perspective: the Need to Evaluate the Impact of the 1980s Economic Crisis on Latin American and Caribbean Women*, IDB unpublished paper, Washington, April

Humphrey, John (1987), *Gender and Work in the Third World, Sexual Division in Brazilian Industry*, London, Tavistock Publications

Humphrey, John (1989), 'Novas Formas de Organização do Trabalho na Indústria: suas Aplicações para o Uso e Controle da Mão-de-obra no Brasil.' *Padrões Technológicos e Processo de Trabalho: Comparações Internacionais*, mimeo, São Paulo, DEP/EPUSP

IBGE (1992), *Pesquisa têxtil*, Rio de Janeiro

IDB (1990), *Economic and Social Progress in Latin America, 1990 Report*, Washington, IDB, October

IDB (1991), *Economic and Social Progress in Latin America, 1991 Report*, Washington, IDB

INDEC, *Population Census*, various numbers, Buenos Aires

INDEC, *Household Survey*, various numbers, Buenos Aires

Jacquette, J. (ed.) (1991), *The Women's Movement in Latin America*, Boulder Colorado, Westview Press

Jelin, E. (ed.) (1991), *Family, Household and Gender Relations in Latin America*, London and Paris, Paul Kegan/UNESCO

Kergoat, Danièle (1982), *Les Ouvrières*, Paris, Le Sycomore

Kergoat, Danièle (1984), 'Division Sexuelle due Travail et Qualification'. *Cadres*, CFDT, No. 313

Lobo, Elisabeth S. (1991), 'Lutas Operárias em São Bernardo do Campo', in *A Classe Operária tem Dois Sexos: Trabalho, Dominação e Resistência*, São Paulo, Editora Brasiliense

Maruani, Margaret (1992), 'Ouvrages de Dames', in Guy-Patrick Azémar (ed.), *Ouvriers, Ouvrières: Un Continent Morcelé et Silencieux*, Paris, Editions Autrement, Série Mutations No. 126

Milkman, Ruth (1987), *Gender at Work*, Urbana and Chicago, University of Illinois Press

Mitter, S. (1991), 'The Impact of New Technologies on Women's Employment:

Horizon 2000', project proposal presented to UNU/INTECH, Maastricht, Holland

Moser, C. *et al.* (1993), *'Urban Poverty in the Context of Structural Adjustment: Recent Evidence and Policy Responses'*, World Bank, TWURD WP No. 1, Washington, DC, February

Novick, M. and E. Lavigne (1988), 'Nuevas Tecnologias de Gestión: una Alternativa Hacia un Nuevo Modelo de Empresa?' in CEIL, *Documentos de Trabajo*, N. 20, Buenos Aires

Pearson, Ruth (1986), 'Female Workers in the First and Third Worlds: the 'greening' of women's labour', in Kate Purcell, Stephen Wood, Alan Waton and Sheila Allen (eds), *The Changing Experience of Employment. Restructuring and Recession*. London. Macmillan, BSA Series Explorations in Sociology No. 22

Perez, C. (1985), 'Microelectronics, Long Waves and World Structural Change: New Perspectives for Developing Countries', *World Development*, Vol. 21, No. 3

Phillips, A. (1983), 'Review of Brothers', *Feminist Review* No. 15, (quoted by Jenson 1989)

Powers N. (1992), 'Increased Poverty, Neo-liberal Economics and Democracy in Argentina: Exogenous Influences on the Public's Response', unpublished paper presented at the LASA XVII International Congress, Sept. 24–27, Los Angeles

PREALC, Monetarismo Global y Respuesta Industrial: el Caso de Argentina, Working Document No. 231. Buenos Aires, 1983

Reich, M., D. Gordon and R. Edwards (1980), 'A Theory of Labour Market Segmentation', in A. Amsden (ed.), *The Economics of Women and Work*, Harmondsworth, Penguin

Revista Textil, various numbers

Roldan, M. (1992), 'Un Debate Pendiente: Innovaciones Tecnologicas 'Blandas': Reconversion Industrial y Desregulacion en el Contexto Latino-americano de los '90. Hacia una Perspectiva 'Sensible al Genero'?' unpublished paper presented at the LASA XVII International Congress, Sept. 24–27, Los Angeles

Rowbotham, S. and Mitter S. (eds.) (1994), *Dignity and Daily Bread: New Forms of Economic Organising Among Poor Women in the Third World and the First*, London, Routledge

Saboia, João (1991a), 'Emprego Nos Anos Oitenta. Uma Década Perdida', Trabalho Apresentado no Seminário 'Modelos de Organização Industrial. Politica Industrial e Trabalho', mimeo, São Paulo, ABET, 11–12 April

Saboia, João (1991b), 'Emprego, Renda e Pobreza no Brasil na Década de Oitenta. Transformaçãoes conjunturais e estruturais', Trabalho Apresentado no Seminário Internacional de Politicas Económicas e Mudanças Estruturais na América Latina, mimeo, Salvador, 4–6 November

Sales de Melo Soares, Rosa Maria (ed.) (1988), *Gestão da Empresa, Automação e Competitividade. Novos Padrões de Organização e de Relações do Trabalho*. Brasília, IPEA/IPLAN

Schmitz, H. (1985), *Technology and Employment Practices in Developing Countries*, London, Croom Helm

Schmitz, H. and J. Cassiolato (eds.) (1992), *Hi-tech for Industrial Development: Lessons from the Brazilian Experience in Electronics and Automation*, London & New York, Routledge

Sen, A.K. (1987), 'Gender and Cooperative Conflicts', mimeo, Helsinki, World Institute for Development Economics Research

92   Liliana Acero

Sen, A. (1990), 'Gender and Cooperative Conflicts' in Irene Tinker (ed.), *Persistent Inequalities: Women and World Development*, New York, Oxford University Press

SENAI (1987), *Inovação Tecnológica e Formação Profissional na Indústria Têxtil*, by A. L. Ribeiro and M. H. de Lima, São Paulo

The Population Council and the International Centre for Research on Women (1988), 'Concepts and Classifications of Female-headed Households: Implications and Applications for National Statistics', Notes for Seminar I of Seminar Series, 'The Determinants and Consequences of Female-headed Households', New York

Touraine, A. 'A Historical Theory of the Evolution of Industrial Skill', in C.R. Walker (ed.) (1962), *Modern Technology and Civilization*, London, McGraw Hill, and reprinted in Davis and Taylor (eds), *Design of Jobs*, Harmondsworth, Penguin, 1972

UNEP (1991), 'Environmental Aspects of the Textile Industry: a Technical Guide', prepared by Prasad Modak, Paris, March

UNICEF (1987), *The Invisible Adjustment*, Santiago de Chile, UNICEF

UNICRI (1991), *Ser Niño en América Latina: de las Necesidades a los Derechos*, Mendez E. García and M.C. Bianchi (eds), Buenos Aires, UNICRI Publication No. 42, Galerna Ed.

Visao (1992), 'As Maiores Empresas do Brasil', *Revista anual de informação*, Rio de Janeiro and Sao Paulo

5 Changes in textiles

Implications for Asian women

Pavla Jezkova[1]

INTRODUCTION

This chapter is a summary of a recently completed study by UNIDO which combines inputs from research with commissioned studies covering technology changes in the textile and garment industries worldwide, plus three country surveys followed by seminars in Bangkok and Dhaka.[2] The study focuses mainly on the impact of changing technologies in the textile and garment sector on the female labour force in Bangladesh, Thailand and Indonesia. References to Asia's newly industrializing and advanced economies, in which the textile and garment industry has already undergone restructuring, provide a longer time perspective for the analysis. The study is one of UNIDO's responses to concerns of developing countries about the future of their textile and clothing industries.

Advanced technology has challenged the producers in developing countries by undermining their cost advantage and presenting them with new parameters of competition. Due to the nature and speed of technological innovations and the accompanying organizational changes, developing countries are finding it more difficult to keep up and the technology gap between the developed and developing countries is increasing. These trends affect not only the direction, composition and volume of international trade in textiles and garments, but also the industrialization process and labour markets at a country and regional level.

A key question for the Asian countries involved is the likely impact of these changes on the size, composition and skill levels of the female labour force. The textile and clothing sector has been one of the most important industrial employers of female labour globally. This has enhanced the social and economic status of women. Since technology has played an important role in the 'demand pull' for female labour in the textile and garment sector, changes in this demand variable are of particular concern to women.

SCOPE AND METHODOLOGY

Investment in industrial human capital can be an expensive and uncertain proposition, since there is a considerable gestation period before investment benefits can be realized. A longer-term development horizon is necessary to formulate appropriate strategies which could sustain and enhance the potential of the large female labour force which has recently emerged in the textile and garment industry. In order to grasp the present situation and predict what may occur in the future, the textile and garment industries have to be placed in a broader context of industrial development associated with technological and labour market restructuring. Empirical studies of industrial development in the Asian region have identified four development stages (see Table 5.1), characterized by changes in four parameters:

- natural and social resource endowments;
- the level of industrialization;
- technological capabilities and human resources; and
- government policy environment.[3]

Although the focus of the study is on technology, it is important to view all four parameters as interdependent variables which affect not only the overall industrialization process but also the development of industrial sectors and the position of women within them.

These phases do not inevitably succeed one other, but they can be recognized as common features of industrialization in the more advanced countries in the Asian region. The four-phase model provides a useful analytical tool to be applied to the empirical evidence presented in the study. In terms of their overall level of industrial development, Bangladesh would be in the first phase and Indonesia and Thailand in the second phase, with Thailand on the verge of transition into the third phase. Japan and the newly industrialized economies are in the third and fourth phase.

In the study, technology includes machinery and equipment, know-how or skills, information on new trends, and forms of organization. The role of women is considered in the light of a quantitative and qualitative assessment of women's participation in the production of textiles and garments, including where possible a discussion of the economic and social constraints which have produced gender bias. Due to the lack of data on women's contribution in terms of economic indicators such as productivity or share in the value added, more general indicators such as participation rate, occupational mobility, educational achievements, etc. had to be used.

The impact of new technology which is considered here includes any

Table 5.1 Characteristics of four development stages of the textile and garment industry

Parameters	Stage I	Stage II	Stage III	Stage IV
Use of endowments: competitiveness	abundant natural resources (cotton, silk) and/or low cost labour	abundant natural resources (cotton, silk) and/or low cost labour	human capital and technology	high technological capabilities (invention, adaptation, application) and highly-skilled manpower; key role of support infrastructure
Composition of MVA (manufacturing value added): industrial structure	light consumer industries; mass production of low VA (value added) products benefiting from economies of scale; dominance of state-owned enterprises	diversification – horizontal expansion: same products and factor inputs – vertical expansion: higher VA products	dominance of intermediate and capital goods branches; consolidation/streamlining; shedding labour-intensive industries and processes	dominance of service sector including a large proportion of industry related services previously included under industry; vertical integration and cooperation; concentration on high VA products for the upper-end market
Technological capabilities: level of technology; HRD/training; position of women	semi-automatic labour-intensive technology using abundant unskilled labour force; apprenticeship and on-the-job training sufficient; opportunity costs of manufacturing labour force are close to zero for men and women alike; preference for women based upon the nature and tradition of tasks	mix of labour and capital-intensive technology; increasing importance of vocational qualifications and in-service training; increasing occupational polarization between male and female labour force; opportunity costs of labour in the light, low VA industries are higher for men than women; preference for women based upon cost advantage	increasing automation to compensate for rising labour costs; demand for semi-skilled and high-skilled production labour force; increasing demand for management and marketing expertise; increasing occupational and wage disparity between women and men due to educational and training differences; low cost of female labour loses its prime importance as other factors enter the cost structure; women are leaving the industry for the service sector	highly automated; use of the newest technology responding to changing market conditions rather than changes in factor costs; highly educated or trained manpower; emphasis on multi-skilling; organized in-service training or retraining, and R&D; lack of technical education marginalizes women in industry; more opportunities in the supportive services
Government policies: social/economic; women specific	import protection/infant industry argument; employment creation policies; labour legislation including selective protection measures for female labour force	export promotion; incentives for foreign investment; infrastructure; localization policies; selective protection measures for female labour force	provision of enabling environment for local and foreign investors; cooperation with industry in training and education; promotion of equal employment opportunities and wages equality between men and women; social services	cooperation with industry on training and technology development (science parks, projects); promotion of women's social and economic status (provision of social services and non-discriminatory legislation)

change in the position of women in the textile and garment industry, both quantitative and qualitative. The indirect impact of technologies in use in other countries on the competitiveness of Asian developing countries is as important as the direct impact from the introduction of new technologies in Asia. The indirect impact is actually of more immediate relevance for Bangladesh, Indonesia and Thailand.

TECHNOLOGICAL AND ORGANIZATIONAL DEVELOPMENTS

Understanding technological transformation requires an assessment of the time sequence of innovations, the degree of their interdependence, the improvements achieved by their introduction, and the cost and employment implications. Technological innovations in the textile and garment branch are reviewed separately, since technological change in the industries differs in character and speed. Organizational changes, on the other hand, generally apply to both branches.

Technological change in the textile industry

Technological changes in the textile industry during the last forty years can be broadly divided into three phases. High-speed spinning frames and looms, with reduced vibration levels, were developed in the 1950s and early 1960s. The most radical alterations in the core technology of spinning and weaving came in the late 1960s and during the 1970s, with the introduction of rotor spinning and shuttleless looms. This was the period when new technology was sought to increase productivity and thereby to combat the cost-based competitiveness of lower wage producers from Asian countries. From the late 1970s onwards, the changes in the textile industry of the developed countries have been characterized by the introduction of microelectronics based technology and the automation of industrial processes.

The new technologies have allowed the various production stages to become one continuous process of interrelated activities, resulting in higher quality and flexibility and thus a faster response to changing market conditions. The full exploitation of these technological improvements is dependent on further complementary changes in organization and management. During the 1990s, rapid response to market conditions is likely to become an even more important force behind technological innovation and is likely to focus on increases in speed and flexibility rather than on cost-cutting.

Investment costs associated with technology improvements in the textile sector have risen considerably. About US $1 billion per year has been invested in the European Union, and twice as much in the USA, throughout the late 1980s and early 1990s. These levels could double in the coming years. The impact of automation on employment has also been significant. During the last 15 years, employment in the textile and clothing industry in the entire EU area has declined by 40 per cent, and the forecast for the 1990s is a loss of 700,000 to 1 million jobs in the textile sector alone. The occupational structure has also changed, with the proportion of operators and unskilled labourers decreasing while the share of technical and management staff increases. The new technologies require specialized skills in textile engineering, maintenance, design, computer science, and marketing.

Technological change in the garment industry

The pace of technological innovation in the garment industry was slow up to the beginning of the 1980s. The main innovations before 1980 were in sewing technology, with faster and more durable machines and the development of attachments for specialized tasks, which later resulted in the emergence of task-dedicated machines. In the pre-assembly phase the introduction of fast, automated cutters in the late 1970s replaced the operator-driven hydraulic die cutting machine.

The major technological changes occurred in the 1980s, when micro-electronics penetrated all stages of garment production to some degree. The most significant innovations took place in the pre-assembly stage, where computer-aided design (CAD), computer numerical control (CNC) cutting systems, and computer-aided manufacturing (CAM) led to material and labour savings. In the assembly stage, which accounts for 80 per cent of the manufacturing value added (MVA) and of the workforce in the industry, technological change has so far been relatively modest. The main improvements have been microelectronic control units which are attached to the standard industrial sewing machine to handle the more complex tasks. These can either be used to speed up production on task-dedicated machines or to increase the flexibility of multi-purpose machines. The major technological innovations of the 1990s are likely to build on these developments.

The introduction of computer-based technology has increased the cost of clothing machinery enormously, yet nearly sixty advanced CAD systems are already in Hong Kong, the Republic of Korea and Thailand alone, with over 60 per cent of these having been installed in the last three years.

Organizational changes in textiles and clothing

Organizational changes complement the technological drive towards greater market responsiveness. These changes affect not only production itself, but also the relationship between suppliers and buyers. The emphasis in the organization of production is shifting to a multi-skilled workforce, closer management–workforce cooperation, and increasing reliance on externally supplied industrial services. There is also a tendency towards vertical integration within the textile and garment industry. In the field of buyer–supplier relations, textile producers, garment makers and retailers are working together in design teams. Price is no longer the only important determinant of sourcing: elements such as quality, timely delivery and technical cooperation between buyer and supplier play an increasingly important role. The buyer–supplier relationship is also intensified by the reduced lead time and shortened production runs. This means that close proximity to the markets and availability of efficient international telecommunication and transport networks have become an important competitive factor for the producer countries.

EMPIRICAL EVIDENCE FROM COUNTRY CASE STUDIES

The following characteristics of the textile and garment sector were identified in the case studies of Bangladesh, Thailand and Indonesia.

Resource endowments – the textile industry

The presence of natural resources – mainly cotton, but in the case of Thailand also silk – was an important initial factor in the emergence of the textile industry in Bangladesh (when it was a part of India), Indonesia and Thailand. In all three countries the development of modern textile manufacturing, especially for export, was based on extensive use of abundant low-cost labour. This factor has made the industry an important source of employment and secured it a competitive advantage in export markets. Bangladesh and Indonesia have retained this relative advantage, but this is no longer the case for Thailand.

In Thailand, local raw material production has not grown sufficiently, and cotton yarn is now imported on a large scale, as well as man-made fibres. The quality of domestic raw silk is also hampering the modernization of handloom production, but joint R&D efforts are being undertaken by the Government and private business to introduce new varieties of raw silk suited to more advanced technology. In Indonesia, local production of man-made fibres has been facilitated by the local availability of oil and timber. While the production of man-made fibres has developed sufficiently to cover most of the textile industry's requirements, most of the raw cotton is imported.

The garments industry

The modern garments industry developed much later than the textile industry in all three countries. At the initial stage of the import substitution period, the industry benefited from upstream linkages with the textile sector in Thailand and Indonesia. In Bangladesh, with no substantial local demand for manufactured garments, the industry was export-driven from the start. Today, Bangladesh and Thailand rely increasingly on imported textiles, because local textile producers are no longer capable of providing the quantity, quality and variety of cloth required for export garments. In Indonesia, local fabric still satisfies almost 80 per cent of the industry's demand.

In all three countries the competitive strength of the garment industry has been built upon a cheap labour force, predominantly women.

The sub-sector's role in manufacturing

In Bangladesh, the textile branch accounts for some 35 per cent of MVA, down from over 50 per cent in the early 1970s. In Thailand and Indonesia (which are further along the path to a modern, diversified manufacturing sector) the textile sector accounted for 11 per cent and 10 per cent of MVA, respectively, at the end of the 1980s. The industry is still one of the largest employers of manufacturing labour in Bangladesh but has been surpassed by other industrial branches in Thailand and Indonesia. Its significance as an export earner has declined in all three countries. In Thailand and Indonesia this can largely be explained by the diversion of output to the local market.

In Bangladesh, textiles continue to be produced largely by traditional cottage industries (the handloom sector) although the pre-liberation period in the early 1960s saw a rapid expansion of integrated mills. Small-scale industries also play a very important role in Indonesia and Thailand (silk production). Indonesian microenterprises have made more technical progress than those in Bangladesh and Thailand. In Thailand, however, improvements in the organization and management of subcontracting have increased the number of home-based silk producers and contributed to the growth of the silk industry. Public ownership of large-scale enterprises is more pronounced in Bangladesh than in Thailand and Indonesia, where local and foreign investment (private or joint ventures) dominate.

The MVA share of the garment industry is quite modest in all three countries: 1 per cent in Bangladesh, 7 per cent in Thailand, and 1.8 per cent in Indonesia. But the trend is still upwards, and the branch is one of the major contributors to foreign exchange earnings in spite of its low MVA share, especially in Bangladesh. Cheap, mass-produced clothes remain the main export item. In the Indonesian and particularly the Thai garment industries, there is now a trend towards quality products based on local design and diversification. In all three countries, small and medium-size enterprises predominate, often subcontracting for foreign firms which are responsible for high value added, industry-related, services such as design, distribution and marketing.

Technological capabilities in textiles

Overall, technology levels in the textile industry in the three countries have not changed much since the 1960s. Technological stagnation is most evident in Bangladesh. There is as yet no sign of automation in the large-scale mills, and traditional handloom weaving predominates in the informal sector, although semi-automatic Chittaranjan looms have been introduced on a modest scale.

In Thailand and Indonesia, advanced technologies are now being intro-duced, especially in foreign-owned mills producing synthetic textiles. But these technologies cover only isolated aspects of production, such as spinning. There are as yet no integrated modern mills. Thai producers have partly compensated for the lack of technological progress by better organization and maintenance. Efforts are also being made to modernize the traditional Thai silk industry. In Indonesia, power looms have become common in cottage industries.

In all three countries, there is a traditional female presence in the textile industry, although in Bangladesh women were traditionally confined to yarn processing and excluded from weaving activities. This explains the unusually low share of women in the textile sector in Bangladesh, about 10 per cent compared to about 80 per cent in Thailand. No figures are available for Indonesia, but the rate can be estimated at between 40 and 60 per cent.

Small enterprises and subcontracting are important for female employ-ment in all three countries. The introduction of a semi-automated loom in the traditional handloom sector, and the formation of female cooperatives, have created new employment for women weavers in Bangladesh. But in the 'modern' sector, outdated technology and a heavy reliance on physical strength are real obstacles to increasing female participation. The preva-lence of traditional values and strong competition from men in the saturated labour market makes it even harder for women to increase their share.

In Thailand, it is too early to judge the effect of the recent modernization of the traditional silk industry on overall female employment in this sector. It is, however, possible that some of the newly-created opportunities for female factory employment, mostly for young and unmarried women, could be at the expense of women working as subcontractors from their homes. In Indonesia, the available information suggests a decrease in employment opportunities in the traditional weaving sector and in small enterprises as the result of modernization and competition from the modern, large-scale sector. The growth of the modern sector seems to have compensated for this loss so far, but this is unlikely to continue.

Technological capabilities in the garments industry

Technology levels in the garment industry are on the whole relatively low. Most Thai and Indonesian firms still use standard industrial sewing machines, and only the large Thai establishments producing high-quality clothing have introduced computers for design, special sewing operations and inventory control. Garment production in Bangladesh uses simple operator-guided electric machines, although some firms in Export Processing Zones (EPZs) are beginning to use computerized attachments. Local establishments make extensive use of second-hand machinery.

Female employment in the garments industry has grown rapidly, with the demand motivated by the presence of an untapped pool of cheap labour, particularly suited to the nature of production and the low-skill technology. This has in some instances, especially in Bangladesh, been enhanced by a 'supply push', with economic necessity forcing women to sell their labour well below the rate acceptable to men. Widespread subcontracting has facilitated the growth of female employment in Thailand and Indonesia.

Since unsophisticated mass production still predominates in the textile and garment industry, it is not surprising that the issue of human resource development receives relatively little attention in the three countries (although Indonesia does have a textile technology institute and a modest textile/garments training programme). The situation is also slightly better in transnational firms, which are more aware of the increasing importance of skills improvement.

In-plant training is generally confined to simple on-the-job training for new employees by more experienced machine operators. Where more structured training programmes are available, they tend to concentrate on the middle and high level technical and managerial staff. Women tend to be seriously under-represented at these levels, although in Indonesia a relatively large number of women occupy middle or high-level positions in the garments industry. This is primarily explained by their well-established role in traditional garment making.

The trend towards diversification and higher value-added products which is associated with technology improvements results in skill polarization. This tends to marginalize women in quantitative and qualitative terms: they are in danger not only of losing jobs, but also of being excluded from operations requiring new skills. These tendencies are not so strongly apparent as in the newly industrializing economies (NIEs), but they can be observed in the garment EPZ of Bangladesh, in the textile and garment industries in Thailand, and in the textile industry in Indonesia. No statistical documentation is available as yet, as these trends have been masked by the increase in the absolute number of employees, both men and women.

Policies in textiles

Import substitution policies formed the basis of the modern textile industry in all three countries. After Bangladesh became independent in 1972, there was a policy shift away from promoting large mills to traditional handloom production, in an attempt to cope with the serious unemployment problem. Also in Indonesia, conscious labour market policies favoured labour-intensive technologies to create much needed employment opportunities.

By the end of the 1970s, export promotion became a major focus of government policies for the industry in all three countries. The background for these policies was the need to increase foreign exchange earnings and to capitalize on opportunities arising from the textile industry relocation strategies of producers in the developed countries and the NIEs. Foreign investors have been attracted by favourable legislation and/or the provision of special facilities (such as the Bangladesh EPZ). Serious attempts to let domestic industries benefit from technology transfer connected to private foreign investment seem to have been made only in Indonesia.

The export promotion drive in all three countries stimulated the demand for cheap female labour, and the supply was increased by the decline of rural job opportunities. The result is a heavy predominance of women in the textile industry in Thailand and Indonesia. In Bangladesh, the number of women in the industry has not grown as rapidly. Men have retained their traditionally predominant role, partly because backward technologies require considerable physical strength and also because of lack of alternative employment opportunities. In addition, labour regulations allowing women to do only work which is 'appropriate to women' leave considerable scope for discrimination in hiring practices, which are still heavily influenced by traditional sociocultural values. The adherence to values which confine women to traditional roles and sanction the gender division of labour affect not only the employers' attitudes but also women's perception of themselves. This is also the case in Indonesia.

Policies in garment manufacturing

Policies for garment manufacturing in Bangladesh have been linked to the export promotion drive from the start, whereas in Indonesia and to some extent Thailand, import substitution provided the original impetus for the industry. In stimulating garment (and textile) manufacturing, the governments have exploited the international relocation and restructuring trends which resulted from technological change and increasing wage levels in the industrialized countries. The Multi-Fibre Arrangement (MFA) and Generalised System of Preferences (GSP) have facilitated an easier access to markets in developed countries for all three countries. In addition, a trade agreement with the USA in 1971 provided Thai garment manufacturers with very favourable export conditions.

It is clear that export promotion of the garment industry has created new possibilities for female industrial employment, which has grown much faster than in the textile industry, especially in Bangladesh. There is also little doubt that the growth of the industry has been built upon the dexterity, easy subordination and low wages of the female labour force. Although the governments in all three countries recognize the present and still untapped potential role of women in industry there are few signs of any significant measures to improve the qualitative aspects of the female labour force. The literacy rates and education levels of women are still well below those of men, and so is women's access to relevant technical and managerial training. Also, special rules covering working conditions for women are neither observed nor endorsed. They are often used not for the benefit of women workers, but to their disadvantage.

THE EXPERIENCE OF JAPAN AND THE ASIAN NIES

The industries of the Asian NIEs have clearly left the low-wage, labour-intensive phase behind and are moving to technology-intensive manufacturing, with the attendant need for highly skilled human resources. Japan is already one step further, at the 'brain intensive' stage of development, marked by the predominance of activities based on knowledge and information taking place outside the manufacturing sector. The trend away from manufacturing towards services is already visible in the NIEs, with increasing employment in the service sector, including activities previously classified within the manufacturing sector. These activities represent highly productive inputs into the production system and have very little, if anything, in common with the traditional notion of services as low-skill, low-production activities.

The textile industry is rapidly becoming marginalized in the process, although a 'hard core' of highly sophisticated textile firms will no doubt remain. The declining share of female labour in the textile industry is indicative of changes in skill requirements, for which women seem to be less prepared than men. The textile branch is thus becoming of relatively small importance as a supplier of female jobs. Skill upgrading or diversification of the female workforce is needed if their share in the textile labour force is to be maintained.

In the garment industry, slower progress in automation has been compensated for by organizational changes and the introduction of computerized management systems. These changes have had little impact on the composition of the garment labour force, which remains overwhelmingly female. While this situation is unlikely to change in the near future, there is a longer-term need for skill improvement and diversification, in view of the industry's need to respond to changes in demand and to anticipated changes in technology.

Women can be seen to be moving into services or into the growth industries. Services would generally be the domain of those with better educational levels, which are definitely rising. In the new growth sectors and branches, women are still predominantly found at the lower occupational levels. An increase can be detected among the higher ranks of professionals, but the numbers involved remain small. A new group of generally better-skilled marginal workers also seems to be emerging: home workers and subcontractors who are dependent on information-intensive activities. The most vulnerable group is older married women doing unskilled work: their skill/education levels being too low to be of much use in the rapidly-changing economy.

The educational and training systems are responding with varying means and degrees of success in the individual economies. But women are still a minority of the students in the subjects that matter, particularly with regard to the skills and knowledge needed in manufacturing. The evidence about specific training for textiles and clothing in Hong Kong and the Republic of Korea suggests that although women's representation in some of the courses is quite impressive, their representation in the subjects required for higher technical and managerial posts remains very low.

Women appear to be better represented in education and training for services. Seen in the broader perspective of a shift towards service-dominated economies, the situation is therefore not altogether unfavourable for women, even if they have to cope with other obstacles, such as biased hiring practices, which have not been discussed here. However, there is a need to further increase the participation of women in the relevant types of education and training, while paying particular attention to those female workers in low-skill positions who are likely to be marginalized in the process.

EMERGING ISSUES

The UNIDO study outlines three important areas to be challenged by strategies for the textile and garment industries and the workers they employ. These are:

- technology;
- human resource development; and
- the social environment.

Different gender-related problems emerge at each phase of development.

Technology

No measurable direct impact of technology changes in the textile and garment industries on the female labour force can be detected at present in the three developing countries under examination. Very little if any technological change has actually occurred in either industry in these countries over the last twenty years. Indeed it could be argued that it has been the indirect impact of the adoption of technological innovations in the more advanced countries which has affected the female labour force in the textile and garment industries in these countries. The adoption of new technologies in the developed and newly industrializing economies in the past thirty years resulted in a relocation and sourcing strategy which benefited textile and especially garment producers in many developing countries, including Bangladesh, Thailand and Indonesia. This led to large increases in female employment based on low labour costs.

The situation is now changing. The technology gap between industrialized and developing countries is increasing in importance. Cost advantages are no longer sufficient to establish competitive strength on the international textile and garment markets. Only a few of the new technologies generate sufficient cost savings, for firms in the developed countries, to threaten the low-wage advantage of developing countries. But this is not to say that technology developments in the industrialized countries are without implications for developing country producers. Demand factors such as quality, variety and just-in-time response are becoming equally important in determining the competitiveness of textile and garment producers in developed countries' markets, which are the destination for most of the developing countries' textile and garment exports. The comparative advantage of the developed countries in these factors, because of the use of advanced computer-based technology, has already started to compensate for their labour cost disadvantage.

Producers in Bangladesh, Thailand and Indonesia are at present reluctant to invest in new technology, especially in the garment sector. Given the existing product specialization and market conditions, their position has so far been rational. The high investments associated with the new technologies have to be critically assessed in the context of the techno-economic environment. This is particularly the case in Bangladesh and Indonesia, where the opportunity cost of capital is high and potential savings in labour costs are small. In addition, the scarcity of skilled labour and the weakness of the supportive industrial infrastructure pose limitations to the effective use of the new technologies. In Thailand, the situation is different. The cost advantage has been eroded by rapidly rising wages and the need for technology changes is more urgent.

In the near future, however, manufacturers in all three countries will have to come to grips with computerized technologies. An assessment of the possibilities for incremental technological improvements as well as a review of marketing strategies will be necessary. The scope for selective improvements is larger in the garment than in the textile industry, due to the greater interdependence of technology changes in the textile production. It could also be argued that in the clothing industry, improvements in the organization and skills components of technology could yield a higher and faster return on investment than production automation.

In all three countries, but especially in Bangladesh and Thailand, technological innovation in the textile industry has the potential to provide new employment opportunities for female labour in the near future. For example, improved handlooms and 'women-friendly' automation in textile mills in Bangladesh, and automation in silk yarn production in Thailand, could both increase the demand for female labour. In addition there are many physically demanding tasks now performed by men which could be made accessible to women if technology such as hydraulics were used in lifting, loading, and moving materials. However, male workers and trade unions may resist such changes, and the introduction of machines to perform tasks previously performed by male labour does not, as experience shows, automatically lead to women taking over. In Indonesia, stronger reliance of the garments industry on domestic textiles could boost the demand for labour in the textile industry, even if labour-saving technologies are introduced.

Human resources development

Whatever strategy is adopted with respect to technology and marketing, skill development should be an immediate concern because of the long gestation period for investments in human resources. The emerging trend points towards a shift from the mass production of standard products, using narrowly-skilled workers, towards more specialized products using a broadly skilled workforce and universal, multi-purpose machines. Skills and know-how not only have to be improved, but are also required in areas which transcend a traditional industrial framework, because managerial and marketing expertise are increasing in importance. Hence, in estab- lishing training programmes and institutions, both the short and long-term skill requirements of the textile/garment sectors have to be considered. Moreover, the long-term trend for the textile and garments industries to diminish in importance as providers of employment for women, to be replaced by high-tech industries and the services sector, has to be offset by forward looking strategies for industrial human resources development.

As producers are not likely to invest in what appears as a high risk proposition in the present business environment, governments will have to assume the role of initiator, coordinator, and cost-sharing partner of R&D and training schemes. This is of crucial importance in the development of the relevant skills and know-how, as proved by the experience of the NIEs. At the same time, the experience of these countries shows that the business community – for its own good – should take an interest and participate in the design and execution of human resource development measures. Fairly advanced technologies are beginning to make an impact on the large-scale textile industry in Indonesia and Thailand, and the 1990s will no doubt see their rapid diffusion. At the same time, both changing forms of organization and international market conditions require a new range of non-technical skills. Coping with these developments means investing in human resource development now.

The experience of Japan and the NIEs demonstrates the importance of a universal primary education and widespread secondary school attendance as an essential building block in the process of industrial skill development.

As the complexity and speed of technological changes increase, formal education has to be complemented by specialized training and R&D which are more closely related to the production system. In-service training thus becomes an important vehicle for skill development and adaptation to the changing technology environment in the later phases of industrial development. Major efforts will be needed to upgrade the present learning-by-doing type of training, which is limited in duration and scope and of highly variable quality. In-house training should be formalized and be part of a long-term overall personnel management plan. Refresher courses will have to be an integral part of training in order to keep abreast of changes in technology, fashions, and market conditions.

There is little information concerning women's participation in the process of industrial skill development. It may however be assumed that they are severely under-represented both in the relevant types of post-primary education and in-house training. In Bangladesh, there is even a very serious backlog in primary education. Completion of secondary school is generally seen as the minimum requirement for managerial posts, and vocational technical training for the technical posts. On-the-job training and special upgrading courses are essential and can compensate for the lack of formal education, but only up to the level of a one line production supervisor. Production posts above that level and managerial posts are filled by direct recruitment. If women are to make a greater contribution to growth in the textile and garments sector in the future, then their access to education and specialized technical and non-technical training must be improved. The increasing importance of non-technical skills could be to the advantage of women, since the textile and garment industry characteristically contains a large number of jobs which are not necessarily the traditional preserve of men.

Social environment

The surveys of all three countries have highlighted the importance of a social environment conducive to the enhancement of women's economic status. Gender bias institutionalized in traditional social norms, legal frameworks and recruitment practices affect both sides of the supply and demand equation for the female labour force. Evidence, especially from Bangladesh and Indonesia, has shown how a male-dominant culture can be an obstacle to the fuller integration of women in the industrial labour force, and to social equity.

However, in situations where choices for economic survival are limited, the purely economic necessity for women to contribute to the family income or to work for their own existence takes precedence over cultural and religious values. Although Bangladesh and Indonesia are both predominantly Muslim societies, low household incomes, especially in Bangladesh, have forced an increasing number of women to look for employment in manufacturing.

An aspect of gender bias which is harder to overcome is the perception of women's inability to carry out certain tasks associated with a higher degree of skills and responsibility. This is shown, for example, by the different attitudes among garment producers in Dhaka and the Bangladesh EPZ with regard to training and certain types of female employment. The cross-cultural impact of foreign enterprises can serve as a vehicle of change in the perception of women as industrial workers. Considerable effort will however be required to improve women's access to higher-level employment, even in the most advanced countries, such as Japan. On the other hand, the example of Indonesia shows that there is some scope for women to make careers in those industries where women have traditionally played a key role.

Legislation on the conditions of work should be closely geared to the actual circumstances of female participation in the industrial labour force. Social justification for protectionist regulations specifying work 'appropriate' for women and limiting female working hours often have a genuine basis. But those that only distort equal access to job opportunities, diminish women's career opportunities and make female labour too expensive should be changed.

The areas identified for strategic gender-sensitive intervention by government, private sector and donor agencies can be grouped as follows:

- industrial planning and policy advice including human resource development strategies;
- advice and assistance in the choice and transfer of technology;
- advice on organizational improvements;
- planning and implementation of in-service and vocational training; and
- additional gender-sensitive research in industrially more advanced countries on the effects of industrial and labour market restructuring.

NOTES

1 Pavla Jezkova was the UNIDO staff member responsible for the production of the study summarized in this chapter.
2 'Changing Techno-economic Environment in the Textile and Clothing Industry: Implications for the Role of Women in Asian Developing Countries', UNIDO PPD.237(SPEC), February, 1993. The study was supported by the

Government of Switzerland, which financed the country case studies in Bangladesh and Thailand and the follow up seminars, and the Government of the Netherlands, which financed the Indonesian case study. While the verbatim extracts and Table 5.1 are used with the permission of the United Nations Industrial Development Organization, the précis reflects the views of the writer and is not an official document of UNIDO.

3 Empirical evidence has shown that the sharp increase in demand for female labour in the textile and, especially, garment industry in the newly industrializing countries of Asia was associated with the rapid growth of manufacturing at the expense of the agricultural sector; an export-led industrial strategy enhanced by favourable market conditions at that time; low skill labour-intensive technology; the nature of the production tasks, and low opportunity cost of female labour. On the supply side, there were changes in areas such as education and the cultural and religious values influencing the social and economic status of women.

6 Information technology and women's employment in manufacturing in eastern Europe

The case of Slovenia

Maja Bučar

INTRODUCTION

The specific problems faced by Slovenia as a new sovereign state in the transition from a socialist self-management economy to a more market dominated one have affected many aspects of women's employment. These changes cannot be separated from the impact of information technology. It is hoped that this study will provide insights into the problems faced by an economy such as Slovenia, and that parallels might be drawn with the ongoing transition processes in the other central and eastern European countries.

Slovenia is a small central European country with 2 million inhabitants and an area of 20,256 square kilometres. It is the most developed part of ex-Yugoslavia, with the highest living standard, an intensive manufacturing sector and very active foreign trade. It has traditionally been open to the world and, in comparison with other central and east European countries, enjoyed an active flow of commodities, people, information and technology from and to the industrialized countries.

There have been rapid changes in the ownership structure of the Slovene economy in recent years. Of 13,309 operating enterprises at the end of 1991, some 75 per cent were private, 19 per cent were public and 5.6 per cent had mixed ownership. Despite these changes, the economy is to a large extent still dominated by public enterprises, which account for 78 per cent of total revenue and employ 88 per cent of the labour force. Many of these enterprises will be privatized or restructured by 1995. The November 1992 Privatization Law provides for the mandatory privatization of all public enterprises in manufacturing within a set period. The privatization process is expected to have major implications for the organizational structure of the Slovene economy.

There is a tradition of Slovene women working in paid employment, dating back to World War II. In 1952, women made up a third of the workforce. By 1990 the figure was as high as 46.5 per cent. There is however a clear gender pattern of employment: in the same year women provided 73.5 per cent of the workforce in what are classified in Slovenia as 'non-economic' activities (public administration, education, culture, health services, social services, etc.)[1] and 41.3 per cent of the workforce in 'economic' sectors.

The high participation of women in the active labour force can be explained by a number of factors. Relatively dynamic economic development after the war demanded the recruitment of additional workers. The income of a single provider was also not sufficient to support a family and secure a decent standard of living. With the rise in women's educational level, the number of women willing to be full-time housewives decreased even further. As long as there was work available, it was regarded as 'natural' to look for a job on leaving school, and to continue working after marriage and childbirth.

As in a number of other socialist countries, the employment of women was supported by labour legislation. Though some labour rights have been curtailed, there has been no change in the laws guaranteeing equal status for women in terms of renumeration, protection, promotion and various employment benefits. Legally, therefore, equal treatment is guaranteed, although this does not prevent companies from advertising for 'men only'. Some special protections for women have also been retained.[2] Talk of abolishing maternity protection has been limited, even among conservatives, by the fear of further lowering the birth rate, which has been declining in the last five years. The net reproduction rate in 1990 was 0.71 per cent. On the other hand, no extension of maternity leave or increase in benefits is realistic, given the severe economic crisis. In the current debate in Slovenia, women's right to continue working on the same terms as men has been asserted by intellectual and professional workers, but it is less popular among working-class women who, in some industries, are seriously affected by various job-related health hazards.

Unemployment figures are rising, due to the economic crisis, but it is no worse among women than among men,[3] perhaps because they had been employed in larger numbers in 'non-economic' (service) sectors. Employment levels in these sectors have fallen less markedly, and have even begun to recover. One official of the Agency for Employment said that less bankruptcies have occurred in typically female industries, because women are more willing to accept lower pay rather than losing their work and are more flexible in looking for alternative jobs, even ones which do not fit their qualifications. Such observations are of course impressionistic.

However, there is no evidence thus far that women are being discriminated against in labour cuts.

The severe recession at the beginning of the 1990s was caused by the shock of the double transition – to an independent state and to a market-oriented economy. Most of the damage was caused by the collapse of trade with the states of ex-Yugoslavia, by the loss of transport and other infrastructure links with the south, by the aggression of the Yugoslav Army in Slovenia in the summer of 1991, by the wars in Croatia (Slovenia's second most important foreign trade partner) and Bosnia and Hercegovina (which brought some 70,000 refugees to Slovenia). These alone would have created economic difficulties. Moreover, the Slovene economy has been going through ownership restructuring, fighting an everlasting war with inflation, introducing a new currency and modernizing its industry.

Since 1989, GDP and industrial production have been falling, although there were more encouraging indications regarding industrial production in the second half of 1993, when particularly the manufacture of consumer goods showed positive growth. Less satisfactory results were to be observed in the area of unemployment,[4] which is expected to continue to increase in 1994, as the result of privatization and the bankruptcies of a number of large companies.

High unemployment figures and general lack of financial resources have made restructuring extremely problematic. Signs of stress had become apparent by the late 1980s, when it was obvious that many of the large conglomerates would have to reorganize and modernize. With the gradual introduction of new technology and new managerial practices, a number of companies, particularly medium-size ones, successfully survived until the beginning of 1992. The break with other ex-Yugoslav republics has in many cases led to a halt in the restructuring process and transformed it, for the time being, into a holding action.

TECHNOLOGICAL RECONSTRUCTION

Under these circumstances, it is difficult to talk about any major trend as regards the introduction of information technology in Slovene manufacturing. The general lack of new investment has affected the rate of introduction of new technologies. However, the situation is somewhat different in those companies which have had either long-term cooperation deals or joint ventures, since they have had to follow the technological changes in their partner companies, and have often received financial assistance from the foreign partner to introduce new production technology.

Research in technology transfer has fallen with the slow-down in technological restructuring. Before 1988, a number of research projects were dealing with the introduction of information technology (IT) and its effects in various sectors. Since then, there has been practically no economic research in this field. One major research project, in 1988, studied the planned rate of introduction of computer assisted design (CAD) and computer assisted manufacturing (CAM) technologies in the metal processing industry. This showed that the process of technological change was very slow, and varied substantially from company to company. Even in the metal processing industry, which research had identified as likely to make many changes, as many as two thirds of the companies said that they had no plans to introduce CAD/CAM before mid-1990 (Duhovnik *et al.*, 1988; Stanovnik and Kuntin, 1989).

Where the introduction of information technologies has already taken place, most of the new technology went into the design departments and very little into the actual production, with the exception of some experimental applications. It was also noticeable that suggestions for the introduction of new technology came predominantly from the engineering side. Management has simply listened to the technical cadre in implementing technical change, with little economic or organizational analysis. This has meant that there has been little organizational or personnel changes, so that the full benefits of the information technologies could not be exploited, which in turn has led to a degree of disenchantment among management. Any financial and economic benefits from the introduction of information technologies in this piecemeal fashion would not be noticeable for two to three years, and by then other economic factors such as the high inflation and interest rates and overvalued currency had often undercut them.

Most labour cuts observed in this study were not the result of the new technology, but were indicators of over-employment in administration in the past, or were caused by the loss of markets and the consequent fall in production levels, and organizational rationalization. The effects of new technology can be expected to be felt within the next few years, when such technology is introduced on a more significant scale.

Although the data from the 1988 project is relatively old,[5] the low investment rate over the past few years means that the situation in Slovene industry has not changed dramatically. What has altered is managerial perception on the importance of new technology.

PROFILES OF SELECTED SECTORS

Despite the lack of statistical data, by conducting interviews in one company in each of the sectors in which many women work, it was possible to make an approximate assessment of what is happening to Slovene women. Eight sectors were identified in which 50 per cent, or nearly 50 per cent, of the workforce are women in 1990 (see Table 6.1). No consideration was given to the technological intensity of these sectors. These eight sectors were then analysed as to their importance in the national economy (their share in industrial production, in imports and exports), the educa- tional structure as compared to the average in industry and salary level.

Only two of these sectors (manufacturing of electrical machinery and apparatus, and the chemical industry) have experienced a fall in production which is above the average for industry as a whole.[6] All the others show relatively good results, as reflected in Table 6.2.

Table 6.3 shows the educational structure of the workforce in each of the selected sectors. Unfortunately no breakdown of these statistics by gender is available, but it is striking that these sectors, in which the share of women is high, have a very poor educational structure. On average 49.7 per cent of all those employed in industry have basic education (8 years of elementary school or less), but of our selected sectors, only the chemicals sector has a lower percentage (48.9 per cent), and in the manufacturing of textile yarns and fabrics 64.1 per cent of the workers have only this basic education. These figures also reflect the relatively poor educational structure of

Table 6.1 Selected industrial sectors in Slovenia

Sector	% of ind. prod.	% of exports	% of imports	% of women in workforce 1990	1992
Manufacture of electrical machinery and apparatus	11.3	15.9	11.3	51.0	49.2
Chemicals	8.6	6.8	7.4	50.3	50.3
Textile yarns and cloth	2.9	2.5	2.8	64.0	62.7
Textile products	7.4	3.2	2.0	84.4	83.5
Leather and fur manufacture	1.3	1.9	1.0	47.0	43.7
Leather products	2.2	3.1	1.9	75.0	76.4
Food products	11.3	3.2	5.1	45.9	44.0
Tobacco	0.3	0	0	64.8	67.4
Total	45.3	36.6	31.5		

Table 6.2 Production in selected industrial sectors, 1989 to first 9 months of 1992 (1991 = 100)

Sector	1989	1990	1991	Jan–Sept 1992	relative wage
All industry	127.5	114.2	100	86.9	100.0
Manufacture of electrical machinery and apparatus	134.0	114.9	100	80.1	98.1
Chemicals	120.2	112.0	100	70.2	117.6
Textile yarns and fabrics	159.7	131.2	100	93.0	78.9
Textile products	124.7	111.7	100	93.1	88.5
Leather and fur manufacture	127.5	111.0	100	113.6	118.0
Leather products	160.4	133.0	100	116.3	84.2
Food products	104.0	104.6	100	90.4	109.7
Tobacco	133.7	108.0	100	121.2	134.2

(a) average wage in the sector, as a percentage of average wages in all industry

Slovene industry, which will undoubtedly have serious repercussions for technological and organizational restructuring.

It is interesting to note that neither the rate of industrial production nor the educational structure seem to affect the wage level in individual sectors (cf. Tables 6.2 and 6.3). It is nevertheless noticeable that the three sectors in which wage levels are lowest (manufacturing of textiles and fabrics, textile products, and leather products) have the highest percentage of women workers. This is despite the fact that output in the leather products sector has been good. This would confirm the opinion of the official from the Agency for Employment, who argued that women are prepared to accept lower wages just to keep their jobs.

METHODOLOGY

One company was selected in each of the eight selected sectors. No special attention was paid to the size of the factory, yet most were medium or large factories and would be well known in their branch. They were 'social' companies, meaning that the capital was still predominantly public. They could therefore be considered typical of the sector, and employment levels in these companies had not been affected by privatization. In each company, an interview was carried out with the general manager or the personnel manager. The following questions were asked:

Table 6.3 Educational structure of the workforce in selected sectors

Sector	No schooling	4–7 yrs elementary	Elementary	High School	2 year college	University
Manufacture of electrical machinery and apparatus	0.9	19.9	29.8	40.9	4.1	4.5
Chemicals	1.0	17.9	30.0	41.1	3.9	6.1
Textile yarns and cloth	1.6	31.2	31.3	32.2	2.3	1.4
Textile products	0.7	20.8	35.4	40.9	1.4	0.7
Leather and fur manufacture	1.7	30.5	26.8	35.1	3.1	2.9
Leather products	0.7	22.5	34.5	40.5	1.2	0.6
Food products	1.9	22.9	27.1	42.3	2.7	3.1
Tobacco	1.5	20.2	37.1	34.4	2.8	4.0
Total industrial workforce	1.4	22.3	26.0	44.6	3.0	2.7
Total national workforce	1.3	16.7	20.0	50.5	5.9	5.5

- Have you introduced information technology in your company and, if so, in which phases (planning, manufacturing, administration, accounting)?
- Has the introduction of information technology had any quantative impact on the level of employment of women and, if so, on what job profiles?
- Has information technology had any qualitative effect (e.g., better working conditions, more satisfactory or creative work) on the employment of women, and, if so, on what job profiles?;
- What were the major ways of dealing with technologically redundant workers?
- Has any training been provided to aid women to adjust to the new technology?
- What new skills are required, if any, when recruiting new workers, as the result of the information technology?

In spite of the relatively general character of the questions, there was some reluctance to be interviewed or to provide exact figures. This was probably because of the social disapproval of firing workers. The perception is that you do not lay people off if you are doing well. Also, usually the only people with the authority to answer the survey questions were general managers who, because of severe work pressure, found it difficult to allocate time for an interview.

During the interviews, many of the representatives of the companies requested that the name of the company should not be mentioned. The results have therefore been combined, and names and exact figures have been eliminated.

EXTENT OF TECHNOLOGICAL CHANGES

In all the interviewed companies, various reasons had contributed to redundancies. The direct effect of technology was a minor factor and was seldom an isolated one. The standard procedure seems to be that department leaders examine the working process, decide how many workers are required for its smooth operation and gradually eliminate the redundant workers. The major factor determining the size of the workforce is the size of the market. The personnel departments have figures on the number of people who have left the company (early retirement, lay-offs), but no data on why certain jobs were no longer necessary. So no exact figures on the quantitative impact of the information technologies can be obtained, though impressions can be gathered from the discussions with the managers. These indicated that very few of the selected companies had a long-term plan of technological modernization and reorganization prepared in sufficient detail to include the personnel changes which would be required.

This was not because of any lack of willingness on the part of the management, but rather because of the general economic environment which, over the last few years, has been changing rapidly and requiring so much day-to-day improvization that long term planning could be carried out only in very broad terms, if at all. On the other hand, the gradual nature of technological modernization (caused also by scarce financial resources) had its positive side. Technology was introduced step-by-step in various departments within the factory, allowing for the gradual restructuring of employment. Workers would be moved from one part to the other and attempts were made to find other positions within the factory. The introduction of new technology was thus never seen as a major factor causing job redundancy: it was the loss of Slovenia's markets in the other republics of ex-Yugoslavia which dealt the most severe blow. This required an overnight adjustment of production and employment levels, and the adaptation was made even more difficult and complex by the general economic recession being experienced by Slovene economy.

In most of the companies some information technology had been introduced, mostly starting in 1989 or 1990. In electronics, and the pharmaceutical side of the chemicals industry, the introduction of new technology was seen as an on-going process. Companies typically started gradually with the introduction of new technology in administration and accounting, moved on to planning and production preparation, and continued into production itself. In no case can we talk about major technological change, let alone of flexible automation or CAM. What we found is a piecemeal approach, depending primarily on the availability of financial resources.

However there were two exceptional cases. In one the formation of a joint venture with a foreign partner required the existing plant to undertake a programme of overall reorganization and technical modernization. This led also to job redundancies in practically all parts of the company.

In the other example technological modernization in manufacturing was initiated in the development department, mainly because of the demand of foreign partners for higher quality products. From development and design stages, new technology moved on to the production floor. Today this firm has more than sixty fully-automated machines coordinated by a central programming station. Gradually, information technology is also being introduced to other sectors such as production support (various production calculations and optimizations, production documentation), purchasing and sales, storage facilities, accounting and financial services, and business planning. Productivity in the preparatory phases of production, which had previously been time-consuming and quite rigid, had risen markedly. Information technology allowed for much greater flexibility and the economical and rapid production of even small batches of particular designs.

All of the companies had introduced some information technology in accounting and general administration. It is not possible to draw firm conclusions on the basis of such a small sample, but it does seem that companies which had introduced new technology more systematically, and had applied it to the production stages, had also been better able to face the shock of losing the ex-Yugoslav market: the quality level of their production was sufficient to enable them to gradually increase exports to developed countries. In one case, while the physical volume of production had declined, on the quality side they had successfully progressed and consequently had kept their export orders. They were convinced that, without new technology, there would have been no export development and the number of jobs which could have been kept would have been even lower.

In all of the companies, employment had shrunk since 1990. Depending on how much they were affected by the loss of the ex-Yugoslav market, the cuts in the labour force varied from 20 per cent to as much as 50 per cent. Since the interviews were conducted in typically 'female' enterprises, the majority of those made redundant were women. But there was no evidence to indicate that workers' gender had been significant. Where data was available it confirmed that the gender structure of the workforce had not changed.

Yet it was argued that the introduction of information technology had led to redundancies at various levels of production and in support activities. Better organization of the production process had meant a reduction in routine jobs, and the introduction of computers in accounting and administration led to major cutbacks on employment in these phases, affecting women in particular. Accounting and administration had been areas of massive over-employment. The relatively low cost of labour, combined with red tape, resulted in large administration departments by western standards, filled with women employees.

The major mechanism for dealing with redundancies, in practically all the companies, was early retirement. Retirement legislation permits companies to retire workers who do not yet meet the age or work experience requirements, by 'buying' the missing work years for them. Some workers who had been found a new position decided to quit the job, and yet others were given redundancy compensation. Natural attrition accounted for some workers leaving, and almost no new workers had been recruited in the past years.

In the introductory phase of new technologies, all companies provided additional training for workers with sufficient interest and background education to acquire new skills. Training was usually organized internally, in special courses run either by the supplier of the equipment or by the technical personnel of the company itself (this depended primarily on the size of the company). In one case, a foreign partner provided some training on their own premises. For workers with a very low educational level (or even illiteracy), there was no solution but redundancy. In general, the higher the initial educational level of the employees, the easier was the retraining process and less the need to declare the worker redundant.

Some of the companies have been recruiting on a small scale. This recruitment has largely been confined to workers with a very high educational level. This is gradually changing the skills structure, but it is not necessarily lowering the proportion of women employees, since many of the newcomers are women with college or university degrees. The employment policies of all companies looking for new workers recognize the need for a better-educated labour force: high school seems to be a minimum requirement. One reason is that rapid changes in the organization and technology of production require the ability to adjust quickly and to be able to understand the ongoing changes. People with higher basic education are expected to grasp new skills and knowledge faster and to be more easily trained. Familiarity with information technologies, especially computer literacy, is an advantage but not a prerequisite, since most personnel managers feel that this knowledge can easily be obtained on the job and with internal training (except of course for the job profiles dealing specifically with the programming or maintenance of computer equipment).

There is extensive legal protection and social assistance for workers who are threatened with redundancy. There are also schemes to promote employment, including:

- additional financing for new job creation;
- subsidies to maintain existing jobs;
- loans for new productive investments;
- additional financing to provide all-year-round employment for seasonal workers;
- financial help for educating new (unskilled) workers;
- financial help for additional training; and
- financial help for adapting work stations and technical equipment for disabled persons.

Many of these programs do not have sufficient finance, and so are not able to achieve much at present. In 1993, all programmes were stopped in the middle of October for lack of funding.

The Agency for Employment is trying to introduce programmes for the unemployed to help them learn new or additional skills. These programmes include:

- basic education courses;
- special training for particular jobs for which there are openings;
- language and computer training; and
- management training (how to set up your own small scale business, etc.).

Unemployed people who wish to start their own business can receive a lump sum in lieu of unemployment compensation.

AN ASSESSMENT OF SLOVENE EXPERIENCE

Slovenia has been going through the formation of a new national economy, with all the required mechanisms, at the same time as it makes the transition from a socialist economy to a market economy. The second transformation may be somewhat easier for Slovenia than for some other central and east European countries, since the Yugoslavian self-management system was closer to the market system than state planning. Companies, especially in Slovenia, had considerable independence in their business decisions and already had some direct contacts with foreign partners. This made them much more open to western styles of management and production organization.

Many companies also have long-term cooperation agreements with foreign companies and have therefore been part of an international chain of production. This has exposed them continuously to new technology. The current failure to incorporate information technology in manufacturing on a larger scale is not due to any lack of unawareness of the impact such technology could have on productivity and quality, but rather to the scarcity of financial resources.

The use of information technology in manufacturing in Slovenia is determined primarily by the availability of resources and by the export orientation of the specific manufacturing company. Even from the limited sample in this study, it can be concluded that information technology has usually been introduced in companies with a strong export orientation. The motivation was not 'internal', indeed the last reason for introducing new technology would be to save on labour costs. But there was a demand for quality products, which could not be met without information technology.

Slovenia's aim of rapid integration in the international marketplace is shared by many other ex-socialist countries. Their domestic markets have low purchasing power and the formerly well-developed trade within COMECON (the economic association of communist countries) has crumbled. They are therefore turning to the west: aiming at the developed countries of western Europe first, and then also at all other developed markets. The possibilities of competing on the basis of inexpensive labour only are very limited, because of the quality requirements in developed markets. It is thus to be expected that there will be a dynamic escalation of information technology in all export-oriented sectors and companies, and especially in those companies where foreign capital is involved. One purpose of the active promotion of direct foreign investment by the governments in ex-socialist countries is to secure the necessary financial resources for the modernization of the manufacturing sector.

In the Slovene case the sectors or companies in which there has been direct foreign investment, or long-term cooperation contracts or subcontracting, have been much quicker to use information technology than those concentrating on the domestic market (or the ex-Yugoslav market). These export-oriented companies have fared the best. Although modernization, both technical and organizational, has been a long-term process, they were better fitted to deal with the changed circumstances and the drastic loss of the Yugoslav market. They have been able to find additional export markets in a relatively short time, and have had to reduce their workforces less sharply than companies focusing on the domestic market. Domestically orientated companies found that their type and quality of production was not suitable to the developed markets. Their workforces were usually less qualified and therefore more difficult to retrain and, most important, they lacked the financial resources for technological modernization.

This is certainly something other central and eastern European countries are likely to face or are already facing. The modernization of their manufacturing sectors will be determined by the availability of financial resources from either direct foreign investment or foreign aid. This will of course change labour relationships as well. Work, which was once a common right in socialist societies, is already becoming a privilege. Even if the unemployment rates which have accompanied the transition to a market economy are not extreme in comparison to the developed market economies, the relatively short time span in which this phenomena has developed, and the poor support system for the unemployed, makes the situation dramatic.

Another characteristic of these labour markets has been the participation of women. Our analysis has shown that, in Slovenia, unemployment has no consequences specific to women, at least not at this stage. Even where large portions of the workforce are made redundant, the proportion of women in the remaining workforce did not change much. However, people with lower educational and qualification levels were hit harder, and will continue to lose their jobs first and have a harder time in finding new positions. Assuming that women's overall level of qualifications is lower, the increased introduction of new technologies could result in gender segregation of the redundant workers, with women being the first to go. Current evidence does not yet support this conclusion.

A more worrisome question raised by the Slovene example, is the entire approach to the technologically redundant workers. As shown, legislation does not differentiate between types of redundancy (economic or techno-logical). Company managements also talk only in terms of redundancy, without ascribing any reason. The unions have no knowledge or experience in dealing with technology issues, which are left to technical management. The standard explanation of all sides is that, so far, technology has not been seen as the major reason for job redundancy or a major factor affecting working conditions.

Yet one cannot help wondering what is going to happen if the expected influx of foreign investment and the ongoing technological modernization is not matched by a greater understanding of its potential consequences for the workers. Are we to repeat all the mistakes the developed economies have made, or can we approach these issues in a more systematic manner? One fears that with the present extremely low status of workers[8] in Slovenia, and probably in other ex-socialist countries as well, the negative consequences of the introduction of information technologies will not be averted. This would have serious implications for women workers.

What is needed if such developments are to be avoided is better knowledge of the way this process has developed in the western economies. The next step would then be to see how to adapt these lessons to the circumstances in the ex-socialist countries, and to try to mobilize various pressure groups, such as unions, women's organizations and various popular movements, to promote the issue of the quality of the work and the need to be aware of where technological modernization is taking us. These pressure groups are all relatively new: 'old' unions are trying to rehabilitate themselves, and the women's groups do not yet have a coherent and popular programme. These group's demands are much more a reflection of their party affiliation than the needs of their women workers. For example, the Women's Alliance of the Christian Democratic Party worries about traditional family values and fights abortion, while the student women's group fights for the rights of lesbians. The specific position of a woman as a worker is nobody's particular concern. This is exacerbated by the low participation of women in politics. Under the previous regime, equality was not a problem, at least officially, so it was considered that there was no need for a special 'women's policy'. Under the new regime, there are so many 'serious' problems that gender is again considered unimportant. As Barbara Einhorn shows in *Cinderella goes to Market* (Einhorn, 1993), this is a common feature of all ex-socialist countries.

The introduction of information technology is undoubtedly necessary in the Slovene and other ex-socialist economies, but we should approach this issue with an awareness of gender perspectives and with sufficient knowledge to eliminate its negative consequences for employment, for both women and men. The experiences of women workers in developed market economies and in some of the newly industrializing countries would be very relevant in this process.

NOTES

1 Slovenia is gradually adopting the NACE (Nomenclatura statistique des activités économiques dans la communauté européene) standard in its statistics, but not all the figures are yet available in this classification, so it has been necessary to use the old National Classification of Economic Activities.

2 Night employment is regulated, and mothers and pregnant women are prevented from undertaking night work and jobs which could be detrimental to their health. Slovene legislation allows twelve months of paid maternity leave: in the first six months after a birth either of the parents can decide to stay home with the child. There are also special provisions for single mothers (prolonged maternity leave), for twins or children with disabilities. Fathers seldom take paternal leave. The traditional perception is that mothers should undertake most of the parental obligations when a child is very young.

3 In 1993, 48 per cent of the workforce were women, and 44.2 per cent of the unemployed were women.

4 In 1992, employment in the business sector declined by more than 9 per cent. In the private sector, employment and self-employment increased by 8 per cent, but in absolute figures this meant only 4,800 new jobs. According to statistics from the Agency for Employment, the unemployment rate in September 1993 was 14.6 per cent. Some 44.1 per cent of all registered unemployed as of October 1993 were women, of whom 39.7 per cent were under 26 years old and 22 per cent had never had a job.

5 Since then, some data on information technology has been collected, but only for manufacturing sectors which employ few women workers (metal processing, machine building). The rate of introduction of new technologies was very low in these as well.

6 This is partly the result of the loss of ex-Yugoslav markets, but is to a large extent also the reflection of the collapse of a giant corporation, ISKRA, which disintegrated in 1991, with various units going bankrupt. The chemical processing industry has problems both on the supply side and in demand. Much of its raw material was coming from other parts of ex-Yugoslavia, and its major markets were in East and Central Europe, which are themselves experiencing serious crises.

7 All tables are compiled by the author from various official publications of the Statistical Office of the Republic of Slovenia.

8 The transition phase is characterized by poor protection of labour rights: previous legislation provided a very high level of protection and has therefore been nullified in the process of market reforms, and new legislation is still not fully in place. The pool of unemployed also exerts sufficient pressure for those still having a job not to 'rock the boat'.

REFERENCES

Duhovnik, J., P. Stanovnik, and G. Stanič (1988), *Računalniško podprto konstruiranje*, Ljubljana, Institute of Economic Research

Einhorn, Barbara (1993), *Cinderella Goes to Market*, London, Verso

Stanovnik, P., and B. Kutin (1989), *Ekonomski vidiki robotizacije*, Ljubljana, IER

7 Restructuring and retraining

The Canadian garment industry in transition

Charlene Gannagé

INTRODUCTION[1]

In 1986, on International Women's Day in Toronto, a contingent of garment workers from the International Ladies' Garment Workers' Union (ILGWU) marched under a new banner designed especially for the day. They were celebrating what appeared to be a new beginning. They had successfully won an industry-wide strike. They had thrown off the yoke of a male- dominated union leadership, with more rank and file women active on the stewards' council. Their participation marked an important shift in contemporary feminist politics toward a more inclusive movement that recognized the importance of combining issues of class, gender and ethnicity.

By 1993, following the passage of the United States–Canada Free Trade Agreement (FTA), and in anticipation of its extension to include Mexico in the North American Free Trade Agreement (NAFTA), garment workers were again on the streets. They were protesting the exploitative conditions of industrial homework, seen to be on the increase in some of the larger cities of Canada.

How had the Canadian garment industry changed? Were immigrant women entering a new period of militant unionism or being thrown backward to an earlier time when sweatshop conditions prevailed? What new strategies are favoured by garment workers in the face of debates about the need for retraining in a competitive global economy?

The purpose of this chapter is to provide an overview of the Canadian garment industry in transition. It begins with a brief analysis of the theoretical literature, drawn from both Marxist and feminist debates about the restructuring of work, especially as these debates have helped to shape political responses to the restructuring process. The paper presents evidence to suggest that the Canadian garment industry is in transition, with new corporate strategies existing alongside more traditional forms of manufacturing. It considers the role of governments in the restructuring process, especially the way in which the Canadian state has encouraged continental economic integration with the United States and Mexico. This chapter seeks to understand how feminist anti-racist initiatives in educational policy place the needs of immigrant workers at the centre of the retraining debate.[2]

FIELD WORK

The initial field work for this study involved four factory sites and seventy in-depth taped interviews with immigrant women sewing machine operators, packers, bundlers, spreaders and pressers. To help with language interpretation, I worked with women who were familiar with the working class immigrant communities. Women workers were interviewed in English, Chinese, Vietnamese, Portuguese, Italian and Spanish.

Interviews with rank and file workers were supplemented with an analysis of union records, participant observation in the union office, regular attendance at union meetings, and by interviews with plant managers, union representatives and industry specialists. Tours of factories were conducted in Canada and the United States.

The interviews were carried out in two stages between 1985 and 1987, and again in 1990, following the introduction of the FTA. In the later stage, I returned to one of the factories to interview a smaller sample of men who worked as cutters, shippers and material handlers. From 1987 to 1992, I kept in touch with developments in the industry by observing the monthly meetings of the Fashion Industry Liaison Committee (FILC), a municipal committee convened by city councillors representing the fashion district from the New Democratic Party (NDP). The mandate of the committee is to lobby city, provincial and federal governments on behalf of the fashion industry. This committee includes community college educators, representatives from the garment unions, retailers and garment manufacturers.

REVIEW OF THE LITERATURE

Canadian political economy tradition

The Canadian political economy tradition has its roots in left nationalist debates about the character of the Canadian state and its relationship to Canada's industrial base. Rianne Mahon made an important contribution from within this tradition by examining the role of the Canadian state in regulating textile imports in exchange for the sale of Canadian staple products and resources. She examined the process whereby Canadian textile capital became increasingly consolidated, so that only a few companies dominated the domestic market (Mahon, 1984). More recently, the literature has shifted to an analysis of the government's role in helping to set the stage for intercontinental integration and rationalization of the major industries in which Canadian women are employed (Cohen, 1987). Thus far, little attention had been paid to the restructuring of Canadian garment capital, which is perceived to be scattered among small manufacturers with little political power. A labour-intensive industry, the garment industry has remained highly protected, with unions often allied with small manufacturers to save the industry from import penetration.

As this paper will demonstrate, the industry is in transition. Changes in the industry demand new strategies.

Labour process perspective

The labour process perspective has drawn attention to the political culture of work organization and the historical transformation of managerial control (Braverman, 1974; Burawoy, 1979; Edwards, 1979). The feminist contribution has been to extend the boundaries of workplace studies to understand the way that gender relations have transformed organizational theory and workplace struggles (eg., Cockburn, 1985 and Coyle, 1982 (England); Steedman, 1986 (Canada); Lamphere, 1979 (United States)). My own contribution has called for a new feminism that combines issues of class, gender and ethnicity. Based on a case study of a unionized garment factory, my earlier research examined women's double day of labour and the barriers to women's active participation in the union (Gannagé, 1986).

Global feminist perspective

The global feminist perspective focuses on global labour markets and the international division of labour. The unequal relationship between core and periphery countries is explained within the context of a global manufacturing system divided along gender and racial lines. Swasti Mitter (1986) is especially concerned with the world-wide subcontracting process made possible by new developments in technology and the mobility of capital within transnational enterprises. The increasing casualization and marginalization of women's work in the quasi-legal sector characterizes the fragmentation of work as capital moves operations from North to South (see also Nash and Fernandez-Kelly, 1983). Women's resistance through participation in non-governmental organizations is highlighted as a major catalyst for social change.

International labour studies

A newly emerging approach to labour studies examines work relations in both developing countries and the first world (Munck, 1988; Cohen, 1991). Recognizing that different historical patterns of industrial development have occurred, this approach analyses the labour process, the role of unions and the way in which the state has shaped workplace struggles. According to Elson (1991), male-biased approaches ignore gender relations, especially the role of women in the development process.

Each of these perspectives has been influential in shaping the discussion about the nature of industrial restructuring around the globe. In Canada, immigrant workers in the clothing industry are uniquely positioned because of their experience of two cultures across national boundaries, their history of struggle, and their spirit of survival in the face of tremendous difficulties created by the new industrial giants and their political representatives in government.

NEW MANAGERIAL STRATEGIES

Cloakmakers in the ILGWU, primarily from eastern Europe, resisted changes to the organization of their work in 1966. A story in the Toronto Star carried the headline, 'Garment workers fight mass production'.[3] Referred to as the 'Artex rebels', a dozen skilled craftsmen in Toronto protested that factory owners threatened to hire non-union labour to open a sportswear shop. The skilled tailors feared that their jobs would be lost if the conventional method of making the whole garment were to be replaced by a new section system used widely in the men's clothing industry. Their fears were gender based. At the time, new employees were mainly Italian, Greek and Portuguese immigrant women. The union struck a compromise to protect the existing cloak shops which used the conventional method, while allowing new shops in the sportswear industry to introduce the section system.

In the 1990s, the demographic characteristics of the labour force, ownership patterns, and style of work in the Canadian ladies' clothing industry have changed. Technology has been introduced as part of a massive restructuring process which has transformed the industry from top to bottom. The restructuring process is multifaceted and has proceeded with government and manufacturers working in tandem. In less successful operations, new technology has been used by management to downsize, while more successful enterprises have expanded overtime, shift work and part-time work. With an increasing reliance on technological innovation in factories whose owners could afford to modernize or received government aid to do so, the occupational structure of the workforce has shifted from both male and female skilled craft work in the cloak and dress industry, respectively, to female-dominated assembly line production, section work and industrial homework in the newly-created sportswear industry.

The restructuring process, begun in the late 1960s and early 1970s, accelerated with the passage of the FTA. During the year following the introduction of the FTA, from June 1989 to June 1990, the clothing industry lost 23,000 jobs, an 18 per cent decline in employment. The Canadian Labour Congress (CLC), the main labour federation in Canada, estimates that in the first two years under the free trade agreement with the United States, 582,000 fewer jobs were created in the Canadian economy than could be expected under average conditions (Canadian Labour Congress, 1993: 116).

Reskilling or deskilling?

Gender relations have changed at the top of the pyramid structure as well as at the bottom. Changing attitudes in business have seen more women assuming managerial positions. Daughters and wives of owners are becoming divisional heads and paid employees of the company, instead of 'helping out' fathers and brothers.

Jobs have been created in business services, warehouse distribution and import houses. A new strata of white collar clerical personnel are employed in offices of human resources management. The rationalization of the office to meet the pressure of just-in-time delivery threatens the employment of this largely non-unionized clerical workforce. Electronic data interchange systems have eliminated the need for clothing retailers to keep costly inventories. Rapid response and fast turnover to fill special orders entail a closer interface between manufacturer and retailer. The demand for increased productivity and greater flexibility is passed onto the already vulnerable white collar workforce (Dagg and Fudge, 1992).

The more skilled aspects of pattern making and grading have been taken out of the hands of male cutters to become highly trained positions for computer operators and programmers. In owner-managed factories, trusted family members, or even the owner, use computer aided design systems. A few senior cutters have been pushed into middle management positions. Some openings have emerged in the highly-paid mechanical field, positions that have been given to men (see also Cockburn, 1985).

Computer aided design and manufacturing has made it possible to design and cut patterns in Canada and transfer the assembly work to states in the United States or offshore where labour standards and wages are lower. Women are employed in the less challenging aspects of this traditionally male-dominated craft, in laying and cutting the fabric.

Automated material handling systems, used in some shops since the early 1970s, carry the work to sewing machine operators, eliminating the jobs of bundle girls. With a press of a button, a hanger drops down beside a sewing machine operator. She sews a single seam or dart and presses the button again. The automated conveyor belt transports the garment to the next operator for the next operation.

Piece work

In the sewing room, young women are expected to perform more than one operation. They are rotated from job to job to meet the employer's requirement for a flexible workforce, while older workers do the same job day in and day out. An administrative apparatus based on prescribed rules and procedures, fewer supervisory personnel and the reliance on conveyors to control the pace of work has made it easier for management to track workers' performance. Electronic monitors built into the individual work stations are used to check the speed of sewing machine operators.

On the factory floor, changes in the social organization of work have given rise to new forms of wage payment. Because of the transitional character of the industry in Canada, no single method of calculating piece wages predominates in a largely piece work industry. Multinational firms have developed standardized methods of wage payment, used in subsidiary firms. More than one method for calculating the wage may exist. Workers in the cutting room may be paid by the hour, while those who work as sewing machine operators may be paid under an incentive system. Various accounting procedures are used to pay piece wages, ranging from the traditional ticket system of quality control to more complex calculations of workers' output based on the standard allowed minute. In a multi-ethnic work environment, numerically-based accounting systems increase the demand for English literacy and mathematical numeracy.

Workers' resistance to the intensification of work may take the form of individual responses such as absenteeism or job shopping. Coordinated resistance on the shop floor, such as slow downs or work stoppages, is used to enforce workers' demands for improved conditions during contract negotiations. A cutter reported that some women in his factory engaged in mischievous play, sewing garments backwards or with the stripes upside down if management practices seemed especially harsh or unfair. These activities were timed to cause the most havoc, usually when the company was under particular pressure to meet special orders or production deadlines. A shop steward reported that in her factory, where turnover was especially high, management paid workers a special bonus for recruiting family members or friends. Some workers expressed reluctance to comply with such requests when piece wages were so low.

The ethnic division of labour

Forty-five per cent of the workers in the garment industry are immigrants, the majority of whom are women whose first language is neither English nor French. The latest wave of immigration has brought visible minority women from third world countries to Canadian garment factories.[4] Third world immigration is seen as part of a global restructuring of the international migration system. Canada shares with the United States, Australia and New Zealand a relative openness to ethnically diverse immigration from third world countries (Simmons, 1990). Immigrants have fled the ill effects of structural adjustment programmes or poverty in their home countries (George, 1992). Once they enter Canada, they join a labour market that is already structured both ethnically and on class lines (Li, 1988). As they look for a better life for themselves and their children, immigrant workers face new managerial strategies and government policies that threaten to take away their livelihood and the limited gains that workers have achieved in recent years.

On the factory floor, a combination of different methods have been used by clothing manufacturers to maintain control of an ethnically diverse workforce. In one factory that I toured, East Asian immigrant women from Vietnam, China and Hong Kong were assigned the 'more delicate tasks' off the assembly line. With less opportunity to earn bonuses, they reported that their take home pay was lower. Ethnicity can be used by management to favour one ethnic group over another for special treatment or privileges. Black immigrant women reported differential treatment in terms of lay-offs and recall. In another factory, Italian immigrant workers with a history of union experience were laid off, while more recent Vietnamese refugees did not lose their jobs. The tolerance of ethnic traditions in the workplace may be a cooptive method of winning the confidence and loyalty of new immigrant workers. In a factory where turnover was a problem for management, Muslim workers were allowed to take time from their work to pray in the lunchroom, and were granted time off work to observe their holy days.

THE GARMENT INDUSTRY IN TRANSITION

The manner in which firms are restructuring is extremely diverse and includes the radical transformation of long-standing enterprises as well as the rapid growth of new enterprises. The case studies presented below illustrate both the breadth of that process and the specific ways that companies have tried to improve their own market position relative to their competitors. Changes in managerial styles, from entrepreneurial to corporate, new ownership patterns, and the global context of garment manufacturing mark a dynamic transition. Multinational firms have grown, declined and revived alongside smaller family-owned businesses. Large clothing com- panies have acquired their own retail chains, bought out their competitors, integrated vertically or sought international fame through designer-driven franchise operations and product licensing. Large garment firms have expanded too quickly and tied their fortunes to an economy in decline: some manufacturers closed their retail outlets in Canada to offset losses in the United States. Others, like Mr. Jax, closed their manufacturing houses.

The threat of factory closure has spelled trouble for unions. Some firms have sought to undermine already established collective agreements through wage freezes or capital flight across provinces and to low wage economies in the United States, the Caribbean and the Far East; the extension of free trade to include Mexico creates another opening for capital mobility. Some firms have co-opted unions by using employee pension funds to finance rapid expansion schemes.

The rapid change and multiple threats have paralysed union organizations and hindered their recruitment of members, which has created fertile ground for the growth of non-union contract shops and subcontracting to industrial homeworkers (Cameron and Mak, 1991; Dagg and Fudge, 1992; Leach, 1993). An inquiry into the conditions of clothing workers revealed that visible minority workers in non-unionized contract shops were especially disadvantaged when their factories closed without notice, leaving them with no jobs and no severance pay (BASIC, n.d.).

At the bottom of this class structure are the growing proportion of women who take work into their home. The ILGWU interviewed thirty industrial homeworkers, who were primarily Chinese-speaking. Most of the homeworkers were paid less than the minimum wage. Half of them reported difficulty in getting paid for work completed. Many women were being helped at home by their children (Dagg and Fudge, 1992: p. 24). The ILGWU has reported a two-thirds loss in membership since 1986. The expansion of garment manufacture to new localities outside urban centres, and even outside the country, poses tough challenges in organizing the unorganized.

Dylex in Toronto

Dylex is a pioneer in multinational retailing. The company began by manufacturing sportswear, marketed through retail outlets it purchased in Canada and the United States. The company met with success until it ventured into the United States and bought some failing retail chains (Foxmoor, Brooks and T. Edwards) at a time when the economy was heading into a downturn. In 1985, Dylex had 2,700 retail stores in Canada and the United States. By 1991, the conglomerate was down to 1,500 stores. The company showed a heavy loss in its Canadian operations in 1986.[5] By the first half of 1991, they recorded a loss of 37.6 million dollars and were closing their Town and Country women's retail chain in Canada and their Club International, recently acquired from Monaco Group, in the United States.[6] In 1991, the company announced a twelve month wage freeze among its 20,000 full-and part-time employees.[7] Despite these losses, Dylex is considered to be a major stakeholder in the Canadian retail market with a strong balance sheet in 1991, with 117 million dollars in cash at hand,[8] and control of about 10 per cent of the Canadian apparel retail market.

Alfred Sung and the Monaco Group

While Dylex sought to acquire retail holdings, the emphasis of Alfred Sung and the Monaco Group was designer-driven. The Monaco Group based its strategy on the promotion of a single designer, Alfred Sung, who is known throughout Canada and internationally. His name was used in marketing and promotion not only in women's clothing, but also in a variety of products manufactured under license by other companies. Some 30 per cent of the Alfred Sung label was manufactured in-house, 50 per cent was manufactured by Canadian contractors and the rest was manufactured overseas, primarily in Hong Kong.[9] When the Monaco Group posted a loss in 1991, Alfred Chan and brother Edward Tan, for Etac Sales Ltd, bought the rights to the Alfred Sung label to market Alfred Sung clothing world-wide for fifty years. Etac is able to improve profit margins by using Asian manufacturers and distribution networks in Shanghai, Hong Kong and Tianjin.[10]

Tan Jay: from Winnipeg to Toronto

Peter Nygard, owner of the Tan Jay line, has also captured international fashion headlines. Nygard is well known for his lavish Hollywood-style extravaganzas both in Canada and the United States. He is also famous for placing whole page advertisements in Winnipeg newspapers to present his case against union organizing drives.[11] The Manitoba labour board has ruled that Tan Jay had committed unfair labour practices, including the refusal to deduct union dues, to allow the union access to the plant and to pay into the union's retirement and health and welfare funds. The labour board ruling followed a history of intimidatory practices used by the company against its immigrant workforce, many of them from the Philippines. The company was ordered to pay the union and illegally laid off employees $150,000 in monies owed and fines.[12]

Tan Jay employs fifteen hundred workers and has also opened factories in Montreal and Thunder Bay, with research and design facilities in New York and Los Angeles and extensive offshore operations throughout the Orient (Ghorayshi, 1990). Much of Nygard's success has been under-written by his political acumen in lobbying for favourable terms from federal government assistance programmes to finance the restructuring of his four factories in Winnipeg. He has now moved his corporate head-quarters to Toronto.

Mr. Jax Group of Vancouver

Another feature of the Canadian garment industry is the expansion of new fashion centres outside the traditional Montreal, Toronto and Winnipeg needle industry. Vancouver's Mr. Jax is an example of a fashion group that initially had trouble breaking into the eastern retail market. In 1986, Mr. Jax listed on the Toronto Stock Exchange and purchased West Coast Woollen Mills in British Columbia. The mill made woollen worsteds and would become Mr. Jax's domestic fabric supplier.[13] In 1987, the Mr. Jax Group acquired Surrey Classics.[14] But by 1990, unable to sustain its expansion, Mr. Jax was in the red, looking to sell to a multinational company who could take advantage of the United States market.

Mr. Jax Group employed 1400 people across Canada, had six companies with retail outlets and real estate holdings plus a state-of-the-art factory housed in a recently purchased building on Vancouver's waterfront. In the year ending 30 November, 1990, it posted a loss of 5.9 million dollars. In January, 1991, it announced the closing of the Surrey Classics Division.[15] One hundred and ninety workers were affected by the closure.[16]

Government strategies

The restructuring of Canadian garment capital has been supported by federal government policies designed to improve the competitiveness of Canada's manufacturing base. The previous regulation of imports as an industrial strategy did not work. Despite the government's 'protection' of the domestic clothing industry, the industry showed a decline in employment prior to the FTA, which could in part be attributed to rationalization and new technology. Following the introduction of the FTA, industrial homework increased. As mentioned, some small companies, unable to compete, have opened import houses or have become non-union shops in a subcontracting nexus.

The federal government helped manufacturers modernize their operations with grants through the now defunct Canadian Industrial Renewal Board. Non-Canadian multinational corporations have established branch plants in Canada under the auspices of the also defunct Foreign Investment Review Agency (Mahon, 1984). Work sharing (with the help of unemployment insurance), subsidized training programmes and tax shelters were also provided through government assistance programmes (Ghorayshi, 1990).

The Free Trade Agreement

In 1988, the political and economic stage was set for the introduction of the FTA, which would have disastrous consequences for workers, unions and small businesses in the ladies' clothing industry. The FTA has helped to shift the Canadian clothing import structure from low cost countries to the United States. The agreement opened the Canadian market to manufacturers based in the United States while helping big clothing firms in Canada to move production south of the border; it also helped large clothing manufacturers-turned-retailers in Canada to ship their manufactured apparel goods duty free to their existing retail outlets in the United States. American exports of apparel to Canada (not including production contracted abroad by US firms) increased dramatically by 26 per cent in volume and 14 per cent in value in the first nine months of 1991, following the introduction of the FTA, although the total market for apparel was down considerably, with the total volume of imports from all sources declining by 7 per cent, and by 11 per cent in value terms (Beatty, 1992: p. 14).

THE WORKFORCE

Training and retraining

Along with participation in restructuring the industry, the government's policy regarding labour has emphasized the need for the workforce to retrain. Federal government initiatives have called for a national educational strategy for 'competitive' training to keep pace with global restructuring. New job opportunities in the 1990s, according to the Hudson Institute study commissioned by the federal government, will see a decline in blue collar jobs and a shift to a service economy with highly-skilled jobs, especially in the fields of health care, transportation and finance. The emphasis on retraining has been at best elitist and narrow, highlighting the technical requirements of industry rather than the educational development of workers. New technology has been seen to benefit workers with university education most:

> Even jobs in manufacturing are becoming like service jobs. Workers need greater technical skills to supervise, maintain and reprogram computer-assisted equipment and robots. They must deal with new materials on the job and oversee quality control for the goods they produce. More workers are spending more time on design work, marketing distribution, maintenance and finance. These jobs require good communication skills and problem solving abilities.
>
> (Minister of State, Multiculturalism and Citizenship Canada, 1990: 16)

The new training strategy calls for a 'continuous learning culture to complement formal education' (ibid., 1990: p. 25). Employers will be expected to fulfil training needs through employer-assisted training programmes, as a form of 'employment insurance' for all employees made vulnerable by changes in technology (ibid., 1990: p. 11). This contrasts with the general lack of industry training in Canada. Silvia Ostry estimates that Canada spends about 0.6 per cent of payroll costs on training. This is half of what the United States spends and a fifth of what Japan spends. Canada also lags in research and development.[17]

Sectoral analyses of the clothing industry have elicited manufacturers' support for the long-term development of human resources (Industry, Science and Technology Canada, 1991). Suggestions focus on apprenticeship programmes for pattern makers, middle management training and industry support for both young and established designers. Job development strategies that do not include the long-term educational goals of immigrant workers perpetuate a class-biased programme.

For years, the working knowledge and self-expression of tailors and seamstresses had been appropriated by managerial strategies to wrest control of the labour process, to transform it and to break the autonomy of craft workers. Today the majority of immigrant workers who obtained or maintained employment were not using their skills, they were losing their skills or their skills were not transferable. Their work was labelled 'unskilled' despite the working knowledge that workers obtained on the job, the transformation of their skills within the labour process and the development of collective skills they shared with their workmates. (Gannagé, 1989–90).

The women

Some South Asian and Latin American women that were interviewed had professional experience as nurses, teachers and even doctors in training prior to immigrating to Canada. There were women from Northern Italy who had been apprenticed in garment manufacture and knew how to make the whole garment; black women from the Caribbean, too poor to purchase clothes, who had learned how to sew out of economic necessity; and many Portuguese women from the rural Azores who had no previous industrial experience and came to Canada as economic refugees. High school aged daughters of immigrants contributed to the family income by working in the sportswear industry.

Let me introduce some women shop stewards in the factories that I studied, women who had battled against traditional notions of femininity to hold union positions.

Gina is a skilled tailor who knows how to design patterns for dresses and make the whole garment, but she is not using these skills because she works in a highly sectionalized garment factory. In 1959, she immigrated from Italy to Canada. She worked for the same company for over twenty years until the employer declared bankruptcy. During her employment, she had two children and took time off work for six months and five months respectively. Her mother lived with her and helped with childcare. In 1981, she found a job as a serger. Her starting salary was only $4.00 an hour. Her years of experience as a sewing machine operator enabled her to master her new job in about a week. After $3\frac{1}{2}$ years, she earns $5.60 an hour.

Isaura, from the rural Azores, has a grade three education. She immigrated to Canada in 1960. She worked at night, cleaning offices and factories. She eventually applied for a day job in a pickle factory where she worked for three months before she was laid off. After four years and a second child, she found a job as a busheller (removing loose threads before garments are shipped) in a factory located in her neigh- bourhood. The supervisor taught her how to use an industrial sewing machine and after eleven years she earns $6.80. When the company installed an automated conveyor belt, she was assigned a job previously done by two people. She handles 1,275 units a day. Her job involves lifting and stretching. She suffers from soreness in her muscles and varicose veins in her legs.

In Bev's home country in Ghana, it was common for women to work outside the household as traders in the market. She received most of her education up to secondary school in Ghana. She followed her husband to England, where she worked for five years as a key punch operator. When she came to Canada in 1971, she applied for a job in a bank but was told that she lacked 'Canadian experience'. She obtained work in a muffler factory and then in a plastics factory. In 1983, she found a job in a garment factory as a machinist. Her starting salary, after twelve years in Canada and plenty of 'Canadian experience', was $4.00 an hour. When her husband became ill, she applied for a 'less strenuous job' in the examining area where she put her mathematical skills to use measuring the sizes and checking the quality of garments. Her basic salary without bonus was around $170 a week and during a good week she was able to earn $180 take-home pay.

Rosa has a grade five education and learned how to sew dresses at school in Italy. She immigrated to Canada in 1960 and for ten years worked in a non-unionized pyjamas factory. When the factory moved, she found another job. She has worked as a sewing machine operator for twelve years. She can operate four industrial sewing machines: single needle, double needle, serger and a special machine for making plaquets. She knows how to sew all the parts on the blouse but has never been taught how to inset the collars and sleeves. At home, she sews the whole garment for family members. She works in a piece work factory. For every 100 units she earns $5.17 for sewing the hem of the blouse and $3.65 for plaquets on the cuff. Workers receive a minimum guarantee of $4.50 an hour plus a cost of living bonus negotiated every year between the employer and the union. In 1986, she earned $6.87 an hour. When she came to work in this factory in 1974, 75 to 80 workers were employed, and in 1986 only 23 workers remained. Rosa learned to operate more and more machines as fewer workers were left to perform the subassembly operations. She has been laid off five times in one year: 'I have a house. I have a family. I have to work to live . . . I can't afford to stay home.' When I visited her in the summer of 1986, she did not know when she would be called back to work.

Family considerations were an integral feature of immigrant women's working lives. Childcare was viewed as a basic necessity; unemployed women relatives, older daughters and grandmothers traditionally provided childcare when government programmes were inaccessible or non-existent. The lack of accessible childcare outside traditional family networks caused some married women to delay or interrupt their labour force participation, while grandmothers left the industry to 'help out' daughters with children. The lack of both childcare and the protection of citizenship pushed refugee women to combine family responsibilities with industrial homework without the benefit of union protection.

The men

I returned to the field after the introduction of the FTA to understand the working conditions of the men in the industry: how had the industry changed? What were the skills that they had brought to the industry? Were they using their skills? Were they adapting their skills to garment manufacture? Two of the four factories that I initially set out to study had closed and I wished to know what kind of training programmes immigrant workers wanted. Evidence for the next section of the paper is based on in-depth interviews conducted with male workers at Jersey Garments, a sportswear factory in operation since 1975.[18]

Despite the FTA, Jersey Garments had continued to be profitable. The employer had bought an exclusive franchise for a sportswear line from the United States that made jerseys, sweatshirts and other athletic clothing. This was so successful that he introduced a second part-time shift, and workers were making overtime wages during the week and on Saturdays.

The men who worked in the factory included East Asians from Vietnam and the Philippines, blacks and West Indians from the Caribbean, and Spanish speaking workers from Latin America as well as workers from eastern Europe and Israel. The immigrant men that I interviewed criticized the employer's unwillingness to invest in human resources and train workers for careers in the industry.[19] Most men reported that they learned on the job by watching others and developing their own working knowledge. Men were a minority in the sportswear industry, and were primarily employed as cutters, mechanics, materials handlers and shippers. The men were paid higher wages than the women, but their wages were much lower than the wages of other male workers in the Canadian manufacturing sector.

The men that I interviewed had a number of skills that they had learned in their home country, but which they were not using. Some were enrolled in post-secondary education prior to immigrating to Canada: one had studied dentistry, two had trained in auto mechanics, another had trained to be an electrician. Some previous occupations included work as a bricklayer, radio broadcaster, x-ray technician, and typesetter. In the majority of cases, workers had to drop out of high school because of financial need. Those who had trained as apprentices could not find well-paying jobs in their home countries, others found that their skills and training were not recognized in Canada or they could not afford to take courses for accreditation. Some talked about holding down more than one part-time job to make ends meet.

Paulo is Spanish speaking, from Peru, and has 17 years of cutting experience. He is 40 years old and earned $12.25 an hour in 1990. He learned cutting in his uncle's factory while studying to become an electrical engineer, prior to immigrating to Canada in 1976. He just recently received his Canadian citizenship. His wife stays home to look after their two small children. They cannot afford to purchase a home in Toronto on their single income. At weekends, the family participates in the activities of the Spanish-speaking community.

Walter is from Trinidad. He is 26 years old and employed as a material handler. He was recently promoted to inventory control and is considered a manager, with two employees under his supervision. He earns $9.00 an hour. He shares a small basement apartment with his wife, young son, his sister and her husband. They share expenses and everyone in the household helps with childcare.

Samuel immigrated from the Philippines. He works in the shipping department and earned $10.23 in 1990. A union activist, he has resisted promotion to supervisor. He works at a second job where he earns $7.16 an hour. He works sixteen hours a day, five days a week. He is 54 years old and has been with the company for nine years. His wife and three children work and help to pay for the mortgage on a small condominium in a subsidized housing development. They live in downtown Toronto. His wife's parents also live in the household.

The men wanted to learn more at work and to be appropriately compensated while training on the job. Paulo, with seventeen years experience in cutting, was eager to upgrade his skills in computer-training and pattern-making. He suffered an injury at work and welcomed the opportunity to use a computer. Samuel, aged 54, felt that he was 'too old' to move from his present job in shipping and inventory control to start over again. To keep busy, Walter often asked the mechanic if he could help him. With his previous training in auto mechanics, he had an understanding of how machines work and welcomed the opportunity to work full-time as a mechanic. Walter described to me, in great detail, the chart he had developed to organize his shipping orders, including lot and dye numbers, fabric content, type of weave and so on. He was very proud of his ingenuity and skill in developing a chart to help him organize his work. It is now technologically possible with the development of electronic data processing for inventory control (EDI) to eliminate the most challenging aspects of his job, and the need for the skills which first won him a promotion to management. No longer in the union, he has unwittingly lost his only opportunity for minimal job protection.

For the first time in the recent history of the union, the men in the industry compared their wages with those of the women in a non-competitive way. The men spoke of the need to strike alliances with the women, most of whom were earning wages of $6.50 an hour, some with eight to twelve years experience. Gender politics extended from the workplace into the home front. One worker supported his wife in her attempt to receive Canadian accreditation for her nursing skills and wondered whether such feminist retraining programmes could be expanded to include immigrant men. On the job, male workers lamented that women employed as cutters continued to do the same job day in and day out at lower wages than the men, thereby weakening the cutters' bargaining position. Patriarchal attitudes at home posed dilemmas for women. The son in one cutter's household would not allow his mother to be interviewed because she was 'busy' with family responsibilities.

For most of the men who participated in my study, family responsibilities were an integral aspect of their lives. Mutual support within the family context helped the men to continue working during hard times. With the erosion of government social programmes and the universality of such programmes under attack, enormous pressure is placed on working class families to absorb more of the cost and care of dependents (McQuaig, 1993).

The nature of men's work in the industry determined the kind of resistance open to them. They were under pressure to increase their productivity. Paid by the hour, they usually stretched out their work during slack periods in order to look busy. When accidents occurred at work, they were reluctant to take time off work or file for workers' compensation for fear of losing their employment. For men employed as cutters, hand and finger injuries were prevalent. Shippers reported back strains and muscular injuries. The employer kept a personnel record on each employee. One worker's personnel record was used by the employer to discourage him from filing for compensation when he was injured on the job.

IMPLICATIONS FOR SOCIAL POLICY

The restructuring process that has occurred in the Canadian garment industry has seen a decline in men's labour force participation and the downgrading of employment standards for the vast majority of women immigrant workers. Following the completion of my research, a report presented to Labour Canada made a number of recommendations to mitigate against the worst effects of industrial restructuring and technological change, especially related to health and safety and the reorganization of work (Gannagé, 1987). An earlier version of these recommendations was translated and sent to workers who had participated in the research project. The recommendations on skills training continue to be relevant for developing educational programmes for immigrant workers. Lifelong learning and paid on-the-job training are important to a democratic educational programme. So is accessibility: in the case of immigrant workers this means that such programmes need to consider the childcare and language needs of the workers, and the double day which most of them work.

Garment and textile unions are developing a united front to save jobs. Inter-union alliances and community coalitions will continue to extend their efforts to unorganized workplaces and to join forces across national boundaries to include workplaces that have relocated. The building of cross-border linkages has begun with union militants and feminist activists in the United States, Mexico and Canada organizing against NAFTA (Moody and McGinn, 1992).

At home, grass roots initiatives aimed at eliciting government support for retraining have encouraged new forms of labour–feminist cooperation. These initiatives have focused on lobbying governments at the federal, provincial and municipal levels. Labour advocates in the New Democratic Party have been the focal point for union activities, both provincially, where the NDP was in power, and municipally, where NDP city councillors represent the fashion district. As the discussion below indicates, some of the planning has been initiated and implemented.

Short-term programmes include English as a Second Language and basic mathematics classes for immigrant women. Immigrant workers whose previous professional or trade skills are not recognized have been helped by community based programmes for visible minority women to receive accreditation. Long-term training could include paid educational leave, similar to the collective agreements of the Canadian Auto Workers, for workers who wish to pursue more advanced degrees or certifications or for workers whose training would directly benefit the employer (Gindin, 1991).

In the Spring of 1991, the FILC announced a Toronto Sews project using the City's new Fashion Incubator. This project involves a training facility with the latest state-of-the-art technology to provide technical support to young designers from Toronto fashion schools. In June 1991, David Sobel and Susan Meurer completed a consultant's report for the FILC in which they concluded that more hands-on training programmes in the workplace are needed, not only for designers and middle managers, but also for rank and file workers who wish to upgrade their skills without losing pay. In an unprecedented move, two major international unions in the industry, that were formerly rivals, the Amalgamated Clothing and Textile Workers' Union and the ILGWU, have pooled their resources to share in the development of the Apparel and Textile Action Centre. They are pressuring manufacturers to take advantage of federal and provincial grants to provide paid hands-on training in the workplace.

In another development, the International Ladies' Garment Workers' Union, in conjunction with the National Action Committee on the Status of Women, have organized to protect immigrant women employed as homeworkers through a homeworkers' registry. They have targeted Canadian and multinational retailers in a labour–feminist coalition, established to lobby the provincial government to improve employment standards legislation for low-wage homeworkers.[20] Training programmes with childcare facilities will be an important outcome of the provincial labour strategy.

The increase in factory closures signalled the need for the Workers' Information Action Centre, founded by the City of Toronto, to inform non-unionized employees of their legal rights under the provincial Employment Standards Act. The plight of non-unionized workers, employed under near sweat-shop conditions, was described in the Report of the Inquiry Into Garment Factory Closings. The inquiry, held by the BASIC Poverty Action Group with the assistance of the Woodgreen Community Centre in Toronto, included legal specialists, prominent journalists, municipal councillors and organizers from the labour movement to hear and publicize the testimony of workers employed at Lark Manufacturing, a contract shop in the East End of Toronto which was threatened with closure.

CONCLUSION

No single managerial strategy exists in the Canadian garment industry. In a transitional phase, the industry is unevenly developed with multinational interests existing alongside family-owned businesses and non-union contract shops. Following the introduction of the FTA, there has been a dramatic decline in union membership. New technology, economic integration with the US and a deepening recession have contributed to the present economic malaise in Canadian manufacturing. In the face of a growing economic crisis that shows no signs of improving, garment and textile unions have struck alliances with each other and with community organizations in lobbying efforts to increase immigrant women workers' access to government retraining programmes. The struggle to develop an educational strategy with a feminist anti-racist orientation continues to be a major concern for union militants and labour educators concerned about the class-bias of current retraining programmes.

NOTES

1. I am grateful to Chris Huxley, Swasti Mitter and Sheila Rowbotham for their encouragement and helpful comments on earlier versions of this paper. I am especially indebted to the men and women from the union for their participation in this study. Their names have been fictionalized. Special thanks to the International Ladies' Garment Workers' Union for their cooperation and to the owners of the factories who allowed this study to be undertaken. The research was made possible with seed money from the McMaster University Research Board, a postdoctoral fellowship and Canada Research Fellowship from the Social Sciences and Humanities Research Council, held at York University, and by a grant from Labour Canada, from the Technology Impact Research Fund (TIRF). Of course, the final responsibility remains mine.
2. The ILGWU wanted to understand how technological innovation affected the working lives of its members. Grants from TIRF, under the federal government auspices of Labour Canada, offered the unique opportunity for academics to work with unions to develop labour-related research projects on new technology. The focus on new technology is part of a broader project that involves a book on industrial restructuring with specific reference to the garment industry. The book addresses a number of related themes including the implications of economic integration, gender and skill, systems of wage payment and the social policy implications of restructuring as it relates to health and safety issues.
3. *Toronto Star*, 26 November, 1966: p. 64.
4. See Seward (1990). Recent demographic trends indicate a decline in immigration from Europe, with new immigrants coming from Asia (including East Asia, South Asia and South East Asia), the Caribbean and Latin America (Simmons, 1990; Frideres, 1992).
5. *The Globe and Mail*, 25 November 1986: B22.
6. *Financial Times of Canada*, 9 December 1991: p. 12.
7. *The Globe and Mail*, 24 January 1991: B9.
8. *The Globe and Mail*, 9 April 1992: B9.
9. *The Globe and Mail*, 1 March 1986: A10.
10. *Report on Business Magazine*, November 1991: pp. 70–80.
11. *Winnipeg Free Press*, 25 May 1985: p. 5.
12. *Winnipeg Free Press*, 26 January 1985: 3; 24 January 1985: pp. 1, 4.

13 *The Globe and Mail*, 25 May 1987: B5.
14 *Apparel*, September–October, 1987: p. 27.
15 *Style*, 15 April 1991: pp. 1, 4.
16 *Style*, 21 January 1991: p. 3.
17 *The Globe and Mail*, 23 December 1991: B4; see also Sharpe, 1993.
18 The name of this factory has been fictionalized.
19 For a discussion of the distinction between 'multiskilling' and 'multitasking', especially in relation to the issue of skills development, see CAW-Canada Research Group on CAMI (1993).
20 *Now Magazine*, 2–8 December 1993: pp. 17–18.

REFERENCES

BASIC Action Poverty Group. (n.d.) Report of the Inquiry into Garment Factory Closings held on 9 September 1989 at the Woodgreen Community Centre in Toronto

Beatty, Stephen (1992), 'The Americans are Coming!' *Apparel*, January/February: pp. 12, 14

Braverman, Harry (1974), *Labor and Monopoly Capital: The Degradation of Work in the Twentieth Century*, New York, Monthly Review Press

Burawoy, Michael (1979), *Manufacturing Consent*, Chicago, University of Chicago Press

Cameron, Barbara and Teresa Mak (1991) 'Working Conditions of Chinese Speaking Homeworkers in the Toronto Garment Industry: Summary of the Results of a Survey Conducted by the International Ladies' Garment Workers' Union'

Canadian Labour Congress (1993), 'Two Years Under Free Trade: An Assessment' in Graham S. Lowe and Harvey J. Krahn (eds), *Work in Canada: Readings in the Sociology of Work and Industry*, Nelson, Canada, Scarborough: pp. 115–119

CAW-Canada Research Group on CAMI (1993), *The CAMI Report: Lean Production in a Unionized Auto Plant*, Willowdale, CAW Research Department

Cockburn, Cynthia (1985), *Machinery of Dominance: Women, Men and Technical Know-how*, London, Pluto Press

Cohen, Marjorie Griffin (1987), *Free Trade and the Future of Women's Work: Manufacturing and Service Industries*, Toronto, Garamond Press

Cohen, Robin (1991), *Contested Domains: Debates in International Labour Studies*, London, Zed Press

Coyle, Angela (1982), 'Sex and Skill in the Organization of the Clothing Industry' in Jackie West (ed.), *Work, Women and the Labour Market*, London, Routledge and Kegan Paul

Dagg, Alexandra and Judy Fudge (1992), 'Sewing Pains: Homeworkers in the Garment Trade', *Our Times*, Vol. 11, No. 3, June: pp. 22–25. Reprinted in Graham S. Lowe and Harvey J. Krahn (eds) (1993), *Work in Canada: Readings in the Sociology of Work and Industry*, Nelson, Canada, Scarborough: pp. 190–194.

Edwards, Richard (1979), *Contested Terrain: The Transformation of the Workplace in the Twentieth Century*, New York, Basic Books

Elson, Dianne (ed.) (1991), *Male Bias in the Development Process*, Manchester, Manchester University Press

Frideres, James S. (1992), 'Changing Dimensions of Ethnicity in Canada' in Vic Satzewich (ed.), *Deconstructing a Nation: Immigration, Multiculturalism and Racism in '90s Canada*, Social Research Unit, Department of Sociology, University of Saskatchewan at Saskatoon: pp. 47–67

Gannagé, Charlene (1986), *Double Day, Double Bind: Women Garment Workers*, Toronto, Women's Press

Gannagé, Charlene (1987), 'The Impact of Technological Change on Toronto Ladies' Clothing Workers: Selected Case Studies of Material Handling Systems', Final report submitted to Labour Canada on behalf of the International Ladies' Garment Workers' Union

Gannagé, Charlene (1989-90), 'Changing Dimensions of Control and Resistance: The Toronto Garment Industry', *Journal of Canadian Studies*, Vol. 24, No. 4: pp. 41–60

George, Susan (1992), *The Debt Boomerang: How Third World Debt Harms Us All*, Boulder, Westview Press

Ghorayshi, Parvin (1990), 'Manitoba's Clothing Industry in the 1980s: Change and Continuity', in Jim Silver and Jeremy Hull (eds), *The Political Economy of Manitoba*, Regina, University of Regina Canadian Plains Research Centre

Gindin, Sam (1991), 'Time Out: Reducing Working Time to Our Benefit', in *Our Times*, Vol. 10, No. 2, March: pp. 34–35

Industry, Science and Technology Canada (1991), *Fashioning the Future: Building a Strategy for Competitiveness. Report on Phase II of the Fashion Apparel Sector Campaign*, July

Industry, Science and Technology Canada, (n.d.), *Fashioning the Future: Fashion Apparel Sector Campaign, Framework for Phase III*, Ottawa

Industry, Science and Technology Canada, *1990–91 Industry Profile: Apparel*, Ottawa

Industry, Science and Technology Canada, *1988 Industry Profile: Clothing*, Ottawa

International Ladies' Garment Workers' Union *et al.* (1991), *Fair Wages and Working Conditions for Homeworkers: A Summary*, November

International Ladies' Garment Workers' Union, Ontario District Council (1987), brief to Ministry of Industry, Trade and Technology, Industry and Trade Policy Branch, Province of Ontario, 21 October

Lamphere, Louise (1979), 'Fighting the Piece Work System: New Dimensions of an Old Struggle in the Apparel Industry', in Andrew S. Zimbalist (ed.), *Case Studies in the Labor Process*, New York, Monthly Review Press

Leach, Belinda (1993), '"Flexible" Work, Precarious Future: Some Lessons from the Canadian Clothing Industry', *The Canadian Review of Sociology and Anthropology*, 30, 1 February: pp. 64–82

Li, Peter S (1988), *Ethnic Inequality in a Class Society*, Toronto, Thompson Educational Press

Mahon, Rianne (1984), *The Politics of Industrial Restructuring: Canadian Textiles*, Toronto, University of Toronto Press

McQuaig, Linda (1993), *The Wealthy Banker's Wife: The Assault on Equality in Canada*, Toronto, Penguin Books

Minister of State, Multiculturalism and Citizenship Canada (1990), 'Creating a Learning Culture: Work and Literacy in the Nineties' based on the report 'Workforce Literacy: An Economic Challenge for Canada' by the Hudson Institute, Ottawa, National Literacy Secretariat, Ministry of Supply and Services

Mitter, Swasti (1986), *Common Fate, Common Bond: Women in the Global Economy*, London, Pluto Press

Moody, Kim and Mary McGinn (1992), *Unions and Free Trade: Solidarity vs. Competition*, Detroit, Labor Notes

Munck, Ronaldo (1988), *The New International Labour Studies*, London, Zed Books

Nash, June and Maria Patricia Fernandez-Kelly (eds) (1983), *Women, Men and the International Division of Labor*, Albany, State University of New York Press

Seward, Shirley B. (1990), 'Immigrant Women in the Clothing Industry', in S. Halli, F. Trovato and L. Drieger (eds), *Ethnic Demography*, Ottawa, Carleton University Press: pp. 343-362

Sharpe, Andrew (1993), 'Training the Workforce: A Challenge Facing Canada in the Nineties', in Graham Lowe and Harvey Krahn (eds), *Work in Canada: Readings in the Sociology of Work and Industry*, Nelson Canada, Scarborough: pp. 108–114.

Simmons, A. (1990), 'New Wave Immigrants: Origins and Characteristics', in S. Halli, F. Trovato and L. Driedger (eds), *Ethnic Demography*, Ottawa, Carleton University Press: pp. 141–159

Sobel, David and Susan Meurer (1991), 'Sowing the Future: Training in Toronto's Garment Industry: A Report to the Fashion Industry Liaison Committee', Toronto, May

Statistics Canada (1989), *Clothing Industries*, Statistics Canada Catalogue Nos. 34–252, Ottawa

Steedman, Mercedes (1986), 'Skill and Gender in the Canadian Clothing Industry, 1890–1940', in Craig Heron and Robert Storey (eds), *On the Job: Confronting the Labour Process in Canada*, Kingston, McGill-Queen's University Press: pp. 152–176

Textile and Clothing Board (1987), *Report on Textiles and Clothing*, Ottawa, Ministry of Supply and Services

8 Computerization and women's employment in India's banking sector

Sujata Gothoskar

INTRODUCTION

The pattern of Indian women's employment has changed markedly since the 1970s. The sectors in which women have worked throughout the century, plantations, mining and manufacturing, have not been the areas of growth. Indeed in the better-paid and unionized jobs the proportion of women in the workforce has declined drastically. Women have been increasingly pushed into unregulated non-unionized jobs, with the exception of electronics and the service sector.

Banking and insurance have provided new areas of opportunity for women, and nationalization has been a key factor in countering some aspects of gender discrimination. As Table 8.1 shows, in areas such as electricity, construction, trade, transport and communication, finance and insurance, and community services, employment in the public sector is an important factor in boosting women's employment. However recent national and international policies, which have led to the dismantling of the public sector, are affecting those limited openings. It is therefore urgent not simply to develop the means for retraining women but also for women to participate in creating alternative economic strategies.

Changes in the quantity and quality of women's employment in banking can be accounted for by a number of factors operating simultaneously. There are deeper social changes taking place in the country *vis-à-vis* women's education and employment; changes in government policies regarding this and other sectors; changes in management policies, especially after the nationalization of banks in 1969; the effects of internationalization; and the technological changes taking place in this industry. This study will focus primarily on the effects of technological change, and will include material on how women employees perceive these changes and what they feel themselves about retraining and improving their working

Table 8.1 Changes in women's employment in some major sectors 1975–1988 (thousands)

	1975			1988			% change (total)
	Public	Private	Total	Public	Private	Total	
Agriculture	14.8	391.0	405.8	48.3	465.4	513.7	+26.6
Mining	57.7	24.9	82.6	60.4	17.6	78.0	–5.6
Manufacturing	53.9	399.4	453.3	105.8	448.5	554.3	+22.3
Electricity	10.2	0.3	10.5	25.6	0.6	26.2	+150.5
Construction	43.2	23.4	66.6	71.7	5.1	76.8	+15.3
Trade	2.5	16.6	19.1	9.0	17.9	26.9	+40.8
Transport and communications	50.5	1.8	52.3	125.9	2.8	128.7	+146.1
Finance and Insurance	35.2	8.2	43.4	124.2	22.4	146.6	+237.8
Community Services	861.1	236.6	1,097.7	1,553.5	389.5	1,943.0	+77.0

Source: Indian Labour Year Book

conditions. Moreover, it is important to consider how unions, cooperatives and workgroups can strengthen women's positions and overcome the stereotyping which persists even in new fields.

Two key questions have to be asked about the impact of new technology: how can the gains women have made in the financial sector be safeguarded, and how can improvements be made in the qualitative aspects of employment?

RESEARCH METHODS

I approached the unions in eleven Indian and foreign-controlled banks, and in the nationalized Life Insurance Corporation, between April and October of 1992. I talked to between 5 and 9 employees and union activists in each of the banks and the LIC. I also talked to at least 2, and in some cases 4, of the management personnel in each institution. Some found it a little difficult to identify with the focus of the study, while others saw its value and suggested that I meet the women employees too. I met several women, both employees and union committee members, who immediately identified with the concerns expressed. We had lively discussions at the workplace, in union offices, in their homes and at the Workers' Solidarity Centre Office. Much of this chapter draws heavily on the experiences, insights and analyses of the women employees, and some of the male employees and unionists. I also met the management personnel – some from the Personnel Department, others from the electronic data processing (EDP) department. The management's response varied from attempting to evade questions ('it is our policy not to give information'), to not coming for appointments or giving cautious public relations type answers, or even open hostility. However I also went to the Banks' Training College and to the National Institute of Bank Management, where material on training and retraining were made available to me and lively discussions followed.

Generally speaking, very little statistical information or quantitative data about employment in the finance industry was available from most of these sources. Despite efforts to gain a balanced picture of the situation, I have had to rely mainly on knowledgable, experienced and active employees and their biting, insightful comments, descriptions and accounts, which were supplemented by a structured questionnaire which they filled out. We had a series of meetings to discuss these questionnaires.

THE BANKING INDUSTRY, HISTORY AND TECHNOLOGICAL CHANGES

Historical overview

The antiquated Indian banking system has its roots in the nineteenth century. The character and structure of the system has, however, changed substantially since 1969, when the major banks were nationalized. Prior to nationalization, banking was concentrated in urban areas. It was clear that a better banking system was needed to promote the economic goals of the new Indian state. Rural markets for industrial goods could not be developed so long as money lenders, charging usurious rates of interest, were the main source of rural credit. Moreover, the 'green revolution' depended on farmers finding substantial sources of credit to pay for fertilizers and hybrid seeds.

Since the mid-1970s, there has been a spectacular growth in the spatial distribution of bank branches and in the size of their deposits and advances. According to experts in banking this transformation has no parallel anywhere in the world (Anantharam Iyer, 1991). After nationalization, there was also a change in recruitment policy. For the first time, the doors of the banks were opened to everyone, irrespective of family status, caste, community, religion or gender. Recruitment was placed on a more systematic basis, with merit assessed by aptitude tests conducted by an external agency in a relatively impartial manner (Deekshit, 1991).

As the size of the banking sector increased, the industry became difficult to manage. Computer technology offered a possible solution. In India, a small number of industrial houses and a few educational, research and development institutions started using computers in the early 1960s. During the late 1960s and 1970s, service-oriented industries such as airlines, railways and insurance companies introduced computers to 'improve their functioning' and 'to provide better customer service' (Anantharam Iyer, 1991). Banks in India did not, however, introduce computers on a large scale because of the fear that these would result in retrenchment and unemployment (Goodman, 1991). For a long time Indian banks faced very little competition and operated in a protected economy. Thus no long-term policy or perspective for the banking sector was formulated: it was simply treated as part of the public sector. This is now changing. Well-computerized foreign banks are beginning to compete seriously with the nationalized banks. They aim at a profitable and wealthy part of the market and, in contrast to the nationalized banks, do not recognize any social responsibilities to small account holders or to a rural and semi-urban clientele.

Technological changes, legislation and bargaining

In India, the main agents affecting the introduction of new technology have been the unions, management and the workforce. The government has played a very indirect role in the process. In the early days of the massive introduction of computer technology into industry and services, union policies on new technology were basically defensive. They focused almost entirely on the immediate consequences of technological change on the workforce, especially the aspect of possible job losses.

However, these attitudes and the strategies of unions *vis-à-vis* computerization have begun to change, especially since the 1980s. Management in many places has been able to convince workers and unions that competition is becoming increasingly harsh, and computerization is not only inevitable for the health and survival of the unit but also beneficial to employees, because it may improve the competitiveness of the enterprise, enhance job security and improve employment conditions. Many unions which have consistently opposed computerization have had to face their members who are keen on technological changes. As one EDP employee who is also a unionist put it, 'As a unionist I would oppose computerization, as an employee I would welcome it. That is my dilemma.'

Consequently, unions today are increasingly seeking to influence the process of technological changes so that new technology can be introduced in such a way as to benefit workers and minimise its adverse consequences. The last decade has seen several 'technology agreements' or 'computerization agreements', along with routine collective bargaining agreements which contain clauses related to technology. Despite these agreements, most managers in India, including those in the public sector, have consistently regarded all aspects of technological changes as matters falling within the area of managerial prerogative. When consultation with unions has occurred, these have been far from fair since unions have lacked the requisite know-how and information.

The Reserve Bank of India (RBI) installed its first computer in 1968, and a larger one in 1979. But the United Commercial (UCO) Bank, the Standard Chartered Bank, Lloyds' Bank, Grindlays, and others had installed accounting and other machines before 1966. Operations such as payrolls had been computerized fairly early on. Some head offices began to use computers by the beginning of the 1980s.[1] In September 1983, two of the major banking unions – the All India Bank Employees Association (AIBEA) and the National Confederation of Banking Employees (NCBE) – signed an agreement with the Indian Banks Association (IBA), representing 58 bank managements. The unions wished to maintain surveillance of the process and to protect job prospects in the banking sector, but the final settlement was self-contradictory. On the one hand there were restrictions on computerization, with numerical limits on the numbers of mainframe computers, and even on the number of accounting machines which might be used in rural branches, but there was also a loop-hole which allowed the banks to use 'such number of mini-computers as are warranted by their needs and exigencies'.

The 1983 agreement provided an opening for individual banks to make their own computerization agreements, and many foreign banks immediately took advantage of this 'openness' to negotiate agreements giving them a free hand to introduce new technology, despite the careful restrictive approach of the AIBEA and NCBE.

In March 1987 the AIBEA and NCBE signed a new settlement with the IBA. The settlement was similar in its approach and concerns to the 1983 agreement. Although it allowed for an extension of new technology in both the operations computerized and the equipment used, the concern was largely still with ways of restricting and controlling the use of computers to protect existing staff and preserve the prospects for future staff. The agreements also provided some additional allowances and protection for pregnant women. Taking advantage of the 'openness' clause in the 1983 and 1987 agreements, some of the AIBEA's own affiliates agreed to the installation of automatic teller machines and fax machines, which were beyond the purview of the industry level accord.[2] There are signs that the AIBEA has been forced to reverse its earlier relatively liberal stance on computerization because of the campaign spearheaded in recent years by its arch rival, the Bank Employees' Federation of India (BEFI), which has been seeking recognition from the IBA.

However it would be misleading to look at the unions alone in explaining the slow rate of technological innovation. A highly-placed bank executive commented that the management of the banks lack perspective, because of the protection they had enjoyed, and were not really serious about computerization (Goodman, 1991). There is also uncertainty among bank managers about the implications of computerization in terms of the hierarchy and their own positions. Employees of many Indian banks, including the State Bank of India and Bank of Baroda, said that management 'just dumped these machines here. They are hardly used, and some don't work.' A comprehensive policy seems completely absent. In contrast, the multinational banks have computerized almost totally, with the unions unable to have any say.

IMPACT OF COMPUTERIZATION ON THE WORKFORCE

Some of the general issues that have concerned unions and employees, especially women, in the wake of the introduction of new technology in the banking and finance sectors have been:

- Prospects of job losses and declining employment levels.
- Increase in workloads.
- Pressure for flexibility.
- Changes in job contents.
- Increase in insecurity in the workplace, and loss of union power.
- Increase in the proportion of 'non-bargainable' staff (i.e. those without an automatic right to unionize) as compared to the 'bargainable' staff.
- Changes in grading and pay.
- Changes in information and control.
- Changes in the autonomy of employees.
- Changes in health and safety conditions.

Job losses

There have not been visible losses of employment in either the banking or insurance industries, due to the massive expansion and diversification in the two industries and to the high proportion of nationalized enterprises, in which workers are generally protected against job losses. Some of the foreign banks have undergone massive expansion in terms of the number of their branches and their areas of operation. In fact, in January 1992, 12 foreign banks sought permission to open 44 more branches in various major cities of India (*Economic Times*, 1992). There has however been a reduction in the rate of recruitment in the nationalized banks. According to a recent study covering three banks and two insurance companies, the growth of new jobs has dwindled. As the use of new technology expands, labour savings are likely to increase further in some operations (Chopra, 1991). The three developments that are likely to displace workers, and women in particular, are voice recognition, optical character recognition and artificial intelligence (Rajan, 1990). An employee at the Hong Kong bank observed that the entire category of typists had already been abolished.

It is possible to discern a tendency to reduce the proportion of 'bargainable' staff in both nationalized and foreign banks. The Banque Nationale de Paris reduced its bargainable staff from 200 employees in 1979 to just 135 in 1992, by not recruiting staff at the lowest levels and by asking about 35 employees to accept the so-called Voluntary Retirement Scheme (VRS) because computerization was expected to reduce the need for their labour.

Increase in workloads

New technology could lessen the repetitive and heavy nature of certain operations. However, most employees in the insurance and banking industry, especially in the foreign banks, have experienced serious strain and heavy work-loads. According to an employee working in the cash department of the Citibank,

> Before computerization we used to do 30-40 cash entries per day; now we have to do more than 100. There is a greater pressure of work – more work and more responsibility. The speed has increased enormously.[3]

According to experienced unionists in ANZ Grindlays Bank, computerization, coupled with non-recruitment and non-replacement of retired staff, has led to a tremendous increase in workloads, 'after 20 years of employment, people are bound to be completely fagged out. Then the management will term them "unsuitable", "old" or "unfit"'. The personnel officer of Grindlays, who disagrees with the union on everything else, admitted, 'Since the emphasis is entirely on productivity and efficiency, there has been intensification of work. Employees' efficiency levels have gone up ten-fold'. Personnel officers at the Life Insurance Corporation (LIC) confirmed this picture.

Pressure for flexibility

Over the last decade and a half, management has consistently sought to have flexible manning levels. They have argued that they need operational flexibility in order to respond quickly to changes in the market, to introduce technological innovations, and to deal with fluctuations in the flow of work. This, they say, can be achieved by employing a core of secure, permanent, multiskilled, full-time employees and a 'periphery' of marginal, generally single-skilled workers who may be employed part-time or temporarily, and directly or indirectly, in a variety of 'new' ways (Huws *et al.*, 1989)

Computer technology demands functionally flexible multiskilled workers rather than specialists. The strategy of increasing flexibility in the employment system frequently targets women workers, who occupy the lower rungs of the job hierarchy. They are often forced to change work stations or leave the firm. Professionals and specialists, a majority of whom are men, benefit from the strategy.

Changes in job content

Changes in work methods caused by the introduction of computerization affect the content of work as well as the skills needed by employees. The direction of changes is, however, not uniform. Two divergent tendencies can be observed. In routine transactions, certain skills of a mechanical nature, which nevertheless require a measure of mental effort and concentration, are no longer required or are needed less. The skills replacing them are equally mechanical but call for less mental effort. The level of skills required for the performance of routine transactions therefore actually falls, although the degree of attention and concentration required will be just as high or even higher. In contrast, in the area of customer services, computerization offers potential for an increase in both the necessary range and level of skills, for example, searching for, extracting and assimilating relevant information in response to a request. The realization of the potential is, however, contingent on the relevant organizational decisions being taken by management (Ozaki *et al.*, 1992)

The impact of new technology on work content and the skills required of workers also depends on how rigidly jobs are defined and demarcated and on the skill levels of the existing workforce. Various studies seem to show that, in places where the tasks of workers have already been defined broadly and flexibly, with much overlapping, the reorganization of work after the introduction of new technology has been comparatively smooth and workers' resistance relatively minor. In places where the skill level of workers is high, technological change tends to strengthen the tendency towards the integration of planning and production tasks. Where skill levels are low, there seems to be a trend towards polarization of skills. Computerization is also creating skills that are largely transferable from one enterprise to another, such as the skills of computer programmers (Ozaki *et al.*, 1992).

Product innovations have generally led to an increase in the importance of formal skills. The informal skills, learned on the job, that characterized women's work are not seen as important. The professional and technical jobs increase in number and importance, and formal theoretical knowledge is becoming more important for employees in the banking sector (Tremblay, 1991). In India as elsewhere, categories such as junior clerks and tellers are becoming less important in the overall workforce as Automated Teller Machines (ATMs) multiply (Rajan, 1990).

An employee working at the bill discounting department in Citibank, Bombay, says:

Earlier, when a bill was brought to us, we made manual entries. The customer would present the bill. We had to scrutinise it, and then send it to the liability department for their approval. In the liability department, each client had one big card which showed her status. After approval, it was sent back to us for processing. That is:

1 calculate the interest using a calculating machine;
2 make debit/credit tickets;
3 balance the amount; and
4 send the tickets to the journal keeper, who would balance all the amounts.

Each department had a journal keeper. Now, we still have to scrutinise a bill. Then we key it into the programme – the bill programme. The computer shows the credit limit automatically. The ticket is then given to the officer, who takes it to the Credit Approval Committee. There are no manual interest calculations, no manual tickets, no journal-keeper.[4]

There are positive aspects of computerization as well. Although employees used to do the posting of debit and credit, they

did not necessarily know much about whether and why a particular debit or credit was passed. There is greater knowledge about these things now. There is also greater access to other types of work. Earlier I did not endorse documents. I do so now.

According to the personnel manager of the LIC, work had not been enriched or tasks enlarged, because jobs were set and functions well-defined. 'Computerization has made the jobs easier rather than interesting.' The personnel officer at the ANZ Grindlays Bank, in contrast, was adamant that employees' skills had increased ten-fold, but he was actually referring to their productivity or efficiency. He agreed however that many jobs have been 'realigned'. For example, in bill discounting, work that was previously done by a team is now done individually by workers with their own machines. An employee at Grindlays comments, 'Earlier, there was greater interaction between employees. Team work was good work. We learnt more about the work. Now there is no time to look around, help or seek help from colleagues. You just sit there and bang at the keyboard'. The management of Grindlays argues that employees used to spend most of their time with books (e.g. tabulations) and now spend more time with customers. The unionists at Grindlays dismissed this claim, 'There have been no changes. Work has become more monotonous. The brain is getting more dull.'

Many employees expressed mixed feelings about computerization. While it relieved some work pressures and strains of particular types, it has made work dull. It increased efficiency, but decreased the feeling of team work and sharing. Work might be less arduous, but it also becomes less varied. Computerization is supposed to increase customer interaction, but many employees experienced a reduction, and all complained of an increased work tempo.

Increased insecurity and loss of union power

Deskilling contributes to a feeling of powerlessness *vis-à-vis* the employer. This feeling was expressed more definitely by employees working in foreign banks than by those employed either in the nationalized banks or the nationalized LIC. Four women employees in the Banque Nationale de Paris said that the closure of some branches and their awareness that they had not been given computer training at a time when nearly all the banking operations had been computerized had made them 'very scared.' All four were later made redundant.

At ANZ Grindlays, insecurity was said to have increased, with early retirements and no recruitment for the last four to five years, 'That itself creates insecurity. If there is a reduction, then it creates panic.'

Citibank employees reported feeling, on the one hand, that their workload was generally too heavy, and, on the other hand, that any temporary reductions made them fear that work had been contracted out. They said that contract workers had been employed for specific tasks, without informing the employees or the union. This has become possible because of computerization.

The feeling of insecurity has also increased because unions have been considerably weakened. The women who were forced to take the VRS (Voluntary Retirement Scheme) by the Banque Nationale de Paris say:

> There is virtually no union in the BNP. The union officials were bending backwards to sell the VRS to us. We didn't want to resign. We wanted to fight it out. But how can you do that without the firm backing of the union?

Even when a union is strong, women may not be protected against discrimination.

Increase in the proportion of 'non-bargainable' staff

Control over the workforce provides the basis for controlling production processes, output levels, and scheduling. Over the years, this control has been loosened as unions have come to play a role in areas such as work intensity, output levels, health and safety, which were and still are considered to be 'management prerogatives'. One of the strategies available to wrest control back is to weaken unions, both numerically and in terms of the functions which the unionized workforce performs. This is one reason behind the dramatic and continuous increase in the non-bargainable category of workers, as compared to unionised workers. This casualization process has occurred in the banking and insurance industry as well as in manufacturing.

The number of workers in the bargainable categories is being reduced,[5] for instance by using contract couriers in place of employing messengers. In 1973, 18.7 per cent of all workers in the banking industry were officers. By 1987 this had grown to 26.7 per cent. Over the same period, the percentage of clerical workers fell slightly, from 55.9 per cent to 52.4 per cent, and the percentage of workers in more subordinate positions fell quite significantly from 25.4 per cent to 20.9 per cent (Borkar, 1991).

In almost every industry in India, computer programmers are in the non-bargainable category. Computer programmers are usually in a position to anticipate changes and may use their knowledge to keep other workers and unions informed. Most new recruitment is done in the 'officer' category, though often these new employees do the same work as the bargainable employees. In industries where the union has refused to co-operate with computerization, the management recruits 'officers' to do the work of data entry operators etc. The unionists are increasingly feeling that they have to bargain with the management about the content of work in the bargainable and non-bargainable categories, and be vigilant about any infringement.

Changes in grading and pay

There seems to have been no attempt to redefine a new grade structure in the banking and insurance industry after computerization was introduced. In the Banque Nationale de Paris a 'promotion agreement' was signed in 1987, under which all the clerical staff were promoted within three years to the status of Special Assistants, a supervisory category with an extra wage allowance. Everybody, including the lower grade staff, received the allowance, and there was a substantial increase in basic pay too. But there was no attempt at evolving a new grade structure, nor any training to equip employees to deal with the new type of work. All employees, including the women, have gained financially but there has not been any change in their job definition or real status.

All the banks have some allowance for EDP staff or computer operators.

In the LIC the allowance was Rs 100. In the Hong Kong Bank only the most senior employees in the department got the allowance, although almost all the employees have to work on the terminals. The Union Bank of India employees who work on the computers get an allowance of Rs 350 per month. The Hong Kong Bank employees get an allowance of Rs 400. In the words of one computer operator in the Bank of Baroda, 'EDP staff are definitely graded highly in the Bank'.

Changes in information and control

Traditional craft workers often knew far more about their jobs than managers or supervisors, which gave them a lot of freedom as to how the work was done. But computers have enormously increased management's ability to collect and analyse information – about product performance, market trends, customers, sales, finance, and of course about employees. The tendency has been for management to learn more about how work is done, and to specify more tightly how jobs should be done – both in terms of method and speed.

> Every minute of your time is being recorded. How many words did you key in? How much time was required for posting debits and credits, for bill discounting? However, we cannot access information that is not in our jurisdiction. If one tries it, it is invalid; but the fact that you tried will be recorded in the computer. If one looks at it dispassionately, one would have an eerie feeling.

Employees felt that they were being watched and intimidated, increasing the sense of insecurity. Unions have not claimed a right to have access to information relevant for negotiating. Employees in ANZ Grindlays bank found such a demand difficult to even imagine. 'Management has total control over all information. Profits, costs etc. are under secret code. They have all the information about us though.'

Changes in health and safety conditions

The introduction of new technology has also created a range of new hazards for the workers. The development of new materials, processes and substances, without adequate information being made available about their impact, may be creating problems which will not be perceived for many years. Increases in the scale and pace of production have contributed towards stress, especially where there is also inadequate support or training or an unfair distribution of workloads.

Some specific health and safety problems have been shown to arise from the introduction of computer-based equipment. Visual Display Units (VDUs) have been known to cause a number of health problems, especially if operated continuously for a long time. 'Video blues', eye problems, musculoskeletal problems, painful conditions such as tenosynovitis, varicose veins, ulcers, nausea, headaches, and skin diseases as well as reproductive problems such as miscarriages, stillbirths, birth defects, infertility, menstrual problems and low sperm counts have been very extensively documented (Labour Research Department, 1985). However, none of the bank employees had been given any health training. Most employees complained of eye strain, headaches, or a heavy feeling in the head, but they worked at the terminal from 9.30 a.m. to 4.30 p.m. with only breaks for lunch and tea in between. Three women in Citibank had had mis- carriages, though none of them had any personal or familial history of miscarriages. Of the forty women interviewed only one had heard that working on the computers continuously could cause health problems. None of the training sessions had mentioned this problem. Though information on the health and safety aspects of working with computers is widely available, employees were ignorant of health hazards. This indicates their lack of access to information relevant to women, the unwillingness of management to share it, and the indifference of the union to issues of health and safety. This is a serious issue, especially because the number of women working on computers is increasing rapidly.

WOMEN'S EMPLOYMENT IN BANKING

As Table 8.1 showed, there has been a marked increase in women's employment in the financial sector since the 1950s, in both public sector companies and private foreign-controlled banks. The increase has been most marked in metropolitan cities. By the mid-1960s the number of women entering the banks increased significantly, intensifying in the 1970s and early 1980s.

Despite this increase, women are still concentrated at the clerical level, and the general picture is changing only very slowly. Women officers in banks are a recent phenomenon, which has become a little more significant since 1975 because of direct recruitment and promotions (Kanhere, 1991). Even in EDP activities, the share of women is low. A recent study of Indian banking notes that in one bank women constituted only 5 per cent of the EDP staff, about 12 per cent in another bank and 7 per cent in an insurance company. Women were not recruited as programmers (Chopra, 1991).

As Table 8.2 shows, there are considerable differences between indiividual banks, which women employees attributed to the historical development of personnel recruitment policies in the particular banks.

Table 8.2 Women employees in Indian nationalized banks, 1985 and 1990 (%)

Bank	Officers		Clerks	
	1985	*1990*	*1985*	*1990*
Allahabad Bank	3.5	3.66	9.7	11.03
Andhra Bank	9.1	9.54	19.2	21.88
Bank of Baroda	5.1	7.93	17.8	18.12
Bank of India	5.2	5.06	20.7	20.60
Bank of Maharashtra	6.3	6.75	29.9	31.62
Canara Bank	3.7	4.12	25.5	27.57
Central Bank of India	3.9	4.63	17.7	20.10
Corporation Bank	6.2	6.78	32.2	33.47
Dena Bank	1.8	2.02	17.9	18.9
Indian Bank	5.6	5.95	24.1	21.34
Indian Overseas Bank	5.9	5.56	17.9	18.43
New Bank of India	4.5	4.61	17.8	17.59
Oriental Bank of India	8.1	7.96	17.4	15.98
Punjab and Sind Bank	2.8	2.69	8.1	9.58
Punjab National Bank	4.1	4.45	16.0	16.54
Syndicate Bank	8.2	8.15	26.6	27.49
ICO Bank	4.1	3.00	11.6	11.90
Union Bank of India	5.9	6.27	18.8	22.15
United Bank of India	0.6	0.85	5.9	8.20
Vijaya Bank	11.8	12.23	20.3	21.22
State Bank of India	1.7	2.33	12.8	15.44
State Bank of Bikaner and Jaipur	1.6	1.89	7.8	7.66
State Bank of Hyderabad	3.1	3.88	13.7	16.78
State Bank of Indore	1.1	1.29	10.7	11.77
State Bank of Mysore	3.9	3.68	22.7	25.96
State Bank of Patiala	2.1	2.88	16.7	17.79
State Bank of Saurashtra	0.8	1.16	8.6	9.91
State Bank of Travancore	7.5	9.00	35.4	35.99
Total	3.9	4.9	17.3	18.77

Source: Documentation at the National Institute of Bank Management, Pune

Computerization and women in foreign banks

The effect of computerization on women bank employees, both clerical and officer grades, is of considerable significance as the process of computerization is soon to be intensified. A glimpse of the possible impact may be discerned from an analysis of foreign banks, in India. According to a unionist in Citibank,

> In 1970, out of a total workforce of 200, there were only ten women. Now, in 1992, 70 per cent of the workforce are women. This includes programmers as well as women officers. Management feels women are better on computers as they have routine clerical ambitions. Women really do more work and their *frustration* level is higher.

(Presumably, he means their endurance is higher.) A union official in Banque Nationale de Paris confirms this:

> Our managements' latest policy seems to be to recruit young girls and train them on computers. In our latest recruitment in January and April 1992, ten new employees were recruited. All ten were girls. Now we have women on all the customer counters. They are eager to learn, more sincere, obedient, less union-minded and also provide better customer service.

A militant unionist at the Grindlays bank said that, in Bombay, the proportion of women employees had increased from 5 per cent in 1970 to about 50 per cent in 1992. Figures from Grindlays management showed that about 35 per cent of their workforce, nation-wide, were women. This is a higher proportion than in most of their nationalized counterparts (see Table 8.2). According to a union official at Grindlays:

> Earlier, the policy of multinational banks was *not* to recruit women employees. But over the last few years, they have changed. Management realised that women are more submissive, overworked, and have less time for union work. Besides, because of general socio-economic development, women do much better, especially in cities like Bombay.

The points which bank managements generally present in women's favour include:

- women employees are sincere and diligent and meticulously complete their work;
- they are time-conscious;
- they do not shirk responsibilities;
- they perform all types of jobs well;

- they are less involved in union activities;
- they are less often involved in frauds and corruption.

(Mankidy, 1986a)

An active woman unionist in the Hong Kong Bank confirmed the high recruitment rate of women, but explained it as due to the fact that women are better qualified and tend to put in greater effort. The better-qualified women apply for bank jobs, while similarly qualified men would tend to go in for jobs, such as engineering and computers, which employees regard as more challenging and which have better prospects in terms of job satisfaction and pay. Another reason which was suggested is that women resign sooner than men. Of the twenty-seven girls recruited in the 1991 batch, three had left within the first year. The pay levels of new recruits are considerably less than for a senior person, so it is less expensive for the management to have a fresh supply of new recruits. The Hong Kong bank has about 500 employees in the head office, of whom more than 350 are women, including more than half of the officers.

However it is not clear whether this source of employment will persist. The RBI's National Clearing Cell in Madras has already extended its 'instant credit' facilities to Saturdays.[6] Because of the increasing involvement with foreign share markets and banks and the time difference between countries, it may not be too long before the hours of these and other facilities are extended to Sundays and night shifts. This would have a significant impact on the recruitment, employment and promotion of women. In Canada, where computerization has reached fairly advanced levels, banking jobs are coming to be more frequently occupied by men (Tremblay, 1991). Amin Rajan, in his study of the finance sector at an international level (1990) observes that, 'In the short term technology has created job opportunities for women. In the longer term, however, this process is likely to disadvantage women.'

THE QUALITY OF WOMEN'S WORK

The banking and insurance sectors today offer more prospects for jobs for women – both qualitatively and quantitatively. However there are some common problems faced by women managers, officers and clerical groups in banking and insurance, in the course of their careers. These include the burden of the dual role, sexual harassment in the workplace, the refusal of men to accept women as colleagues or seniors, the need to work twice as well as men to gain recognition, and the lack of solidarity among women.

According to a study by Kamala Srinivasan (1991) 50 per cent of women complained that extra work is always shunted to women. They also complained about sexual harassment from colleagues, managers, or customers. Women also felt dissatisfied that they were not sent out for training. Some obstacles arise from women's specific difficulties in demanding promotion – because promotions are linked with transfers; or they have difficulties in working late; or because women shy away from responsibility, having a low opinion of their own abilities and a negative attitude to accepting recognition (Mankidy, 1986a). Some women employees feel that these constraints are intensified by being forced to adopt the behaviour of the 'successful manager or officer' which has been established by men. They argue that women could find their own strategies which would achieve the same result (Mankidy, 1988).

One way of improving prospects for women could be to restructure the work, for example with flexible working hours, part-time job assignments, split location positions performed partly at home, and job-sharing (Mankidy, 1988). Some of these suggestions have already been tried out elsewhere, for example in Japan, where the results for women have not been entirely positive. None the less, examination of this experience could be a basis for working out alternatives which do not disadvantage women (International Labour Office, 1989).

WOMEN'S NEEDS AND ASPIRATIONS WITH REGARD TO EMPLOYMENT AND TRAINING

Technological change usually involves changes in job content, making many traditional skills obsolete and creating a demand for new types of skills. Training and retraining ensure not only that the enterprise obtains the optimal benefits from new technologies, it is also an effective way of protecting the employment of workers affected by technological change and other structural changes.

Workers, and the trade union movement, are divided about training. Some unions, such as the BNP (Banque Nationale de Paris) union, seem to have relinquished not only any initiative, but also responsibility for both the employees who are being forced to quit and those who are allowed to stay. Despite the 1986 agreement giving the union a right to participate in determining and formulating the training, there has been no move from the office-bearers of the union, all men, to take the initiative. One union officer said that they 'had not realised the importance of this clause at the time. And now it is too late.' Women employees at the BNP were almost desperate to be given retraining. They were too young – about 39 to 42 years of age – to retire. They saw no other way to retain their employment. They were also keen to learn new skills.

The union in Citibank, on the other hand, participated actively in the computerization process as well as the training process. But even in Citibank there seems to be no long-term view as to the type of jobs and skills which will be required in the future. The younger recruits have been given a one-week training course in computer languages, which they did not use in the year following the course. They were then given a very brief, functional on-the-job type course. As one senior woman employee now working in the Bill Discounting department says: 'We were given a half-day "familiarity with the word-processor" course, and printed sheets telling us what to press for which function.'[7] The Citibank women employees felt they knew too little, apart from their own little work area, and they wanted to know more so that they would not be adversely affected when it came to promotions. The attitude of women at the Hong Kong bank was similar. The ANZ Grindlays Bank Employees' Union had a very different perspective, 'We have completely opposed computerisation. There are no skills involved in operating computers. It only deadens your mind. We cannot participate in such a process. We believe in struggle.' In the Indian banks, the younger women and those between 30 and 45 years old seemed keen on their jobs as careers, whereas many in the 30–45 age group had many more responsibilities at home – although some of the latter felt that learning about computers at work would also help them to assist their children in their studies, since computers have been introduced in many schools. Many women felt that learning to use computers, and being in the EDP department, would protect them against transfers to remote areas, as EDP departments are located only in the metropolitan cities.

Most of the older women, especially those above 50, felt they would not be able to cope with any new retraining. They would undertake it if it was necessary for the job. However, a small minority of women above 50 years of age also seemed keen to take up a new challenge. As one woman put it,

> As women, we are used to challenges, at home, at work, in combining the two roles, and in relationships with in-laws, neighbours, community, children, colleagues, and bosses. As we grow older, these challenges become routine matters. When you no longer have in-laws, when children are well settled elsewhere, when neighbourhood relationships are settled and repetitive, what do we do? We are used to challenges. New skills are merely one such challenge. Why not take it up?[8]

Another woman disagreed, but from a very different point of view.

I'm not sure that computer skills are any skill at all. What are we doing? The generalised use of computers is only a means of deskilling and flattening us all. Very soon using computers will be like using our pencils. Then all of us will be declared unskilled and redundant again. We need to do something else.[9]

In the Banque Nationale de Paris, thirty-seven people had to leave under the Voluntary Retirement Scheme, including ten women. At the same time they recruited ten young women to work on the computers at the customer counter. A 39 year old woman who was forced to take the VRS explains the strategy thus:

For over two years, we were given very little work and we were shunted about from one department to another, one floor to another. We were treated like *badli* (casual) workers and were made to feel redundant and easily disposable. We pleaded to the management that we be given training on the computers. But they declined. We have a seniority of over twenty years, our pay levels are quite high, thanks to our earlier struggles. We are very confident and know our management inside out. Why should they want us any more?

Another woman activist working in the BNP says,

they would have to spend money giving us training. Now they've killed so many birds with one stone. One, the new girls are already trained. Two, the girls start at a much lower rate, about half our wage levels. Three, they are new, more enthusiastic to please the management. Four, the management has succeeded in creating an atmosphere of terror and uncertainty. These young girls are bound to be affected by this atmosphere and work with heads bent. Five, they have no experience with this management and are not affected by the union movement. The management has succeeded in throwing out all the active members of the union. Those active workers that remain are likely to be promoted to the management category.

On the issue of computerization and training, there seems to be fairly divergent views among bank managements too. By and large, the nationalized Indian banks seem to feel that 'it is better to retrain a banker in computer skills than train a computer specialist in banking'. To this end, the Indian Banks' Association has developed training packages for various types of personnel. The National Institute of Bank Management has a very wide range of training programmes for top management, and every bank has its own programmes for their staff. The foreign banks again seem to operate differently. In contrast to the BNP management, the Grindlays bank has not introduced an early retirement scheme, and has retrained its existing personnel. However according to the Personnel Department at the ANZ Grindlays, it is likely that the bank will insist that new recruits have some knowledge of computers.

One woman employee who had attended a training course arranged by the management at a professional computer training institute, said,

> The whole management approach to training is like their approach to our work – extraction. In both it is the superiors or the experts laying the ground rules, without any input or participation expected from us. Participation is only a hindrance, a point of delay, precious time wasted. I had a feeling of being steam-rollered rather than of having learnt something.

Another suggested:

> Workshops should be organized in such a way that women are collectively given the space to handle PCs, and with manuals explaining what needs to be done. One can have experts in at crucial times like an introductory familiarizing talk, and when we feel we need someone to guide us, but not experts breathing down our necks like supervisors on an assembly line.[10]

In fact, the women felt that such training sessions would also achieve a great deal from the point of view of the management.

The crux of the problems created by technological changes appears to be that the entire strategy is still technology-centred. Behind the technology-centred approach is a mechanized world-view in which computers, a machine carrying out the brain work of the human, are superior to people.

> In one of the training sessions we were told how computers may be used to level the hierarchies and authorities that exist in the workplace. But in practice a new hierarchy has been created, alongside the earlier one. You can do only this, and can have access to only this, while the authorities have a greater range of activities and access to greater areas of information.[11]

Despite their criticism of the training programmes organized by the management, the women employees are extremely keen on learning new things and new skills. In fact, the new generation of bank and insurance employees, including women, are very serious about their work and career-conscious. Reports of workshops with women clerks, officers and managers have indicated both the problems women face and their commitment to face these challenges for a better career. A senior unionist who has been active in the bank unions notes a shift,

> The attitude of the employees is changing. They no longer look at the unions as an expression of their aspirations, but as an agency which will deliver the goods. They are with the union because they mistrust the management. Their real interest however is their career.[12]

The unions too have begun to organize workshops for women employees. These workshops discuss the problems women employees face in their multiple roles, how women deal with these, and what their experiences are. Similar workshops are organized by the National Institute of Bank Management (NIBM), for women managers. Women clerical staff, officers and managers have reacted to these positively. One woman working in the EDP Department at the insurance corporation observes,

> We feel the thirst for more knowledge and better career prospects. Stagnation somehow scares us. Training programmes and institutions which acknowledge this, and our dilemmas and situation, are well received. But there are fewer of those than we need.[13]

In some of the courses in the National Institute of Bank Management, women managers are encouraged to talk about their ideas and suggestions as well as their experiences as women in banking. Many other unions and management training institutes are organizing similar courses. Women feel that this needs to be done more systematically and more often, so that a greater range of issues and diverse sections of women employees might be covered.

WOMEN EMPLOYEES ORGANIZING

The interests of women employees have been expressed in different ways. In the early 1980s the Women's Wing of the All India Conference of Bank Officers' Organizations (AICOBOO), open to women officers only, was formed. However the issues that concern them relate to all women employees. According to one of the spokeswomen of the Women's Wing,

> There is a pressing need for women to form strong pressure groups to see that the right to education and employment do not remain merely on paper. The problems of working women can be dealt with more effectively through collective action.

> (Amberkar, 1985)

The discrimination experienced by women working in banks is mainly in terms of the lack of infrastructural facilities, the transfer policy, and assumptions that women would not be interested in training or in promotions. The Women's Wing of the AICOBOO has been taking up these issues systematically. One outcome of their work has been the charter of demands they submitted to their union confederation. These included:

- Infrastructural facilities such as crèches and day care centres.
- Provision of hostels for working women, accommodation for divorced, separated and widowed women with children.
- Special leave with a lien on service, for up to say five years, to meet certain contingencies specific to women, extending this facility to men also whenever required.
- Provision for a woman with a child less than three years old to work for fewer hours and receive proportionate pay.
- Family pension and voluntary retirement for men and women after twenty years of service.
- Provision for flexi-hours and part-time employment in suitable cases.
- Although maternity leave (12 weeks in all) is regarded as fairly satisfactory, additional provisions required are medical benefits, hospitalization, leave for the purpose of child care, paternity leave for at least ten days, further leave also for those who have to look after an infant in special circumstances.
- Discrimination exists in our laws with regard to women . . . especially with regard to taxation, which needs to be looked into.

(Mankidy, 1989)

The specific demands put forward by the Women's Wing include a uniform transfer policy in all banks for women officers, and a cell to deal with women's issues in every bank's personnel department. They are currently trying to formulate demands relating to training programmes and time off for women to do union work.

Similarly the All India Bank Employees Association (AIBEA) has initiated a women's wing of the union to take up issues specially affecting women. The Reserve Bank of India has a Women's Forum for the same purpose.

The unions in the LIC have begun to organize women-only meetings and workshops. The Insurance Employees Association decided in 1991 to organize women employees more effectively, as the number of women employees was increasing day by day, with over 75 per cent of the new recruits being women. The association has demanded crèche facilities, special leave and better working conditions for women, and the removal of hidden discrimination.[14]

The demands put forward by the Punjab National Bank Employees Union include:

- Inter-region transfers of women on a priority basis.
- Arranging pre-promotion training programmes for women who want to take tests relating to promotions.
- Displacement on promotion to be avoided.
- Protection for pregnant women who work on computers.
- Women should be given temporary transfers on request during pregnancy, etc.[15]

The unions and the management have begun to acknowledge the separate needs of women employees and the specificity of the issues they face. Yet women employees' concerns and aspirations have not been adequately addressed by either. The training programmes organized by management do not include the vast majority of women employees. A 1986 study by the IBA showed that only 20 per cent of staff received some training in any one year (Madhukar, 1986). Officers of the NIBM reported that the situation had not changed since then.

The sessions organized by the unions are at a mass level and do not allow for the much-needed interaction and sharing of experiences. These too are organized fairly erratically. One senior woman employee notes,

> Both types of programmes – union and management – seem one-sided rather than multidimensional. In the union workshops and meetings, we are addressed as union members; in the management training programmes we are bank employees. But all of us are much more than that. We are employees, we are women, we are home-makers, we are thinking and feeling human beings, we are ambitious and much more. Training programmes need to keep this perspective in mind.[16]

Women feel the need for different types of inputs too. In the wake of liberalization and globalization and the changes in Indian banking, they want to know what is happening in the banking and finance sectors in other countries in terms of women's employment and organizing, what the experiences of women in those countries have been and what strategies they have used. Many women employees, including women officers, also feel that they would like to know and interact with women in other sectors too. As a young insurance officer said, 'What is happening to women nationally is of concern to us and is going to affect us.'

Such interconnections between the women's wings of the banking and insurance unions and the women's movement in the country and outside have begun to be explored recently, and a few women employees at all levels have begun participating in women's movement conferences. However, there is as yet no reciprocal interest from the women's movement in the concerns of employees in banking and finance. Developments in this area would also strengthen the links between the various forums and organizations that represent the interests of women bank and insurance employees. This would also necessarily include a wider forum for national and international solidarity for the exchange of information, strategies and forms of organization.

CONCLUSION

The last decade has seen a systematic rise in the employment of women in the banking and finance sector. The result of a multiplicity of factors, including: profound social changes taking place in India regarding women's education and employment; the changing policies of management, especially after the nationalization and reorganization of the LIC and of major banks; the policies of the Indian government; international changes in banking and finance and, not least, the technological changes being effected in the industry.

Computerization has had positive and negative implications for the workforce. It has affected employment levels and workloads and brought increasing pressure for flexibility. It has changed the content of work, and brought reduced job security and a shift towards more non-bargainable employees, which affects the nature and stability of the union. There have been changes in grading and pay, and in the means by which the workforce and information are controlled. The autonomy of employees and their conditions of work, and health and safety, have been affected also.

These all have a specific impact on women employees, who are being recruited in large numbers in the banking and finance sector, mainly in the clerical category. Women employees are increasingly looking at their work in terms of career prospects and are keen on learning new skills and advancing in their careers, despite severe limitations. They are organizing themselves into unions and separate women's caucuses within and outside unions.

While the rate of recruitment has slackened in India since the mid-1980s, there has not yet been a reversal, as has happened in some western countries. Women employees feel the need to broaden their vision by relating to each other and sharing information about national and international trends. This is an important basis for both interaction with the national women's movement and for international solidarity and sharing of experiences and working on future strategies.

This is especially relevant in the context of the introduction and extension of new technology in workplaces, as new technology has made the globe a much smaller place in terms of the spread of technologies and management strategies. Women employees need a constant process of discussion and strategy formulation if they are not merely to respond to these changes, but to become more proactive, to make suggestions and changes to suit their short and long-term interests.

NOTES

1 *Bank Flag*, Journal of the All India Bank Employees Association, Bombay, March, 1981.
2 *Economic Times*, 'IBA decision puts banks in a fix', Madras, 6 May 1991.
3 This quotation has been paraphrased.
4 This quotation has been paraphrased.
5 For instance, in 1970, Citibank had 2.33 bargainable workers for every 1 non-bargainable worker: in 1991 the proportion was 1.63:1, although the management had verbally agreed to a ratio not lower than 1.75:1. In the Banque Nationale de Paris the proportion used to be 5 bargainable for every 1 non-bargainable worker. Now it is 1.5:1.
6 *Business and Political Observer*, 26 May 1992.
7 This quotation has been paraphrased.
8 This quotation has been paraphrased.
9 This quotation has been paraphrased.
10 This quotation has been paraphrased.
11 This quotation has been paraphrased.
12 This quotation has been paraphrased.
13 This quotation has been paraphrased.
14 Circular of the All India Insurance Employees' Association, 23 January 1991.
15 Leaflet of the Punjab National Bank Employees' Union, 7 September 1991.
16 This quotation has been paraphrased.

REFERENCES

Amberkar, G. (1985), 'Women's Wing of All India Confederation of Bank Officers Organisation', paper presented at the National Seminar on Women's Movement in India – a review of achievements and issues, SNDT, Bombay

Anantharam Iyer, T.N., E. Venkateshwara Rao, and M. Sitaram Murthy (1991), *Computerisation in Banking Industry in India*, Indian Bank, Madras

Borkar, D.G. (1991), 'The Numbers Game–Bank Employment', *Economic Times*, 30 May

Chopra, O.P. (1991), *New Information Technologies and Employment in India's Finance Sector*, World Employment Programme Research, ILO, Geneva

Deekshit, G.R. (1991), 'An Uneasy Look at Bank Nationalisation', paper presented at the national seminar on 'Revitalisation of Indian Banking under Threat of Privatisation', organized by the All India Bank Employees Association (AIBEA) in Bombay, 4 April

Economic Times (1992), 4 January, Bombay

Goodman, S. (1991), *New Technology and Banking: Problems and possibilities for developing countries, a social actor perspective*, Research Policy Institute, University of Lund, Sweden

Huws, U., J. Hurstfield and R. Holtmaat (1989), *What Price Flexibility? The Casualisation of Women's Employment*, London, Low Pay Unit

Indian Labour Year Book, Chandigarh/Simla, Ministry of Labour, various years

International Labour Office (1989), *Conditions of Work Digest*, Vol. 8, Home work, 2/1989, ILO, Geneva

Kanhere, U. (1991), 'Bank Officers' Trade Unions and Women Officers', in Chetana Kalbagh (ed.), *Women and Development*, Vol. 1, New Delhi, Discovery

Labour Research Department (1985), *VDUs Health and Jobs*, London, LRD

Madhukar, R.K. (1986), 'Human Resources in Indian Banks', in *Indian Banks Association Bulletin*, Bombay, September

Mankidy, A. (1986a), *Women Employees: A New Dimension to Human Resource Management in Banks*, Indian Banks' Association, special issue

Mankidy, A. (1988), *Towards Better Functioning of Women Managers in Banks*, National Institute of Bank Management, Pune

Mankidy, A. (1989), 'Women Employees: a New Variable in Industrial Relations in the Banking Industry, *Management and Labour Studies*, Vol. 14, No. 2, April

Ozaki, M. *et al.* (1992), *Technological Change and Labour Relations*, ILO, Geneva

Rajan, A. (1990), *Information Technology in the Finance Sector: An International Perspective*, Technology and Employment Programme, ILO, Geneva

Srinivasan, K. (1991), 'Women in Banking and Professional Struggles', in Chetana Kalbagh (ed.) *Women and Development*, Vol. 1, New Delhi, Discovery

Tremblay, Diane-Gabrielle (1991), 'Computerization, Human Resources Management and Redirection of Women's Skills', in I.V. Eriksson *et al.* (eds), *Women, Work and Computerization*, Amsterdam, North Holland

9 Information technology, gender and employment

A case study of the telecommunications industry in Malaysia

Cecilia Ng Choon Sim and Carol Yong

INTRODUCTION

Ever since the Industrial Revolution there has been an ongoing debate over the impact of technology on employment. This debate continues today in what is widely recognized as the second industrial revolution – information technology. The objective of this chapter is to examine the impact of information technology on women's employment in Malaysia. Malaysia is a useful country to look at, given the present acceleration towards rapid industrialization and the government's intention to make information technology (IT) one of the key technologies in the nation's bid to become a developed country by the year 2020. The chapter also aims to explore the importance of gender, in relation to other factors such as ethnicity, in the stratification of occupations and jobs under the impact of computerization.

The above issues are discussed in relation to the telecommunications industry, on the basis of a case study of a major telecommunications company in Malaysia. Besides looking at new questions such as VDU-related health and safety issues, the case study also examines the role of unions in augmenting opportunities for women in the IT industry and in office employment.

Information technology and employment: the debate so far

The impact of IT on employment is not necessarily uniform. It can reduce clerical work to tedious and repetitive jobs and it can create innovative work and create new skills. It can fragment and control work and workers and it can broaden and allow more autonomy. The computer rationalization of production can be robust and more democratic, or algorithmic and more authoritarian (Albin and Appelbaum, 1988). Clearly, the direction of change in the organization of work depends on the strength and articulation of office workers themselves.

Struggles by office workers in Canada, France and Mexico reveal that the flexibility of IT can allow for worker participation in the design of information systems (Clement, 1991; Ormos and Blameble, 1989). Strong trade union demands coupled with a more open government (e.g. in the Scandinavian countries) can provide channels for participation from all levels of office staff in the planning of technological change. Feminist computer professionals are already combining participatory principles in the design of systems (Greenbaum, 1991). In Malaysia the struggles of office workers focus mainly on economic gains rather than political changes, as will be discussed later.

The impact of the introduction of IT cannot be analysed apart from its immediate context of social relations and the existing organization of work. The extent of the impact will also vary depending on the type of machines being installed, the period of installation and the existing labour processes which are being automated (Baran and Teegarden, 1987). Previous studies have tended to consider the impact of IT on clerical staff as an undifferentiated group, but different levels of office workers, men and women, and different ethnic groups may be differently affected. And while the new technology skills are being polarized by gender, it is also evident that women are entering computer professions in both the developed and developing countries, leading to class polarization within the female labour force itself.

It is also important to look at the broader social, economic and political context, as this is reflected in relationships at work. Since society is based on hierarchy, and technology is a medium of power, one needs to understand how power is negotiated. This means that deskilling and intensification of work are not inevitable consequences of technological change, but neither will technology automatically create better opportunities.

Industrialization, information technology and employment in Malaysia

As Malaysia enters into a new phase of industrial development under the Sixth Malaysia Plan (1991-1995), information technology has been singled out as one of the five key technologies which will launch Malaysia as a developed country and support the industrial culture needed to sustain industrialization.[1] This new approach to industrialization will:

> emphasise the development of export-oriented, high value-added, high technology industries . . . the objective of the industrial policy is to move towards more capital-intensive and technologically sophisticated

industries producing better quality and competitive products that are integrated with the markets of developed countries . . . and, in the long run, industrial development will emphasise greater automation or other labour-saving production processes to reduce labour utilisation.

(Government of Malaysia, 1991: pp. 137–139)

Malaysia has been transformed from an economy based on agriculture to one with a substantial industrial base. The share of agriculture in GDP has declined significantly, from 40.5 per cent in 1955 to 18.7 per cent in 1990. Conversely, industry's share rose from 17.5 per cent in 1955 to 27 per cent in 1990. Moreover, the move towards privatization encouraged by the World Bank has made the private sector the main engine of growth. There has also been a shift in the gender and ethnic composition of the labour force.[2] In line with the New Economic Policy, there has been an increase in the employment of Malays from rural areas in urban employment sectors. At the same time, with the opening up of export processing zones and the present tight labour market, more and more women are joining the labour force.

EDUCATION AND TRAINING

Computers in schools

The shift from an agricultural to an industrial economy, and the stress on IT as a key industry, has led to a shortage of computer professionals. Government policies aimed at rectifying this shortage operate at both secondary and tertiary levels. A computer literacy programme called Computers in Education (CIE) was established in 1986 by the Malaysian Institute of Microelectronic Systems and the Ministry of Education. The idea was to introduce computers into schools. The programme now covers 1,359 secondary schools, including 41.6 per cent of schools in the Federal Territory, but just 4.4 per cent of those in Sabah and 2.6 per cent of those in Sarawak.

Primary school computer clubs have also been encouraged. In 1990 the total membership of these clubs was 34,493, or just 1.4 per cent of students. Female students, the majority of whom were non-*bumiputras*, comprised almost half of the total membership. The clubs were also concentrated in the Federal Territory. Similar clubs in secondary schools serve about 5 per cent of the total school population. Once again, half of the members are girls. Given the rather limited coverage of these schemes, it is hard to believe that 'by the year 2000, those who have gone through our education system, would be computer literate and would be able to integrate themselves into the newly emerging information society' (statement by the Finance Minister[3]).

Private computer colleges and schools

In line with the demand for more computer personnel, private institutes have been offering courses and training in this field. A 1992 survey of seven of the principal private schools and colleges, conducted by the authors, showed an increasing number of students enrolling in computer courses or related subjects. Of these seven private institutes, five offered a Diploma in Computer Studies and a Certificate in Computer Packages and Software programmes; one offered courses in Electrical Engineering and Electronics (Diploma and Certificate), while the last one offered classes in selected computer packages. Between 1987 and 1992, 957 males and 1,207 females graduated in computer packages and software programmes, and 2,234 males and 1,637 females in computer courses or studies. Only nineteen females completed electronics courses, compared to 476 male graduates. Thus despite the opportunities for women in computer education and training in the private sector, women study software programmes rather than competing for higher qualifications in computer studies and electronics/electrical courses.

Universities and colleges

At the tertiary level there are almost equal numbers of female and male students. However female students have a preference for the non-technical and non-vocational disciplines. At the university level, although more women have been enrolling in science and technological courses, female students still dominated the arts and applied arts (Government of Malaysia, 1991: pp. 420–421). Women constituted 65 per cent of the students in arts, 45 per cent in science, 22 per cent in the vocational and 36 per cent in the technical streams in 1990. Sex-based socialization and stereotyping of women's education and skills training is declining, but it is still a reality today.

Academic programmes offered by tertiary institutions in the area of computing, informatics, information technology and related fields have grown largely because of national policies that have encouraged their development. A number of universities offer degree courses in computer science programmes. The Universiti Utara Malaysia has started a School of Information Technology, and the Kolej Tunku Abdul Rahman offers a diploma in computer science. There were 4,215 students in computer related courses in tertiary institutions for the 1990-1991 academic year. Female students comprised 51.4 per cent of total intake, 47.6 per cent at the degree level, 55.5 per cent at the diploma level and 29 per cent at the Certificate level.[4]

Projections for 1990-1995 are that 10,478 professionals and semi-professionals will graduate at the tertiary level, and another 12,750 semi-professionals from private institutions, but this will still be 3,224 short of the IT personnel required.[5] According to the MNCC survey (n.d.), there will be shortfalls in the areas of IT management (41 per cent), systems analysts (22 per cent), programming (27 per cent), operations (10 per cent) and specialists (18 per cent).[6]

Trends in new technology employment

The rapid increase in employment associated with the new technologies, between 1975 and 1990, is shown in Table 9.1. The number of systems analysts grew nearly fifteen-fold (from 172 to 2526) during this period while computer programmers increased thirteen-fold (from 335 to 4353), and automatic data processing and machine operators increased ten-fold (from 1038 to 10709).[7]

The trend towards increased employment in computer-related jobs actually masks two divisions. Firstly, jobs become differentiated between 'high-skilled' and 'low-skilled' work, that is between systems analysts, programmers and the like in the professional and technical category and automatic data processing and machine operators on the other. If the other clerical workers, a growing percentage of whom are using computers, are included, the direct and indirect low-skilled groups in 1990 were about 40 times the size of the high-skilled category (Table 9.1). Hence the majority of computer-related jobs are still in the direct and indirect low-skilled category.

Another trend is polarization in terms of gender. Women's share in the direct high-skilled jobs increased from 42 per cent in 1985 to 45 per cent in 1990, reflecting healthy inroads made by women in this professional category. On the other hand their share of the low-skilled data processing operators declined – from 91 per cent in 1975 to 75 per cent in 1985 and 62 per cent in 1990. Yet it is clear that low-skilled new technology employment is predominantly female and will continue to remain so.

TELMAL: GENDER AND OFFICE EMPLOYMENT

TELMAL,[8] is a telecommunications agency established in 1948 under the

Table 9.1 Employment by selected occupation and sex, peninsular Malaysia, 1975 and 1990

Skill level and occupation	1975				1990				% change 1975–1990		
	Male	Female	Total	%female	Male	Female	Total	%female	Male	Female	Total
1 Direct high-skilled											
Systems analysts	91	81	172	47	928	1,598	2,526	63	920	1,873	1,369
Computer programmers, statistical and mathematical technicians	335	–	335	–	2,883	1,470	4,353	34	761	–	1,199
Total	426	81	507	16	3,811	3,068	6,879	45	795	3,688	1,257
2 Direct low-skilled											
Automatic data processing and machine operators	91	947	1,038	91	4,067	6,642	10,709	62	4,369	601	932
3 Indirect low-skilled											
Clerical supervisors	5,011	419	5,430	8	16,612	6,346	22,958	28	232	1,415	323
Stenographers	4,220	22,962	27,182	84	883	46,130	47,013	98	-79	101	73
Bookkeepers, cashiers, and related workers	2,665	710	3,375	21	1,757	2,205	3,962	56	-34	211	17
Correspondence and reporting clerks	40,983	26,854	67,837	40	75,149	122,931	198,080	62	39	358	192
Statistical clerks	–	–	–	–	462	560	1,022	55	–	–	–
Total	52,879	50,945	103,824	49	76,863	178,172	255,035	70	45	250	146

Source: Department of Statistics, Labour Force Survey (unpublished data)

Ministry of Posts and Telecommunications with the dual functions of telecommunications operations and the supervision of such operations. As part of the structural transformation of the economy, TELMAL was corporatized in January 1987 and became a Public Listed Company in October 1990, with 20 per cent of its shares open to the public.

The basic services provided by TELMAL, are telephone and telex services, but it also provides radio and data communication services, with plans for more advanced services in line with the IT strategy of the government. In 1991, TELMAL announced that it planned to spend more than RM 5 million (approximately US$ 2 million) on personal computers, printers and application software 'in a move to increase the productivity of the staff'. In its 1991 Annual Report, TELMAL proudly pointed out that the company has become the largest user of IT in the country.

TELMAL's turnover is expected to reach RM 6 billion by 1995, compared to RM 3 billion in 1991. Profits have also dramatically increased since TELMAL was privatized. In its first year of incorporation TELMAL chalked up a pre-tax profit of RM 181 million. This jumped to RM 550 million in 1990 and soared to RM 1,079 billion in 1991. TELMAL workers have been urged to work harder to achieve profits of more than RM 2 billion in the next two or three years.[9]

This stupendous growth is in line with the nation's desire to be an information society and the regional communications centre. It is estimated that the telecommunications industry in Malaysia will grow by 15 per cent per year, outstripping the estimated growth rate of telecommunications in the Asian region of 7.5 per cent for the period 1990–1995. Global telecommunications are expected to grow by only 5 per cent per year over the same period.[10]

COMPUTERIZATION IN TELMAL

Although TELMAL embarked on computerization in the early 1970s, there has recently been major upgrading and the development of new systems to provide more functions and utilize more up-to-date technology. This includes designing and developing an integrated customer service order system, upgrading the systems for billing, financial management, human resource management, material management, and corporate and marketing information and areas of technical and network operations. Despite the attempts to computerize, the actual rate of diffusion is not very high. The proportion of our respondents who used computers 'most of the time' in their office tasks ranged from 72.5 per cent to as low as 6.3 per cent, depending on the respondent's task and gender. About 26.7 per cent of female respondents, and 42.6 per cent of the male respondents, spent one to four hours on the computer a day, while 69.9 per cent of the females used computers for five to eight hours per day, compared to 53.4 per cent of the male respondents. The perceived importance of their computer-related tasks differed according to gender. Women office workers ranked hands-on responsibilities such as directing mail and telephone messages, reading letters, processing records and data entry as their most important tasks, while male office workers were most involved in processing and maintaining records, data entry, information gathering and writing original materials. It seems that men are more involved in jobs requiring 'mental' concentration, as compared to the more routine tasks of the women. Table 9.2 depicts the ranking of office tasks in terms of frequency on the importance and the extent of computer usage of the respondents by gender.

Computerization and employment

As of October 1990, there were 28,015 employees at TELMAL compared to 28,168 in 1988. Thus there has been a slight reduction in staff (minus 154) despite the expansion of services and the customer base, and the substantial increase in profits through the years. Women comprised 24 per cent of the total staff in 1990. Some 78 per cent of all employees were Malays, compared to 9 per cent Chinese and 11 per cent Indians. The overall domination of Malays is a legacy of the colonial bureaucracy and recent state economic policies to narrow the ethnic gap, particularly in the urban sector.

Six per cent of the female staff and 4.8 per cent of the men are in the 'executive' category. This gives the impression that women are being given better opportunities to advance to leadership positions.[11] However, on closer examination, most if not all of the top decision-making positions are held by Malay men. Of the female executives, 90 per cent are Malays, while 75 per cent of the male executives are Malays. Only 4 per cent of executives are Indians, and 16 per cent are Chinese. This contrasts to the situation in other sectors, particularly in the finance and computer vendor and service industries, where top management is predominantly male and Chinese. Five per cent of all staff, and 5 per cent of all Malay staff, are executives, whereas 9 per cent of the Chinese staff and just 1.6 per cent of the Indian staff are in the executive category. The majority of the Indian non-executive employees are labourers or lower level technicians.

Thus ethnic and class differentials are as important (and sometimes more important) than gender differentials. In TELMAL, the hierarchical occupational ladder prevents the majority of men and women from

Table 9.2 Ranking of office tasks and computer usage at TELMAL by gender

| Female respondents | | Male respondents | |
Tasks (in order of importance)	% use computer most of the time	Tasks (in order of importance)	% use computer most of time
1 Directing mail & telephone messages	60	1 Process and maintain records	59.8
2 Read letters or enquiries	50.9	2 Data entry	64.6
3 Process and maintain records	53	3 Information gathering	41.4
4 Data entry	72.5	4 Write original materials	41.0
5 Information gathering	42.3	5 Prepare charts, diagrams	45.7
6 Write original materials	52.9	6 Statistical computation	50.8
7 Statistical computation	51.5	7 Production control	34.8
8 Text input	56.5	8 Write standard materials	42.4
9 Filing	9.4	9 Billing	56.0
10 Write standard materials	51.7	10 Spreadsheet	55.1
11 Spreadsheet	72.5	11 Money handling	56.0
12 Prepare charts, diagrams	65.6	12 Support services	14.0
13 Money handling	55.6	13 Filing	7.8
14 Billing	52.8	14 Proofread/edit	28.6
15 Create a filing system	22.6	15 Bookkeeping	45.0
16 Fill in forms	11.3	16 Read letters or enquiries	–
17 Production control	30.0	17 Directing mail & telephone messages	6.3
18 Proofread/edit	35.3	18 Text input	19.8
19 Develop forms	49.1	19 Fill in forms	7.7
20 Bookkeeping	30.0	20 Develop forms	33.3

climbing to the top or being recruited to that limited space, but it remains easier for Malays of either sex or for Chinese men. Indians are barely represented, and in fact remain at the bottom of the non-executive levels. Feminist theories of work have to consider the complex interrelationship of the forces contributing to segmentation in employment and take account of how these operate in relation to specific sectors in society, rather than just focusing on gender *per se*. Table 9.3 shows the distribution of selected executive and non-executive employees, and of employees in computer-related occupations, by ethnicity and gender.

To a large extent, the gender differentiation of employment at TELMAL reflects the pattern at the national level. Decision-making at the executive level is dominated by men, particularly at the most senior levels. The technical slots are also the domain of men while women are concentrated in data-entry, clerical and telephonist occupations. While there are equal numbers of men and women in computer-related jobs, the majority of women are lower level data processing operators. Women are in a relatively strong position at the level of systems programmers, but the main decisions regarding computerization remain with systems analysts, three-quarters of whom are men.

Table 9.3 Distribution of selected employees in TELMAL by ethnicity and gender

Category	Malay		Chinese		Indian		Total	
	Male	Female	Male	Female	Male	Female	Male	Female
Executive	790	375	197	34	52	8	1,039	417
Non-executive								
Technical	6,292	1,019	905	187	643	46	7,840	1,252
Clerical	1,168	2,216	102	149	99	44	1,369	2,409
Manual	4,692	101	256	21	1,573	33	6,521	155
Teleprinter	34	212	1	24	3	34	38	270
Telephonist	596	1,032	34	201	34	132	664	1,365
Computer-related Jobs								
Systems analysts	97	33	9	2	1	2	107	37
Systems programmers	31	20	4	3	1	–	36	23
Computer operators	36	17	1	4	4	1	41	22
Data processing operators	10	97	–	9	3	9	13	115

The internal labour market

Internal promotion seems hard to come by for women employees. Of the female respondents, 64 per cent had been in their jobs for less than 10 years, 27 per cent for eleven to twenty years, and 9 per cent had been in the same jobs for more than 21 years. This was completely different for the male respondents, 94 per cent of whom had been in their jobs for less than 10 years. Men were promoted after working an average of 4 years, compared to 9.5 years for women.

Only about 25 per cent of women from the telephonist, clerical and managerial categories were 'quite satisfied' or 'very satisfied' with their chances of advancement in the company. None of the women computer operators was very satisfied with their promotion prospects, compared to 25 per cent of their male counterparts. When four new data centres were established, 'outsiders', mainly male, were recruited rather than relying on internal recruitment and promotion. Yet the TELMAL 1991 Annual Report recognized the importance of career opportunities and upgrading to lower level staff. It noted quite proudly that in the past year there had been twenty-two promotions from non-executive to executive levels. While this could provide an incentive to the lower staff, it should also be noted that this represented just 0.08 per cent of the total non-executive staff in the organization. The promotions were seen as reflecting the substantial increase in revenue per employee, from RM 80,500 in 1990 to RM 93,000 in 1991.

Computerization and employment

What is the impact of computerization on employment? According to the union president of TELMAL, management had stated that computerization has meant that between four and five thousand workers, mainly at the technical and clerical levels, are no longer required. However, there have apparently been no lay-offs so far, partly because of the strength of the union, and partly because of the political repercussions. Of the total West Malaysian non-executive employees in TELMAL, 94 per cent are Malays. Laying these workers off would be political suicide, as Malays provide the urban support base to the government. Indeed in the early to mid-1980s, public sector employment expanded considerably, relative to the other sectors, with the intake focused on the Malay population who are expected to provide support to the state.[12]

But it seems that while the union can save people, it does not necessarily save jobs. Nor does the union have a say in the hiring of new or contract staff. In early 1991 there was an intake of telephone operators in the

Table 9.4 Respondents' satisfaction with their chances of advancement in the company, by gender and occupation (%)

| | Computer operators including data entry operators | | Telephone operators (all women) | | Clerical (typists, clerks, secretaries, accounts assistants) | | Management | |
	Male	Female	Male	Female	Male	Female	Male	Female
Not satisfied	25	77	–	44	61	56	21	26
Quite satisfied	50	23	–	32	21	32	50	48
Very satisfied	25	–	–	24	18	12	29	26

international section, to meet rising customer demand. However, these workers, mainly women, were employed on a contract basis without the benefits enjoyed by regular staff.

Computerization has in fact displaced labour in some cases. For example, the development of the rather sophisticated Customer Automated Services System (CASS) has led to the elimination of many routine clerical and technical tasks. The mechanized service order system automatically processes, records, updates and stores all information about the subscriber, eliminating time-consuming paperwork. Previously it took at least three months (if one was fortunate) to obtain a telephone line. With CASS, one can be confident of receiving a line within three days.

When computers were introduced to billing in 1986, clerical workers who used to write and type bills became redundant, and were relocated to other branch offices. Data entry operators were then hired to key in bills more rapidly. However with on-line billing from the various payment centres, under CASS, these data entry operators will one day themselves be redundant. The upgrading to a digital switching system, has also made some telephone operators redundant, and a cable plant assignment system has reduced manual technical intervention. One of the CASS managers estimated that 200 staff had been redeployed to other sections, while new outside staff, mainly systems analysts and programmers, had been recruited.

Changes in work organization, job content and skills

Office automation affects different levels and types of workers differently. The first applications of IT in TELMAL involved the simple mechanization of high-volume activities such as processing forms, billing subscribers and answering phone calls. These early systems involved key-punch operators using batch systems, typists and telephonists. The shifts from manual to computerized activities were fairly straightforward as task fragmentation, or Taylorization, had already routinized these functions. Thus this early phase of automation conformed to the pre-existing division of labour in a rationalized bureaucracy. The result was task fragmentation and the intensification of work, which was decentralized into geographically separated and gender segregated units.

Routine keyboarding was functionally and spatially separated from the rest of the clerical work. In a sense, the technology demanded spatial separation, due to the convenience of the computer infrastructure being centrally located. As a result of this fragmentation, the present data entry operators, some of whom were previously key-punch operators or typists, work on the machines all day, in shifts and with set production standards monitored by the computer.

In the TELMAL main office, forty-five data processing operators work three shifts, with a break of twenty minutes in the morning and a one hour lunch break. Often they work overtime after office hours and on Sundays. These workers, most of them women, are required to key in between 10,000 and 14,000 keystrokes per hour, and their productivity chart is posted on the wall the next morning. Tension and pressure to perform permeate the small crowded workplace. Adding to the tension are restrictions preventing them moving freely or speaking to their colleagues during working hours. One of the operators said:

> With privatization there is more pressure to work. Work gets faster and the room is very cold and small. We have to do overtime a lot especially at the end of the month. I feel very tired . . . my eyes, my head, my back are all painful. When I go home I have to do housework again. Many women here have had miscarriages, but I do not know the exact number. We want a better place to work, an increase in pay and more staff. Before, the extra work was subcontracted out. But now this has stopped due to an increase in costs. It is cheaper to pay us overtime.

Similar intensification and control over work is also experienced by the international telephonists at TELMAL. Previously, these telephonists seem to have had more control over their work processes. They were required to write down customer information and bookings on ticket slips and collect the tickets, check, arrange them by country and then send the final accounts to the billing section. With the introduction of computerized exchanges in 1985–1987, and with privatization, they feel their work has intensified and that there is more control over what they do. Now they have to fulfil a quota of 3,000 calls per day or to complete a call within ten seconds. A computer checks their productivity, and makes a monthly report on their performance. At the same time, the telephonists, all female, prefer the present system which is easier to handle as the equipment is less heavy and cumbersome. Only now there is more work and they feel more pressured to perform. During one interview, one of them said:

> My work is now more efficient with computers. However I have to answer more calls. There is more work and I have to work faster and non-stop. When I reach home I am so tired I do not want to answer any more phone calls! However my chances of promotion are poor. It is very difficult and I feel frustrated.

Typists, clerks and secretaries have been spared this intensification and loss of control. Although there is rationalization and increasing specialization, the work has become easier. This is especially so for small work groups performing both clerical and typing activities, such as the mobile maritime service group, which handles ship to shore communication charges. The five female clerks, under a female supervisor, work in a separate room. They check through an average of 1,500 dockets per month and used to type up the relevant information on typewriters. With the introduction of two personal computers in 1989, the work load has become lighter and easier. In fact there is a request for each typist to have her own personal computer. The person we interviewed seems to like her work and working environment – there is freedom of movement in this small and decentralized work group, although this is more restricted now with privatization. According to her,

> I like my work and the environment here. However there are more restrictions now. For example, we cannot take an afternoon tea break – there are specific times for breaks now. We cannot relax as people are eyeing you, or we are afraid that people are eyeing you. There is now more pressure to perform.

The information in Table 9.5, gathered from the respondents' responses, reflects this mood.

The above discussion suggests that the introduction of computerization in TELMAL has brought about changes in work relations and organization among the various categories of office staff. The effects of the first stage of office automation seem to be in line with the Braverman hypothesis that, for certain categories of workers, tasks are fragmented, and deskilled so that production becomes more controlled and centralized, with increased occupational segregation. But this does not mean that the organization of office work is technologically driven. There is simply a meeting of interests between capital and automation, the computer builds on processes which were already present. In other words, computerization extends and intensifies the pre-existing division of labour so that productivity and profits can be increased. However, some are not affected, others have their work transformed in the classical Braverman fashion, and there are some who are still involved in a variety of tasks and skills without undue loss of control over their work.

Reorganization of work

Recently, with the introduction of integrated and more sophisticated systems, there seems to be a reorganization of work which is reversing some of these

Table 9.5 Respondents' perceptions regarding productivity, freedom of movement and decision making

| | Computer operators | | Telephonists | Clerical | | Management | |
	Male	Female	Female	Male	Female	Male	Female
Productivity							
The computer keeps track of my productivity quite a bit/a lot	75	62	93	40	43	38	19
The computer has increased my work output quite a bit/a lot	100	95	97	94	83	80	80
Freedom of movement							
I can take breaks when I want to:							
– never	25	50	96	29	33	16	29
– once in a while	50	50	4	68	60	74	56
– often	25	0	0	3	7	10	15
I can talk with other workers from where I sit							
– never	0	22	61	6	3	4	12
– once in a while	50	61	39	41	61	28	44
– often	50	17	0	53	36	68	44
I can walk around when I want to							
– never	25	39	97	15	14	6	7
– once in a while	25	50	3	53	62	40	51
– often	50	11	0	32	34	54	42

% agreeing with statement

Decision-making

I can make decisions about my work flow

– never	25	56	96	32	41	10	14
– once in a while	25	28	2	44	31	31	32
– often	50	16	2	24	28	59	54

I can make decisions without the supervisor's OK

– never	25	56	84	32	36	16	23
– once in a while	75	44	13	50	51	60	42
– often	0	0	3	18	13	24	35

My opinions are listened to by management

– never	25	39	88	9	32	12	7
– once in a while	75	61	11	74	51	60	58
– often	0	0	1	17	17	28	35

I am asked for my comments on proposed office changes

– never	75	72	67	59	63	52	30
– once in a while	0	28	27	29	22	28	44
– often	25	0	6	12	15	20	26

trends and creating new work processes. However it is difficult to evaluate the new organization and processes as the integrated systems have just been introduced. Nonetheless, it is clear that certain data processing functions will soon be eliminated. The data entry operators who are inputting the billing information from the Post Office will soon become redundant, when the Post Office is connected on-line to the CASS system. These operators will have to be redeployed. When the billing system for employees' clinic bills is computerized, typists will no longer be needed there. According to one of the respondents, typists and clerks are a dying breed in her particular section. New staff are accounts assistants, with accounting certificates or diplomas.

New skills can also be added to workers' functions, as has happened with the book-keeping clerks. With integrated accounting, previously fragmented tasks in the various accounts units are more integrated. In TELMAL's international section, the book-keepers used just to 'input' the receipts from various sources e.g. salaries, allowances, refund, leave, fines etc. These would then be sent to the central accounts section which would produce daily and monthly reports (output). Since 1987, a new section called 'Input/Output' has been created, and staff have acquired new skills in areas such as preparing balances and budget forecasts. The male book-keepers in this section work as a team and enjoy their work as they can 'see what they are doing'. While there is more work, they do not mind as it gets done more efficiently and there is no pressure as they are their own bosses. In another sense, there is also less work, as the earlier routine paper work has been eliminated. According to one male book-keeper: 'Although I have more work to do I learn something new. I can see what I am doing as I have now my own programme for budget forecast. I have more control over my work now.'

With more advanced systems, the centralization of command seems to allow for more decentralized control, and thus more flexibility at the middle and clerical levels. At the middle level, systems analysts, pro- grammers and their end users have been found to work together, albeit mainly in implementing new systems on a trial basis. It is possible that clerical staff, as end users, could meet with the systems designers to change existing systems or to suggest new ways of obtaining information. At the lower levels, the position of the pure typist is being eliminated as clerks take on their responsibilities. Here again, earlier fragmented tasks are reunited into single multitask operations. Clerks become more independent as they are put in charge of specific operations.

An example is a senior clerk who handles international accounts dealing with leased circuits. Previously he had a few typists in his section to write the bills, with each typist completing twenty billings a day in triplicate. It took more than a month to generate the bills to the 270 subscribers (500 circuits). However with the integrated billing system, the time spent on manual labour has been cut by 80 per cent and he feels that his staff is now redundant. This is because he can now key in the information himself and the computer will generate the bills. This has simplified his work and he feels there is more control. He has also learnt new computer skills in the reorganization of the work processes in his section. While the work has become lighter, privatization has meant that staff have to be more disciplined as quotas have to be met every month.

In another accounts section dealing with pay, the introduction of the human resource management system has made the payment of salaries, income tax, housing loans, and other payments to staff more efficient. The time required to process changes has been reduced from ten weeks to two weeks, the workload has been reduced and tasks are centralized. Where previously the various kinds of information were typed up by different typists who specialized in their own little area of work, now there are only two clerks, who have to do everything. According to the chief clerk:

> The clerks are independent now and can run the whole show. By having to relate to more agencies, they also pick up more skills. They are more competent. However, sad to say, there is no increase in their salaries or grade structure.

Typists are also made redundant with the clerks taking over their jobs, and in fact typists who retire or resign are not replaced. Although the work is easier there is more pressure to perform in a profit-making company, and more reports to prepare. This chief clerk has worked for twenty-six years in the company, and reached her maximum grade nine years ago. In fact she is doing the work of an accounts officer. However it is difficult to get promoted as: 'Promotions are based on the book. Only with a Diploma can one be promoted to be an accounts assistant. I have taken computer classes outside my working hours to improve myself, but all this is not recognised.'

The introduction of IT in office work does not inevitably entail work intensification or deskilling. The negative consequences fall mainly on the shoulders of data entry workers and typists, whose work is routine, monotonous and highly stressed. They also suffer more in terms of health and safety due to the nature of their working conditions. At the same time flexible multifunctional jobs are possible, at least in certain clerical sections.

Our survey of the clerical workers' skills revealed that women ranked abstract and interactive skills (concentration, cooperation with others, problem solving, good memory) above technical skills such as good spelling and good grammar. In fact the performance rating of telephonists at TELMAL focuses primarily on these 'invisible' skills and abstract, interactive and caring characteristics, such as knowledge of the company, initiative, cooperation, patience, and ability to communicate (Table 9.6). This affirms the positions taken by Goodman (1985), Lie and Rasmussen (1985), and Pullman and Szymanski (1988), who criticise current discussions of office skills for focusing too much on routine, and on tasks which are easily visible, measurable and male constructed. However despite TELMAL's recognition of the importance of these traits in its telephonists, they are not customarily categorized as skills, and are thus not rewarded accordingly.

Union demands and gender issues

In TELMAL, the union seems to be an important arena in which social conflict is negotiated, particularly in collective bargaining. Some of the union members felt that it was important to be in the union to fight for their rights, as management did not care about the workers. Some of them voiced their opinions about management during our interviews: 'They only care about workers' output and do not inform workers about health and safety issues regarding computerization. Management and union are far from each other.' Because of the strength of the union, the collective agreement negotiated as a result of privatization guaranteed that no jobs would be lost. Moreover, when the company was floated on the stock exchange, the union also negotiated for shares to be sold first to the workers. The union was successful in obtaining shares which were allocated proportionately according to the occupational grade of the workers. While this was a victory, it was a small one due to the huge disparity between shares allocated to executives and lower level employees, even those who had served for a long time. The lowest-ranking worker was only allotted one unit of RM 5,000, even if he or she had worked for thirty years in the organization. Clerical workers were entitled to three units, supervisors to four units, and executives were entitled to between ten and thirty units each. However, the union has recently been seeking an extra share for the lower level workers. According to our clerical interviewees, the allocation was unfair as those who really worked hard, for example the labourers, did not get what they deserved, compared to the executives who received the maximum benefits.

TELMAL workers have also won year-end bonuses. Worker consciousness, at least for economic gains, seems to be fairly high. During the research, many of the staff, aware of the increased profits that the company had made in 1990, were preparing to take to the streets to demand their

Table 9.6 Ranking of skills most important to TELMAL workers

	Telephonists		Clerical workers	
Skills	Skills	Very important (%)	Skills	Very important (%)
1	Accuracy	96	Accuracy	72
2	Good memory	93	Good memory	69
3	Tact and diplomacy	87	Concentration	64
4	Concentration	87	Problem solving	60
5	Ability to communicate	82	Cooperation with others	58
6	Cooperation with others	82	Tact and diplomacy	48
7	A good sense of timing	81	An eye for detail	46
8	An eye for detail	81	A good sense of timing	45
9	Good spelling	64	Ability to communicate	39
10	General knowledge of the workings of the firm	62	Ability to coordinate workflow	38
11	Explaining policies and procedures	61	Explaining policies and procedures	37
12	Good grammar	60	A good knowledge of workings of company	36
13	Problem solving	56	Good grammar	36
14	Ability to coordinate workflow	60	Ability to read other's handwriting	32
15	Proper dress	45	Knowledge of maths	29
16	Ability to read other's handwriting	44	Ability to format (text, charts)	27
17	Knowledge of maths	25	Creativity	27
18	Creativity	14	Good spelling	22
19	Ability to format (text, chart)	3	Proper dress	20

Source: List of skills adapted from Pullman and Szymanski (1988)[13]

bonuses. Indeed, management appears to recognize the vital role of labour in 'their contribution to the success of privatization'. As stated in the 1989 report: 'Union activities are encouraged in the genuine belief that these contribute to healthy industrial relations and provide for the effective resolution of issues on a collective basis.' It seems that employment prospects and working conditions will to a large extent be determined by how social conflict is resolved. In the case of TELMAL, at least during the transition period (which fortunately occurred during a period of high growth), capital was open to trade union demands since it also realized the vital contribution of labour to its corporate goals. The direction of change also depends on the level of trade union consciousness of the leadership and members, who are at the moment more bent on economic advantage than broader political goals such as worker participation and democracy. Perhaps this is not surprising, since trade unions' voices have become somewhat muted due to repressive and anti-labour measures of the state.

The TELMAL union is not making gender issues a priority: the tendency is for gender to be either subsumed under economic demands or influenced by ideological constructs and images of the role of women. Rather than recognizing the undervalued skills of office workers and the difficulty they face in going up the career ladder, given the level of redundancy as a result of computerization, the union has been satisfied simply to retain their grade which is one of the lowest in the job hierarchy. They start with a basic salary of RM 407 per month with annual increments of RM 17, compared to a starting salary of RM 2,002 with annual increments of RM 66 for officers.

Much the same applies regarding health and safety. The union has asked for a hazards allowance for workers exposed to microwave and/or radiation emissions, rather than for the participation of workers in the safe and ergonomic redesign and reorganization of such systems. The majority of the women workers will not know how, if at all, radiation affects their reproductive health. Respondents who worked with computers, particularly those in their forties, complained of headaches and stress. Due to stress, they say that there is a tendency for them to eat too much. While the union has training sessions on health and safety aspects of computers and VDU, these sessions reach only a few workers, and the VDU hazards which affect mainly women workers are not priority issues. According to our interviews, management is reluctant to release workers for training sessions because of target outputs and deadlines.

Women employees are still viewed primarily as homemakers. While there are positive union demands in relation to pregnancy and day care centres, the specific training activities which have been recommended for women workers are in Home Economics and Domestic Science classes.

The union's failure to take up gender issues, and women's lack of interest in the union, reinforce one another. Several female union activists we interviewed said that women are scared to join the union. Apparently women are unaware, have too much work to do, and are afraid to appear in the forefront. Some workers feel that the union is not doing much, particularly for those at the lower levels. Women are poorly represented in union leadership positions – there were only four women out of a total of sixty-four members at the Executive Committee level. Moreover, according to a Malay woman union leader, it is difficult for women to join union activities, especially outside office hours, because of the need to find a babysitter and resistance from some husbands. Nevertheless, she is keen to start a women's wing to make the women realize their rights and act upon them. According to her, another problem in the union is the pro-Malay orientation of members, who vote according to ethnicity rather than on the quality and commitment of the candidate.

However unions are not the only means of dealing with office workers' concerns with computerization. Non-union initiatives can and have been taken by women's groups to bring the issues and problems to the fore. For example, an education and training programme regarding the social and health impact of computers has been initiated by the Women's Development Collective, a women's group based in the capital. A major conference was organized in November 1993, which brought about 170 office workers together to share their experiences and problems. This will be followed by a series of smaller workshop sessions for more intensive sharing and action. An increased awareness of current issues is emerging which, it is hoped, will lead to more networking among women office workers facing new technology.

CONCLUSION

Malaysia's aim to leapfrog to a developed status within the next three decades has resulted in IT being given significant prominence with the state taking a leadership role in the ongoing formulation of a national IT policy. This has been coupled, since 1984, with extensive privatization, which has also affected the telecommunications industry. By examining this industry it is possible to consider the gendered impact of IT on office workers in Malaysia and also to trace the class and ethnic dimensions of this process in relation to employment, skills and work organization.

IT has brought about changes in the employment pattern of office workers in the country, creating new opportunities in some occupations, while putting other jobs at risk. Overall, there has been a tremendous increase in IT-related jobs, especially at the professional and technical levels, due to the government's focus on hi-tech industry since the mid-1980s.

With the structural shift in the economy from an agricultural to an industrial base, and the present high economic growth, there has been a severe shortage of IT professionals. There are attempts by the government to rectify the shortage by introducing more computer and IT related courses at the tertiary level. It is interesting to note that more women are now enrolling in such courses, pointing to a possible gender balance among IT professionals in Malaysia in the near future.

The data also shows that some occupations have been much reduced or eliminated with the onslaught of the first phase of automation. Machine card punchers were inevitably made redundant with the introduction of modern computers. New jobs for data entry operators and computer professionals have been created. However, with the advent of more integrated systems, our case study suggests that the era of the data entry operator could be over. But it would be premature to predict their demise altogether; the increased flexibility of IT allows for decentralization in the preparation and data entry part of information processing. Several developing countries have benefited from the advent of telework, whereby data entry work has been internationally relocated to save labour costs in the developed countries (Pearson, 1991).

The evidence in the case study runs counter to the assumptions about the consequences of computerization at the office level which underlie both the pessimistic 'capital accumulation logic' approach and the technological euphoria which equates technology with wellbeing. The stage of socio-economic and political development within each society and the pre-existing division of labour are important mediators of how IT and its different phases are implemented. In these stages, IT has differential effects on employment, work organization and labour processes. In some cases, the fragmentation and rationalization of office bureaucracies exist already, and computerization makes use of and intensifies these processes. According to our empirical findings, Taylorization is usually, but not always, associated with the first phase of computer implementation. But in some cases there are no radical changes in work, and in others, previous fragmented tasks become integrated. Small work teams, with more personal control over one's work (despite centralization), have been made possible with the flexibility of microprocessor technology in the second phase of integrated systems.

Different categories of workers are affected differently. The combination of computerization and privatization in TELMAL has led to increased stress for the lower level staff, especially the data entry operators and telephone operators, whose work has been intensified with high quantitative targets. On the other hand, although clerks and secretaries have increased workloads, they would appear to have more control over their work, which has become more flexible with computerization.

Thus the second phase of computerization, with advanced integrated systems, could create the conditions for different ways of working, particularly in the clerical and middle-level occupations. These new ways of working (e.g. flexible team work, the happy family in the company) are, in part, recognized as corporate strategies in human resource management. But the skills and traits which these new work methods demand, such as communication skills and flexibility, are not readily recognized or rewarded.

The realization of improved working conditions depends on the negotiating power and the collective and political strength of different levels of workers. Given the hierarchical and patriarchal setup in TELMAL, devoted to 'service to business', the generally repressive labour policies, and the union leadership's pledge of industrial harmony, the struggle will be a long one. Non-union groups, such as women's groups, can also take up the demands of office workers and highlight their problems, particularly the health and safety concerns of the less skilled workers.

Employment for women office workers is also changing. Women are not being inevitably pushed into low-skill dead end jobs as a result of automation, as the argument that capital makes use of existing patriarchal relations has asserted. The trends are more diverse. On the one hand, it is true that the clerical workforce is slowly becoming feminized, and that lower level data entry operators are largely women, who work under highly stressed conditions. Women's position in the labour force is still secondary and ideologically constructed, and skill polarization by gender will continue to be common. On the other hand, in the Malaysian IT and telecommunications industry, more than in other technological fields, women are slowly making headway into middle level professional and management positions. Malaysian women seem to be taking advantage of the educational system, which is heavily promoting computer studies, although they still predominate in the software programming side while men are in the more lucrative fields such as electronics engineering and management. Moreover a gender-segmented labour market will ensure that decision-making positions and processes are male dominated, with male Malays in command in the public sector, co-existing with their male Chinese counter- parts in the private sector. Gender segregation, as well as stratification among women along class and ethnic lines, will probably continue in the Malaysian IT sector.

NOTES

1 The other four key technologies are automated manufacturing technology (AMT), advanced materials, biotechnology and electronics (Government of Malaysia, 1991: 203–204).

2 Malaysia is a multi-ethnic country comprising Malays and indigenous groups (55 per cent), known as *Bumiputra*, Chinese (34 per cent), Indians (10 per cent), and other ethnic groups (1 per cent). Political power is held by a multi-party coalition of communally-based parties dominated by the elites of each ethnic group, who use ethnicity to advance their own political and economic power in the country. The 1971 New Economic Policy provided for 'positive discrimination' for the *Bumiputras* as they were perceived to be economically backward compared to the other ethnic groups.

3 *The Star*, 12 August 1992.

4 This information was obtained from the Curriculum Development Centre, Computers in Education Unit, Ministry of Education, Malaysia.

5 *New Straits Times*, 7 September, 1992.

6 The survey covered 789 organizations. The shortfalls are expressed as percentages of the current staff levels in these fields.

7 These figures fall a little short of the number of IT personnel reported by the National Institute of Public Administration, INTAN. According to this report, out of 18,199 IT personnel in 1990, 64 per cent worked with corporate users in the private and public sector and 36 per cent were in the computer vendor industry (Yusof and Chan, 1991).

8 TELMAL is a fictitious name. The study was conducted in 1991 and 1992. A survey questionnaire was administered, using group interviews, with a total of 340 male and female respondents. These represented 30 per cent of office personnel at the headquarters who used computers at least two hours daily. Respondents ranged from data entry operators to executive employees. In addition, several respondents representing the various categories of staff were selected for in-depth interviews.

9 *New Straits Times*, 7 May 1992.

10 *New Straits Times*, 26 August 1992.

11 At the national level (1990) only 0.6 per cent of working women are in managerial positions, compared to about 3 per cent of working men (Government of Malaysia 1991). It augurs well for TELMAL that women are better represented at the management level.

12 The urban private sector is mainly dominated by non-Malays, although there have been ongoing efforts to redress this balance since the promulgation of the New Economic Policy in 1971. Urban centres have historically been opposition areas, and some analysts have seen this opposition as coming from the non-Malay, particularly Chinese, voters.

13 Pullman and Szymanski, 1988, of the Labor Institute in New York categorized clerical skills as either 'technical', 'interactive' or 'abstract'. Abstract skills are aspects dealing with accuracy, concentration, eye for detail, memory, and creativity. Technical skills deal with spelling, grammar, maths and formatting, while interactive skills are associated with communication, coordination of

work, tact, knowledge of the company, and explaining procedures. They point out that the compensation for clerical jobs, as 'women's jobs', tends to be determined in terms of routine tasks such as filing, keyboarding, or answering telephones. The other technical, abstract and interactive skills noted in Table 9.6 are important and necessary in performing computer-related jobs, but are underestimated as skills, and hence 'hidden or invisible'.

REFERENCES

Albin, Peter and Eileen Appelbaum (1988), 'The Computer Rationalization of Work: Implications for Women Workers', in Jenson, Jane *et al.* (eds), *Feminization of the Labour Force*, Oxford, Polity Press

Baran, Barbara and Suzanne Teegarden (1987), 'Women's Labor in the Office of the Future: A Case Study of the Insurance Company', in Lourdes Beneria and R. Catharine (eds), *Women, Households and the Economy*, New Brunswick, Rutgers University Press

Clement, Andrew (1991), 'Designing without Designers: More Hidden Skills in Office Computerization?', paper presented at the 4th conference on Women, Work and Computerization, 30 June – 2 July, Helsinki, Finland

Goodman, Sara Ellen (1985), 'Computerization and the Skill in Women's Work', in Agneta Olerup *et al.* (eds), *Women, Work and Computerization: Opportunities and Disadvantages*, Amsterdam, North Holland

Government of Malaysia (1991), *Sixth Malaysia Plan 1991–1995*, Kuala Lumpur, Government Printers

Greenbaum, Joan (1991), 'Participatory Design – the Head and Heart Revisited', paper presented at the 4th conference on Women, Work and Computerization, 30 June – 2 July, Helsinki, Finland

Lie, Merete and Bente Rasmussen (1985), 'Office Work and Skills', in Agneta Olerup *et al.* (eds), *Women, Work and Computerization: Opportunities and Disadvantages*, Amsterdam, North Holland

MNCC: Malaysian National Computer Confederation (n.d.), *Malaysian IT Survey 1989*, Selangor, Petaling Jaya

Ormos, Marta and Maya Blameble (1989), 'Strategies of Introduction of Office Auto- mation in Mixed and Traditionally Female Jobs within Two Work Units of the French Electricity and Gas Public Utility companies', in Kea Tijdens, *et al.* (eds), *Women, Work and Computerization: Forming New Alliances*, Amsterdam, North Holland

Pearson, Ruth (1991), 'Gender and New Technology for Women: New Work for Women?' paper presented at the International Workshop 'Women Organising in the Process of Industrialization', 15–26 April, The Hague, Netherlands

Pullman, C., and S. Szymanski (1988), 'The Impact of Office Technology on Clerical Worker Skills in the Banking, Insurance and Legal Industries in New York City: Implications for Training', in Kea Tijdens *et al.* (eds), *Women, Work and Computerization: Forming New Alliances*, Amsterdam, North Holland

Yusof, Johor, and Chan Yet Meng (1991), 'Status of Human Resource Develop- ment in Informatics in Malaysia', country paper represented at the Regional

Conference on Informatics (Information Technology) Human Resource Development, IIP, UNESCO, 2–4 July, Kuala Lumpur

10 Women in software programming
The experience of Brazil

Fatima Janine Gaio

INTRODUCTION

The extraordinary technical progress in microelectronics, coupled with the convergence of a diverse set of technologies, has favoured the pervasive diffusion of information technologies (ITs). As the neo-Schumpeterians have pointed out, such a process involves extensive structural changes, threatens previous economic, social and organizational paradigms with 'creative destruction', and heralds new ones. But this revolutionary process seems, so far, to have left women behind. The broad 'conventional' pattern of feminine employment has not been significantly altered. Women tend to be found clustered in low-skilled and low-paid jobs, and to be systematically excluded from the techno-scientific occupations. This picture may change in the future, at least in some areas of IT such as the production of software.

Software production, a core component of IT, is a labour-intensive, design- and science-based activity. It is an area in which both industrialized and developing economies could reap considerable economic benefits. The question addressed in this chapter is whether its growing commercial importance could create a window of opportunity for women, and so change the conventional pattern of women's employment in developing countries. The outcome will depend on the direction of movements in three dimensions: the participation of women in software activities; whether the employment offered in these activities, and particularly to women, suffers deskilling; and the level and nature of software activities on both the internal and external markets. The international competitiveness of the software and computer services industry plays an increasingly crucial role in developing countries, and thus has a significant influence on the total volume of employment which the industry can offer. The optimum out- come for women would be their increasing participation, at higher levels, in a skill-intensive and growing industry.

SOFTWARE AS A TECHNOLOGY AND ITS PRODUCTION PROCESS

This section will seek to relate recent changes in software production to changes in work organization, and consider the implications for job opportunities for women. The background here is the ongoing labour process debate around the question of whether the long-term trend in productive processes is in the direction of deskilling and job fragmentation. But there are a number of differences between software development and more conventional production systems, so that theories based on the latter may not provide an adequate framework for understanding the evolution of software production, and software-related occupations.

Software programming as a technology and occupation

Software production is a design-intensive process producing logical and non-material products whose core function is to incorporate coded knowledge and structural flexibility into products and processes. The idiosyncrasies which arise from the non-material nature of software are magnified at present because the industry, and the technology, have not yet matured.

Software can best be understood in the context of its evolutionary interdependence with user requirements and hardware.[1] The dynamic interplay of these three components has influenced the pace and direction of the generation and diffusion of IT-based systems, as well as generating a series of imbalances and bottlenecks. There have been exceptional improvements in the cost and performance of electronic components and hardware, due to a continuous flow of technological innovations. Software production, in contrast, has remained an essentially labour-intensive activity, based on intellectual skills. This evolutionary 'desynchronization' has been exacerbated by steep increases in the variety and complexity of software which is required.

In the 1970s there was growing apprehension that a 'software crisis' might hinder the diffusion of ITs. The 'crisis' was substantiated by a range of forecasts such as the reversal of the comparative cost relationship between hardware and software, with software being responsible for an increasing share of system costs;[2] a growing gap between the demand and supply of software products and services; and a scarcity of skilled labour.

The 1970s could be called a turning point in the development trajectory of software. Its recognition as a major bottleneck in the IT complex was paralleled by, and influenced, significant technological, economic and social changes. The technological evolution in hardware accelerated, with the advent of semiconductors and microprocessors, coupled with increasing integration and miniaturization of electronic components.[3] This made it possible, in the late 1970s, to launch microcomputers, creating a potential mass market. An independent economic sector developed, specializing in the development and selling of software, with packages (software products) as the major growth area. There was a growing managerial emphasis on controlling the software development process, together with a tendency to apply industrial scientific management principles to job fragmentation and deskilling.

The evolution of software as a computing occupation

From the 1980s on, as information technologies have become more central to business strategies, three broad trends have emerged. First, productivity and reliability in software production have continued to be constraints, and there has been increasing emphasis on the concept of software engineering. Second, there has been an increasing emphasis on the adequacy of emerging systems to meet the needs of users. Software development, and its evolution, have come to be seen as an interactive process in which both users and producers have significant roles. Third, there has been a growing shift to 'downsizing', i.e. to decentralize computer resources to user departments, and transfer applications from mainframes to microcomputers linked by telecommunications networks. The two latter trends, in particular, are bound to create major disruptions in organizations and to change the composition of the computing staff they require.

Despite these trends, most labour process analyses of software development work relate to mainframe computers. Since the emergence of centralized data processing installations, mainframes have been the focus of attention. These computers have the aura of complex high-tech, and the staff directly linked to them have had a high status. Complementary tasks, such as the operation of input and output devices, have been regarded as subsidiary activities which involved much lower skills and, therefore, are much more easily subject to scientific management practices. From the outset, data-entry has been seen as a clerical job with low educational requirements and skill levels, and thus as 'appropriate' for women (Braverman, 1974). Friedman (1986) has observed that the Braverman/ Kraft hypothesis of task fragmentation and deskilling does apply to data entry work. Data entry has been deskilled to the point of alienation, producing both physical and mental health hazards.

Although more 'flexible' management strategies have been adopted in computing, a hierarchic structure seems to remain (e.g. systems and applications analysts, analyst/programmers, programmers, computer operators, data preparation and data entry staff).[4] Women's participation is greatest at the bottom of this pyramid. Case studies by Soares (1989) in local firms in Brazil showed that women accounted for the major share of employment only in jobs related to data entry. In the largest firm studied, around 60 per cent of the data entry and data preparation staff were women. In another firm, women were responsible for 40 per cent of total computing jobs, but while 87 per cent of data entry employees were females, only 37 per cent of programmers and analysts were women. These findings appear to support the broad scenario outlined by Cockburn (1985), that the generation and diffusion of information technologies has not substantially altered the traditional association of women's employment with low skill and education requirements, low status and low paid work.

But there is also scattered evidence that some national software markets and areas of work may provide more conducive environments for women's employment, and should be interesting for future investigations.[5] For example, recently, software was evaluated as a very promising area, in India and in the USA, for females as professionals and managers.[6] In Brazil, from the late 1980s to the early 1990s, women have accounted for about 50 per cent of graduate degrees in computer science and mathematics, conventionally seen as predominantly male areas.[7]

The limitation of mainstream labour process theory, as applied to software development work, is that it has focused on some kinds of 'hard' technical knowledge, and so has found that automation and scientific management will lead to deskilling.[8] It has tended to overlook the 'soft' technical knowledge involved in areas such as the analysis and basic design of systems, the complex work of modelling a problem to be computerized, communications and interactions tasks, and keeping a software product in tune with the evolving environment it is supposed to reflect.

Evolving and expanding software requirements are bringing major changes for software development occupations. The emergence of analyst-programmers, already noted by Friedman and Greenbaum (1984) in the 1980s, not only entails a reversal of the Braverman/Kraft fragmentation hypothesis, it also points to reskilling of the labour force. The new occupational structure of development work entails different sets of skills, changing the content of programmers' and analysts' work and combining parts of them in new job descriptions. The analyst–programmers may be an indicator of new trends in the division of labour and job contents.

Analyst–programmers would be more closely linked to the technical 'know-how' of computing, being responsible for the detailed design of systems. A new category of professionals appears likely to emerge – the business or information analysts. Probably at the top of the hierarchy of development work, these will be senior staff who combine a deep knowledge of business with the technical know-how of computing. These professionals would be responsible for identifying strategic new applications of information technologies and specifying the systems requirements in close interaction with users. Their work could be called the phase of basic design, or the 'know-why'.

With the increase in more advanced applications, another new kind of professional is emerging in development work: 'specialists' with specific knowledge in the application fields being modelled.

THE SOFTWARE AND COMPUTER SERVICES SECTOR

This section provides a brief picture of international markets for software and computer services, and contrasts the Brazilian experience in the sector with the theoretical strategies for developing countries suggested by the current literature.[9] The question here is whether the total volume of employment which this industry offers to both men and women in a country such as Brazil can be maintained at significant levels. If it cannot, women's entrance to this high-status work will not have a significant effect on the overall profile of women's employment.

The international context

As observed by the OECD (1989), many of the existing interpretations of the software sector are based upon quantitative and simplified structural analyses which do not reflect the industry's intricate differentiation or dynamic nature. Quantitative analyses[10] have generally been applied to the relatively more mature 'computer services' segments, such as commercial electronic data processing (EDP) and general purpose computer systems.

Because there has not been any thorough understanding of the supply sector, there has been a tendency to associate the industry structure with the USA model, as an international benchmark. The USA is both the leading world market for computer services and the major software exporter. The USA is the most conducive market for producing standardized software products, due to its large internal market, closeness to sources of technical change in complementary technologies (e.g. computers, microelectronics and telecommunications), and tight labour markets. The local software and hardware producers, led by a small number of large firms, have played significant roles in the industry's success. The independent industry is active in various market segments, but their market share has been higher in packages for microcomputers.[11]

The OECD (1989: Table 2, pp. 24–25) has presented a broad picture of the world market for computer services and software. In 1987, it was estimated that the total revenues of the industry would amount to US\$ 78199.6 million (m), of which about 61 per cent would come from software (US\$ 47667.3m), with the USA, Japan, France, Germany and the UK accounting for around 77 per cent of these sums. The USA alone earned about 50 per cent of world revenues. The participation of newly industrializing economies was very small. Brazil, India, South Korea, Mexico, Singapore and Taiwan together represented only about 6.5 per cent of the world market (US\$ 5068.2m) and 5.4 per cent of the total software market (US\$ 2575.9m). Brazil was the most important country within this group, with a market of US\$ 4217.6m (83 per cent of this group) and software turnover of US\$ 2186.2m (about 85 per cent).

The literature regarding the computer services markets has often stressed software and software packages as a source of significant economic opportunities. However, it is debatable whether the USA phenomenon has been replicated even by other industrialized countries. As Correa (1989) noted, the national markets of both industrially advanced and newly industrializing economies are generally highly dependent on software imports, particularly in the segments of systems and utilities and applications tools. In cross-industry packages, trade is increasingly internationalized, and the few standard products traded in the internal markets come from foreign sources.

In the literature it is generally argued that software could be a point of entry to information technology for developing countries, due to its labour-intensive nature, relatively low capital requirements, and slow rhythm of technical change (see e.g. Ernst, 1981; Hoffman, 1982; O'Connor, 1985). Two main strategies have been recommended: to concentrate on the production of applications solutions, exploiting the 'natural' market reserve created by diversified market conditions, and to generate export opportunities by reaping the benefits of low-waged labour as a comparative advantage (UNIDO Secretariat, 1983; Kopetz, 1984; Narasimhan, 1984). The export-led strategy of India, since the 1980s, shows that there is room for international outsourcing. India's software exports have grown remarkably, and are expected to reach US\$ 350 m by 1993, but this is still a very small share of the world market revenues. Indian export activities have been based primarily on subcontracting programming and writing components for large systems designed abroad.[12] There are already indicators of the Indian experience being followed by countries such as Singapore, Taiwan and Russia.

The Brazilian experience[13]

Brazilian industrial development in general has been associated with Government intervention, under a broad 'import-substitution' policy. From the mid-1970s to 1990, Brazil pursued a policy of promoting an indigenous IT complex within its economy in an integrated manner. The strategy aimed at 'self-reliance' through fostering the accumulation of internal technological capabilities in combination with local entrepreneurship. This strategy proved to be too ambitious.

The policy measures were gradual, focusing on the supply side and favouring the hardware industry, while software activities were not assigned a high priority. Yet there was some early recognition of the importance of devising a specific policy for software (SCSS, 1981), and the promotion of an indigenous software industry was a goal. Particular emphasis was given to the production of packages for locally-manufactured mini and microcomputers.

Until the mid-1980s, the main policy instruments included a registry of computer programmes combined with Government procurement of local products; import control coupled with a refusal to accept any legal protection for intellectual property rights (IPRs); and making approval of manufacturing projects for microcomputers conditional on the use of indigenous operating systems. In addition, a three year diploma course in computer science was established at the university level, with a practical emphasis. The objective was to accelerate the education of skilled personnel for software development. It is not equivalent to a full degree course, which takes 5 years.

By 1987, the revenues of the computer industry as a whole amounted to US\$ 2,578m, and total employment to 30,947. Local hardware firms, manufacturing in the 'market reserve' segments of mini and microcomputers, were already responsible for around 53.4 per cent of this amount and for 76.2 per cent of the total labour employed in the industry. The indigenous microcomputer segment was characterized as the most dynamic in the industry (SEI, 1987; DEPIN, 1991). But local demand for software was still largely met by imports, particularly in the mainframe and microcomputer segments (SEI, 1986).[14] Some 90 per cent of software turnover was estimated to come from imports, channelled mainly through subsidiaries of multinational corporations (MNCs). Local private firms had 19.6 per cent (US\$ 450.3m) of the computer services market in 1987, and employed 26,388 people. The internal market for computer services does not appear to have been conducive to fostering local firms' activities, yet local services firms, with revenues amounting to less than one third of the revenues of the local computer industry, generated more employment than the computer industry.

Another important feature of the Brazilian computer services market is the strong presence of public firms, which mainly act as captive (i.e. 'in-house') data processing bureaux for Government institutions. The revenues of these firms rose from US$ 484.2m (26.9 per cent of the total market) in 1985 to US$ 789.9m (a 34.3 per cent share) in 1987. This was about twice the revenues of local private firms.

The policies which provided supply inducements for local computers in the domestic market also promoted the externalization of demand for software products and services, without creating any comparable conducive market for local software products. Imported packets continued to dominate the market. Effective control of software imports would in fact have jeopardized the expansion of the local hardware industry, particularly in the microcomputer segment, which was the actual centre of the Brazilian informatics policy. No clear rules for the internal market were adopted, and there was increasing internal and external political pressure for liberalization. The 1988 Software Law merely provided a legal framework for the *de facto* market liberalization which was already in place. Thus, in practical terms, software activities have never been the subject of effective 'infant industry' protection. Local firms operating in this sector have been exposed to international competition from the early stages.

The Brazilian case provides some empirical evidence as to the validity of the main software strategies being suggested for developing economies. First, Brazil does not provide any significant evidence to support the conventional theoretical view that economies endowed with low-waged skilled labour enjoy comparative advantages in software. On the contrary, in the early stages of the diffusion of information technologies, when cross-industry packages tend to predominate, the demand tends to be met through imports.

Second, in 1993 around 15 Brazilian software houses were exporting software, mainly to the USA and the European Union, either through joint ventures with foreign partners or by establishing subsidiaries abroad. The majority produced cross-industry packages for microcomputers, with total revenues estimated at US$ 20 to 30m.[15] Although this could be seen as a very modest result, these firms have proven to be internationally competitive, carving out niches in highly internationalized market segments. Following what Schware (1992) called a 'two-legged' model, they have struggled to accumulate technological and marketing capabilities in the internal market and have then moved to exports. Whether such a strategy will remain successful and can be expanded on is an interesting topic for future research.

Table 10.1 The local private sector for software and computer services in Brazil, 1985–1987: distribution of revenue, employment and number of firms by market segment

Main activity	Revenues US$ million		Average annual growth rate of employees		No. of firms
	1985	1987	%	1987	1987
Total	253.9	450.3	33.2	26,388.0	289
Software	22.6	35.0	24.4	1,949.0	91
% total	8.9	7.8		7.4	
Data processing	193.6	320.2	28.6	20,568.0	107
% total	76.3	71.1		78.0	
Training	2.0	8.0	100.0	429.0	17
% total	0.8	1.8		1.6	
Consultancy	4.6	16.5	89.4	1,292.0	41
% total	1.8	3.7		4.9	
Trade & maintenance of computers, peripherals and software	13.3	20.8	25.1	657.0	26
% total	5.2	4.6		2.5	
Other services (including systems integration)	17.8	49.8	67.3	1,493.0	7
% total	7.0	11.0		5.6	

Source: Elaborated from ASSESPRO (The Brazilian Association of Processing Services Firms) (1988).

Note: Data covers ASSESPRO members only.
In this survey, firms declared their revenue by main type of activity.

Finally, the evidence of Brazil confirms that applications solutions have been a major area of opportunity for local firms, but are not a sufficient base for promoting the dynamic growth of an independent software sector. The software industry has, in practice, remained stalled at an incipient stage. To a large extent, local opportunities in applications software have remained limited to the 'in-house' activities of IT users. The predominance of imported packages in the internal market has limited the scope for local production at a number of levels. Not only the existing distribution channels, but also users, have shown a marked preference for well-finished and well-known international brands, and a reluctance to interact with local producers of still amorphous products. Such interaction is necessary to the development of new applications. Thus imports also seriously undermine the future prospects of local information technology initiatives, by reducing both firm-level learning and the positive employment externalities for computing personnel.

AN ANALYSIS OF PATTERNS OF WOMEN'S EMPLOYMENT IN SOFTWARE ACTIVITIES

Supposing that there are relevant opportunities for software activities coupled with a competitive local software industry offering significant volumes of employment, and that it has not been deskilled to the level of clerical work, the next dimension to be considered is the current patterns and the future prospects for women's employment in the industry.

Women's employment has tended to be associated with low skill and education requirements. Information technologies, thus far at least, do not seem to have led to any substantial alteration in this pattern, but the 'soft' side of information technologies (in technological and economic terms) that software represents may well offer a 'window' of opportunities for women. At the moment, this window may be 'ajar', although women still face difficulties in building up their career paths, on both technical and managerial grounds.

This section will analyse the patterns of women's employment in software in Brazil, and their likely prospects in the future. It is based mainly on case studies of three large Brazilian firms, undertaken from mid-1992 to early 1993. Employment figures for computing personnel were gathered, and interviews were conducted using a semi-structured questionnaire. Practical difficulties in carrying out this kind of work in Brazil limited the type of data which could be gathered, and meant that the analysis is basically qualitative. Quantitative data is used to illustrate the issues examined. For more details, see the appendix to this chapter.

A profile of the Brazilian firms studied

Software activities are hard to define, atomized and highly heterogeneous at a number of levels, and the software production process is not yet well understood. The complexity grows if one considers also software-related occupations, which tend to be spread throughout the economy. The skills required in these occupations are changing, and change is accelerating as the diffusion of information technologies progresses.

In Brazil no aggregate statistics or previous systematic analyses covering the field are available. Moreover, in our empirical work, some firms, particularly private firms, refused to divulge information. The empirical work was mainly undertaken in three large state-owned companies. Generalizations to the Brazilian market as a whole should therefore be undertaken with caution.

Company ALPHA is a computer services company, with revenues of US$ 207m and 5,037 employees. Company GAMMA is similar but smaller, with revenues of US$ 40m and 1,697 employees. Both are public computer services companies, operating as captive bureaux for Government institutions. They work as 'conventional' data processing bureaux, with a centralized structure based on mainframes, operating mainly in a 'batch' mode. However firm ALPHA, in particular, is under increasing external pressure to diversify its services, with a strong emphasis on decentralizing computer resources, coupled with the development and implementation of more advanced verticalized applications, and on their adequacy to rapidly evolving user requirements.[16] BETA is a chemicals and petro-chemicals firm which is a very large information technology user. In 1991 it was the second largest employer in Brazil, with 70,000 employees. By national standards, its software activities and computing resources are remarkably decentralized.[17] It is a science based firm, with a strong commitment to technological self-reliance, within what could be termed an 'engineering' mentality.

As can be seen in Table 10.2, both ALPHA and GAMMA employ large numbers of workers at the operational level of data processing, and women account for a significant share of these jobs. In firm ALPHA, around 54 per cent (2,703) of all employees are computing staff, 78 per cent (2,115) of whom work at the operational level. About 52 per cent (1,100) of jobs at this level are held by women, representing around 79 per cent of their total employment as computing staff. Their share is even higher at the base of the operational pyramid, in data entry (DE), data preparation (DP) and as production control technicians (PCT). Around 56 per cent (1,000) of jobs in these categories in GAMMA are held by women. In GAMMA, 69 per cent (1,166) of all employees are computing staff, of which 67 per cent (785) work in electronic data processing (EDP) operations. Women account for around 47 per cent (371) of all EDP jobs, but their share is higher at the base of the operational pyramid, with 54 per cent (350) of the jobs in DE, DP and PCT. Approximately 76 per cent of all computing jobs held by women are in operations.

ALPHA employs 148 programmers, 375 application analysts and 65 systems analysts, to carry out its development work.[18] Women account for 32 per cent, 27 per cent and 15 per cent of these categories, respectively. GAMMA employs 28 EDP documenters, 55 programmers, 165 organization and methods analysts and 133 EDP analysts, of which 61 per cent, 35 per cent, 33 per cent and 23 per cent, respectively, are women.

Table 10.2 Educational requirements and numbers of operational and development (a) computing staff

Job Category	Education	Total	Female	Female %	Male
		FIRM ALPHA			
Data entry	I(b)	780	447	57	333
Data preparation	I	904	492	54	412
Production control technician	II(c)	115	61	53	54
Teleprocessor operator	II	19	6	32	13
Computer operator	II	238	89	37	149
Production analyst	III(d)	59	15	25	44
Computer programmer	**II/III(e)**	**148**	**47**	**32**	**101**
Application analyst	**III**	**375**	**100**	**27**	**275**
System analyst	**III**	**65**	**10**	**15**	**55**
Sub-total		2,703	1,267	47	1,436
		FIRM BETA			
Data entry	I	6	2	33	4
Computer operator	II	38	1	3	37
Computer programmer	**II**	**92**	**11**	**12**	**81**
EDP analyst	**III**	**358**	**67**	**19**	**291**
Sub-total		494	81	16	413
		FIRM GAMMA			
Data entry	I	307	193	63	114
Data preparation	I	271	126	46	145
Production control technician	II	76	31	41	45
Computer operator	II	105	19	18	86
Production analyst	III	26	2	8	24
EDP documenter	**II**	**28**	**17**	**61**	**11**
Computer programmer	**II**	**55**	**19**	**35**	**36**
O&M organizations & methods analyst	**III**	**165**	**54**	**33**	**111**
EDP analyst	**III**	**133**	**30**	**23**	**103**
Sub-total		1,166	491	42	675
Total		4,303	1,792	42	2,511

Source: Elaborated from data supplied in 1992 by firms ALPHA, BETA and GAMMA.
(a) Figures for development staff are printed in bold text
(b) Level I education repressents the first 8 years of general education (ages 7–15)
(c) Level II education is the subsequent 3 years of education (ages 16–18)
(d) Level III refers to tertiary graduates
(e) ALPHA requires programmers at the c level (its career top) to have a graduate degree. None of the firms said that they required analysts to have a degree in computer science, but they did require a degree plus complementary training in the computer science field.

For firm BETA, the figures in Table 10.2 refer only to computing staff located in the firm's headquarters. According to these figures, the composition of its computing staff is very different from ALPHA and GAMMA, with operational workers accounting for a negligible share of about 9 per cent (44) of total computing staff (494), and data entry being practically non-existent, whereas on the development side it has 92 programmers and 358 EDP analysts. The participation of women is even lower than in the two previous firms, at 12 per cent and 19 per cent, respectively, of operational and development jobs. According to data reported by Duarte Pinto (1993), the firm actually employs a total of 1,500 people in computer-related job categories, of which 326 were programmers and 562 were EDP analysts. This is only about 2 per cent of the corporation's total staff. There are 1,852 professionals located at the company's headquarters and holding graduate degrees in natural and applied sciences (e.g. geologists, geophysicists, chemists and engineers). It is striking that only 6 per cent of these, (111 jobs) are held by women, a much lower share than in computing occupations. At least in the short term, male dominance is likely to continue in software development work for such technical and scientific fields. The interviews conducted for this study, however, focused mainly on personnel involved with commercial data processing and mainframes.

Labour turnover in these firms tends to be very low, with internal labour markets. Permeability with external markets is also low, so that the opportunities for career progression inside the firm become a quite important issue. Although seniority within these firms may not be considered as a formal criterion for career promotion (or progression), it appeared to be quite relevant to the progression of computer-related occupations. Nonetheless, institutional rigidities could be observed, varying between firms and over time. There was some job mobility, not only within software development occupations, but also from the operational staff to development occupations. The latter movement was particularly visible in ALPHA and GAMMA, which have many operational employees.

The management of the production process corroborates the findings of Friedman (1986) and Friedman & Cornford (1989). At the operational level, scientific administration principles prevail, although the corresponding instruments (e.g. time and motion studies), are generally not implemented. At the level of development work, more 'flexible' managerial practices were observed, both in terms of organizational structures and mechanisms for staff control.

In contrasts to the 1970s' pattern of pools of programmers, separated from the analysts, most of the development work was organized in teams, specialized according to the type of product. This creates opportunities for master-apprentice, on-the-job learning and for job mobility. No standard structure was found for job categories, job titles or organizational roles in these firms, and job titles do not always reflect the actual job contents. For instance, in BETA and GAMMA, the broad title of EDP analysts covers staff working with both systems and applications software, although these were clearly conceived of as suboccupations, and were in fact located in different departments. The fusion between analysts and programmers, as observed by Friedman and Greenbaum (1984), is taking place although the two categories retain distinct titles.

As a senior EDP analyst at BETA remarked, the conventional wisdom or 'rule of thumb' has been that two programmers are required for every analyst. In these firms, however, there are many less programmers than analysts (see Table 10.2). In ALPHA there is one programmer for three analysts, in BETA the proportion was 1 to 2. To say the least, employment prospects for programmers are less than dynamic.

The subcontracting of computing activities has recently become a major issue for Brazilian user corporations. The effects will be felt primarily at the bottom of the operational pyramid, where women tend to be concentrated. For instance, in 1992 the data entry work which ALPHA subcontracts was estimated to require 1,029 workers per month, almost twice the stable labour force (565) actually working in this activity. The data preparation work which is outsourced was estimated to require 113 workers, which is only about 20 per cent of the stable labour force.

Thus unskilled and semi-skilled computing jobs are tending to be placed on a flexible and unstable contractual basis. This has negative implications not only for the nature of employment on the operational side, but also for job mobility from operational to development work. The less skilled tasks of software development may also be subject to the same tendency, as can be seen in Indian software exports (Schware, 1992).

These firms employ significant numbers of skilled computing staff. The opportunities for career advancement which they offer are essentially on internal labour markets. But these companies follow, in broad terms, one of the basic principles of scientific administration – the separation of conception and management from execution activities. Their organizations have hierarchic levels (e.g. managerial and supervisory positions), and the occupations are also split into levels with a pyramid structure. Although these companies offer some scope for job mobility, it is likely that these conventional and rather rigid organizational structures inhibit both the social and technical changes necessary for the diffusion of information technologies, as well as limiting the opportunities for women to progress in their careers.

The participation of women in software occupations

The occupational structure of development work is quite complex and job fluid, with considerable room for change and mobility. Development work seems to be affected by a combination of evolving skills requirements with informal social networks and high degrees of autonomy at the organizational level.

The evidence from these firms is that women's employment is concentrated at the base of the pyramid of computing jobs. Women in operational work tend to be found mainly in data entry, data preparation and as production control technicians. These jobs involve clerical-like tasks, with low skills and low education requirements. To use Cockburn's terminology, these jobs require the 'know what' kind of technical skills, with very few chances of career advancement. She also remarked that women generally tend to be reluctant to engage in technical careers:

> It does not spring from inadequacy or lack of interest but from a keen perception of the costs involved: isolation, discomfort, harassment and, often, wasted time and energy. . . . Technology and the relations of technical work have to change before most women will choose to engage with them.
>
> (Cockburn, 1985: p. 13)

The data shown in Tables 10.3 and 10.4, for firms ALPHA and BETA, does show that women are the 'occupational losers' in computing jobs. For instance, although experience and time in the company were said to be important criteria for promotion, women tend to stay longer in these firms and to concentrate in the lower levels of each job category, an indicator that their careers advance more slowly than those of men.

Women's career progression: rising to challenges

Although the statistical picture found in the case studies does not paint a rosy picture for women, the qualitative interviews with seventeen women working in software occupations may be grounds for a more optimistic perspective. In most cases they had found room for career progression, including moves from operational to development activities. Far from being reluctant, their professional attitudes were determined and competitive.

In spite of being in relatively disadvantageous positions, the vast majority of the women interviewed valued the job stability and fringe benefits such as subsidized medical assistance and children's schooling, as well as the rather flexible working hours of the occupation.

Table 10.3 Firm ALPHA, computing staff, distribution of job categories by sex and employment time

Job Category	Less than 3 years			3–5 years			More than 5 years		
	Female	% Female	Male	Female	% Female	Male	Famale	% Female	Male
Data entry	10	50	10	224	47	248	213	74	75
Data preparation	21	37	36	181	62	110	290	52	266
Production Control Technician	4	19	17	9	56	7	48	62	30
Teleprocessor operator	1	20	4	0	0	5	5	56	4
Computer operator A	0	0	10	18	41	26	66	44	83
Computer operator B	0	0	3	0	0	2	5	31	11
Computer operator C	0	0	2	0	0	0	0	0	11
Production analyst	5	45	6	1	17	5	8	20	33
Computer programmer A	9	27	24	11	42	15	6	46	7
Computer programmer B	4	19	17	6	33	12	9	53	8
Computer programmer C	0	0	3	0	0	12	2	33	4
Application analyst A	30	34	59	10	31	22	5	29	12
Application analyst B	6	24	19	10	31	22	6	35	11
Application analyst C	7	23	23	5	19	21	12	36	21
Application analyst D	1	8	12	5	15	28	4	14	25
System analyst A	1	14	6	2	29	5	2	18	9
System analyst B	1	50	1	1	17	5	1	17	5
System analyst C	1	17	5	0	0	2	0	0	7
System analyst D	0	0	0	0	0	5	1	17	5
Total	101	28	257	483	47	552	683	52	627

Source: Data supplied in 1992 by firm ALPHA

Table 10.4 Firm BETA, computing staff, distribution of job categories by sex and employment time

Job Category	4 Years			5–9 Years			10–14 Years			15–19 Years			20 Years		
	Female	% Female	Male	Female	% Female	Male	Female	% Female	Male	Female	% Female	Male	Female	% Female	Male
Data entry	0	0	0	0	0	0	0	0	1	2	40	3	0	0	0
Computer operator I	0	0	0	0	0	0	0	0	4	0	0	1	0	0	0
Computer operator II	0	0	5	0	0	4	1	50	1	0	0	5	0	0	17
Computer programmer I	0	0	0	0	0	3	0	0	1	0	0	0	0	0	0
Computer programmer II	0	0	1	6	13	39	2	14	12	3	38	5	0	0	20
EDP analyst I	9	22	32	21	24	67	2	50	2	0	0	2	0	0	0
EDP analyst II	2	50	2	12	29	30	3	18	14	1	14	6	1	11	8
EDP analyst III	0	0	1	1	33	2	3	19	13	4	9	43	7	18	31
EDP analyst IV	0	0	0	0	0	0	0	0	0	0	0	19	1	5	19
Total	11	21	41	40	22	145	11	19	48	10	11	84	9	9	95

Source: Elaborated from data supplied in 1992 by firm BETA

In contrast to Friedman's findings in the USA (Friedman, 1986), operational activities have served as a significant route for women entering computing occupations. Of the seventeen women interviewed, eight had taken this route to building up their career paths, albeit with great difficulty. As L.U., an EDP analyst at GAMMA who started in data preparation remarks, 'Either you join the company in a good position or you have to endure a lot of pain'.

The pioneers in the early 1960s had to face explicit prejudice. Three analysts at ALPHA, now in their mid to late fifties, had started as key punch operators (I.S. and M.L.) or in data preparation (A.M.). All have children and have raised their families as the sole 'breadwinners' while working, sometimes in two different places, and at the same time earned their university degrees through evening courses. In the mid 1960s they were offered a first opportunity to attend courses in computer programming and, at the same time, were explicitly discouraged from pursuing it. As I.S. puts it:

> When programming emerged in Brazil as a profession, it brought a pattern established abroad. Then, it was clearly set as male's work, whereas data entry jobs were regarded as appropriate for women. At that time, men working in the latter were also discriminated against. People often wondered whether they were gay or physically disabled.

A.M. also recalls her first experience with programming, quite illustrative of the kind of resistance these women had to endure:

> In my first chance to attend a programming course, the teacher asked me what the hell I was doing there. My stay was conditioned on remaining silent so as not to disturb my male colleagues. I was allowed to develop the final project. My programme was the last to be tested and the only one that worked with no problems. Then the teacher recognized that, in spite of being a woman, I was capable of programming, inviting me to undertake a more advanced course. For a woman to succeed, she had to work extra hard. I believe that when the labour market began to expand the prejudice against women diminished.

Contrary to Cockburn's hypothesis, women in Brazil have not been reluctant to follow these pioneers in pursuing computing careers. In fact most of them seem to have learned to play the game according to the males' rules, that is, to be assertive and to compete fiercely to get what they want. The professional behaviour of C.L., a senior EDP analyst at BETA, is illustrative of such an attitude. She joined the firm in 1980. Very early in her career she was chosen to be a project leader. For the last 6 years she has been a junior manager of development teams, now working with the development of systems to support managerial decision-making. C.L. is very assertive in defining her entrepreneurial attitude, 'Women who gain a bit of prominence are "phallic", that is, they compete aggressively like men. They are courageous, do not escape from conflict but, quite on the contrary, face it upfront.'

The division of work in the domestic sphere does not seem to have gone through any radical changes either. Ten of the women interviewed have been raising children. A few of them said they had delayed having children because they were afraid of being devalued professionally. Those who were married or had partners tended to classify them as 'very supportive', although the women continued to carry the main responsibility for house-work and childcare. Nevertheless, the vast majority of these women seem to cope very well with their professional and domestic lives. The sad side of these rather 'successful' stories is that, in many cases, the responsibility for 'rocking the cradle' is, in fact, taken over by other women working as full-time house servants, because men generally do not share these responsibilities.

Some of these women, either intuitively or consciously, are initiating changes in the hierarchic social relations at work. For instance, six out of the eight women interviewed with managerial experience had been adopting a participatory style, involving cooperative work and democratic relations. The initiative of L.U., an EDP analyst at GAMMA, is remarkable. She was assigned to supervise a group of data entry personnel at a client location. She encouraged them to work as a team and to take the decisions of how and when to carry out their tasks. L.U. notes that:

> People became highly motivated to work. Women, in particular, loved to participate in the decisions about their own work and the flexibility they got. Only one man did not adjust to the scheme. He was used to working individually and complained to the operational director at GAMMA headquarters. My experience is that women are more discrim-inated againt at the operational level than in software development work.

Beyond the mainframe: a future for women?

In contrast to the conventional labour process view, an important finding from my research was that, in both operational activities and the more 'noble' software development work, occupations have not been sex-typed. The only areas which seem to remain the realm of men are those in close contact with mainframes.

In the literature it is generally argued that the primary allegiance of computing staff has been to the technology itself, not the organizations that employ them. This appears to be quite applicable to personnel such as systems analysts, whose technical and social prestige have been supported mainly by the hardware manufacturers, which guarantee a stable environment for their career progression by producing a continuous flow of new generations of computers, within a stable framework of upwards compatibility (as pioneered by IBM in the 1960s).

A.L., an EDP analyst at BETA, who had worked for five years as a systems analyst in an end-user department, gives some evidence of the kind of environment that surrounds these hi-tech machines:

> I was assigned to give support to the operating system, very close to the machine, within a social climate permeated by machismo. Men think of themselves so highly, that they believe they are indispensable. The machine is at the centre, while users are looked down upon as rather 'dumb'. Besides being left behind, the work was not that attractive to me to the point of continuing to endure such a macho environment. I managed to be transferred to a group providing support to users, as soon as it was created in my department. This is a promising area: the future is one of increasing integration with users, which will alter the professional profile of software development labour.

Friedman identifies areas involving more communications, interface with users, and client support as likely to be conducive for women to develop their expertise. Although these areas have become central to software evolution since the 1980s, he notes that there could be a danger of segregating women in them, under the label of 'feminine-type' occupations. Despite the danger, this is a highly valued type of work and a very promising scenario for women. Interaction with users is not only a promising area for women, but also a core component of technical progress in software. In fact, user–producer interactions are central to the evolution of technologies, particularly, as Lundvall (1988) noted, in the case of rapidly changing and complex products. The quality of exchange, with the development of direct cooperation links based on mutual trust, is central. However only in the 1980s has this activity been brought to the fore in software, with increasing concern about the effectiveness of the systems being designed to users' needs. Brooks claimed that:

> The hardest single part of building a software system is deciding precisely what to build. No other part of the conceptual work is as difficult as establishing the detailed technical requirements, including all the

interfaces to people, to machines, and to other software systems. . . . Therefore, the most important function that the software builder performs for the client is the iterative extraction and refinement of the product requirements. For the truth is, the client does not know what he wants. . . . Complex software systems are, moreover, things that act, that move, that work. The dynamics of that action are hard to imagine. So in planning any software-design activity, it is necessary to allow for an extensive iteration between the client and the designer as part of the system definition.

(Brooks, 1987: p. 16)

A.C. and E.C., two senior EDP analysts at BETA, share a rather more radical view: users could even assume leadership of the process. As A.C., who integrates an experimental team of business analysts, asserts:

I believe that computing experts tend to keep a distance from users. In the process of identifying and specifying the systems' requirements of new applications, users should participate actively in the development team and, eventually, lead the process.

This is also the approach advocated by the users' support groups of BETA's Service of Informatics Resources in Rio. Their aim is to endow end-users with the technical capacity to be self-sufficient to develop their own applications. Implicit in this radical approach is the socialization of technical knowledge, which has potential to diminish the social power that computing experts have been able to concentrate in their hands in the past decades.

E.C., one of the leading figures in this way of thinking, notes that:

In many national meetings about the function of technical support to users, I observed a significant participation of women ahead of this process. We tend to have an ability to establish empathy, as a core element for generating relations based upon personal credibility and emotion.

CONCLUSION

To summarize, since the software crisis of the 1970s the industry has gone through far-reaching technical, economic and organizational changes. Work organization has evolved from the Tayloristic approach of the 1970s to a rather more flexible management style in the 1980s. However these changes have not been able to counter the continuing desynchronization of progress in hardware and software. The occupational structures in the industry remain fluid. The sexual division of labour in computing jobs does not seem to have crystallized, although women do tend to be clustered at the base of the hierarchic pyramid. Although they face difficulties in building their career paths, there seems to be room for upward mobility into more skilled occupations and development work. On the other hand, even in firms studied, which emphasize job stability, a trend towards diversifying work relations can already be foreseen. The growth in the outsourcing of less skilled activities, which are being turned into casual work, is likely to seriously jeopardize this window of career advancement for women.

With regard to software development work, at least in the short term, women may continue to have only a minor share of total employment. There are indications of gender polarization of the work, with men tending to be clustered closer to the machinery, where technical expertise associated with mainframes has been assigned a high social prestige. Small processor platforms (e.g. microcomputers, workstations) have so far had lower organizational prestige. These, and activities involving close interaction with users, seem to offer more conducive environments for women. Since the epoch of the powerful centralized mainframes is passing, and software is moving further from the machinery towards the modelling of problem-solving in close contact with users, women may well become core agents in the technical and social changes necessary for the further diffusion of information technologies. Whether this will have a significant effect on the overall profile of women's employment in developing countries will depend also on factors affecting the viability of indigenous software activities and, increasingly, deploying an internationally competitive software and computer services sector.

APPENDIX

Field work methodology

This appendix briefly describes the methodology followed in the empirical investigation of the employment opportunities for women in software development work.

Software is a complex subject in both technological and economic terms, and an analysis of software-related occupations is even more difficult. In Brazil, the scarcity of data is a critical issue. No aggregate statistics about the computer services and software sector are available, and software-related occupations are not even recorded in the official statistics. Moreover, these occupations tend to be spread throughout the economy.

Because of lack of generalized data, and limitations in time and resources to undertake an extensive survey, it was decided to carry out case studies in large Brazilian user companies. Three large public firms granted access to their employment data and gave permission for primary data gathering through qualitative interviews with women working as software development staff. All information was to be kept strictly confidential.

Table 10.5 Basic features of the women interviewed

Person	Job Title	Year of admission	Education degree
		Firm ALPHA	
SC	Application analyst D	1975	Economics, M.Sc. Computer Science
VM	Application analyst D	1975	Business Administration
IS	Application analyst D	1975	Business Administration
AM	Application analyst B	1975	Business Administration
ML	Application analyst B	1975	Diploma Computer Science
TC	Application analyst A	1981	Diploma Computer Science
MA	Application analyst D	1975	Business Administration
AP	Computer programmer C	1980	Mathematics
		Firm BETA	
AC	EDP analyst III	1975	Mathematics, M.Sc. Computer Science
EC	EDP analyst III	1975	Physics, M.Sc. Production Engineer
CL	EDP analyst III	1980	Telecommunications Engineer
VG	EDP analyst II	1968	Business Administration
AL	EDP analyst II	1978	Electric Engineer
KT	EDP analyst I	1984	Diploma Computer Science Business Administration
		Firm GAMMA	
EL	EDP documenter	1982	Computer Science
DE	Computer programmer	1981	Diploma Computer Science
LU	EDP analyst	n.a.	Economics

Note: EDP (electronic data processing) covers a broad range of job categories.

Seventeen women, all working in software-related activities, were interviewed using an open-ended questionnaire. Each interview lasted two to three hours. They were asked to approach the following subjects:

- To discuss their education and career history, at the technical and managerial levels.
- To express their opinions about segregation at work.
- To relate their difficulties and opportunities in relation to job mobility, internal and external to these companies.
- To discuss the relation between raising a family and following a professional career.

Some basic characteristics of the women interviewed are presented in Table 10.5. It is important to remark that ten of these women have been raising children, and that eight of them have had managerial experiences.

NOTES

1 For analyses of the software evolution which focus on technological and economic forces see, for instance, Valdez, 1988, who offers a detailed historical approach, and Gaio, 1990, working within a neo-Schumpeterian theoretical framework.

2 OECD, 1984, Annex 2, reproduces a series of these 'stylised' estimates of the reversal of hardware/software cost ratios. These estimates were very popular from the late 1970s to the early 1980s.

3 For an in-depth analysis of the evolution of electronics components see, for instance, Dosi, 1984.

4 The labour process literature tends to claim that, once the gendering of work has been established, it becomes a persistent pattern which is quiescently accepted as a 'natural' sexual division of labour (e.g. Davies, 1979; Milkman, 1987).

5 The available analyses of women's employment in computing occupations tend to focus on data entry work, where women have always predominated. Very little attention has been given to gender patterns in software development jobs. There is some evidence that women have had only a minor portion of these jobs, and some scattered comments in the existing literature.

6 In India, according to Mitter and Pearson, 1992: p. 23, 'There is no overt discrimination in the field of software programming. There is a general consensus among the management that women stand a better chance of receiving a position of seniority in this area than in other fields of science and technology.' In the USA, Johnson, 1990, remarked that a recent survey of 100 corporate human resource directors highlighted systems analysts, managers and programmer analysts as the most promising jobs for women in computing.

7 Although it was not possible to get aggregate data on the question, and course titles are not standardized, in 1989-1991 the proportion of computer science and mathematics graduate degrees awarded to women ranged from 40 to 50 per cent in three respected Brazilian universities.

8 Kraft, 1979, hypothesised that, whilst women pioneered programming as a profession, they were then systematically excluded until its job content had been substantially deskilled to resemble clerical tasks. The vast majority of labour process analyses until the late 1980s and early 1990s concentrated on software development for mainframes. In this field, at least, the validity of Kraft's hypothesis is at least debatable. Firstly, even if we admit that there has been some fragmentation and deskilling, software development remains a science-based and design-intensive activity, with much lower degrees of formalization than industrial production systems. Secondly, although women's participation in this activity remains minor, it is an important source of employment and offers a viable 'window' of opportunities for women to get access to the 'soft' side of technological competence.

9 This section draws heavily on Gaio, 1992.

10 For examples of this quantitative approach, see Katz, 1987, IDC-C&L, 1987 and OECD, 1989.

11 Although the software industry remains fragmented, there is a tendency for revenues to concentrate in a small number of firms, mainly due to a significant level of acquisitions and the remarkable growth rates shown by some cross-industry packages for microcomputers (Katz, 1987). Recently, in the USA, above-average growth rates (about 4 per cent per year) can also be observed in emerging segments such as educational and entertainment packages (the so-called 'edutainment') for the home personal computer market.

12 With regard to Indian software exports, 1987 and 1989 figures and 1993 world market estimates are derived from Schware, 1992, pp. 148, 143, and the 1993 estimates are from Gargan, 1993, p. 1. For detailed comparative analyses of the Indian and Brazilian experiences in software see, for instance, Mitter and Pearson, 1992 and Schware, 1992.

13 For studies of the evolution of the Brazilian informatics industry see, for example, Tapia, 1990, Evans, Frischtak and Tigre, 1991, Meyer-Stammer, 1992 and Schmitz and Cassiolato, 1992.

14 The import control scheme established in 1975 was restricted to transactions which involved remittance of payments, so that it had little impact on the intrafirm software transfers between local subsidiaries of MNCs and their parent companies. This was in fact the main channel of imports. In 1986, 74.5 per cent of the products registered in the Registry of Computer Programs were imported and traded by MNCs, while 24.9 per cent were locally developed products. Of the local products, 71.7 per cent were applications solutions.

15 For more details about the local firms exporting software, see Ponde, 1993.

16 For a detailed analysis of firm ALPHA, see Vasquez, 1993. The firm is linked to a federal Government institution, which is responsible for a significant part of the social services provided by the State. ALPHA provides computer services at the national level. In 1992, besides its headquarters in Rio, it had 22 regional data processing centres located in the main state capitals of Brazil. Historically, these regional centres have had very little autonomy, performing only the basic tasks of receiving the original documents from local users and the first phase of data entry.

   In 1988, ALPHA started a process of decentralizing its operational capacity, despite considerable resistance from its main office because of the loss of institutional power. In 1992, one of its main positive outcomes was the decentralization of technical support, creating a more conducive environment for closer interaction with local users (e.g. training, hardware installation and maintenance and local software development). Nevertheless, the company still has a largely centralized structure inherited from the 'epoch' of mainframes. The vast majority of their computing and development resources are still located in Rio, including three of its five UNISYS mainframes. In addition, the firm has around 2,000 general-purpose micros. Its data entry is based on about 840 micros. Although it is still processing in a batch mode, ALPHA has a comprehensive telecommunications infrastructure.

17 For a thorough study of the evolution of software in BETA, with an emphasis on the adoption of process innovations, see Duarte Pinto, 1993. The firm has 35 EDP centres spread around Brazil. Its processing capacity consists of 39 mainframes (26 IBM and 13 DEC), 60 superminis and 331 workstations. It has a significant telecommunications infrastructure, including 16 satellite circuits.

18 Software development is usually carried out by teams, in the following, somewhat simplified, phases: analysis of the problem being modelled for computerization, including user needs and constraints, as well as economic and technical feasibility studies; the specification of the system requirements; the design of the system and its components; implementation and testing; and maintenance. This work also involves the preparation of supporting documents such as user's manuals, installation instructions, and procedures for operational activities.

REFERENCES

ASSESPRO (1988), PERSSONA Survey, working paper, ASSESPRO, Rio de Janeiro

Braverman, H. (1974), *Labor and Monopoly Capital: The Degradation of Work in the Twentieth Century*, New York, Monthly Review Press

Brooks Jr, F.P. (1987), 'No Silver Bullet: Essence and Accidents of Software Engineering', *Computer*, April

Cockburn, C. (1985), *Machinery of Dominance – Women, Men and Technical Know-how*, London, Pluto Press

Correa, C.M. (1989), *The Legal Protection of Software – Implications for Latecomer Strategies in Newly Industrialising Economies (NIEs) and Middle-income Countries (MICs)*, working paper, Paris, OECD

Davies, M. (1979), 'Woman's Place is at the Typewriter: the Feminization of the Clerical Labour Force', in Z. Eisenstein (ed.) *Capital Patriarchy and the Case for Socialist Feminism*, London, Monthly Review Press

DEPIN (1991), *Panorama do Setor de Informatica*, series estatisticas, Brasilia, Vol. 1, No. 1, SCT

Dosi, G. (1984), *Technical Change and Industrial Transformation: the Theory and an Application to the Semiconductor Industry*, London, MacMillan

Duarte Pinto, P.E. (1993), *Um Estudo do Processo de Difusão de Engenharia de Software: o caso da PETROBRAS*, M.Sc. dissertation, Rio de Janeiro, COPPE/UFRJ

Ernst, D. (1981), *The Software Market Conditioning Factors and Possible Future Trends – an Analysis Undertaken from a Third World Perspective*, Vienna, UNIDO

Evans, P., Frischtak, C. and Tigre, P. (eds) (1991), *A Informatica Brasileira em Transicão: Politica Governamental e Tendencias Internacionais nos Anos 90*, Rio de Janeiro, IEI, UFRJ

Friedman, A.L. (1986), *Software Industry and Data Processing in the U.S.A.: Work Organisation and Employment Structure*, report for the Directorate-General for Employment, Social Affairs and Education, Bristol, Commission of the European Communities

Friedman, A.L. and Cornford, D.S. (1989), *Computer Systems Development: History Organisation and Implementation*, Chichester, Wiley & Sons

Friedman, A.L. and Greenbaum, J. (1984), 'Wanted: Renaissance People', *Datamation*, September

Gaio, F.J. (1990), *The Development of Computer Software Technological Capabilities – a Case Study of Brazil*, Ph.D. thesis, Brighton, Science Policy Research Unit, University of Sussex

Gaio, F.J. (1992), 'Software Strategies for Developing Countries: Lessons from the International and Brazilian experience', in H. Schmitz and J. Cassiolato (eds), *Hi-tech for Industrial Development: Lessons from the Brazilian Experience in Electronics and Automation*, London, Routledge

Gargan, E.A. (1993), 'India Booming as a Leader in Software for Computers', *New York Times*, 29 December

Hoffman, K. (1982), *Microelectronics and Industry in the Third World: Policy Issues and Research Priorities*, working paper, Brighton, SPRU, University of Sussex

IDC-C&L (1987), *Computer Services Industry 1986–1996 – a Decade of Opportunity*, working paper, London, Department of Trade and Industry

Johnson, M. (1990), 'Women under glass', *Computer World*, 3 December

Katz, R. (1987), *La Industria del Software en Estados Unidos: Structura y Comercializacion del Producto*, Buenos Aires, CALAI

Kopetz, H. (1984), *Guidelines for Software Production in Developing Countries*, Vienna, UNIDO

Kraft, P. (1979), 'The Industrialization of Computer Programming: From Programming to 'Software Production', in A. Zimbalist (ed.) *Case Studies on the Labor Process*, New York, Monthly Review Press

Lundvall, B.A. (1988), 'Innovation as an Interactive Process: from User–Producer Interaction to the National System of Innovation', in G. Dosi, *et al.* (eds) *Technical Change and Economic Theory*, London and New York, Pinter Publishers

Meyer-Stammer, J. (1992), 'The End of Brazil's Informatics Policy', *Science and Public Policy*, April

Milkman, R. (1987), *Gender at Work – The Dynamics of Job Segregation by Sex During World War II*, Chicago, University of Illinois Press

Mitter, S. and Pearson, R. (1992), *Global Information Processing: The Emergence of Software Services and Data Entry Jobs in Selected Developing Countries*, working paper, Geneva, ILO

Narasimhan, R. (1984), *Guidelines for Software Development in Developing Countries*, IS 439, Vienna, UNIDO

O'Connor, D.C. (1985), 'The Computer Industry in the Third World: Some Policy Options and Constraints', *World Development*, Vol. 13, No. 3, Elmsford, NY

OECD (1984), *Software: A New Industry*, working paper, No. 17, Paris, OECD

OECD (1989), *The Internationalisation of Software and Computer Services*, No. 17, Paris, OECD

Ponde, J.L. (1993), *Competitividade da Industria de Software*, working paper, Campinas, NEIT/IE/UNICAMP

Schmitz, H. and Cassiolato, J. (1992) (eds), *Hi-tech for Industrial Development – Lessons from the Brazilian Experience in Electronics and Automation*, London, Routledge

Schware, R. (1992), 'Software Industry Strategies for Developing Countries: A "Walking on Two Legs" Proposition', *World Development*, Vol. 20, No.2, Elmsford, NY

SCSS (1981), *Relatorio da Comissão Especial de Software e Servicos*, Brasilia, SEI

SEI (1986), *Diagnostico do Mercado de Software no Pais*, working paper, Brasilia, SEI

SEI (1987), *Panorama do Setor de Informatica*, special edition, Vol. 7, No. 16, Brasilia, SEI

Soares, A. dos S. (1989), *A Organização do Trabalho Informatico*, MBA dissertation, Sao Paulo, PUC-S.P

Tapia, J.R.B. (1990), 'Protecionismo ou Integração Competitiva? Os Caminhos da Politica de Informatica Brasileira para os Anos Noventa', in *Table Ronde Internationale Innovations Technologiques et Mutations Industrielles en Amerique Latine: Argentina, Brasil, Mexico e Venezuela*, Paris, 12-15 December

Tierney, M. (1991), *The Formation and Fragmentation of Computing as an Occupation: a Review of Shifting Expertise*, Edinburgh PICT working paper No. 25, Edinburgh, Research Centre for Social Sciences, University of Edinburgh

UNIDO Secretariat (1983), *Problems of Software in Developing Countries*, Vienna, UNIDO

Valdez, M.E.P. (1988), *A Gift from Pandora's Box: The Software Crisis*, Ph.D. thesis, Edinburgh, University of Edinburgh

Vasquez, C.R. (1993), *Evolução da Produção de Software: Novas Ocupações, Oportunidades de Emprego e o Trabalho da Mulher (Estudo do Caso DATAPREV)*, M.Sc. dissertation, Rio de Janeiro, COPPE/UFRJ

11 Something old, something new, something borrowed ... the electronics industry in Calcutta

Nirmala Banerjee

INTRODUCTION

The background

In the 1960s, when the idea of using computers in economic activities was first floated in India, there was a wave of protest from trade unions and political parties who feared the impact of automation on future employment prospects. By the 1990s, computers had been partially accepted in some major service industries, particularly the communications industry, and to some extent in banking and financial services. However because these had also been some of the fastest growing sectors of the Indian economy, employment there continued to grow in spite of the technological changes. The period since the 1960s has also seen the government beginning to emphasize the minimization of employment discrimination against women, at least in the public sector. Since most of the growth industries mentioned above were under public management, women's employment in those industries grew faster than in other sections of the economy. It has therefore been easy to conclude that, as in most other countries, the deploy- ment of electronic technology has on the whole been 'gender friendly'.

In the 1990s, Indian policy makers have somewhat belatedly awakened to the growth potential of electronic goods manufacturing, and the potential uses of computers in other manufacturing industries. Between 1982 and 1992, (the period covered by the VIth and VIIth Indian plans), the value of output of the electronics manufacturing industry grew at about 30 per cent per annum. Even so, India produces less than 1 per cent of the world's production of over US$750 billion worth of electronic goods (Planning Commission, 1992: para 5.18.1: p. 116).

The Indian industry is dominated by consumer electronics, especially television sets, whose import content remains very high. In other branches, particularly in controls and instrumentation, India has created a considerable capacity for the manufacture of hardware, but utilization remains low because of the lack of capabilities in systems designing. Another fast-growing section of the industry is software production, mainly for export markets. The eighth plan noted that this industry had only touched on its true potential because of the limited geographical coverage by quick and easy communications facilities (ibid.: p. 117). It has often been observed that, compared to the size of India's national product and its general industrial development, the Indian electronics industry is still a long way away from realizing its full potential.

Although policy makers are not very optimistic about any immediate dramatic improvement in this situation, they agree that even at its current rate of growth, the industry is likely to generate a substantial number of jobs in the near future. Estimates vary widely: a recent well-researched study by the Institute of Applied Manpower Research (IAMR) under the sponsorship of the Department of Electronics of the Government of India estimated that between 1992-1997, there would be 177,000 new jobs in electronics manufacturing alone.[1] These estimates probably erred on the cautious side. At the other extreme were the estimates printed in the economic press in 1991, when the industry was given a boost through a few concessions announced in the central budget. Their somewhat euphoric predictions indicated that, over the following five years, the industry and its secondary links could generate as many as 2 to 2.5 million additional jobs.[2] Even if one discounts this euphoria, the lower estimates of the IAMR still compare well with the annual additions to registered Indian manufacturing employment (CSO, 1991, Statement I: p. 8).

In the past, women have claimed about 30 per cent to 40 per cent of additional manufacturing employment in the Indian electronics industry (Sen and Gulati, 1987: p. 13; Piore, 1991, Table 4: p. 204). If this trend continues, even the IAMR estimates would mean that the total registered factory employment of women would increase by at least 25 per cent (CSO, 1991). Thus even if Indian women may not be doing as well in these industries as their counterparts in many of the newly industrialized Asian countries, (ILO – ARTEP, 1990, Table 5.9: pp. 81–82),[3] they do have a special interest in the further development and spread of the technology in this country.

Objectives of the study

At this juncture there are uncertainties not only about the likely size of the additional employment in this field in India, but also about the nature of those jobs, the kind of labour that would be required for them, and the prospects of it being available and actually drawn from among women.

In the past, changes brought about by the new technologies in the worldwide employment scenario were very much in the pattern posited by Braverman (1974). Skilled jobs, mainly the jobs of men in the manufacturing industries of developed countries, were depleted through automation. On the other hand there was an expansion of low-skilled jobs particularly in the manufacture of electronic components – especially the microchip – where untrained young women in several developing countries had an advantage. Microelectronic technology itself was in a state of rapid transition, and its capacity for industrial use was not fully appreciated. Producers of electronic equipment had therefore been unwilling to invest in large capital-intensive plants and had preferred to use labour-intensive operations located in countries where cheap, docile, and therefore mainly female, labour was readily available. India missed out on these earlier opportunities because of the unwillingness of the then government to accommodate large multinationals on terms comparable to those offered by competing countries. The scale of operations and the pace of technological changes have now altered sufficiently to make it profitable for large producers to introduce a degree of automation in these industries. In a recent interview in India, Apple International's business manager for South Asia said that, 'There are no more lines of young women dropping components into boards. Labour content in computers is dropping dramatically.'[4]

On the other hand, use of information technology enormously increases industrial efficiency through its capacities to link distant markets, economize on inputs and inventories and streamline product designing. It has played a major role in the worldwide expansion, over the last two decades, in the output and employment of many manufacturing and service industries (James, 1985; Sayer, 1986). In several developing countries which participated in this boom, women provided the major share of the additional labour (ESCAP, 1987). Again, largely because of its governmental policies, India did not participate in these developments in a major way (Bagchi and Banerjee, 1986). But now India is rapidly shifting towards a more open economy, and the question is whether Indian women will get similar opportunities in the expanding industrial sector.

The potential created by the enormous flexibility of the microelectronic technologies and of machines embodying them opens up another vista of employment opportunities which has not been fully appreciated in India. Since the same equipment can be used for a large variety of designs and production processes, producers can switch between different designs as well as scales of operations without a significant loss of efficiency. They are therefore in a position to serve large, diversified and sensitive markets without significantly adding to their unit costs. For this process to work, however, it is imperative that the labour working on those machines is educated in, and at ease with, the technology, and is also well informed about market trends for the final products. Moreover, for a smooth transition from one product or process to another, the workers need to work in close cooperation with the management. In other words, far from being mindless assemblers, the workers need to feel an active partnership in the production, and indeed be a kind of artisan, using both their own skills and their creativity (Piore and Sabel, 1984).

In the literature regarding the impact of these technologies on labour processes, the trends of deskilling and feminization of employment, on the one hand, and the creation of artisan-type jobs on the other hand, have been widely noted. But they have usually been regarded as consecutive steps in a universal and uniform process in which the specific location of a given economy is considered to be a function of its level of development. One comes across scholars suggesting that experiments such as that of 'Little Italy' are easily reproducible in India, now that the appropriate machinery is locally available (Sanyal, 1992).

However, as several recent studies have pointed out, there have been marked differences in the impact on labour processes of these new technologies, even between countries at apparently similar stages of development (Gordon, 1988; Lauridsen, 1991). It has also been pointed out that the pace and form of utilization of available technologies are crucially dependent on the institutional background of a given economy (Freeman and Perez, 1988) and that one can seriously question how far the experiences of one country can be reproduced in another with a different set of institutions (Belussi, 1991).

This study explores the nature of the jobs that are being created in microelectronics in Calcutta in the 1990s. Its thrust is to analyse the economic as well as the institutional factors determining the actual course of events.

The study is confined to a few units of Calcutta which produce the following products:

1 black and white and colour television sets;
2 electronic micromotors; and
3 software.

Regional characteristics

Before discussing these case studies, it is necessary to point out some basic characteristics of this region. First, Calcutta has a large pool of educated persons including a substantial number of computer experts. The local industry has, however, not been able to use them to any great extent, and many of them have looked for jobs abroad. At the same time, as will be discussed later, facilities for basic training in computer languages and usage are not very good in this region.

Second, in Indian manufacturing generally, and particularly in Calcutta, there is a long tradition of production work being farmed out to ancillaries and subcontractors. Much of the work is done by self-employed persons through the mediation of these contractors and middlemen (Bose, 1978; Banerjee, 1988). The system is sustained by the high unemployment and underemployment rate among the many illiterate and semiliterate workers in the region. Studies of Calcutta's economy indicate that the city attracts workers from a rural hinterland with a radius of over 150 kilometres, which includes parts of Bangladesh (State Planning Board, 1991: supplementary Vol. 1, maps 4 & 5).

Third, the Indian electronic industry has not made any headway in international markets, but it has a large domestic market, thanks mainly to India's numerically large middle class. Also, in the last two decades there has been a marked increase in the average proportion of incomes spent on non-food items in both rural and urban India. Within that group, durable consumer goods claim only a small share, but this share has expanded considerably over the years. Although West Bengal, including Calcutta, is still below the national average, the increase in its figures is of an equally large order (see Table 11.1).

Lastly, perhaps more than other comparable regions within India, Calcutta

Table 11.1 Percentage share of non-food items and of durable goods in per capita consumer expenditure, all India and West Bengal, rural and urban

	1972–73		1987–88	
Items	*India*	*W. Bengal*	*India*	*W. Bengal*
Total non-food				
Rural	27.2	22.6	36.2	29.0
Urban	35.2	35.8	44.1	42.4
Durable goods				
Rural	2.1	1.1	3.6	2.5
Urban	2.2	1.1	4.2	2.1

Source: Sarvekshana, January 1979 and July–September 1991

suffers from several crucial infrastructural bottlenecks. Producers here are not assured of an uninterrupted power supply. The communications system leaves much to be desired. Small industrialists complain about difficulties in obtaining credit. These factors have had an impact on the way industries here are organized and on the pace of their adoption of new technologies.

Methodology

A significant section of the electronics-based manufacturing industry in this region is in the public sector. Units under the umbrella of WEBEL (West Bengal Electronics Development Corporation) are yet to run on proper commercial lines. In the private sector there are also too few units for a sample study. This analysis was therefore based on detailed interviews with, first, the chairperson of WEBEL, and then through the introductions provided by him, with the entrepreneurs, managers and some workers of several firms in the selected industries.

THE CONSUMER ELECTRONICS SECTOR

Three registered manufacturers

For manufacturing television sets, public policy has long favoured either semi-government or private medium-size and small firms. There are many firms manufacturing black and white as well as colour television sets, cassette players and two-in-ones (a transistor and a cassette deck in one unit) in the Calcutta region, though not all of them have been continuously in production. For this study, three firms were examined, of which one was medium-size and the others were small enterprises. Later, following leads which they provided, some non-registered producers of black and white televisions were also examined.

The medium-size registered firm was able to produce around 200 colour and 1,000 black and white televisions per month. It had a fixed investment of around Rs 20 million and a workforce (including management, office and sales staff) of 150. It had started well, with financial support from semi-government financial institutions at less than market rates of interest. It had also acquired a good reputation for the quality of its products. However, for the last year or more, it had been closed because of mounting losses.

The smaller two firms were each able to produce around 200 black and white 14-inch television sets per month under their own brand names. Each had started with an initial fixed investment of approximately Rs 2.5 to 3.0

million, raised under public schemes for assistance to small entrepreneurs. At their peak production each had had a workforce of around 50, but lately both had been in financial difficulties, and with unsold stocks mounting they had drastically cut down on their production and retrenched some of the workers.

In spite of the differences in sizes, the three firms were all basically assembly plants: over 70 per cent of the value of the final products consisted of costs of intermediate goods: these were imported either from abroad or from other parts of India (this included the case to house the set).

In all three units, around two-thirds of the workforce were women with secondary education, but none of them had any formal technical training. The men in production work were generally less educated than the women. The white collar workers were all graduates, and some had technical qualifications. Monthly earnings of the workers ranged from Rs 1,000 to Rs 1,200 for the women and Rs 1,500 to Rs 2,500 for the men, depending on the level of skills and experience. The employers especially mentioned various measures, such as regular salary grades and holidays, which they had taken to build up a modern, stable workforce.

The reasons given by the entrepreneurs of all three units for their poor performances were twofold. First, the demand projections made for the television industry by the government (Government of India, 1984) had been highly misleading. On the basis of experience in the developed countries, the latter had assumed that each household would replace its television set after five years. In practice, almost all households had continued to use theirs for ten years or more. Second, they complained that in spite of repeated representations from the industry, the state government continued to levy sales tax on the component parts at a rate way above that of other regions producing similar units within India. This meant that West Bengali products could not compete with those coming from other regions, even after the latter had paid transport costs and entry taxes. In West Bengal the minimum wages fixed for the engineering industry were also higher than those in Kerala and Uttar Pradesh, which were the two main competitors of West Bengal in this industry.

The illicit units

The main threat for these units however appeared to originate elsewhere, and though the registered units knew about it, they were perhaps not aware of its full magnitude. The market for smaller black and white televisions was being flooded with sets made by unlicensed or private units run on 'cottage' or 'sweatshop' lines. The larger illicit units were owned by television parts dealers, who sold parts imported under licence as well as those smuggled in from Nepal or Bangladesh. The television sets were assembled in the back rooms of the dealers' shops. Most of their workers were unskilled women, working under the supervision of a few semi-skilled workers who had themselves learned the work by rote in some registered television plant. The women were paid piece rates, earning around Rs 550 to Rs 750 per month. The supervisors earned around Rs 1,500; they were also the sales staff. These television sets usually came complete with some well-known brand name.

The competitive advantage of the unregistered units came from several sources: they could avoid sales taxes on the components by utilizing smuggled or cannibalized parts or by fudging their accounts. There were little or no overheads. The average wage rates of all workers were significantly below those of their counterparts in the registered units. Therefore their prices at the time of our enquiry were as low as Rs 1,400 per set, while the registered units could not bring down their prices for a comparable set below Rs 2,000. As a result, the products of the unregistered units were taking over the low-priced end of the market in rural and semi-urban areas around Calcutta.

These dealer-made sets were definitely of an inferior quality, since the makers had neither the equipment nor the expertise for quality control. They nevertheless found a ready market, partly because of the significant price advantage and partly because they were being pushed in a wide market by the vast army of repair workers, who visited the dealers to buy parts for local repairs. These mechanics often persuaded their neighbours and acquaintances to buy the cheaper sets through them, by giving some kind of a guarantee of quick service in case of a breakdown. For this they got some commission from the dealers and also a lot of poorly paid but frequent repair orders. Occasionally the mechanics would themselves produce a similar unit on their own from cannibalized parts.

Part of this illicit production was going to meet the growing dowry demands, which had increasingly come to include televisions in the list of essential gifts at the time of weddings. The hard-pressed parents of the brides were often relieved to get a cheaper product and were not too concerned about its quality.

The look-alike problem

Competition from look-alikes, which are locally known as number two products, has hit the local production of a large variety of electric, electronic and mechanical products including electrical plugs, switches, light bulbs, electrical fans, radios, cassette players, automobile parts, sanitary fittings and so on. This development is engendered mainly by the character of the labour and capital that are to be found in this region. The region has a large pool of semi-skilled informally trained workers who learn the basics of all kinds of skills by observing older workers, whom they assist from childhood. They thus become experts at making running repairs to almost any machine. They are however incapable of building up their own legitimate production units because they lack access to adequate technical know-how and also to the social connections and confidence that appear to be necessary for raising capital and getting licences, permits etc.

In addition, as the traditional hub of trading activity in eastern India, Calcutta's credit scenario is dominated by traders. The informal credit market that runs in parallel is probably almost as large if not larger than the formal one; it specializes in providing short-term, unsecured, and extremely expensive credit (the interest rate can be as high as 4 per cent to 9 per cent per month).[5] This credit is used mainly for trading activities, but can also be diverted for other purposes with similar credit requirements. These highly volatile but readily-available credit facilities encourage the establishment of any legitimate or illegitimate productive activity, provided it requires little fixed capital, has a low gestation period and a quick turnover. The parts dealers with their own retail outlets appeared to fill this bill ideally. They could tailor their production to fit the demand and not build up unnecessary inventories or other overheads. Since their production was in any case illegal and likely to be banned at any time, the producers were themselves less interested in building up a steady clientele than in a quick sale. Quality was not a consideration for them.

For the licensed units, the fact that the cost of intermediate goods was a large proportion of the final cost of their product meant that they had little scope for improving the cost efficiency of their operations. Nor could they reduce their per unit overheads by increasing the scale of their operations, because they could not get a toe-hold in the faster-growing market of first-time rural or semi-urban buyers. Moreover, the link between the unlicensed producers, parts buyers and repair mechanics cum local sellers provided the customers with a cheap and regular servicing facility which the more distant licensed producers were in no position to offer.

The result is that the consumer electronics industry in the region has remained in limbo. The technically qualified producers with licensed units are unable to develop the potential of the industry because they have failed to make a mark on the newly expanding markets. On the other hand, the dealer–producers know that theirs is strictly a fly-by-night business, and they have no intention to organize it better. Therefore, in the new liberalized economic regime of India, the local industry is under serious threat from competition from large-scale, modern and efficient units from other areas.

Women workers

In the illicit units, employers were wary of any outside interference from unions. They therefore hired women of their own communities (two of the dealers were Muslims) and their own localities, or others who had been strongly recommended by some reliable mechanics. These women usually had no more than primary education. The employers tried to keep them confined to specific tasks and gave them as little information about the business as possible. They also tried to create a divide between the men and the women by treating the men on a somewhat better footing.

Nevertheless, because the operations were so crowded and small, the women had come to know almost all the aspects. They had become familiar with the men's skills and felt confident that they too could mend a television set or even assemble a complete one. In fact, though they were originally from considerably inferior backgrounds than the women working in the registered units, they had become much more sure of themselves. The few women from the registered units that we met had been laid off on several occasions: they had quietly sat at home waiting to be recalled. The women from the unregistered units knew that their jobs were temporary, and they were constantly on the lookout for some other opportunities.

The problem was their lack of systematic training. Although most of the men mechanics shared this handicap, many had done some kind of an apprenticeship with senior mechanics or repairmen in their localities. So they were more confident about the work and could also inspire more confidence among their customers. For the women to be able to convince customers of their skills, some formal qualifications were necessary. The ones we met repeatedly asked us if we knew of any courses they could take up.

There is however a serious lack of training facilities in this region. According to the report prepared for the Eastern Regional Committee of the All India Council for Technical Education, (1992: pp. 42–69), in the whole of West Bengal there were only 53 places for boys and 45 places for girls in polytechnics which gave a diploma in electronic maintenance and repairs. The entrance requirement for these courses was school graduation with 10 years of schooling. Several private institutions do offer shorter courses, but they are more expensive and have similar requirements.

ELECTRONICS COMPONENTS PRODUCTION

From the seedy backyard sweatshops producing inferior quality television sets, the focus now shifts to a modern, well-designed factory situated about forty kilometres from the city of Calcutta. The enterprise was established in 1989 by a group of local engineers in collaboration with a Japanese firm. It produces electronic micromotors, an item which had hitherto been marketed in India entirely through imports. Of the initial capital investment of around Rs 180 million, the Japanese firm had put up one half and the other half had been obtained by raising loans from several Indian financial institutions. The firm has an assured market, because the Japanese had a contract to take half of its production and Indian demand for the product is growing fast.[6] Although the price of the Indian product was higher than the price at which Taiwanese manufacturers had been dumping the item in the Indian market, the Indian product was considered to be better because it had been designed for Indian conditions. Moreover, after the devaluation of the rupee in June 1991, the entrepreneurs had devised local equivalents for most parts. Whereas nineteen of the thirty-seven parts making up a micromotor were imported previously, now only six had to be imported. The local parts were also said to be better designed and sturdier. The firm had the capacity to produce 5,000 items per shift, but previously, uncertainties in the supply of imported parts had kept production down to only 3,000 per day. The management was confident that, with local parts, they would find a market for all their produce even if the plant was run at full capacity for three shifts a day.

Use of ancillaries

Although the owner/entrepreneurs of the micromotor plant had been closely involved in designing the indigenous parts to replace the imported ones, orders for the production of the parts were being farmed out to several metal and polyurethane fabricating units around Calcutta. I had a chance to visit a few of those ancillary units. Most used standard equipment and the bulk of their work consisted of filling the orders of the micromotor plant. However, managers of the latter unit were quite firm in their resolve not to integrate this fabrication work into their own plant and management. Although they admitted that the use of these ancillary firms might occasionally create quality control problems, or supply bottlenecks if they expanded the scale of their own operations, they felt that integrating the two kinds of operations would increase the cost of the parts. The ancillaries used skilled workers but their wage rates were below those paid by the micromotor plant. And in any case the characters of the two workforces were quite distinct: bringing them together under one management could only lead to labour unrest in the coming years.

An ikebana in Calcutta soil

More important, the micromotor plant had been organized mainly on the Japanese pattern of minimizing inventories of inputs and intermediate goods. If the plant were to start fabricating parts, it would be forced to build up stocks of raw materials and other inputs, because Calcutta's channels of supply are notoriously unreliable. By using several ancillary units for each part, the micromotor plant was hedging its bets and passing on these problems of getting inputs on time to the ancillary units.

The workforce of the micromotor plant was indeed distinctly different from the average manufacturing workforce in this region. Of the 110 workers, nearly half, including one technical manager, were women. In a politically volatile area with traditions of an aggressive labour force, the managers had managed to avoid confrontations by adhering to a strict policy of hiring only local youths. Interestingly, though the plant was located in rural surroundings, there had been no dearth of young people with at least eight to ten years of schooling. In the production of micro-motors, young girls are given a preference everywhere because they are said to be biologically more suited to detect a certain sound that is emitted at one stage of production. The managers had looked for and readily found young unmarried women who had all had at least twelve years of schooling. However they had been obliged to hire an equal number of men, even though the average level of education of the men was three to four years lower. The less educated workers were given six months' of initial training, and the others three months. This training had familiarized all of them with the basic theoretical principles involved in the operation and with the various tasks of production. It had also explained to the workers the potential uses of the product and the nature of the market for them.

It was obvious that all the workers were fully familiar with the entire work process and there was no attempt in the plant to segregate or grade them. The salaries of all the workers varied within a narrow range between Rs 1,000 to Rs 1,035 per month. The Japanese collaborators had taken an active part in the initial training programme and had instilled a basic plant discipline which included a daily open air physical exercise programme for all workers. All in all, the owners had created a small, smoothly-working Japanese island within the more rough and ready world of Calcutta's manufacturing.

Being an exotic island was now posing problems for the management in its plans for expansion. Their assessment was that the initial project had been successful for two main reasons: the elaborate training programme which had cost over Rs 2,000 per trainee, and the fact that they had been able to find at least fifty women willing to be trained. It was the presence of the well educated women which had made the training itself a serious and committed programme. Now there were plans for an evening or night shift, but the managers doubted whether more women would come forward to join the plant. The additional workforce would also have to be drawn from the surrounding villages if they were to avoid future labour trouble. Since it was unlikely that all of those women would come from a single village, each would have to travel alone at odd hours. Women with the requisite educational qualifications would probably come from relatively affluent rural homes and those families would probably be unwilling to send them under such circumstances. The managers too were wary of the risks posed for the women in this project.

The initial training exercise also seemed difficult to replicate. They themselves were now very busy running the ongoing operations, and this time they could not hope to get any Japanese help. Moreover, if there were no women in the next batch of trainees, they were worried that the whole group would be less disciplined or willing to undergo the routine. In spite of a ready market for their product, the managers were thus extremely ambivalent about their plans for further expansion.

Women workers

This would indeed be unfortunate because the work in the plant had been highly rewarding for the women workers. The plant was situated in an area with a considerable Muslim population, and eight of the women were Muslims. The rest were from families in which they were the first generation of women to get secondary education. Going to school had itself loosened some of their inhibitions. It had also meant that they were all unmarried at the age of 19 or 20, when they joined the plant. But it was the work that had given them the confidence to feel that they were as capable, if not better, than the men. They were quite sure that they could now tackle any new skills or techniques that the management might bring in. They were also quite firm about having a lifelong career: several had married since joining and a few had also had a baby, but none of them wanted to give the job up. The only thing they were worried about was the possibility of the plant closing down, and whether the skills that they had acquired would be adequate to get another job.

There were mixed reactions to the early morning physical exercise routine. Several felt embarrassed because local boys teased them, but others pointed out that this was important to create a mood for team work. It was interesting that all of them, including the Muslim girls, came to work on their own bicycles, although girls riding a bicycle are not a common phenomenon in West Bengal.

Views and practices regarding marriage had also undergone changes. One of the Muslim girls pointed out that in her family, two older sisters had been married without dowry as per Muslim traditions, but for her third sister her father had been forced to give a substantial dowry, because the custom was now making inroads in their community. She had decided that she was not going to be subjected to this, even if it meant her staying unmarried. On the other hand, one of the Hindu girls had married a man of her own choice and had insisted that her father should give her some cash instead of the usual ornaments and clothes, so that she and her husband can set up an independent household. There was an easy camaraderie between male and female workers, in spite of there being marked differences of class or religion. There was some giggling about a Muslim girl who was engaged to a Hindu fellow worker, but there was no shock at this breakdown of traditions. In another instance, one girl had been married off by her father, and has Rs 15,000 in dowry, which all the other women found shameful. Several said that they were saving a part of their salary in order to be able to marry whom they liked, and set up a home. It was therefore a pity that this very enriching experience was essentially a product of an alien hothouse and could not be expected to be easily reproduced on a larger scale.

THE SOFTWARE INDUSTRY

According to the several software experts I met, the fact that the industry existed at all in the Calcutta region was a testimony to its robust prospects and the passionate interest in it on the part of the numerous budding experts. The state government levied a 12 per cent sales tax on hardware purchases in West Bengal, while the rate in Gujarat and Karnataka was 2 per cent. The region has long been haunted by a deficient and uncertain electrical power supply and unreliable communications services. Unlike many other competing regions within India, the state government has done little to counter this problem: it had not established a 'software technology park', i.e. a site with a guaranteed supply of infrastructural services which serves as a contact point for prospective customers.[7]

Also, as the eighth plan had pointed out, software expertise in the country would grow faster if the producers had steady orders from domestic customers on which to practise and build up their skills in innovation and the application of the technologies. There was a general complaint that, because decision makers in West Bengal in both the private and public sectors were totally unfamiliar with the potential of information technology, the few orders generated here were being dissipated by being channelled into inexpert hands.[8] Whether this complaint was true or not, the several experts that were contacted were all working either on direct export contracts or on contracts from trans-India consortiums who were working for foreign firms.

Apart from personal discussions with several of these experts, I had a chance to examine the workings and the personnel of two of the local firms. The first was a family-based unit that had been built up by two brothers with the help of a third who was working as a systems analyst in the USA. The unit had been financed with family funds. It now employed six software experts including the owners and one woman who had a degree in computer science. The owners made a point of mentioning how well she had been working, in spite of the tremendous pressure of work and long hours. The second unit was larger and had been established by a senior professional who had worked for a large international banking concern for over twenty years. He had built up contacts in companies working in the Middle East and Europe. The unit had ten technical workers, one of whom was a woman with a two-year diploma in computer science from a university. Another woman had been trained only as a secretary to operate a personal computer, but had gradually picked up some programming skills.

Both firms were in dire need of more modern equipment in order to remain competitive. They were charging hourly rates which were less than one fourth those prevailing in the developed countries, but they were apprehensive that in the near future the bulk of their business, which consists of preparing simple programme packages to suit the needs of individual customers, might be lost, since better ready-made packages capable of adaptations for a broad range of customer requirements are now in the offing. With more modern equipment and greater expertise, they would be able to concentrate on systems analysis, for which the market was more assured. Again their complaint was that in the Calcutta region the financial institutions had little conception of the potential of the business and were very tardy in giving them additional financial support.

Gender-based differences

It was the general opinion that male software experts were much more adventurous. Many of them had no formal training in the field, but had picked up the skills by experimenting and working with knowledgeable friends. The field at the moment was so starved of skilled labour that if anybody showed any aptitude, other technicians were more than willing to teach them. Women who had come into the field, on the other hand, had almost always had formal training. Even so they were reluctant to experiment or innovate unless pushed. Once established however, they did very well.

In order to investigate these gender-based differences, I contacted two training institutes within Calcutta. One was a large all-India semi-government institute which gave intensive training courses as well as doing some software projects for units in the public sector. Here the management felt that their girl students had done extremely well. The institute had been retaining the best students from each class on its own staff, and had found that over the last four years, half of these had been women. Lately they had set up a team of nine experts for a major project to compile software for a large investment body. Five of these had been women. But they had noted that not many girls were being sent for training. Recently, the institute had sought candidates for a nine-month course in Hyderabad, for which each candidate was to get a stipend of Rs 1,000 per month in return for a bond to work for the institute for two years after the completion of the course. Unfortunately they had had no girl candidates from Calcutta.

The other training institute was the computer centre of the local university, which awarded a two-year diploma in computer science. So far five to seven of their annual intakes of twenty students had been girls.

I selected a random list of thirty male and female students from both of these institutes who had completed the course in the last three years. Each was sent a short questionnaire enquiring about their father's occupation, their family size, marital status, educational qualifications, work experience (past employment, locations, approximate salaries, promotions received, reasons for leaving, and reasons for gaps between jobs), methods used to find a new job, nature of present job, and their opinions about the job market for graduates from the course. Twenty-two replied, of whom seven were women. The results showed that all of the graduates were working in occupations related to computer applications. However there were marked gender-based differences both in the backgrounds and in the job experience of the trainees. Table 11.2 sums up the findings. The female respondents apparently came from relatively higher income professional or business families. They also had a better educational background: they had attended better colleges and got better degrees. However, in general their experience of the job market had been inferior: they earned lower salaries, on the average, and the majority were working as teachers in training institutes.

Since all the employers in this industry had asserted that trained women were as good as men, it is possible that the somewhat lower achievement profile of the women trainees was to some extent of their own volition. They might have preferred the training jobs because of their regular hours. Since they had generally come from more comfortable backgrounds, they could afford to indulge their preferences.

Training in the technology

In any case, women's entry into the industry was almost always contingent on their getting formal training, and there was a serious shortage of training facilities in India and particularly in the Calcutta region. Government or university sponsored coeducational institutions offering courses in computer science had 218 places for undergraduates and 101 for graduates. Private institutions offering training courses at all levels had mushroomed, but in 1992 when the Department of Electronics of the Government of India first conducted an all-India public examination for 'O' level accreditation

Table 11.2 Gender-based differences among successful trainees

	Women	*Men*
Family background		
High income	5	5
Medium income	2	10
Educational background		
Very good	3	4
Good	3	8
Medium	1	3
Present Job		
Training institute	4	4
Private sector employer	1	6
Public sector employer	2	3
Own or family business	–	2
Present monthly salary		
≤ Rs 2,500	2	2
2,501 to 3,500	4	7
3,501 and above	1	6

for the students of those institutions, only thirty-seven out of the 1367 students passed all four of the required modules.[9] The performance of eastern India was probably on a par with the rest of the country.

Another hurdle in getting training was the high fees for all of these courses. A six-month course in a semi-government institute used to cost Rs 15,000 per student: that fee has now gone up to Rs 18,000. Universities used to provide highly subsidized courses, but recently the Indian government has decided not to subsidize technical training. As a result the fees for the two-year postgraduate course at a university in Calcutta have gone up from Rs 5,000 to Rs 19,000. The teachers of these courses felt that the parents of girls who might have been willing to pay the previous fees would no longer be willing to pay the new rates since a girl's education is generally viewed less as an investment for her future career than as a general embellishment. And families which might have been willing to indulge the whims of their daughters to the extent of perhaps Rs 5,000 may not be willing to do so when the fees are tripled or quadrupled. If this is so, in coming years one would see even fewer girls going for the really serious but expensive training.

CONCLUSION

The few industries of Calcutta included in this brief review are still far too small to permit any generalizations about the future prospects of micro-electronics in this region. Nor are there any reasons to believe that they were representative of what has been happening in the rest of the country in this field. Nonetheless they did highlight some of the interesting possibilities and problems awaiting India in the near future.

The television industry and the micromotor industry stood in sharp contrast to each other. The former, or at least its fastest-growing sector, was producing a modern product but its work organization and labour relations were particularly primitive. For those entrepreneurs, flexibility in production meant saving on overheads and putting the entire burden of adjustments to shifts in demand on to the workers. Whenever necessary, the latter could be laid off, retrenched or given partial employment, and they were paid piece rates. There was some understanding between the owners and the semi-skilled repairmen-cum-mechanics: but this was just a collusion to deceive the customers. There was little possibility that this understanding would blossom at some future date into the kind of flexible specialization described by Hirst and Zetlin (1991), where a cluster of independent small specialist firms form a loose arrangement in order to share economies of scale in functions such as collecting technical and market information, making bulk purchases of inputs or common marketing of outputs. The semi-skilled self-employed workers were themselves not capable of venturing into independent production. Nor were the dealer–entrepreneurs capable of, or interested in, participating in firmly-based, growth-oriented, long-term investment in the television industry.

In the micromotor firm, on the other hand, the producers had definitely wanted to take what Sengenburger and Pyke (as quoted by Lauridsen, 1991) have described as the 'high road' in labour/capital relations. Workers here were considered a valuable resource which had been carefully nurtured by the company. Its main plans for growth were based on the full and willing cooperation of a committed and polyvalent workforce. The entire firm and its operations had been closely modelled on the Japanese pattern of input control and labour involvement. However they too were finding it difficult to reproduce their model to increase the scale and vertical integra- tion of their operations. In the rough and tumble of Calcutta's manufacturing world, too many of their essential prerequisites such as a disciplined labour force which could be easily trained in new skills, smooth-working channels for communications and input supplies or a reliable and knowledgeable network of ancillaries were in short supply. Absence of these vital aids was not only crippling this one firm but was also likely to inhibit future development of Indian industries in general on the cost-efficient lines posited by this Japanese model.

Workers

For the women workers, however, these industries generally offered prospects of a rewarding career. In the television industry this was because the units were small and informally organized: but in general it was because the technologies themselves offered opportunities for upgrading skills by experimentation, innovation and learning-by-doing. Those among the women who were committed to a long-term career could learn much more than their assigned tasks, and because there was little need for manual strength, they could feel confident that they were in no way inferior to their male colleagues. This feeling, along with their awareness that these technologies opened up a new, hitherto untapped, field has helped materially to alter the outlook of even poorly-educated, semi-urban women.

This outcome is of course quite contrary to what has been written about the soul-destroying and deskilling impact on women of working in electronics manufacturing elsewhere (Elson and Pearson, 1984). But perhaps this was to some extent due to some special characteristics of these women. Even the poorly-educated women in backyard television units were in several senses path-breakers. They were usually the first generation of literate or educated women in their households. They had to have the courage to defy social conventions about marriage and feminine roles. And they were genuinely fired by the need to build up a career for themselves. Working away from home had made them aware that jobs were hard to come by and that one must make the most of one's opportunities.

The importance of these attitudes becomes clear when one considers the case of the women in software manufacturing. Here, in spite of a very favourable job market, well-trained women were allowing themselves to be ghettoized into jobs with relatively poor prospects, apparently because their drive to build up a career had been dampened by their comfortable backgrounds. The tragedy for women was that the urge to have a career and the opportunities for proper training were often mismatched and are likely to remain so in the future.

Education and training

This brings up the possibility that the microelectronics industry in Calcutta in particular, and generally in India, might be hamstrung by the extremely limited opportunities available for proper training in information technology, or even for more computer literacy.

There is now a wide-ranging debate about the links between economic growth and human resource development.[10] Our present case studies and discussions with local technical experts suggest that, at least in the microelectronics field, the links are easily discernable. Here, the Calcutta tradition of younger workers learning skills by imitation does not seem to be adequate, because the technology itself is new to the region and there are few senior technicians who can fully demonstrate the skills to newcomers. Also, the technology's potential for flexibility between products and processes can be realized only if workers are made familiar with the basics of the technological principles and are allowed to experiment freely with the equipment. If this remains an expensive prerogative of a few, then the potentially rich markets in India and abroad for electronic equipment and software would be lost to a local industry producing inferior products.

In the current employment-hungry situation in India, where urban unemployment rates, particularly for women, go up steeply with each level of education (Banerjee, 1992), wasting the opportunities for growth and employment offered by microelectronics-based industries would be nothing short of criminal. However, for the kind of women who, in these case studies, were most keen on furthering careers in this field, the present training facilities are totally inaccessible. They can neither afford the high fees nor are they likely to have the educational qualifications required for entry to the training courses. To overcome this, there is a need for radical rethinking on the training front, in terms of a revision of the existing curricula of the normal school system to include a basic introduction to the technology and to computers. But given the innate inertia of the education system and the general crisis of resources for social development in India, can one hope for quick changes of this order?

NOTES

1 *Electronics, Information and Planning*, June 1992, Table 1: p. 469. In making these predictions, the IAMR had followed a macrodynamic approach taking note of the fact that the industry is known to have a strong multiplier effect on other sections of the economy, which in their turn will expand their demand for the industry's products.
2 *Economic Times*, 10 and 17 August 1991.
3 For example, in Hong Kong and Korea, women's shares in total employment in 1986/87 in the electrical machinery industry were 64 per cent and 55 per cent, respectively.
4 *Dataquest*, Nov. 1991: p. 104.
5 An ongoing study of Calcutta's informal economy conducted by myself and Professor Nripen Bandyopadhyay on behalf of the Centre for Studies in Social Sciences, Calcutta, has brought out various crucial activities being financed through these links between trade and credit.
6 Micromotors are used mainly in cassette decks in India. In developed countries, they are used in a wide range of products including electronic fittings for car windscreen wipers etc.
7 *Dataquest*, March 1992: p. 158.
8 *Dataquest*, February 1992: pp. 117–118.
9 *Dataquest*, February 1992: pp. 46–55.
10 For a comprehensive but inconclusive review, see Behrman, 1990.

REFERENCES

All India Council for Technical Education (1991), *Facilities for Technical Education in the Eastern Region*, Calcutta, Government of India, Ministry of Human Resource Development

Bagchi, A. and D. Bannerjee (1986), *The Impact of Microelectronics Based Technologies: The Case of India*, Geneva, WEP 2-22/WP 169, World Employment Programme Research, ILO

Banerjee, N. (1988), 'Small and Large Units: Symbiosis or Matsyanyaya?', in K.B. Suri (ed.), *Small Scale Enterprises in Industrial Development: The Indian Experience*, New Delhi, Sage Publications

Banerjee, N. (1992), *Poverty, Work and Gender in Urban India*, Calcutta, Centre for Studies in Social Sciences, Occasional Paper No. 133

Behrman, J.R. (1990), *Human Resource Led Development? Review of Issues and Evidence*, Geneva, Asian Regional Team for employment promotion, ILO

Belussi, F. (1991), 'Benetton Italy: Beyond Fordism and Flexible Specialization', in S. Mitter (ed.), *Computer-aided manufacturing and women's employment*, London, Springer

Bose, A. (1978), *Calcutta and Rural Bengal: Small Sector Symbiosis*, Calcutta, Minerva Associates

Braverman, H. (1974), *Labour and Monopoly Capital: the Degradation of Work in the Twentieth Century*, New York, Monthly Review Press

Central Statistical Organization (1991), *Annual Survey of Industries 1987-88. Summary Results for Factory Sector*, New Delhi, Government of India

Dataquest, various issues, New Delhi

Eastern Regional Committee of the All India Council for Technical Education (1992), *Report of the Committee on Availability of Technical Education in Eastern India*, Calcutta, mimeo

Electronics, Information and Planning, various issues, New Delhi Information, Planning and Analysis group, Dept. of Electronics

Elson, D. and R. Pearson (1984), 'The Subordination of Women and the Internationalization of Factory Production', in K. Young *et al.* (eds), *Of Marriage and the Market*, London, Routledge and Kegan Paul

ESCAP (1987), *Women's Economic Participation in Asia and the Pacific*, United Nations Economic and Social Commission for Asia and the Pacific, Bangkok

Freeman, C. (1988), 'Japan, A New National System of Innovation?', in G. Dosi *et al.* (eds), *Technical Change and Economic Theory*, London, Pinter

Freeman, C. and C. Perez (1988), 'Structural Crisis of Adjustment Business Cycles and Investment Behaviour', in G. Dosi *et al.* (eds), *Technical Change and Economic Theory*, London, Pinter

Gordon, D. (1988), 'The Global Economy: New Edifice or Crumbling Foundations', New York, *New Left Review*, 168, March–April

Government of India (1984), *Report of the Commission on the Electronics Industry of India*, New Delhi, Department of Electronics

Hirst, P. and J. Zetlin, (1991),'Flexible Specialisation vs Post-Fordism' *Economy and Society*, Vol. 20, No. 1, London, Routledge

ILO – Asian Regional Team for Employment Promotion (1990), *Employment Challenges for the 90s*, Geneva

James, J. (1985), *The Employment and Income Distributional Impact of Microelectronics: A Perspective Analysis of the Third World*, Geneva, WEP 2-22/WP. 153, Technology and Employment Programme, ILO

Lauridsen, L. (1991), 'New Technologies, Flexibilization and the Changing Capital Labour Relations', paper presented at the Workshop on Adoption of Microelectronics Based Technologies, Centre for Studies in Social Sciences, Calcutta, 9–11 October

Lien, L. (1981),'Women's Work in Multinational Electronic Factories', in R. Dauber and M. Cain (eds), *Women and Technological Change in Developing Countries*, Boulder, Colorado, Westview Press

Murray, F. (1987), 'Flexible Specialisation in the Third Italy', *Capital and Class*, No. 33, Leeds, UK

Piore, M. and C. Sabel, (1984), *The Second Industrial Divide, Possibilities for Prosperity*, New York, Basic Books

Planning Commission (1992), *Eighth Five Year Plan*, New Delhi, Government of India

Pore, K. (1991), 'Women at Work – A Secondary Line of Operation', in Nirmala Banerjee (ed.), *Indian Women in a Changing Industrial Scenario*, New Delhi, Sage Publications

Sanyal, K. (1992), 'Punjee Uttar Adhunikata Marxbad: Ekti Sampratik Upakatha Prasanqe', *Baromas*, Calcutta, April

Sarvekshana, various issues, New Delhi, National Sample Survey Organisation, Department of Statistics, Ministry of Planning, Government of India

Sayer, A. (1986), 'New Developments in Manufacturing: the Just in Time System', *Capital and Class*, No. 30, Leeds, UK

Sen, G. and I. Gulati (1987), *Women Workers in Kerala's Electronic Industry*, Geneva, WEP10/WP45, ILO

State Planning Board (1991), *A Perspective Plan for Calcutta 2011*, Supplementary Vol. 1, Calcutta, Government of West Bengal

12 Women and information technology in sub-Saharan Africa

A topic for discussion?

Mayuri Odedra-Straub

INTRODUCTION

This chapter examines, at a macro level, the current state of the information technology industry in sub-Saharan Africa and the situation of women there in general. From this analysis, a few deductions are made about the role of women in the information technology area, and the impact it is likely to have on them. The paper also poses a number of questions about the relevance of the issue of women and information technology.

Before going any further, it is necessary to ask why we need to look at the issue of women and information technology (IT)[1] anywhere, not just in sub-Saharan Africa.[2] Why is this issue attaining increasing importance? Is it because the technology affects women's and men's work differently? Is there concern because of women's low participation in the IT professions? What about other fields and professions, such as engineering, where women's participation is also lacking? Is it really true that the 'IT world' is dominated by men and that women are discriminated against, as some feminists believe, or is it just that women find it increasingly difficult to participate in various fields because of the greater demands placed on them? Has the focus on women gained importance because there is a shortage of skills in the area and women can play a vital role? Women may have certain skills which men often lack, such as business aptitudes, people and communication skills and management potential, but should these capabilities be exploited to maximize their impact on IT? Is there interest because it is thought that women's jobs are either becoming less skilled or are being displaced by the new technology?

The author has few answers to many of these questions, especially with reference to the African situation. Subramaniam also raises some of the above questions in her report but makes little constructive attempt at answering them (Subramaniam, 1991). Apart from the work done by

Soriyan and Aina (1991), which focused largely on Nigeria, I have found very little literature focusing on the impact of IT on women in Africa.

Few doubt the significance of information technology for economic and social development. IT is widely proclaimed to have the power to allow the developing countries to 'leapfrog' development, and as having the potential to tackle many development problems. Yet few developing countries, especially those of Africa, have succeeded in exploiting this developmental potential. Maybe it is just an illusion that IT helps with the development process. Although no other comprehensive surveys have been done to prove this, the author's own research in the last five years (Odedra, 1990a, b, c, 1992a, b), including field trips to many East and Southern African countries, shows that there is extensive under-utilization, or non-utilization, of equipment. Some major computer-based projects have failed. These signs may indicate why IT is playing little role in Africa, at least at the moment.

As there is little literature on the area of women and IT in Africa, and as difficulties were encountered in conducting a survey to find out what was happening in a few African countries, this paper is largely based on the current status of IT in Africa and the general role of women in these countries. It is important to examine the overall status of women in the existing sociocultural environment before considering the impact, if any, of IT on women.

RESEARCH METHOD

There is little information on the role women play in the IT area, or the impact it may have had on them in Africa. An attempt was therefore made to conduct a postal survey in a few countries to find out what the current position of women, as users, was in this area. A simple questionnaire was prepared in early February 1992 and posted to over 200 organizations in Kenya, Zambia and Zimbabwe. Although even a good response from the questionnaires would not have said much about the impact of IT on women in general in these countries, it would have given us some indication of what role women are playing in some particular organizations – what positions they hold, what qualifications they have, how many women are employed in that area, etc.

By May 1992, less than 5 per cent of the organizations had responded – either to say that they did not want to take part in the survey or to say that they had few women playing any major role in the area. The poor response was not surprising as a previous attempt, for a different project, at conducting such surveys by mail had yielded little. Experience had shown that personal visits to the organizations were required, but it proved difficult to find someone in these countries who would do the job. Those approached made responses such as: 'Women are not playing much role in the IT area', 'There are many other important areas of priority which need to be researched rather than women and IT', or 'IT has made little overall impact on our countries. How then do you expect there to have been some impact on women?' Attempts at finding a paid graduate student who would be willing to do the leg-work produced no results, despite generous compensation in foreign currency.

What is presented in this chapter therefore derives from the author's own research and experience on IT in Africa, and from secondary sources. Using the current status of IT in these countries, and a general picture of the role of women in Africa, some deductions are made about the possible impact of IT on women in Africa.

CURRENT STATUS OF INFORMATION TECHNOLOGY IN SUB-SAHARAN AFRICA

Measured in terms of the number of computers bought, Africa's information technology market has expanded considerably in the past decade. This trend is expected to continue over the coming years. Most major computer manufacturers are represented in Africa, and the technology has penetrated all sectors, including banking, agriculture, mining, transportation, research, defence, medical services, accounting and communications. Systems are primarily used for planning and administrative functions in both the public and private sectors. But the level and sophistication of software applications, and the attitudes, business practices, government policies and regulations concerning the use of computers vary from country to country. Several, including Kenya, Nigeria, Ivory Coast and Zimbabwe, are making some progress, but others such as Uganda and Tanzania have lagged behind.

The growth in the number of computers purchased in Africa has been spurred by the increased availability of computer hardware, the advent of microcomputers, an increase in computer awareness throughout the continent, and help from international organizations such as the United Nations, the World Bank, the United States Agency for International Development and the Canadian International Development Association. There is an increasing emphasis on acquiring and using microcomputers in many countries. For example, Zimbabwe which had less than 10 personal computers before 1980, had more than 10,000 PCs by 1990. Ghana had more than 2,000 microcomputers in the same year, compared with none before 1985.

Although African companies have had little success in producing their own hardware, software houses catering to the local market are emerging, particularly in Kenya, Zimbabwe, and Nigeria. Off-the-shelf software packages have largely been used in African countries because of the lack of programmers to develop in-house applications. However, there is a growing demand for applications appropriate for local needs. While the present quality and sophistication of local software may not be on a par with current world standards, it should improve with increasing demand.

However, although the number of computers has increased rapidly in some places, the process of computerization has not been as successful as it should be in a majority of these countries. There is extensive under-utilization of equipment and major computer-based projects have failed (Odedra, 1990a). Examples abound of systems that are simply not used because of the lack of secondary equipment, suitable electric power, or training. The spread of computers in Africa owes more to hard selling from manufacturers and vendors, the urge to keep up with the latest technology, donations from international assistance organizations (half of the computers in Africa acquired in the early 1980s were 'aid-donated'), self-interest, and pressure from computer professionals than to evidence of their successful use in solving real problems.[3]

In many African countries, there is a notion that, if the more developed countries use the technology and tell us to do so as well, then we should. But there are no IT policies or strategic buying plans which clearly identify the needs that are likely to bring overall benefit to the nation, or which determine what may be achieved with the available resources. Some regula-tory policies covering procedures for the acquisition of hardware and software do exist in a few places. These regulations typically mandate centralized acquisition for the public sector and tax private companies and non-government organizations in order to discourage imports or to raise convertible currency for the state. Such taxes range from 0 per cent in Mauritius to 60 per cent in Kenya. However, a number of countries such as Botswana, Zimbabwe, Nigeria and Mauritius have recently taken initiatives to formulate more comprehensive IT policies.

Although IT has been a mixed blessing in different African countries, overall there have been many negative consequences. Scarce foreign currency has been spent on equipment which is not used. Dependency on multinational corporations and expatriate personnel has increased, and sociocultural conflicts have been introduced. Moreover, what Africa has experienced for the most part so far is not IT transfer but transplantation, the dumping of boxes without the necessary know-how. Donor agencies, in particular, have a reputation for doing this.

A reliable power supply to operate the computers, a well-functioning telephone network to transmit data, foreign currency to import the technology, and computer-literate personnel are all prerequisites for the successful use of IT. Such infrastructural elements remain inadequate in many African countries. For instance, the number of telephones per 1,000 people ranges between 12 and 50, depending on the country, and many of the lines that do exist are out of order much of the time.

Africa lacks computer skills in all areas, including systems analysis, programming, maintenance and consulting, and at all operational levels from basic use to management. Most countries lack the education and training facilities needed to help people acquire the proper skills. The few training centres that do exist have not been able to keep up with demand. Only a handful of countries such as Kenya, Malawi, Nigeria and Zimbabwe have universities that offer computer science degrees. The programmes available in the other countries are mainly diplomas and certificates. As a result of unskilled and untrained personnel, user organizations are forced to hire expatriate staff, who in turn lack the knowledge about local organizational cultures and thus design poor systems. Many African governments and organizations are waking up to this situation, but few serious measures have been taken. Moreover, it will not be enough to merely institute courses; books, teachers and equipment are also required but unfortunately have been overlooked.

Unless managers are computer-literate, poor strategic decisions will continue to be made. The applications of computers in Africa have so far been mainly the result of isolated initiatives without any preconceived strategies or plans. The lack of long-term business plans in many organizations results in systems being purchased but not used properly. Managers need to understand that planning is essential before, not after, hardware and software is bought. At present, the most pressing need in Africa is not new systems, but rather the know-how to effectively use what is already there.

Information technology can be of great advantage in various economic sectors if used for decision making. But computers in Africa are still largely used for routine data processing with very little computer-based decision making. There is still minimal recognition that information is one of the major determinants of economic and social development. One of the reasons for Africa's underdevelopment is bad or ineffective public sector management because of the lack or inadequate use of data. Computers are often introduced to overcome some of these problems but few realize that computerization does not correct ineffective manual systems.

However, the above bleak picture is changing, at different paces in different countries. Computer literacy and awareness is increasing in many countries, and many users have come to believe and accept that computer systems can help organizations make more effective use of financial, managerial and socioeconomic resources. With the cost of IT falling dramatically, and with systems becoming much easier to use and maintain, some of the prohibitive cost and infrastructural problems are being lessened. Many Africans are beginning to take advantage of this. But lack of skills in the area still remains a major problem. Overall, people are learning from their mistakes and are trying to address some of the issues.

Further research is needed, but it is already clear that what Africa needs most is the ability to exploit existing equipment effectively. This will require education and training to develop the human resources needed to integrate the technology into the development process. Development is all about people, their needs and their potential, and not the technical sophistication of technology. Women should be given the opportunity to play an equal role in the education process, but, as we will see, women in Africa are still held back in various ways. The inflow of IT cannot be halted, and there is no reason why it should be. IT can play a role in the development of these countries if some of these constraints can be addressed.

OVERALL STATUS OF WOMEN IN AFRICA

African women have always been active in agriculture, trade, and other economic pursuits, but a majority of them are in the informal labour force. In 1985, women's shares in African labour forces ranged from 17 per cent, in Mali, to 49 per cent in Mozambique and Tanzania (World Bank, 1989). African women are guardians of their children's welfare and have explicit responsibility to provide for them materially. They are the household managers, providing food, nutrition, water, health, education, and family planning to an extent greater than elsewhere in the developing world. This places heavy burdens on them, despite developments such as improved agriculture technology, availability of contraception, and changes in women's socioeconomic status, which one might think would have made their lives easier. In fact, it would be fair to say that their workload has increased with the changing economic and social situation in Africa. Women's economic capabilities, and in particular their ability to manage family welfare, are being threatened. 'Modernization' has shifted the balance of advantage against women. The legal framework and the modern social sector and producer services developed by the independent African countries have not served women well.

Most African women, in common with women all over the world, face a variety of legal, economic and social constraints. Indeed some laws still treat them as minors. In Zaire, for instance, a woman must have her husband's consent to open a bank account. Women are known to grow 80 per cent of food produced in Africa, and yet few are allowed to own the land they work. It is often more difficult for women to gain access to information and technology, resources and credit. Agricultural extension and formal financial institutions are biased towards a male clientele; despite women's importance as producers (this has spurred the growth of women's groups and cooperatives which give loans and other help). Women end up working twice as long as men, 15 to 18 hours a day, but often earn only one tenth as much. With such workloads, women often age prematurely. Harrison correctly observes that: 'Women's burdens – heavy throughout the third world – are enough to break a camel's back in much of Africa' (Harrison 1983).

Female education affects family health and nutrition, agricultural productivity, and fertility, yet there is a wide gender gap in education. Lack of resources and pressures on time and energies put enormous constraints on the ability of women to maintain their own health and nutrition as well as that of their children. As a result, women are less well equipped than men to take advantage of the better income-earning opportunities that have emerged in Africa. Although food and nutrition are women's prime concerns in Africa, and they are the principal participants in agriculture, independent farming by women has been relatively neglected. Women's family labour contribution has increased, but goes unpaid.

In industry and trade, women have been confined to small-scale operations in the informal sector; however vibrant these operations are and despite the trading empires built up by the most successful female entrepreneurs, women's average incomes are relatively low. Women are also handicapped in access to formal sector jobs by their lower educational attainments, and those who succeed are placed in lower grade, lower paid jobs. Elite women who wish to improve their legal and economic status must expect to lose honour and respect (Obbe, 1980). There is often sexism in job promotions and unpleasant consequences if women stand up to men. There is often more respect for male professionals (even from women themselves) than there is for female. Women often suffer employment discrimination because they need to take time off for maternity leave or when a child is sick. Career women often have to work harder at their jobs to keep even with their male counterparts. Despite all these obstacles, women continue to move into different professions, including those traditionally seen as male jobs, such as engineering and architecture. Women can be found at senior levels in many organizations in many countries. They are also taking up various different professions, such as law, medicine, politics, etc. These women may be in the minority now, but things are changing all over Africa.

Social attitudes to women are responsible for the gender differences in both the education system and the labour force, as we will see below. Differential access to educational and training opportunities has led to low proportions of women in the formal sector and their subsequent concentration in low paid production jobs with limited career prospects. So, although women play an important role in African society, they suffer legal, economic and social constraints.

African women and education

Women's participation in national educational systems is again biased due to the sociocultural and economic environments. There is also a lack of genuine political will to ensure that girls are given equal access to education in Africa. More than two-thirds of Africa's illiterates are women. Women are regarded as inferior to men and are not expected to aspire as high as men, especially in what are considered as 'male' fields (engineering, computing, architecture, medicine, etc.). It is largely assumed that educating women would make them too independent; in other words, they would not do what they are expected to do – look after the house, bring up children, and cater to their husband's needs.

In poor countries, extending access to education and training is often difficult when the cultural and monetary costs are high or the benefits are limited. When families face economic problems they prefer to invest their limited resources in the education of boys rather than provide what is considered as 'prestigious' education for girls who would eventually marry and abandon their professions anyway. Nevertheless, girls are increasingly getting some limited education, and the focus of concern is gradually shifting to providing access to the same range of educational opportunities open to boys. In poor families, boys are often given first claim on whatever limited educational opportunities are available, although the global policy climate today is more supportive of measures designed to expand the educational horizons of girls than it was twenty years ago.

Even when parents can be persuaded of the value of sending their girls to school, there remains the problem of helping the girls to complete their studies. Drop out rates in the primary grades are higher for girls than for boys in many African countries. In Tanzania, for instance, half of the school dropouts each year are girls of 12 to 14 years who have to leave school because of pregnancies. Such early pregnancies are often blamed on the absence of family life education and the imitation of foreign life styles.

Very few schools allow pregnant girls or young mothers to complete their education. The other half of the Tanzanian pupils who drop out do so for a variety of reasons, including poverty, traditional norms, increases in school fees and deterioration in the quality of learning. Child marriages are also very common in Africa: although the law in many countries does not allow girls under 16 to be married, parents marry their daughters at an early age so they have one less mouth to feed.

Differences in national and regional educational patterns are in part due to differences in population pressures and resource availability, but they have also reflected differing policy priorities. But there have been signs, in recent years, of a growing international consensus on the importance of investing in education for the quality of life in society and for national development generally (UNESCO, 1991). Table 12.1 shows that, in Africa, as in South Asia and the Arab states, the general literacy rate for women is much lower than for men, and that the gap is not expected to narrow rapidly. The differences between these three regions and the rest of the world may be due to differences in enrolment levels, government expenditure on education or the general sociocultural and economic environment.

The enrolment ratios for both men and women also show some differences (see Table 12.2). Although the number of females who have been continuing on to the secondary level in Africa has increased, and the gap between male and female enrolments is narrowing, the increase in the number of women continuing to tertiary education has been minimal. The figures for Africa are the lowest in the world. As mentioned earlier, in most

Table 12.1 Projected adult literacy rates by sex (% literate adults in the population aged 15 or over)

	1990			2000		
	Both	*Male*	*Female*	*Both*	*Male*	*Female*
Sub-Saharan Africa	47.3	59.8	36.1	59.7	70.2	49.6
Arab States	51.3	64.3	38.0	62.0	73.1	50.6
Latin America & Caribbean	84.7	86.4	83.0	88.5	89.7	87.3
East Asia	76.2	85.7	66.4	82.8	90.0	75.4
South Asia	46.1	59.1	32.2	54.1	66.2	41.2
Developed countries	96.7	97.4	96.1	98.5	99.0	98.0

Source: UNESCO, 1991: p. 26

Table 12.2 Male and female enrolment ratios by level of education in 1970 and 1990 (% estimates)

| | 1970 | | | | | | 1990 | | | | | |
| | First level | | Second level | | Third level | | First level | | Second level | | Third level | |
	Male	Female	Male	Female	Male	Female	Male	Female	Male	Female	Male	Female
Sub-Saharan Africa	56.7	36.0	9.9	4.4	0.8	0.2	73.5	59.9	21.2	13.8	2.8	1.0
Arab states	77.9	46.4	28.1	12.5	6.3	2.0	92.3	74.2	60.2	44.9	15.6	9.5
Latin American and Caribbean	91.9	89.4	26.3	24.6	8.0	4.5	111.4	107.2	55.7	59.6	19.3	18.2
East Asia	107.9	94.5	33.1	23.6	1.6	1.1	124.6	114.9	58.7	47.7	7.3	4.9
South Asia	87.1	53.2	30.7	13.1	7.4	2.2	100.8	75.1	47.8	28.2	12.1	5.3
North America	103.5	102.8	92.6	93.6	52.8	37.8	103.0	101.4	98.4	99.5	66.7	74.1

Source: UNESCO, 1991: p. 53

developing countries, the opportunities for girls to advance beyond the first level of formal education are still significantly less than for boys.

Public expenditure on education in Africa is, in dollar terms, the lowest in the world; not surprising considering Africa's economic situation. However, if we consider expenditure as a percentage of GNP, there is not that much difference between all of the developing nations. Women's enrolment rates are lower in Africa, but the female literacy rate is similar to that for women in the Arab states and South Asia. Such discrepancies might be due to differences in government policies or in the sociocultural environment in these countries.

No statistics are available for the number of women who attend computer science courses in Africa, but it is known that few women in tertiary education are in technical courses. Table 12.4 presents figures from a project carried out by the ILO in association with the Commonwealth Association of Polytechnics in Africa, and summarized by Leigh-Doyle (1991). These figures show the poor enrolment ratios for women in technical programmes.[4] There are marked differences between countries, in both women's polytechnic attendance and in their enrolment in technical programmes in particular. The share of women in all polytechnic courses ranges from 40 per cent in the Gambia to just 2 per cent in Zambia. One striking observation is that 30 per cent of all those attending polytechnics in Ghana are women, yet only 1 per cent of those attending technical programmes are women!

Overall, the figures for women attending technical programmes are low in most of these countries. When the author was teaching computer science

Table 12.3 Public expenditure on education, 1970–1988

| | US$ (billion) | | | | | Percentage of GNP | | | | |
	1970	1975	1980	1985	1988	1970	1975	1980	1985	1988
Sub-Saharan Africa	1.3	4.0	11.0	8.0	7.1	3.1	3.8	4.9	4.3	4.5
Arab states	1.8	8.4	18.0	23.8	27.7	5.0	5.9	4.4	6.0	6.4
Latin American and Caribbean	5.6	13.6	32.7	28.6	38.9	3.3	3.6	3.9	4.0	4.4
East Asia	2.6	6.3	15.5	19.9	24.4	1.9	2.3	2.7	3.2	2.9
South Asia	2.2	5.3	12.8	14.8	24.0	2.6	3.0	4.0	3.4	3.6
North America	83.0	131.3	201.8	293.3	365.7	7.5	7.4	6.7	6.7	6.8

Source: UNESCO, 1991: p. 36

Table 12.4 Student enrolment in selected polytechnics in nine African countries, 1989

	All programmes		Technical programmes	
	Total students	% Female	Total students	% Female
Yaba College of Technology, Nigeria	8,510	25	3,862	12
Kenya Polytechnic, Nairobi	3,488	24	2,627	17
Accra Polytechnic, Ghana	2,498	30	1,083	1
Malawi Polytechnic	1,033	14	664	3
Dar es Salaam Technical College, Tanzania	955	7	955	7
Botswana Polytechnic	621	5	621	5
Uganda Polytechnic	566	9	566	9
Technical Training Institute, The Gambia	532	40	265	11
Northern Technical College, Zambia	195	2	495	2

Source: Leigh-Doyle, 1991: p. 437

to final year degree students at the University of Zimbabwe four years ago, there were only four female students out of a class of 30. The figures for female enrolment ratios in many of the other universities and polytechnics offering computer science or related courses in the East and Southern African states the author has visited were not very much different – around 10 per cent. The female enrolment ratios in some of the private sector training programmes were much higher, nearly 40 per cent, although many of these women were from the ethnic minorities. Although no figures are available, a number of women are also trained privately by their employers in various areas of IT and a few privileged women also obtain their 'computing' qualifications abroad, mainly in the USA or the UK. These numbers are small although they may not be insignificant.

If the figures are to be believed, the 10 per cent female enrolment in African institutions is not that much different to some developed countries such as the UK. The Women in Information Technology (WIT) Foundation of UK found that female enrolments in university computer science courses had dropped from 25 per cent in the 1970s to 10 per cent in 1991 (Classe, 1992). This is very low compared to 45 per cent in the USA and 56 per cent in Singapore, and the figure is difficult to believe from my experience of such courses at universities and polytechnics in UK. The reasons for such a drop, if there is one to begin with, are not clearly stated.

It has often been said that, if there were more female teachers and lecturers who could act as a role model to girls, there would possibly be an increase in the number of girls attending such establishments, especially from the Muslim community. However, we can see from Table 12.5 that there are very few female teaching staff in many of the African poly-technics. The number of women teaching technical programmes varies from country to country. In Nigeria and Tanzania, a large proportion of the female lecturers are teaching technical programmes whilst in Malawi the figure is much lower.

Statistics show that the overall share of females in vocational and technical education in thirty-nine sub-Saharan countries increased by only one percentage point in the period 1970 to 1983, from 27 to 28 per cent of all participants (World Bank, 1988). Few employees in the modern economic sectors in Africa are women, and their participation is linked to their level of education. In industry, women generally hold low skill, low paid jobs with limited opportunities for promotion. Very few women are managers, and although more women are now in senior scientific and professional positions, they still represent a very small proportion of those employed in this category. Science and technology has generally been dominated by men, and women everywhere have found it difficult to make it to the top. The differences in the numbers of women working in technical fields can be ascribed to a variety of causes, rooted in the culture and history of each country.

A number of studies have been done on women's under-representation in the scientific and technical fields worldwide, by ATRCW (1986), Harding

Table 12.5 Distribution of teaching staff in selected polytechnics in eight African countries, 1989

	All programmes		Technical programmes	
	Total staff	% Female	Total staff	% Female
Yaba College of Technology, Nigeria	284	19	179	16
Kenya Polytechnic, Nairobi	270	22	203	6
Malawi Polytechnic	117	12	72	1
Dar es Salaam Technical College, Tanzania	119	15	104	11
Botswana Polytechnic	120	3	114	0
Uganda Polytechnic	100	3	100	3
Technical Training Institute, The Gambia	40	5	34	0
Northern Technical College, Zambia	58	2	57	0

Source: Leigh-Doyle, 1991: p. 438

(1987), Lockheed and Gorman (1987), Byrne (1988), Anker and Hein (1985), Leigh-Doyle (1991), etc. Some of the factors which they state influence women's participation (not in order of importance) are: prejudices about women's abilities and attitudes; their roles; their behaviour and aspirations; culture, politics and society; absence of role models; macho image of science; parental expectations, beliefs, attitude and home environment; teacher attitudes and behaviour; curriculum; career guidance; employer attitudes; lack of education and training facilities; lack of quotas; lack of exposure to technically oriented subjects; group pressures at home and at school; classroom interactions between girls and boys; lack of school books and resource materials; and lack of confidence to try new things. This list is long, and further research would be required to find out exactly which factors influence women's participation in technical fields in Africa.

The under-representation of women in technical education, training and employment is not unique to Africa. The situation in Africa must be seen in the context of the serious economic and developmental problems facing many African countries (Leigh-Doyle, 1991). This, together with the societal attitude to women in general, is responsible for the gender differences both in education establishments and in the workforce. Differential access to educational and training opportunities have led to low proportions of women in the formal sector and their concentration in low paid production jobs with limited career prospects.

However, as elsewhere in the developing world, things are slowly changing for women in Africa. More women are joining the formal sector of the economy (especially the public sector), more girls are continuing to higher education and joining technical courses, more women can be found in the management hierarchy, more women are moving into professions so far dominated by men, and more women are becoming self employed. In the years to come, we will see many changes, although the poor economic situation in Africa will not provide many job opportunities. There will be more competition for jobs and women may lose out, especially where there are domestic and family demands placed on them.

WOMEN AND INFORMATION TECHNOLOGY

As there are neither statistics nor literature on the position of women in information technology in Africa, as users or as IT professionals, or what impact IT has had on them, we can only make some deductions and predictions based on the preceding sections and on literature relating to other regions.

The problems with under-utilization of present capacity, lack of computer literacy and of education and training facilities have been described above. Access to training is limited for both men and women, but men may be given priority for admission in the belief that they are more likely to use their qualifications. Computing is still seen as a man's job in Africa, like many other professions. Men are also meant to be 'better' in many ways, although statistics from Obafemi Awolowo University in Nigeria show that final year female students perform better than their male counterparts in both the computer hardware and software disciplines offered by the university (Soriyan and Aina, 1991).

The previous section showed that the literacy rate for African women is low, and that very few women are entering tertiary education or joining technical programmes. This, together with the figures from the World Bank (1988) showing that the female share in vocational and technical education was only 28 per cent in 1983, may say something about the likely role of women in the IT area in Africa. If overall literacy is low and very few women are joining technical programmes, we would expect the proportion of women in the IT field, as users or professionals, to be low.

Although there are few figures to back this up, from the author's experience in Kenya, Zambia and Zimbabwe, there are very few women at the systems analyst, managerial or consultant levels. The few women who have reached such professional levels are from the ethnic minorities (white Zimbabweans in Southern Africa and Indians in East Africa). Women are badly under-represented in IT management jobs everywhere and it is no surprise that women in Africa, considering their position in society, have not made it. For instance, in the UK, according to research done by ICL and IBM, 32 per cent of trainee systems analysts were women, while only 3 per cent of data processing managers were women. The research also found a marked decline in recent years in female entrants to the sector, without explaining why this is so.[5] The report concludes that:

> Women are as well suited as men, and on some aspects more suited, to work in the new organizational and IT environment where the emphasis is on building relationships and on seeing different connections between people and technology.

One can now find more women programmers and operators in a number of African countries, both in public and private sectors, but there are very few indigenous female lecturers or teachers in computer-related courses. Until last year, only two of the staff of ten at the Computer Science department of the University of Zimbabwe were women – both expatriate. The Institute of Computer Science at the University of Nairobi is known to have recruited its first female lecturer recently. Little is known about the situation in other countries. To the author's knowledge, there are very few African female IT professionals although there are many who are users of the technology. Even less is known about the successful implementation of IT in organizations and what impact this has had on women, especially those whose jobs the automation may have directly influenced. Case studies would be needed to establish the size and direction of the impact of IT.

But, bearing in mind the lack of generalizable evidence, it does appear that the likely impact of IT on women, and the role they are playing in the IT area, may be minimal, considering the general status of women in African societies and their position in the technical fields. With the increased penetration of computers in organizations, both in the public and private sectors in Africa, there must have been some impact, however small, positive or negative, on women. For instance, the introduction of computers in most government ministries (more women in Africa work in the public sector than in the formal private sector), some jobs undertaken by women may have been eliminated by automation and others may have been created. Women do most of the data entry work – although changing technology may eventually make data entry pools obsolete – and therefore jobs may have been created in this area. With so many women working in the services sector (three times more than in industry) in Africa, and the increasing emphasis on automation in this sector, IT is bound to have had some impact on women's employment. Women, who are concentrated lower down in the hierarchy in low status jobs, are often easy targets when it comes to getting rid of people. Their employment is particularly vulnerable to automation because of their concentration in work with low skill requirements.

The introduction of computer-based technology into clerical work can build on women's skills, and may have given them new opportunities to enhance human skills. But in the financial sector – banks and insurance companies – where computer technology has penetrated most in Africa, computerization is believed to have limited employment growth. However, without further information, it would be wrong to reach certain conclusions.

The manufacturing sector is of no great importance in many African countries, and has not been extensively automated. Moreover, the current economic and political crisis faced by Africa will not allow extensive automation or major industrial growth in the foreseeable future. It is therefore difficult to predict what impact IT may have on women working in these areas. It does appear that the impact of IT on women has been different from organization to organization and nation to nation. In some

South East Asian countries, jobs have been created for women in IT manufacturing and assembly, although the importance of cheap female labour is slowly decreasing, whilst in many other countries, such as Japan, automation has reduced the employment opportunities for low skilled women. In Singapore, for instance, where the government's focus is on using IT for national development, nearly 55 per cent of the workers in the IT sector in 1987 were women (Chew and Chew, 1990). This figure is higher than that in some of the more advanced countries such as USA, and is largely due to the Singaporean government's policies and incentives for working mothers. The situation in Africa is very different, and no such impact can be expected there. Direct foreign investment in manufacturing and assembly work, where many of the women in South East Asia are employed, does not exist in Africa. Distance from the markets and poor communications facilities also mean that data entry work has not taken off in Africa as it has in the Caribbean.

CONCLUSION

It is difficult to predict exactly what the impact of information technology has been on African women, or what role they play in the area, due to the paucity of information. However, we saw earlier that IT has had little overall impact on these nations themselves – or on their development efforts – and one may therefore be tempted to conclude that IT may have had little significant impact on African women. Although many developments are occurring in the computer area in Africa, there is a great deal of under-utilization of equipment due to lack of skilled personnel, poor strategic buying plans, and scarcity of foreign exchange to import the hardware and software. There is lack of sufficient computer education and training facilities in many countries, which has further aggravated the problem of lack of skills. Scarce foreign currency has been wasted in many cases and there are doubts whether Africa needs IT at all for its development, as it is largely held back by economic and social structures and value systems which have perpetuated under-development. There is a general feeling that technology alone will not be able to change such structures and many doubt its need.

The majority of African women are involved in the informal economy. They often do not enjoy equal opportunities with men. The attitudes towards women, by both men and women themselves, have often suppressed the development or advancement of women. The existing sociocultural norms have so far restricted girls' and women's access to education, training and employment. Poor grounding in maths and science subjects at primary level, and the lack of exposure to technically-oriented subjects, limit their performance in these subjects at secondary school and their access to technical programmes at the tertiary level. African governments themselves have done very little to promote women's participation in technical education, training and employment. Employers' stereotyped attitudes (especially towards working mothers) regarding women's abilities and competence in technical fields mean that few women are recruited. Silent discrimination and stereotyping also exists in many organizations, with the result that even women already in employment are not always given the opportunity to prove their worth (Leigh-Doyle, 1991). Sex-stereotyping on the part of parents, educators, religion, the media and society at large encourage the impression that certain jobs are exclusively for men. Women's own lack of confidence also influences their entry into certain fields and jobs. Often, it is not the technology which is a problem but the economic, social and political structures which keep women in low paid and low status work, whatever the level of technology.

Women's 'double shift', at home and at work, undoubtedly affects their professional progress. In Africa, the home shift may in many cases include caring for parents, in-laws and younger siblings. In addition, women often have to work twice as hard to prove to men that they are also capable of doing their jobs well. The role of a woman is often taken for granted. Essential activities would come to a standstill but for their participation, especially where the 'women's work' syndrome excuses men from attempting it. There is often a conflict between the three roles of mother, wife and employee, and many feel a sense of guilt and give up employment. The demands on working women and their burdens have in fact increased. So it should not be surprising if women were not taking up employment, although IT may offer opportunities for skilled women, due to the scarcity of skilled computer personnel in Africa.

There is certainly a need for more education and training opportunities for girls and women in Africa, both for overall national development and to improve their quality of life. Before this could take place, however, a major programme would be needed to make policy-makers, parents, educators, employers, and others aware of the importance of girls' and women's education. Women's general literacy rate and scientific and technological knowledge have to be addressed before anything can be done about their computer literacy. However it would be a tactical error to introduce programmes only for women. Women should be able to participate actively in such programmes, without treating them as a segregate population. There is also a need for equal employment opportunities and facilities for working women to enable them both to pursue a career and raise a family.

Given the paucity of information, it is difficult to say whether 'women and information technology in Africa' should be a topic of discussion or not, whether we should first examine other issues concerning women in Africa, or whether Africa needs IT at all. As it is not clear what role women are playing in this area, or what impact the technology has had on them, further research would be required to reach some conclusions. Patterns of employment must differ across the continent, and a thorough understanding of the changes occurring in any one country would require in-depth research. Case studies on the importance of women in IT, and the impact of IT on women, to show the differences in context across countries, may be required. This may help identify the potential of IT for women, whether there are jobs in the area, and, if so, how women are going to reap the benefits. Such case studies could also examine the issue of equal opportunities for jobs. However, any further research should consider class and race, as well as gender: women's participation in the IT area must be seen in the context of the domination of the field by certain classes and races. Examination of such issues would help identify their impact on the majority of the indigenous population. Further research on women's situation in Africa would also help answer some of the questions raised in the introduction.

[This essay, with its more pessimistic assessment, is rather different in orientation from the other contributions to the volume. It seemed to us important that it should be included, in order to reflect a wider spectrum of views on these issues – Editors.]

NOTES

1 This paper will largely focus on the impact of computers on women, although IT and computers will be used interchangeably.
2 From here on referred to as Africa. The North African countries and South Africa are not included in this analysis.
3 [However the discussant to this paper, Dr. S. Wangwe, and others have presented many examples of large organizations in sub-Saharan Africa which have successfully absorbed information technology. These examples underline the lack of properly-grounded empirical research in the field. Eds]
4 Leigh-Doyle does not specify in her work what constitutes a technical programme. As no such distinction is made, it will be assumed that all IT related courses are classified as technical programmes.
5 *Financial Times*, 18 October 1991.

REFERENCES

Akande, J.O.D. (1979), *Law and the Status of Women in Nigeria*, Addis Ababa, Ethiopia, United Economic Commission for Africa

Anker, R. and C. Hein (1985), 'Why Third World Urban Employers Usually Prefer Men', *International Labour Review*, Vol. 124, No. 1, Geneva

ATRCW (1986), *Women and the Industrial Development Decade in Africa*, Addis Ababa, African Training and Research Centre for Women (ATRCW), United Nations Economic Commission for Africa

Beech, C. (1990), *Women and Women into Information Technology*, a report by the British Computer Society

Byrne, E. (1988), *Women in Science and Technology: The Institutional Ecology Approach*, Interim Research Report, Department of Education, University of Queensland

Chew, S.B. and R. Chew (1990), 'Information Technology as a Strategy Human Resource Development', in E.C.Y. Kuo, C.M. Loh and K.S. Raman, *Information Technology in Singapore Society: Trends, Policies and Applications*, Singapore University Press

Classe, A. (1992), 'We're talking sex education', *Computing*, January

Cutrufelli, M.R. (1983), *Women of Africa*, London, Zed Books

Davidson, M.J. and C.L. Cooper (eds) (1987), *Women and Information Technology*, Psychology and Productivity at Work Series, London, John Wiley and Sons

Deakin, R. (1984), *Women and Computing: The Golden Opportunity*, London, Macmillan Press

Eriksson, I.V., B.A. Kitchenham and K.G. Tijdens (eds) (1991), *Women, Work and Computerization: Understanding and Overcoming Bias in Work and Education*, Amsterdam, North Holland

Faruqui, A.M., M.H.A. Hassan and G. Sandri (eds) (1988), *The Role of Women in the Development of Science and Technology in the Third World*, proceedings of the conference organized by CIDA and the Third World Academy of Sciences, Trieste, Italy, October

Frenkel, K.A. (1990), 'Women and Computing', *Communications of the ACM*, November

Harding, J. (1987), 'Gender and Science, Technology and Maths Education: an Overview', *Gender Stereotyping in Science, Technology and Maths Education*, London, Commonwealth Secretariat

Harrison, P. (1983), *The Third World Tomorrow*, NY, Pilgrim Press and Harmondsworth, Penguin

Irvine, J. (1990), 'Women into Information Technology', *Information Technology and Public Policy*, Vol. 8, No. 3, Summer

Kluzer, S. (1988), *Computer Diffusion in Black Africa: A Preliminary Assessment*, unpublished paper, SPRU, University of Sussex, Brighton, UK

Leigh-Doyle, S. (1991), 'Increasing Women's Participation in Technical Fields: a Pilot Project in Africa', *International Labour Review*, Vol. 130, No. 4

Lim, G.K. (1989), 'Women's Participation in the Computer Industry in Singapore', in Ken Tijdens *et al.* (eds), *Women, Work and Computing: Forming New Alliances*, Amsterdam, North Holland

Little, K. (1973), *African Women in Towns: an Aspect of Africa's Social Revolution*, Cambridge, Cambridge University Press

Lockheed, M.E. and K.S. Gorman (1987), *Sociocultural Factors Affecting Science Learning and Attitudes*, Washington DC, World Bank Reprint Series, No. 426

Lovegrove, G. and B. Segal (eds) (1991), *Women into Computing: Selected Papers, 1988–1990*, London, Springer

Mahmoud, F.B. (1991), *African Women Transformation and Development*, Institute of African Alternatives

Mitter, S. (1991), 'Computer Aided Manufacturing and Women's Employment: a Global Critique of Post Fordism', in I.V. Eriksson, B.A. Kitchenham and K.G. Tijdens (eds), *Women, Work and Computerisation: Understanding and Overcoming Bias in Work and Education*, Amsterdam, North Holland

Mumford, E. (1980), *Where are Tomorrow's Top Women Executives?*, Manchester Business School Review, Vol. 4, No. 3

Ng, C. (ed.) (1987), *Technology and Gender: Women's Work in Asia*, Women's Studies Unit, UPM and Malaysian Social Science Association

Ng, C. and J. Othman (1992), 'Information Technology, Gender and Employment in Malaysia', in S.C. Bhatnagar and M. Odedra (eds) *Social Implications of Computers in Developing Countries*, New Delhi, Tata-McGraw Hill

Obbe, C. (1980), *African Women: Their Struggle for Economic Independence*, London, Zed Books

Odedra, M. (1990a), *Information Technology Transfer to Developing Countries: Case Studies from Kenya, Zambia and Zimbabwe*, unpublished Ph.D. thesis, London School of Economics

Odedra, M. (1990b), 'Poor Management leads to Gross Under-utilization', *Computer in Africa*, Vol. 4, No. 5, July

Odedra, M. (1990c), 'Information Technology Transfer to Developing Countries: Is it Really Taking Place?', in J. Berleur and J. Drumm (eds), *Information Technology Assessment*, Amsterdam, North Holland

Odedra, M. (1991), 'Possibilities and Pitfalls of IT', *PC World Africa*, August

Odedra, M. (1992a), 'Africa Ripe for Market Growth Despite Serious Obstacles', *International Computer Update Forecast*, an IDG Communications Publication, January

Odedra, M. (1992b), 'IT in Africa: Boom or Doom?', *PC World Africa*, April

Odedra, M. (1992c), 'Telecommunications in Africa', *PC World Africa*, April

Parikh, I. (1987), *Women in Management: an Annotated Bibliography with Emphasis on Commonwealth Sources*, London, Commonwealth Secretariat

Parikh, I. and P. Farrell (1991), *Approaches to Women Managers' Training*, London, Commonwealth Secretariat

Robertson, C. and I. Berger (eds) (1986), *Women and Class in Africa*, NY, Africana Publishing Company

Soriyan, B. and B. Aina (1991), 'Women's Work and Challenges of Computerisation: Nigerian Case', in I.V. Eriksson, B.A. Kitchenham and K.G. Tijdens (eds), *Women, Work and Computerisation: Understanding and Overcoming Bias in Work and Education*, North Holland

Stamp, P. (1989), *Technology, Gender and Power in Africa*, Ottawa, International Development Research Centre

Subramaniam, P.R. (1991), *The Future for Women in Information Technology*, M.Sc. dissertation, London School of Economics

Tijdens, K., M. Jennings, I. Wagner and M. Weggelaar (eds) (1989), *Women, Work and Computing: Forming New Alliances*, Amsterdam, North Holland

Tng, H. and C.S. Yap (1990), 'Attitudes of Female Computer Professionals Telecommuting', in E.C.Y. Kuo, C.M. Loh and K.S. Raman (eds), *Information Technology in Singapore Society: Trends, Policies and Applications*, Singapore University Press

UNESCO (1991), *World Education Report*, 1991

Virgo, P. (1988), 'The Case for Women into Information Technology Campaign', *Information Technology and Public Policy*, Vol. 6, No. 3, Summer

WIT (1990), *Creating Employment Pattern for the Year 2000*, survey conducted by Women into Information Technology Foundation, UK

World Bank (1988), *Education in Sub-Saharan Africa: Policies for Adjustment, Revitalization and Expansion*, Washington DC, World Bank

World Bank (1989), *Sub-Saharan Africa: From Crisis to Sustainable Growth*, Washington DC, World Bank

Wright, B.D. (ed.) (1987), *Women, Work and Technology: Transformations*, Chicago, University of Michigan Press

13 Gender perspectives on health and safety in information processing

Learning from international experience

Ruth Pearson

INTERNATIONAL TRENDS IN INFORMATION PROCESSING EMPLOYMENT

The nature of employment in information processing is extremely varied. Women's employment reflects the full range of jobs from the low-skilled, low-paid data entry jobs through to the high-skilled, high-status professional jobs of systems analysts and computer programmers, though most are concentrated towards the low-skilled end of the spectrum (Pearson and Mitter, 1993). The dynamics of the adoption and dissemination of computer technology are also varied, reflecting the very different socioeconomic realities in different sectors and countries. In developed countries computer technology has been introduced into most offices in all sectors. The diffusion of information technology in developing countries is much more piecemeal. In many cases diffusion has reflected the pattern found in developed countries, where public sector entities and private corporations have followed a similar pattern of computerization, starting with mainframe computers in the 1970s and progressively adopting microcomputers and PCs during the 1980s.

The bulk of women's employment in computer-related occupations in both developed and developing countries has been concerned with the entry and manipulation of data via computer keyboards. This has long been recognized within developed countries. The fact that telecommunications operate internationally implies that information processing services can be relocated to low wage economies. There is a well-established, if limited, trend to relocate or subcontract office services to low-wage developing countries, where women are employed to enter data at a fraction of the cost of comparable labour in developed countries (Davis and Stack, 1993; ILO, 1990; OTA, 1985; R. Pearson, 1993; Posthuma, 1987). Conversely, highly-skilled software development work is purchased from developing countries' computer professionals, either *in situ* or by importing the professionals on short-term contracts, a process known as 'body-shopping' (Heeks, 1989; Mitter and Pearson, 1992; Schware, 1992).

Studies of these processes have focused on the opportunities they present for less developed countries (LDCs), in terms of employment for school leavers and earning foreign exchange, and on the unsubstantiated expectation that such relocation of work offers the opportunity to 'leapfrog' into a new technology age in which small LDCs could have a knowledge-based comparative advantage (Girvan, 1989; Hanna, 1991).

The discussion of the diffusion of computer technology in developing countries, either through domestic computerization or through the internationalization of data entry or software development, has almost totally ignored the contractual position, wages, training and promotion and health and safety of new technology workers. Given the amount of interest in these issues within developed countries, particularly as regards health and safety, this is a telling omission.

RECONSTRUCTING WOMEN AS 'CHEAP' LABOUR: NEW TECHNOLOGY EMPLOYMENT OR THE SAME OLD STORY?

The few case studies available which detail women's employment in international data entry are based on research in the Caribbean, which has become a major centre for external sourcing, particularly of commercial time-sensitive data for North American corporations (Posthuma, 1987; Freeman, n.d.; R. Pearson, 1993). One of the catalysts for this research was the publication of a major US Congress study on Office Automation (OTA, 1985), which considered 'Offshore Office Work' as an alternative cost-reducing strategy to 'Home-Based Automated Office Work', particularly for data input by well-educated Caribbean workers who earned less than one sixth of their American counterparts. This study makes one passing reference to the fact that 'women comprise 99 per cent of the workers' (ibid.: p. 217). OTA focuses on the cheapness[1] of LDC labour compared with comparable workers in the United States, and draws a parallel with the concept of 'cheap labour' in analyses of offshore manufacturing during the previous decades. The report also notes the availability of high quality and productive labour (ibid.: p. 223). Both host governments and employers have tended to see the relocation of work as an opportunity for developing countries, since it is a labour-intensive activity involving very little capital outlay, which offers numerous benefits to the host countries:

It is a 'clean' industry, without the heavy equipment, large space requirements, and pollution often associated with other industrial enterprises.
The industry provides, at the very least, rudimentary training in computer use – a rare opportunity for workers in less developed countries.
Finally, it establishes a foundation on which further advancement in
computer-related industries, such as software development technical
services and data transmission, may grow.

(ibid.: p. 225)

Other issues which have been discussed include the security of data transmitted internationally, the lack of a regulatory framework to control piracy,
national security, the desirability or practicality of imposing tariffs on the
value added to transmitted data (Davis and Stack, 1993; B. Harris, 1989;
Locksley, 1986), and the regulation of trade in services (Ryan, 1990). Both
radical commentators and voices from orthodox financial institutions such
as the World Bank continue to see this form of internationalization as a
cost-free, win–win scenario, in which foreign exchange is generated, unemployed workers are given training and jobs, and the seeds of a new place
in the international division of labour are planted, to flower in the form of
a new comparative advantage in the twenty-first century.

Some criticism of the relocation of computer-based services has been
voiced by those who speak from the standpoint of US labour – organized or
not. The AFL-CIO (American Federation of Labor–Confederation of
Industrial Organizations) has maintained a protectionist position regarding
offshore sourcing in the manufacturing sector, and has extended this to data
entry operations (OTA, 1985: p. 224). More recently the extension of
international relocation to what has been called – provocatively – 'intelligent office work', as well as the contracting out of standard software
packaging and the continuing practice of 'body shopping', has attracted the
interest of professional associations in the West (Heeks, 1989; Mitter and
Pearson, 1992; Schware, 1992).

The OTA report dismisses talk of disadvantages of off-shore data
processing:

The development expert claims that negative reactions, if any, in
developing countries usually come from the more educated sectors and
the labour movement or, as he put it 'people who are not worried about
having a job'. Those citizens of developing countries who view US
investment as exploitative are those who are generally of higher economic status and are not in need of the job opportunities that result from
such investment.

(ibid.: p. 226)

It is significant that there is no discussion of health and safety aspects of offshore office work, given that the same report devotes a whole thirty page chapter (Chapter 5) to 'Office Automation and the Quality of Worklife', which details the risks of stress, and the results of investigation and research on problems with eyesight, musculoskeletal systems, and reproductive systems. These problems are raised in relation to the increasing numbers of home workers who work with computers and visual display units in the United States (OTA, 1985; Di Martino and Wirth, 1990).

It would be fair to say then, that the literature on information technology, computers and employment in developing countries has not been concerned with the health and safety aspects of such employment, even when there is some awareness of these issues in the context of domestic employment.[2]

Since women workers form the vast majority of the workforce in LDCs associated with computer technology (Mitter and Pearson, 1992; Ng, 1991) it can be concluded that once again women are regarded as a cheap and flexible workforce, able to adapt to the new work practices (Standing, 1989; Elson, 1991) which are at the cutting edge of labour relations (Glucksmann, 1986 and 1990).

In this sense, the absence of discussion about the risks to workers' health in LDCs is not surprising, and reflects the very similar positions taken as regards the expansion of women's employment in manufacturing for export in the 1970s and 1980s, when any discussion of the constraints and contradictions of such employment was attacked as self-seeking and unrealistic.[3] Whilst the technology may be new, it would appear that women are in danger of being recreated in a familiar role – that of cheap and abundant labour.

HEALTH HAZARDS OF WORK WITH COMPUTERS AND KEYBOARDS: THE EXPERIENCE FROM AUSTRALIA AND EUROPE

Groups of workers who have suffered from conditions attributed to using new technology have brought the issues into public and political forums by their attempts to gain recognition and compensation for their conditions. An article in the International Labour Review accurately reports:

VDUs have aroused intense debate and often controversy over the implications for workers, particularly the risks to health. Although relatively few countries have passed laws or regulations referring specifically to VDUs, several have recommended codes of practice or guidelines for their use. These cover a variety of issues, such as advance notice, consultation and negotiation procedures with workers or their representatives, training, job design and job security, rest breaks, maximum VDU use, protection during pregnancy, eye care and machine and workstation specifications.

(Di Martino and Wirth, 1990: p. 542)

This gives the impression that there is general agreement in 'several' countries, recognizing the health risks associated with working with computers and related technology, and that there are agreed procedures about prevention and worker protection. It might lead the reader to suppose that these health risks have been defined as industrial injuries for which insured and protected workers are entitled to some degree of compensation.

The reality is quite different. There is an enormous amount of controversy over the medical and legal issues relating to information technology and health risks. The lack of agreement has meant that recent legislation and recommendations within the European Union (EU), have provided much less worker protection than had been expected. It will be worthwhile to survey the medical controversies, and the differing legislative and political debates over repetitive strain injury (RSI) in Australia and the UK. This information will provide a basis for an analysis of the health and safety risks faced by new technology workers in developing countries, from a gender perspective.

Health risks and computer work

Although there is no medical and legal agreement of the degree of risk and vulnerability to various health conditions, the literature has established five types of health hazards which have been attributed to work with computers, and more specifically to the work situation of inputting or manipulating text or data using a visual display unit (VDU) or visual display terminal (VDT):[4]

1   Musculoskeletal; this includes a range of named disorders of the neck, upper limbs, shoulders and back, including tenosynovitis, tendinitis, peritendinitis, bursitis, epicondylitis, carpal tunnel syndrome, dupuytren's contracture, writers' cramp, ganglions, and cervicobrachial disorders (Putz-Anderson, 1988(a); Huws, 1987). These conditions are not identical with the list of thirty separate diseases in the International Classification of Disease Codes, which includes carpal tunnel syndrome, cervicobrachial syndrome, tenosynovitis, and ganglions (cysts), but which makes no mention of repetitive strain injury (Putz-Anderson, 1988(b): p. 601).

2   Deterioration of and problems with visual capacity, including eyestrain and fatigue, loss of focus and mobility, reduction in capacity to dilate pupils, and cataracts (ibid.). The symptoms linked to eye strain include

blurred and double vision, irritability, headaches and migraines, nausea, and discomfort with contact lenses (DeMatteo, 1985).

3 Stress and fatigue; symptoms include short-term problems of fatigue, irritability, depression, headaches, migraine, insomnia, menstrual problems, and accidents, and long-term problems of heart disease, high blood pressure, depression, anxiety, dermatitis, ulcers and fertility problems.

4 Skin complaints including rosacea, acne, dermatitis, telangiectases, pustolosis, urticaria, ostitis and other unspecified changes (ibid.:, and Berg *et al.*, 1990).

5 Reproductive hazards; miscarriages, congenital deformities and fertility problems associated with stress and with emissions of ionising and non-ionising radiation from cathode ray tubes fitted in now obsolete computer monitors (Labour Research, 1984; DeMatteo, 1985; Brandt and Nielsen, 1990).

The literature on reproductive hazards remains deeply contested, and is based on reported or observed clusters of adverse pregnancy outcomes including miscarriages, stillbirths and abnormalities. The 1992 UK Health and Safety Regulations state that:

> There has been considerable public concern among some groups of visual display unit workers in particular due to electromagnetic radiation. Many scientific studies have been carried out but taken as a whole they do not show any link between miscarriages or birth defects and working with VDUs.
>
> (HSE, 1992: pp. 42–43)

We will confine our discussion to the first category, which has been labelled as RSI (repetitive strain injury), since these injuries can lead to a total inability to carry out many tasks (R.M. Pearson, 1990). It is worth noting however that figures issued by the Data Management Association in North America indicate that eyestrain is in fact the most commonly experienced health problem of VDU workers (Bodek, 1987). This finding is supported by data from Malaysia (Ng and Othman, 1991) and Japan (Shiga, 1987).

'If I can't see it doesn't exist': medical controversies over computer-related repetitive strain injuries

Musculoskeletal disorders cause the most severe incapacity amongst sufferers. Although back and shoulder ache feature very frequently amongst surveys of work-related problems of computer clerical workers, the term RSI applies particularly to problems with hands and wrists, and necks. The range of musculo-skeletal conditions which have been reported illustrates that the precise medical diagnosis can fall within a wide range of conditions, and of course can comprise a composite of two or more of these conditions (Bammer, 1990). Despite the frequency with which symptoms are reported amongst office workers, medical opinion remains divided over:

1. whether a term such as RSI has any meaning or usefulness;
2. the medical diagnosis of the symptoms;
3. whether there is in fact a physiological basis, rather than a psychological basis, for the reported symptoms; and
4. whether there is any evidence of causation which would link particular kinds of work with these symptoms.

It is beyond the scope of this paper to present an exhaustive review of the medical evidence and disputes which swirl around this issue, but it is useful to present some of the arguments, since the controversy over the existence and causation of RSI is important in contextualising the link between the gender bias of the new work categories and work organization associated with computers and attitudes to the health and safety of workers in LDCs.

What do we mean by repetitive strain injury?
(It depends on who *we* are.)

In spite of the ubiquity of the symptoms of RSI there is no agreement about definitions or terminology. In Australia, the conditions of tenosynovitis, tendinitis and bursitis have been recorded as compensatable industrial conditions since the 1960s, and 'from the end of the 1970s newly established workers' health centres began to use the term 'teno' to cover all of the repetition injuries they were finding amongst their *predominantly blue collar* clientele' (Hopkins, 1990: p. 367, emphasis added). When the incidence spread to the newly established and expanding white collar segment of the workforce, the term 'repetition injury' began to be widely used by organizations such as the Australian Public Service Association, the National Health and Medical Research Council and the National Occupational Health and Safety Commission. This term was extensively adopted by the media and by many doctors who were not specialists but were required to respond to the increasing number of people presenting with symptoms consistent with what was widely understood by the term.

In the UK however, whilst the term 'repetitive strain injury' is widely used by the media, by sufferers (who have formed an RSI association), and by some doctors and specialists, it has been studiously avoided by the

Health and Safety Executive who prefer to refer to 'work-related upper limb disorders. These range from temporary fatigue or soreness in the limb to chronic soft tissue disorders like peritendinitis or carpal tunnel syndrome. Some keyboard operators have suffered occupational cramp' (HSE, 1992: p. 41).

In the United States the term 'cumulative trauma disorder (CTD) has been used within the occupational health and safety literature. This is a much less transparent term for the general public. Although some agencies do use what is known as the Australian term (repetition strain injury), a lot of occupational medical literature still uses the generic 'musculo-skeletal problems', which is totally neutral in terms of causation' (Putz-Anderson, 1988b). In the USA there is not – as yet – a widely accepted acronym. It has been claimed that the absence of an acronym contributes to the lower rate of recognition and discussion of the problem in that country.

In Sweden, where discussion and remedial policy is well advanced, the terms adopted are ergonomically-related injuries (ERI) or occupational cervicobrachial disorder (OCD), collectively referred to as work-related musculoskeletal disorders. These terms reflect the consensus that occupational labour processes are implicated, but place the emphasis on ergonomic rather than other factors.

These terms are themselves being challenged or refined, not least by medical specialists who are engaged in a fierce dispute about the medical validity of the terminology utilized. Recent (equally disputed) additions to the nomenclature are 'overuse syndrome' (Fry, 1993) and 'refractory cervicobrachial pain' or RCBP (Quintner and Elvey, 1991, cited in Cohen *et al.*, 1992).

There is disagreement as to the meaning of the terms utilized to describe the symptomology (which is not itself disputed), with much specialist medical opinion decrying the 'unscientific' nature of the generic terms employed. Without wishing to enter into this acrimonious dispute, the following extracts convey some of the flavour of the discourse:

> Conventional medicine is not prepared to accept that a physical injury or disease process occurred in an upper limb, or indeed elsewhere, unless there are convincing and reproducible physical signs. The accepted signs of an injury and associated healing are those of tenderness, loss of function and associated histological findings of inflammation . . . until such independent support is forthcoming, the overuse concept should remain an eccentric and unproven hypothesis.
>
> (Semple, 1993: p. 25)

The self-generating term RSI is misleading for there is no scientific evidence proving that repetitive work causes either tissue strain or injury.... The scientific basis of modern medicine demands that disease is caused by a pathological process which, if not identifiable, has a rational hypothesis, thus enabling formulation and designation of appropriate management.... RSI now bears the hall mark of a sociopolitical phenomenon, rather than a medical condition, which on historical precedent, will decline when this basis of RSI is generally accepted.

(Ireland, 1988: p. 5)

Medical explanations of RSI: the doctors' dilemmas

The dispute as to whether the symptoms known as RSI are related to physical injuries, and if so of which type, continues without any sign of a resolution. The position of Semple, that without discernible and replicable physiological signs the patients' symptoms should be dismissed, represents one extreme of the debate. But amongst those who accept that the symptoms have a physiological cause, opinion is widely divided as to whether the explanatory physiological base lies in damage and malfunction of the central or peripheral nervous system (Quintner and Elvey, 1991; Cohen *et al.*, 1992), or in muscle overuse (Fry, 1993), and whether its treatment belongs within the specialism of rheumatology, orthopaedic surgery, physiotherapy, or some combination of these (R.M. Pearson, 1993). These disagreements partly arise from competition between specialisms, and the tendency to work in narrower and narrower specialism rather than to view problems, diagnosis and treatment from a more holistic perspective. It is important to recognize that these problems have only been presented in large numbers within the last ten to fifteen years. In the absence of any sustained and reliable epidemiological studies, the current battles reflect the inability of conventional medicine to respond adequately to a changing pathology of occupationally-related injuries.

'If we can't find it in the body, it must be all in the mind'

As well as denying the existence of RSI, and the dispute over its physiological nature, there is also a broad body of medical opinion which asserts that the symptoms have a psychological cause. This argument asserts that the pain and other symptoms presented by sufferers result from unresolved psychological conflict or emotional disturbance (Bammer and Martin, 1988). This argument is most strongly proposed by Lucire, a female Australian psychiatrist who argues that RSI is a form of conversion disorder or mass hysteria in which patients exhibit neurotic reactions to keyboards and movements which have become symbols of danger to the vulnerable – defined by Lucire as 'eggshell personalities, usually compulsive or dependent people who are powerless and dependent and who cannot otherwise express their righteous rage at their supervisors, employers and spouses, so resort to the use of their exquisitely symbolic pain as a mode of communication of their distress' (Lucire, 1986: p. 325). Needless to say those who support the view that the condition has a psychological basis are also aware that the majority of sufferers are women:

> The condition commonly affects young to middle-aged and predominantly female employees engaged in low paying, monotonous low prestige occupations. The symptoms fail to respond to any form of treatment other than psychological counselling. . . . The treatment of RSI is unrewarding as it requires the patient's acceptance of the psychological basis of their condition. . . . It is surprising how often unsatisfactory social, family, marital and economic circumstances are expressed as job dissatisfaction.
>
> (Ireland, 1988: p. 9)

Some commentators even suggest that sufferers fake physical symptoms which they have learned will earn them an appropriate diagnosis, or present symptoms consistent with hysteria:

> [they] describe 1,000 patients, mostly female workers in offices and factories, and a very typical attitude of the affected upper limb, with half flexion of the elbow, wrist and fingers, without evidence of muscle atrophy. . . . Nowhere do they suggest that this posture is learned, whether consciously or not. Its pattern of incidence is like complaints of *koro* in South East Asian Chinese (sudden anxiety about recession of the penis into the surrounding skin), hysterical overbreathing in teenage girls at pop concerts, or several (other) conditions.
>
> (Patkin, 1993: p. 11)

The last writer goes on to compare 'outbreaks' of ERS with outbreaks of computer-related 'facial dermatitis' in Sweden, angina in computer operators in North Carolina, and mass hysteria at a workplace in Singapore. It should give us pause for thought that the assumption here is that all these events were hysterical manifestations, rather than having a physiological explanation linked to the technological and organizational nature of the labour processes. This view of the nature of RSI cannot be understood without an appreciation of the trajectory of RSI in Australia, which is described below.

RSI: the Australian disease

The rapid growth of manifestations, diagnoses, compensation and dispute about RSI in the mid 1980s resulted in RSI being called the Australian disease, the Australian epidemic, or 'kangaroo paw'. This designation refers both to the emergence of the condition and public debate about it within Australia, and the suggestion, often made quite explicit, that RSI was a condition which was only manifest in Australia, because of the incentive for workers to produce symptoms which would enable them to get compensation.

A number of published studies contain succinct descriptions of the 'Australian disease' (Hall and Morrow, 1988; Hopkins, 1990; Reid *et al.*, 1991; Bammer and Martin, 1988; Meekosha and Jakubowicz, 1991). One version is as follows:

> In Australia between 1983 and 1987 there was an epidemic of upper limb regional pain which was concentrated among workers in occupations which involved either repetitive movement, or the adoption of constrained postures for lengthy periods of time (e.g. process workers and keyboard operators). Although the phenomenon of upper limb pain was observed among process operators in the late 1960s and early 1970s it only achieved epidemic status in 1983 when the first claims began to be made under workers' compensation. The rate of claims increased dramatically during 1984 and 1985, persisted through 1986, and then equally dramatically declined in 1987. The consensus of informed opinion is that the worst of the epidemic has passed.
>
> (Hall and Morrow, 1988: p. 645)

Other accounts of the same phenomena are more cautious about making such an unproblematic link between the availability of workers' compensation and the rise and fall of RSI in Australia. Certainly the 1980s saw a rise in the number of cases recorded, in the number of people seeking compensation, and the number of computer keyboard operatives, particularly in the public service. The number of new notified cases has now diminished. However the assumption of a causal relationship between the availability of compensation and the incidence of RSI is rather suspect.

Part of the story lies in the fact that from the early 1980s the Australian government explicitly recorded the incidence of RSI, and accepted compensation claims on the basis of certification by the claimant's own doctor, who needed only to state that the claimant was suffering from RSI and required a specific period of rest (ibid.: p. 367). In the United States and Britain at that time there was no available source of national information on the incidence of such conditions (Putz-Anderson, 1988b: pp. 604–605).

The absence of public recognition of RSI as an occupational and therefore compensatable disease in other countries meant there was less public awareness of the issues, and this reinforced the view in Australia that there was no comparable condition elsewhere, in spite of extensive, if not systematic, data relating to its prevalence in the United States, Scandinavia, and Japan (Hopkins, 1990: pp. 366–367; English *et al.*, 1989; Bammer and Martin, 1988; Polakoff, 1991)

The reported decline in notified RSI diagnosis in Australia was not the result of a reduction in the incidence of the symptoms of the condition. It was directly related to changes in the compensation procedure, rehabilitation programmes and medical and legal delegitimation of the condition (Meekosha and Jakubowicz, 1991). In many states the system was modified to reduce statutory employer liability and to introduce mandatory rehabilitation programmes. Instead of institutionalizing employer liability, the state has joined forces with those seeking to devalidate claimants' cases by arguing that the condition is psychological in origin. As the medical controversies rage on, workers who have participated in mandatory rehabilitation programmes report a lack of professional support and the exacerbation of their condition by intensive testing procedures. The rehabilitation therapy, officially designed to assist sufferers in regaining fitness to work, has been transformed into an official routine to deny people's perception of their own pain and mobility:

> A major issue for interviewees is the pain involved during and after the key test. . . . Many expressed shock at receiving an assessment that they were fit for work when they had felt sure that the pain they had reported during the test would have indicated that they were not fully recovered.
> (ACT RSI Support Group, 1991: pp. 4–5)

In spite of the apparently positive attitude towards health hazards in the 1980s, the acrimonious debate has altered public and professional perceptions of RSI. The standard explanation that RSI in Australia is the result of the increased pace and duration of keyboard utilization, in ergonomically unsound workplaces, has been undermined (Bammer and Martin, 1998). Alternative hypotheses are that people with RSI are malingerers who don't want to work, who suffer from a form of compensation neurosis (whereby symptoms disappear in the absence of financial gain), that it is a form of psychological hysteria or conversion neurosis (as discussed above), or that RSI is a manifestation of normal fatigue experienced by all sectors of the population with no underlying injury or pathology. These counter hypotheses have a distinct gender bias, as was apparent in the earlier citations referring to dependent personalities, women in repetitive unskilled jobs, and various forms of neurotic dispositions.

Reid *et al.* (1991) have described the experiences of women sufferers of RSI in the increasingly hostile climate of Australia's legal, medical and compensatory systems as a 'pilgrimage of pain' in which women's encounters with the system 'contributed to the chronicity, unemployment, bewilderment and despair reported by so many' (ibid.: p. 602). Their research indicates that the 'polarized environment characterised by doubt, derision and debate' (ibid.) in which sufferers sought advice and treatment, created a situation in which judgements were made about their situation which were directly linked to their gender, family circumstances, body shape and emotional distress. Professionals and experts revealed prejudices about semi-skilled women workers which reflected class and gender conflicts in the wider society.

This is underlined by the recent publication of a number of studies in the medical journals which report on research on 'overuse syndrome' amongst musicians (Fry, 1986, 1988 and 1993; Dennett and Fry, 1988; Lippmann, 1991). These studies have examined the similarities between musicians' 'overuse syndrome' and repetitive strain injury of keyboard and process workers (Bammer, 1993). Although mainly addressing medical analysis, the implications in terms of the prejudices of the experts dealing with RSI are not lost on all writers:

> Much of the heat in the debate over whether occupational overuse exists as a clinical entity has centred on whether the examining physician believes the patient. The problems lie in the lack of objective clinical signs and repeatable investigative tests. Excluding clear cut tendinitis, synovitis and carpal tunnel syndrome, other entities, even as diagnostically straightforward as epicondylitis lack objectivity. When one moves proximally towards the shoulder and neck the problems are greatly increased. . . . The two schools of 'real illness' and 'malingerers' shape up to each other in the courtroom, provide a field day for the lawyers, but do little to help the patients.
>
> How can we get closer to resolving these issues? After all, many of the 'sufferers' are poorly paid manual workers undertaking soul destroying repetitive tasks. They have much to gain from compensation and a respite from occupational boredom. They are also likely to slip inexorably into chronicity.
>
> The search for truth in the patients' symptoms is thus frequently

dogged by the knowledge that they would be advantaged by stopping work and indeed their intellectual powers may preclude a good history in the first place. The position of professional and student musicians is in marked contrast. Here are a group of intelligent, highly motivated individuals who have everything to lose if they develop a disabling pain, and yet their 'work' involves repetitive movements and abnormal postures.

... musicians develop symptom-sign complexes of overuse syndrome indistinguishable from those of less gifted and less motivated workers undertaking work practices which involve comparable hand-arm movements. Ballet dancers develop equally disabling pain and tenderness but in the lower limbs. Again here is another group for whom changing employment would be a disaster.

If we 'believe' the disease to be genuine in dedicated artists, should we not approach the lowly manual worker with more open mindedness? After all, the overuse is genuine and obvious in both groups. The belief in the effects is being driven by our preconceptions of patients and their motivations. Dr Fry has done us all a service by his work into the occupational hazards of the performing arts. It does not provide the incontrovertible proof we all seek, but should make those who espouse the malingering theory to sleep less easily in their beds.

(Harrington, 1993)

Because the 'lowly manual workers' are in fact women keyboard operators, the assumption is that they do not need to work. This is the familiar gendered notion that women's wages are not central for her household, and that paid work is not central to the identity and self image of women in the same way as it is for men. As another medical 'expert' commented, most of the people who consulted him with RSI symptoms were characterized by 'short periods of involvement in the workforce, impulse resignations and unsatisfactory relationships with other workers . . . like the depressed subjects, the women who have conversion reactions frequently reported difficulty with their employers' (Black, 1987, cited in Meekosha and Jacubowicz, 1991).

It is true that women are the majority of RSI sufferers. In 1984, women accounted for 2,800 of the 3,022 cases reported amongst civil servants in New South Wales (Meekosha and Jakubowicz, 1986).

Whilst the debate about the genuineness of the symptoms continues, it is not totally clear that the 'epidemic' in Australia has subsided. The basis for recording the figures has been changed and researchers report that it is now very difficult to obtain data on RSI incidence. Moreover with more public consciousness of the problem, employers are carrying out pre-employment

checks which are aimed at eliminating stereotypically RSI prone appli-
cants, which also has the effect of intimidating other employees from
making complaints or taking action. It may also be that the apparent decline
in incidence relates to better keyboards and changes in the kinds of work
being carried out (Meekosha and Jakubowicz, 1991).

THE RELATIONSHIP BETWEEN RSI AND TECHNOLOGY IN THE WORKPLACE

Some analysis has been carried out to identify the extent to which the
incidence of RSI can be related directly to changes in technology and
the organization of work. Bammer (1987) argues that there are four causes
of repetitive motion injury (an alternative designation to RSI) which can act
alone or in combination: repetitive movements; less frequent, but more
forceful movements; static loading and awkward body postures. Introduction of VDTs into offices has increased three of these risk factors
– rapid repetitive movements, static loading and awkward body movements. Soft touch keyboards allow users to attain much higher keystroke
rates, and the elimination of other actions such as carriage returns, the
application of correction fluid etc. increases the static loading through the
prolonged maintenance of keying positions. Badly positioned and un-
adjustable screens contribute to damaging postures. Additional function
keys increase the need to adopt awkward positions – especially of the wrist
joints and fifth fingers. Ironically the absence of the fourth risk factor,
forceful movements, lessens the risk of tenosynovitis, which is a notifiable
industrial injury in the UK and elsewhere.

These findings have encouraged the view that the ergonomic design of
workplaces and equipment will eliminate RSI, and reinforce the view that
better design is a major reason for the demise of RSI in Australia. However
the research also indicates that there are other factors involved, both in the
construction of risk and in the predisposition of some people, or people
carrying out specific tasks, to RSI. Workers who are in a competitive
situation, who are very self motivated and/or workers who are at the end of
a rigid hierarchy which leaves them little room for autonomy over the pace
of their work, the timing or rest breaks, or decisions over which work
should have highest priority are likely to be particularly vulnerable. Women in
subordinate data entry jobs have limited autonomy – not only in terms of
the allocation of their time, but also in terms of their space and their
physical mobility (Meekosha and Jakubowicz, 1986).[5]

It is too soon to ascertain whether improved workplace and equipment
design, combined with consciousness of the importance of task diversity

and breaks from continuous keying, will eliminate the risk factor even for those workers with the predispositions described above.

LDC EXPERIENCE

To my knowledge there are relatively few studies on which to base any reliable picture of the incidence or prevalence of RSI or other computer-related health risks in developing countries. Many writers make the probably correct assumption that computer operators are vulnerable to the same kind of health risks which have been documented in the advanced countries. Barnes reported that:

> While data entry firms in the UK, Canada and the US are being forced into an awareness of [these] risks by women's organizations, unions and the female workers themselves, the industry in Jamaica still has to catch up. No special attention is paid to the type of seating used, the frequency with which operators are able to get up and walk about, lighting, or anything else.
>
> (Barnes, 1989)

My own study of offshore data entry work in Jamaica confirms the view that there is very little public discussion of health and safety aspects of keyboarding within the sector (R. Pearson, 1993). But, as I argued at the beginning of this paper, given the attention paid to RSI and other health and safety issues in advanced countries, it is surprising that this has not arisen as an issue for wider public discussion. Although there is virtually no literature on the working conditions and health outcomes of offshore contract data entry or data processing workers in LDCs, it is interesting to note that an American company operating in the Philippines boasted to potential customers that 10 per cent of its 800 non-union employees 'are deaf mutes (for the best accuracy)' (N. Cohen, 1992). It may be that the inability to complain about health and safety aspects is as prized as the implied conscientiousness of these handicapped employees.

Ng, whose research is concerned with the introduction of computers into the domestic telecommunications industry, asserts that 'the effects (of information technology) on the health and safety of its users is a major and *less controversial issue*' (Ng, 1991, emphasis added), but she reports no evidence on RSI or other musculo-skeletal problems of data entry or other workers, beyond the statement that 'complaints related to the eyes, hands and wrists, shoulders, neck and back, and general health problems, are commonly registered by these VDU users (ibid.: p. 45). Data about abnormal pregnancy outcomes is also difficult to assess since it is presented without any standard of comparison with a similar cohort of women in different occupational situations (ibid.: pp. 45–47).

There is one study (Soares, 1991) of data entry clerks in a public sector data processing centre in Brazil. This found evidence of problems in arms, upper back, and legs. A significant number of workers were certified as having tenosynovitis, with a larger number displaying the symptoms indicating this condition. Soares notes that the work of these keyboard operators is extremely controlled, with talking and mobility prohibited. Although chair heights were adjustable, the back rests were not. Although the screens were not adjustable, few workers reported problems with their vision, which the researcher suggested may be because they spend less than half of their time watching the screen. Soares also suggests that the high levels of stress, irritability and exhaustion are linked to the facts that women have to do domestic work at home rather than rest and recover from their work-related strains, that they routinely do overtime, and that they spend considerable time commuting to work.

LEARNING FROM INTERNATIONAL EXPERIENCE

Clearly more research is necessary to assess the extent of health problems among keyboard operatives in LDCs, and particular attention must be paid to the specifics of their working routines, tasks and allied problems. In the light of the Australian literature and other studies it is possible to suggest what the parameters of the problems may be.

First, activities in which standards of productivity and speed are the basis for payment, job security, and promotion are likely to be those in which the risk of RSI is greater. However, offshore data entry facilities may in fact be less pressurised than large workplaces in the public or corporate sector, if a continuous flow of work cannot be guaranteed.[6] This is an important observation, since it means that the location and nature of the activity cannot in themselves be used to predict the risk of the workforce, without an accurate assessment of the particular labour process.

Second, we need to take into account that in many countries the widespread introduction of new technology in large corporations coincides with privatization, the deprotection of workers, and the introduction of new forms of work organization (see, e.g. Ng, 1991: pp. 37–40). It is necessary to distinguish between the nature of the technology, the nature of the task and the ways in which the workers are required to carry out the task.

The context in which information technology is introduced will make a difference to the degree to which women have any leverage over how their work is organized and controlled, and the implications of such employment cannot be predicted *a priori*. There are three possibilities: the intensification; decomposition; or recomposition of existing gender and other social relations (Elson and Pearson, 1984). To give just one example, there are plans to promote computers in Saudi Arabia to increase the home-based employment opportunities of tertiary educated women, in order to maintain their seclusion (Kingdom of Saudi Arabia, n.d.).

Third, the extent to which formal worker protection by trade unions is a useful predictor of protection from the health risks of new technology is debatable. There is evidence from the Australian literature that, having been extremely helpful in the earlier phases of the Australian epidemic, the unions failed to combat attempts to psychologize the condition, and have not taken up the long-term issue of what happens to expelled and injured workers (Meekosha and Jakubowicz, 1991). The study carried out by the RSI sufferers reports that 60 per cent found their union to be unhelpful (ACT RSI, 1992). Ng (1991: pp. 36–7) also reports that the union did not see the health and safety protection of women workers as a priority.

But we should also be clear that information technology workers cannot necessarily be expected to take direct action on health hazards. L. Harris (1989) reports that women workers in an American chemical factory in County Mayo, Ireland, refused to take industrial action although they knew that the raw material they worked with had been banned elsewhere because of its supposed carcinogenic qualities. These workers had taken action on other grievances, such as equal pay, but they recognized that the location of the company in Ireland, and thus their employment, was the direct result of the health hazard they were being exposed to. Many information technology workers are in a similar position: they may or may not be informed about the risks of such employment, and may or may not have some bargaining power to address their concerns, but their response is mediated by a complex set of objectives including the need to earn an income and the benefits they obtain from employment in terms of association, socializing and status.

Managerial strategies can exploit these contradictions. In Jamaica, companies followed explicit strategies to prevent the unionization of data entry workers, lest they emulated the well-known and feared militancy of garment factory workers in the free trade zones (R. Pearson, 1993). There has also been a conscious attempt to promote the notion that keyboard operators were different, and superior to, assembly-line production workers (Freeman), similar to the differentiation made between electronics and garments workers in the Mexican *maquiladoras* (Pearson, 1991b). The 'clean' image of information technology work, in contrast to the environmentally hazardous emissions of process manufacturing, can also be utilized to diminish the perceived health hazards associated with computer work.

Such considerations may be central in understanding the responses of low paid semi-skilled workers, but not of professional women working with computers. It is well recognized that many women (and men) who have a much greater autonomy over the ways in which they carry out their work – such as academics, journalists and writers – consistently utilize computers in ways which entail severe risks of developing RSI and other conditions, even though they have access to very up-to-date knowledge of the risks and prevention strategies.[7] Externally imposed pressure and deadlines, as well as an increasingly competitive environment, provide a partial explanation, but self motivation and exploitation must also be factors.

Nor is it axiomatic that the interests of women workers, particularly in LDCs, are antithetic to the strategies of development planners who see the adoption and dissemination of information technology within their economies as the route to long-term economic viability and growth. Sen's model of 'cooperative conflict' (Sen, 1990), which encompasses a situation in which an individual's utility is both in conflict with, and totally inextricable from, that of the wider group might also prove a useful model for conceptualizing the contradictory relationship women have to the risks and benefits from information technology. Such a framework would seem infinitely more realistic than either a totally negative response, which suggests that all risk-bearing employment for women should be prohibited, or one which argues that health and safety issues should be totally subordinated to wider issues of economic growth, employment, and foreign exchange generation.[8]

The experience of advanced countries, particularly of Australia, indicates that new times as well as new technologies require new analyses and new strategies. There were institutional innovations by women in response to the 'epidemic', including support groups such as WRIST (Women's Repetitive Strain Injury Support Team), in Victoria, which not only have provided support and referral advice to sufferers but have played a central monitoring and lobbying role in relation to changes in the institutional and legislative framework. Workplace groups have also organized health and safety circles in an attempt to promote collective endeavours to devise working practices that are more rational, and have devised exercise routines which are both helpful and practicable.

The Australian experience is in a sense a microcosm of the contradictions that information technology presents – to producers, workers and users. The often irrational way in which medical and other professionals have sought to refute the links between technology, work practices and health hazards illustrates most directly the ways in which gendered notions of legitimacy are at the heart of the contradictions which this technology catalyses. It is the role of gender analysis to probe the nature of these contradictions and their gendered manifestations and responses, in order to work towards useful strategic responses.

NOTES

1 The term 'cheap labour' has been deconstructed by Elson and Pearson, 1984; and Pearson, 1988.

2 It is also true that the importance of health and safety aspects of new technology employment in advanced countries is still not universally recognized, outside of a specialized literature. Webster's excellent *Office Automation: The Labour Process and Women's Work in Britain*, 1990, contains no references at all to health and safety issues. Crompton and Jones' pioneering study *White Collar Proletariat: Deskilling and Gender in Clerical Work*, in 1984, was also silent on health and safety. A volume concerned with the social issues relating to information technology (Finnegan *et al.*, 1987) again has no discussion.

3 For instance Linda Lim, who has published a number of reports based mainly on secondary data, in her own name and for UN organizations, on the nature and condition of women's employment in export manufacturing by multinationals has recently insisted that 'feminists who see patriarchy and gender subordination as crucial underpinnings and inevitable consequences of all capitalism refuse to recognize any benefits to women in the Third World from employment in export factories, insisting that such employment intensifies rather than alleviates their gender subordination. The works of Elson and Pearson are popular with this group' (Lim, 1990: p. 116).

4 See OTA, 1985, especially Chapter 7; Putz-Anderson, 1988b; De Matteo, 1985; Shiga, 1987; ILO, 1990; Craig, 1991; English *et al.*, 1989; Bammer, 1987, 1990.

5 Women's lack of physical mobility in the workplace, compared to men, is one of the features of the gendering of work widely reported in studies of industrial and other workers (Humphrey, 1987).

6 My field work in Jamaica indicated that many companies had quite irregular workloads. During slack periods the women keyboard operators had considerable freedom. The situation in the Philippines appears to be rather different.

7 For instance, I suffered from debilitating back ache whilst preparing this paper. I personally know of four women academics and researchers of my generation in the UK who have or have had RSI.

8 These issues are explored in the context of the Jamaican data entry sector in R. Pearson, 1993.

REFERENCES

ACT RSI Support Group Inc. (1991), *Consumers' Perspective of Rehabilitation in RSI Cases; Stage 1 Report*, Canberra, Australia

ACT RSI Support Group Inc. (1992), *Consumers' Perspective of Rehabilitation in RSI Cases; Stage 2 Report*, Canberra, Australia

Bammer, G. (1987), 'How Technologic Change can Increase the Risk of Repetitive Motions Injuries', *Seminars in Occupational Medicine*, Vol. 2, No. 1, March: pp. 25–30

Bammer, G. (1988), 'The Prevalence of Work-related Neck and Upper Limb Disorders Among Office Workers in 7 Countries – a Pilot Study', *Reprints of International Conference on Ergonomics, Occupational Safety and Health and the Environment*, Vol. 1, Beijing, October

Bammer, G. (1990), 'Review of Current Knowledge – Musculoskeletal Problems', in L. Berlinguet and D. Berthelette (eds), *Work with Display Units*, Amsterdam, Elsevier Science Publishers

Bammer, G. (ed.) (1993), *Discussion Papers on the Pathology of Work-Related Neck and Upper Limb Disorders and the Implications for Diagnosis and Treatment*, Working Paper No. 32, National Centre for Epidemiology and Population Health, Australian National University, Canberra

Bammer, G., and Martin, B. (1988), 'The Arguments About RSI: an Examination', *Community Health Studies*, Vol. XII, No. 3: pp. 348–358

Barnes, C. (1989), 'Data Entry Demands', *Sistren Magazine*, Vol. 11, No. 3: pp. 18–21

Bawa, J. (1993), 'Ergonomics in the Office', *Guardian*, Special Report – Computers at Work: p. 17, 22 April

Berg, M. *et al.* (1990), 'Facial Skin Complaints and Work at Visual Display Units', *Journal of the American Academy of Dermatology*, Vol. 22, No. 4: pp. 621–625

Black, P. (1987), 'Psychiatric Aspects of Regional Pain Syndrome', *Medical Journal of Australia*, Vol. 147, 7 September: p. 257

Bodek, N. (ed.) (1987), *The Best of DEMA: Data Entry Management Handbook*, USA, DEMA (Data Entry Management Association)

Brandt, L. and Nielsen, C. (1990), 'Congenital Malformation Among Children of Women Working with Video Display Terminals', *Scan J Work Environ Health*, Vol. 16: pp. 329–333

Castells, M. (1989), *The Informational City: Information Technology, Economic Restructuring, and the Urban–Regional Process*, Blackwell, Oxford

Cohen, M. *et al.* (1992), *The Relevance of Concepts of Hyperalgesia to RSI*, Working Paper No. 31, in G. Bammer (ed.), *Discussion Papers on the Pathology of Work-Related Neck and Upper Limb Disorders and the Implications for Diagnosis and Treatment*, National Centre for Epidemiology and Population Health, Australian National University, Canberra

Cohen, N. (1992), '"Extraordinary" crime records deal attacked', *Independent*, 30 June

Craig, M. (1991), *Office Workers' Survival Handbook*, The Women's Press, London

Crompton, R. and Jones, G. (1984), *White-collar Proletariat: Deskilling and Gender in Clerical Work*, Macmillan, London

Davis, J. and Stack, M. (1993), 'Knowledge in Production', *Race and Class*, Vol. 34, No. 3

DeMatteo, B. (1985), *Terminal Shock: The Health Hazards of Video Display Terminals*, New Canada Publications, Toronto

Dennett, X. and Fry, H.J.H. (1988), 'Overuse Syndrome: a Muscle Biopsy Study', *Lancet* Vol. 1: pp. 905–908

Di Martino, V. and Wirth, L. (1990), 'Telework: a New Way of Working and Living', *International Labour Review*, Vol. 129, No. 5: pp. 529–554

Dobyns, J. (1991), 'Cumulative Trauma Disorder of the Upper Limb', *Frontiers in Hand Rehabilitation*, Vol. 7, No. 3, August: pp. 587–505

Eliasson, G. (1990), 'The Knowledge-based Information Economy', in G. Eliasson *et al.* (eds) *The Knowledge-based Information Economy*, Almqvist and Wicksell International, Stockholm

Elson, D. (1991), 'Appraising Recent Developments in the World Market for Nimble Fingers: Accumulation, Regulation Organization', paper presented at an international workshop on Women Organizing in the Process of Industrialization, ISS, The Hague, April

Elson, D. and Pearson, R. (1984), 'The Subordination of Women and the Internationalization of Factory Production', in K. Young, *et al.* (eds), *Of Marriage and the Market: Women's Subordination in International Perspective*, London, Routledge

English, C.J. *et al.* (1989), 'Clinical Epidemiological Study of Relations Between Upper Limb Soft Tissue Disorders and Repetitive Movements at Work', Final Research Report, Institute of Occupational Medicine, Edinburgh

Finnegan, R. *et al.* (1987), *Information Technology: Social Issues*, Milton Keynes, Open University Press

Freeman, C. (n.d.), 'High-tech and High Heels: Barbadian Women in the Off-shore Information Industry', (mimeo) paper presented to the Fifteenth Annual Conference in the Caribbean Studies Association, Trinidad

Fry, H.J.H. (1986), 'Overuse Syndrome in Musicians: Prevention and Management', *Lancet* Vol. 2: pp. 728–731

Fry, H.J.H. (1988), 'The Treatment of Overuse Syndrome in Musicians. Results in 175 patients', *Journal of the Royal Society of Medicine*, Vol. 81: pp. 572–575

Fry, H.J.H. (1993), *Overuse Syndrome and the Overuse Concept*, Working Paper No. 32, in G. Bammer (ed.), Discussion Papers on the Pathology of Work-Related Neck and Upper Limb Disorders and the Implications for Diagnosis and Treatment, National Centre for Epidemiology and Population Health, Australian National University, Canberra

Girvan, N. (1989), 'Technological Change and the Caribbean: Formulating Strategic Responses', *Social and Economic Studies*, Vol. 38, No. 2: pp. 111–135

Glucksmann, M. (1986), 'In a Class of Their Own: Women Workers in the New Industries in Inter-war in Britain', *Feminist Review*, No. 24, October: pp. 7–37

Glucksmann, M. (1990), *Women Assemble: Women Workers and the New Industries in Inter-war Britain*, London, Routledge

Hall, W. and Morrow, L. (1988), 'Repetition Strain Injury: an Australian Epidemic of Upper Limb Pain', *Social Science and Medicine*, Vol. 27, No. 6: pp. 645–649

Hanna, N. (1991), 'Informatics and the Developing World', *Finance and Development*, December: pp. 45–47

Harrington, M. (1993), 'Response to Hunter Fry', in H.J.H. Fry, *Overuse Syndrome and the Overuse Concept*, Working Paper No. 32, in G. Bammer (ed.), *Discussion Papers on the Pathology of Work-related Neck and Upper Limb Disorders and the Implications for Diagnosis and Treatment*, National Centre for Epidemiology and Population Health, Australian National University, Canberra: pp. 10–11

Harris, B. (1989), 'Does the Third World Need Computers?', *Environment and Planning B: Planning and Design*, Vol. 16: pp. 371–376

Harris, L. (1989), 'Women's Response to Multinationals in County Mayo', in D. Elson and R. Pearson (eds), *Women's Employment and Multinationals in Europe*, Macmillan, London

Heeks, R. (1989), *The Impact of New Technologies on the International Division of Labour in the Indian Software Industry*, Milton Keynes, Development Policy and Practice Group Working Paper

Hopkins, A. (1990), The Social Recognition of Repetitive Strain Injuries: an Australian/American Comparison, *Social Science and Medicine*, Vol. 30, No. 3: pp. 365–372

HSE (Health and Safety Executive) (1992), *Display Screen Equipment Work: Guidance on Regulations*, London, Health and Safety (Display Screen Equipment) Regulations

Huang, D.C. (1990), *Size and Growth Trends of the Information Industry: 1975–87*, incidental paper, Program for Information Policy Research, Harvard University, Cambridge, Mass.

Humphrey, J. (1987), *Gender and Work in the Third World: Sexual Divisions in Brazilian Industry*, Tavistock, London

Huws, U. (1987), *VDU Hazards Handbook*, The London Hazards Centre

ILO (1990), *Conditions of Work Digest*, Vol. 9, No.1/1990, Part 1

Ireland DCR. (1988), 'Psychological and Physical Aspects of Occupational Arm Pain', *The Journal of Hand Surgery* (Aust.), Vol 13–B(1), February

Kandiyoti D. (1988), 'Bargaining with Patriarchy', *Gender and Society* Vol. 2, No. 3

Kingdom of Saudi Arabia (n.d.), *Fourth Development Plan, 1985–90 AD*, Saudi Arabia, Ministry of Planning Press

Kutay, A. (1986), 'Effects of Telecommunications Technology on Office Location', *Urban Geography*, Vol. 7: pp. 243–257

Labour Research, (1984), 'Health at work: 1. Pregnancy and VDUs', Vol. 79, No. 33: December, pp. 299–300

Lim, L. (1990), 'Women's Work in Export Factories: the Politics of a Cause', in I. Tinker (ed.), *Persistent Inequalities: Women and World Development*, New York and Oxford, Oxford University Press

Lippmann, H. (1991), 'A Fresh Look at the Overuse Syndrome in Musical Performers: is "Overuse" Overused?', *Medical Problems of Performing Artists*, Vol. 6, No. 2: pp. 57–60

Locksley, G. (1986), 'Information Technology and Capitalist Development', *Capital and Class*, Vol. 27

Lucire, Y. (1986), 'Neurosis in the Workplace', *The Medical Journal of Australia*, Vol. 145, 6 Oct: pp. 323–327

Meekosha, H. and Jakubowicz, A. (1986), 'Women Suffering RSI: the Hidden Relations of Gender, the Labour Process and Medicine', *Journal of Occupational Health and Safety, Australia/New Zealand*, Vol. 2, No. 5: pp. 390–401

Meekosha, H. and Jakubowicz, A. (1991), 'Repetition Strain Injury: the Rise and Fall of an "Australian" Disease', *Critical Social Policy*, Vol. 11, No.1, Summer

Mitter, S. and Pearson, R. (1992), *Global Information Processing: the Emergence of Software Services and Data Entry Jobs in Selected Developing Countries*, Sectoral Activities Programme Working Papers, Geneva, ILO

Mody, A. and Dahlman, C. (1992), 'Performance and Potential of Information Technology: an International Perspective', *World Development*, Vol. 20, No. 12, December

Moussa, A. and Schware, R. (1992), 'Informatics in Africa: Lessons from World Bank Experience', *World Development*, Vol. 20, No. 12, December

Nelson, K. (1986), 'Labor Demand, Labor Supply and the Suburbanization of Low-wage Office Work', in A. Scott and M. Storper (eds), *Work, Production and Territory*, Allen and Unwin, London

Ng, C. (1991), *Information Technology, Economic Restructuring and their Impact on Women Workers: the Case of the Telecommunications Industry in Malaysia*, Working Paper, Institute of Social Studies, The Hague

Ng, C. and Othman, J. (1991), 'Occupational Health and Safety Among Office Workers: a Preliminary Study', in C. Nicholas and A. Wangel (eds), *Safety at Work in Malaysia*, Kuala Lumpur, University of Malaya

OECD (1986), *Trends in the Information Economy*, OECD, Paris

OTA (1985), *Automation of America's Offices*, Washington, Office of Technology Assessment

Patkin, M. (1993), 'Response to Hunter Fry', in H.J.H. Fry, *Overuse Syndrome and the Overuse Concept*, Working Paper No. 32, in G. Bammer (ed.), *Discussion Papers on the Pathology of Work-related Neck and Upper Limb Disorders and the Implications for Diagnosis and Treatment*, National Centre for Epidemiology and Population Health, Australian National University, Canberra: pp. 11–12

Pearce, B. (1993), 'Is a Change as Good as a Rest?', *Guardian*, Special Report – Computers at work: p. 20, 22 April

Pearson, R. (1988), 'Female Workers in the First and Third Worlds: the Greening of Women's Labour', in R. Pahl (ed.), *On Work*. Oxford, Blackwell

Pearson, R. (1991a), *New Technology and the Internationalization of Office Work: Prospects and Conditions for Women's Employment in LDCs*, Gender Analysis in Development Discussion Paper No. 5, School of Development Studies, University of East Anglia, Norwich, UK

Pearson, R. (1991b), 'Male Bias and Women's Work in Mexico's Border Industries', in D. Elson (ed.) *Male Bias in the Development Process*, Manchester, Manchester University Press

Pearson, R. (1993), 'Gender and New Technology in the Caribbean: New Work for Women?', in J. Momsen (ed.), *Women and Change in the Caribbean*, James Currey, London

Pearson, R.M. (1990), *Muscle Overuse Syndrome (RSI)*, (mimeo), London, Musicians and Keyboard Clinic

Pearson, R.M. (1993), 'Response to Hunter Fry', in H.J.H. Fry, *Overuse Syndrome and the Overuse Concept*, Working Paper No. 32, in G. Bammer (ed.), *Discussion Papers on the Pathology of Work-related Neck and Upper Limb Disorders and the Implications for Diagnosis and Treatment*, National Centre for Epidemiology and Population Health, Australian National University, Canberra: p. 13

Pearson, R. and Mitter, S. (1993), 'Employment and Working Conditions of Low-skilled Information Processing Workers in Less Developed Countries', *International Labour Review*, Vol. 132, No. 1: pp. 49–63

Polakoff, P. (1991), 'Repetitive-motion, Radiation and Eye Concerns Mount at Computer Worksites', *Occupational Health & Safety*, Vol. 60, Part 4, April, pp. 34 and 50

Posthuma, A. (1987), 'The Internationalization of Clerical Work: a Study of Offshore Office Services in the Caribbean', SPRU Occasional Papers No. 24, University of Sussex, Brighton, UK

Putz-Anderson, V. (1988a), 'Prevention Strategies Adopted by Select Countries for Work-related Musculoskeletal Disorders from Repetitive Trauma', in F. Aghazadeh (ed.), *Trends in Ergonomics/Human Factors V*, Amsterdam, Elsevier Science Publishers

Putz-Anderson, V. (ed.) (1988b), *Cumulative Trauma Disorders: A Manual for Musculoskeletal Diseases of the Upper Limbs*, NIOSH, Cincinnati, Ohio, USA

Quintner, J. and Elvey, R. (1991), 'The Neurogenic Hypothesis of RSI', in G. Bammer (ed.), *Discussion Papers on the Pathology of Work-related Neck and Upper Limb Disorders and the Implications for Diagnosis and Treatment*, NCEPH Working Paper No. 24, Canberra, Australia

Reid, J., Ewans, C. and Lowy, E. (1991), 'Pilgrimage of Pain: the Illness Experiences of Women with Repetitive Strain Injury and the Search for Credibility', *Social Science and Medicine*, Vol. 32, No. 5: pp. 601–612

Ryan, C. (1990), 'Trade Liberalisation and Financial Services', *World Economy*, Vol. 13, No. 3, September: pp. 349–366

Schware, R. (1992), 'Software Industry Entry Strategies for Developing Countries: a "walking on two legs" Proposition', *World Development*, Vol. 20, No. 2: pp. 143–164

Semple C. (1991), 'Tenosynovitis, Repetitive Strain Injury, Cumulative Trauma Disorder, and Overuse Syndrome, et cetera', *The Journal of Bone and Joint Surgery* (Br.), Vol. 73-B: pp. 536–538

Semple, C. (1993), 'Response to Hunter Fry', in H.J.H. Fry *Overuse Syndrome and the Overuse Concept*, Working Paper No. 32, in G. Bammer (ed.), *Discussion Papers on the Pathology of Work-related Neck and Upper Limb Disorders and the Implications for Diagnosis and Treatment*, National Centre for Epidemiology and Population Health, Australian National University, Canberra: pp. 24–25

Sen, A.K. (1990), 'Gender and Cooperative Conflicts', in I. Tinker (ed.), *Persistent Inequalities: Women and World Development*, New York, Oxford, Oxford University Press

Shiga, H. (1987), 'Microelectronics and women in Japan', in C. Ng (ed.), *Technology and Gender*, Kuala Lumpur, Malaysian Social Science Association

Smith, I. (1993), 'The Health and Safety (Display Screen Equipment) Regulations 1992', in I. Smith, C. Goddard and N. Randall (eds), *Health and Safety – the new legal framework*, London, Butterworth

Soares, A. (1991), 'The Hard Life of the Unskilled Workers in New Technologies: Data Entry Clerks in Brazil', in H.J. Bullinger (ed.), *Human Aspects in Computing*, Amsterdam, Elsevier Science Publishers

Standing, G. (1989), 'Global Feminization Through Flexible Labor', *World Development*, Vol. 17, No. 7

Webster, J. (1990), *Office Automation: The Labour Process and Women's Work in Britain*, New York and London, Harvester Wheatsheaf

14 Using information technology as a mobilizing force

The case of the Tanzania Media Women's Association (TAMWA)

Fatma Alloo

Africa has been portrayed by the media as poor and powerless. But the media have a role to play in the process of empowerment. The media can enable the people to challenge the powers that be and question the direction they are taking. In Tanzania, women are at the forefront of meeting this challenge. This case study will show the importance of technology in taking control of one's situation. Information technology can be used to destroy the 'poor and powerless' myth, and to mobilize a community for empowerment and social change.

HISTORICAL BACKGROUND

The inception of TAMWA as an association had its seeds in 1979, with a group of women who had just finished journalism school and were beginning work in various mass media institutions. We became aware that we were working very much individually. This method of work was also reflected in the way women's issues were covered in the mainstream press.

We found this situation unsatisfactory and formed ourselves into an informal group to produce radio programmes. The first issue we picked was schoolgirl pregnancies. We produced a total of five programmes on that issue with an in-depth analysis of the social context. These programmes were broadcast, and were very popular both in Kiswahili and in English. Listener response was enthusiastic. This encouraged and inspired us to produce another set of programmes on violence against women, beginning with domestic violence. It was never broadcast because most of the mass media heads were men who refused to see this as an issue. Since they had the decision-making power, we began to become aware of our limitations. Although many of us were demoralized and discouraged, since we had worked so hard on the programmes, the event taught us that we did not have a forum of our own.

Years passed and many of us went our separate ways, but in 1986, after going through many individual trials and tribulations as women, we regrouped and decided to officially launch an association on a formal basis. At that time the association had thirteen members (it has since grown to fifty-five, working in television, radio and newspapers). This kind of urban-based professional women's association is a relatively new phenomenon in Eastern and Southern Africa. Other such associations in the region have been initiated by legal and health professionals (Alloo, 1991).

While waiting for registration, which was to come after a year, we did a stage show on International Women's Day in 1987 to demonstrate different forms of media, including both conventional and popular media. The show was highly successful. We made an impact in the community and especially with the heads of mass media, who until then had not understood what we were really about. We felt that, for the first time, an understanding was beginning to emerge in the community.

We were registered in November 1987, and started a newsletter called 'Titbits' which we produced for ourselves. 'Titbits' covered a wide range of issues and was produced through the initiative of TAMWA members. It became our forum, through which we could express ourselves and respond to a need. Eleven monthly issues of 'Titbits' were produced. In the process, various talents were identified. Eventually 'Titbits' evolved into 'Sauti Ya Siti', which will be described below.

In January 1988 we did a seminar on the 'Portrayal of Women in the Media in Tanzania'. We chose this topic because we needed to understand our situation first. We also looked into how our language perpetuated the negative portrayal of women. The seminar was attended by about sixty women's groups who passed a recommendation that we needed a forum in the form of our own magazine. TAMWA met this challenge and in March 1988, just a month later, we launched our magazine, 'Sauti Ya Siti' – 'Voice of Woman' – which was also named after one of the first prominent woman communicator in nineteenth-century Zanzibar, Siti Binti Saad. Siti was not only a singer, she communicated for justice.

We now produce this magazine on a quarterly basis, in English and Kiswahili versions. We charge more for the English version, so that it subsidizes the Kiswahili version, which we try to make accessible to the rural population. The literacy rate of Tanzanian women is among the highest for women in sub-Saharan Africa (USAID, 1985). 'Sauti Ya Siti' now has a circulation of 10,000 copies. The English edition is distributed via book shops and through subscriptions. The Kiswahili edition requires much more effort. We distribute copies to rural libraries (where each copy is read by an average of thirty persons), schools, ministries, women's groups (those who belong to our network and friends of TAMWA) and through street children, who sell in the regions and earn a commission. The latter sales system is organized by our focal point supporters: women who have trained with us in paralegal work, NGO management, and outreach work. We also target hairdressing salons.

Popular education materials are also distributed in this manner. For example, we produce brochures on the laws which affect women's lives, written in a simplified Kiswahili, with visuals and big letters for the new literates in Tanzania. These are disseminated through legal aid clinics in the countryside.

As we continued, we began to explore other forms of action in accordance with our objective to become a vehicle for increasing understanding of our situation as women and educating ourselves on our rights. In May every year we organize a Day of Action on women's health issues. One of the questions we ask of society is: why is it that so many of us continue to die in childbirth, when we have been performing our reproductive role from time immemorial (Sheikh-Hashim, 1989), and how long will we continue to be denied our rights in terms of appropriate medical care facilities and human rights? This day mobilizes the community over questions pertinent to our situation as women. The people attending effectively raise these issues in their various work places and organizations. We continue to focus these annual events on health, since it is an effective tool for mobilizing women. The process has a multiplier effect in building a gender-sensitized community.

INFORMATION TECHNOLOGY AND TAMWA

As we continue to work in TAMWA, various needs which relate to information dissemination and development education emerged. Generally, as members initiate new ideas, TAMWA undertakes the development of the viable ones (see Figure 14.1).

In producing 'Sauti Ya Siti' we felt the need for a Research and Documentation Unit, together with a Reference Library for material on women. This unit is operational and several basic studies have already been prepared and published by TAMWA, on subjects ranging from sanitation to traditional education. The community involved in the study participates in the evaluation stage.

The growth of TAMWA called for a more rational retrieval, selection and diffusion system. The need was met by installing a programme called 'File Maker' and creating data bases, one for books, and another for unpublished documents and reports. In 1994 the collection included 3,000 books and 2,800 unpublished documents, plus periodicals.

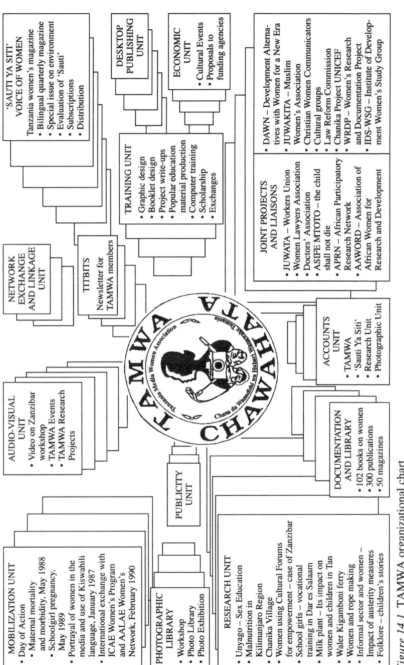

Figure 14.1 TAMWA organizational chart

All documents in the library are classified using 'keywords'. Keywords are terms of constant vocabulary for particular ideas or facts which help describe the contents of a document. The keywords used to classify documents in TAMWA have been selected to reflect the theme and subjects dealt with by the Association. We also take trainees from the Tanganyika Library, who help us with needed expertise, while getting practical exposure to our Association and becoming gender sensitized.

Our Documentation Unit is having a multiplier effect, as it is popularly used by the community, especially the youth. Gender sensitization through basic research is quite effective in empowering both men and women, and it particularly affects young minds. We also have a close collaboration with the Tanzanian School of Journalism, which trains young journalists. Right now (in 1994) the unit is in the process of becoming part and parcel of a non-governmental organization (NGO) Resource Centre, thus planting the seed of a gender-sensitized NGO community with our documentation unit as a basic source.

Another unit is the Audio-visual Unit, whose programmes are used by Radio Tanzania. At the moment, we feed into existing radio programmes using research conducted by TAMWA members. We have developed a small studio on our premises. The target is to launch a community radio in 1995. The Visual Unit is fully equipped and produces video programmes on the issues which are being researched, to show to women's groups as part of a process of empowerment. So far, we have produced three documentations of women's history, the first one being on Siti Binti Saad. This unit is currently producing programmes for television, which has now been introduced to mainland Tanzania. We have also launched artists and artists' groups in our attempt to support young artists and foster aesthetic values in society.

The Economic Unit is another step towards self-sustainability (see Figure 14.2). The goal is for the organization to earn sufficient income to cover its costs. The acquisition of proper office space and the appointment of a full-time administrative secretary have increased these costs. At present most of the funding still comes from donors, with the office costs being met from a 15 per cent administrative charge which is added to every project proposal. To meet the goal of self-sufficiency, entrepreneurship in various forms has found a place in TAMWA. Entrepreneurial activities in 1992 included an alternative fashion show, and the production of African clothing for men and women is now a project. Self-sufficiency is both a financial necessity and, in the long term, a requisite if TAMWA is to have an equal partnership with its counterpart organizations. Reliance on donor funds brings with it the temptation to produce for the sake of satisfying the funders rather than our own constituency, and the risk of losing our freedom to criticize the policies of development agencies. It also commits us to a 'project' approach rather than a 'process' approach, with all the costs in terms of lack of continuity and failure to build up an institutional memory which that entails.

The Children's Unit has transmitted our heritage through a book of children's songs and games. This material comes with an audio cassette. We believe that instead of growing up singing 'London Bridge is Falling Down,' our children should sing our traditional songs, which impart values relevant to us. The Health Unit engages in outreach on AIDS, targeting especially the youth, and engages in debates on reproductive health in order to influence policy decisions at the national level. This is a vibrant unit.

TECHNOLOGY AND THE MEDIA

Media, for us, encompasses all forms of communication, be it theatre, art, dance, songs and folklore or the conventional media such as radio,

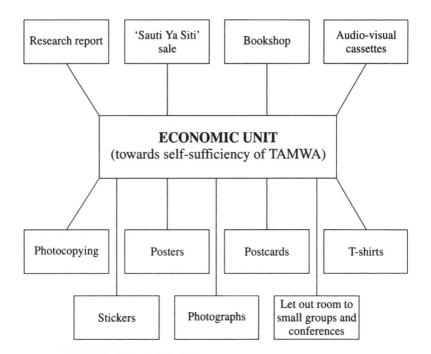

Figure 14.2 TAMWA Economic Unit

television, printed media, etc. When TAMWA was formed, we had a specific definition of the media, and we knew that our forum would be a magazine, 'Sauti Ya Siti'. Our goal was to produce a magazine of high technical quality. This was a conscious decision on our part as an organization. Information technology was to be used in TAMWA, we said, to change our society's behavioural patterns and attitudes towards women. For those of us within TAMWA, working with this technology would demystify our own concepts of technology *vis-à-vis* women. We began with desktop publishing. The Canadian Organization for Development Education (CODE) donated a desktop publishing unit and funded the printing of our magazine fully for the first two years. The support was to be reduced in phases, so as to achieve our goal of self-sustainability.

The desktop unit plays a role, not only in producing a high-tech, quality magazine, but in beginning to give us an income and making the magazine cost-effective. Five years later, TAMWA is producing a magazine, popular education materials (booklets), videos of women's cultural histories, radio programmes, posters, brochures, etc. – all using information technology. Contact has been established with publishers elsewhere in Africa, in India, and with the Women's publisher Kali. Another development is providing feature articles for other publications.

Being in the media ourselves gave us the consciousness that information is power. The 'haves' select how much and what kind of information trickles down to the people through the mass media. The development of this kind of media is a project, not a process. There is no participation from the people, and these media transmit to the people in a one-way, top-down process. This 'beaming down' approach creates dependency and sells us our own images in a distorted way. When we studied the history of conventional media in Tanzania (see, e.g. Alloo, 1988), we found that the print and electronic media was indeed introduced by the colonialists and used as an ideological weapon to control our societies. But the traditional popular media, such as folklore, songs, dance and theatre, could not be controlled by the colonialists, not only because they used the language of the people, but also because the participation of the people was built in (see Mlama and Lihamba, 1988).

As for Africa as a whole, the western media tries to sell us distorted images of ourselves. Africa is portrayed as a problematic continent rather than a continent with problems. Those images of worm-like bodies crawling with begging bowls have been powerful in perpetuating the 'poor and the powerless' ideology. These projections render us powerless and make us believe there is something wrong with our continent. There are similar generalizing images of Asia, portrayed as not so bad except for their 'sex trade and communal violence', and of Latin America, where the 'drug trade' is the problem. All of these images are dangerous. They handicap us in our struggle for self-analysis and dehumanize us in the same way as images which sell the woman as a sex symbol – a commodity. The western media act in this way because, so far, the powers that control these media are commodity-oriented. This media is powerful because it has access to information technology which we in Latin America, Africa, Caribbean, Asia and Pacific (LAACAP) countries lack.

A study of cultural development in Zanzibar revealed not only that the traditional media have remained powerful throughout various colonizing periods, but that conventional media were also powerfully used in the independence struggle. Zanzibar, with a population of around half a million, had 21 newspapers before independence. Their voices played an important role in the anti-colonial struggles of the Islands (Sheriff, 1987).

Throughout Africa, popular media are merging as a powerful tool of empowerment. It is a form which women identify with and use, and have used in the past, for empowerment. For example, we have our traditional cloth, Kanga, which incorporates written messages in the design (Alley-Hamid, 1995). The cloth is worn around the waist. Women wear it to portray feelings towards a spouse, in-law, or friend. This is a powerful media in a culture of silence. This is paralleled by an awareness in the west of the value of technologies such as audio-visual media in empowering women by creating true images of women and showing the oppression of women in patriarchal systems in a global connection.

TAMWA tries to understand these macro-dynamics as it forms strategies for information dissemination at a local level. Lack of access and control of media and information technology exposes us to the dehumanizing portrayal of women. Thus, control of information technology is crucial if we are to transform society through the media.

Until five years ago, Tanzanian government policies restricted the importation and use of these technologies. Thus Tanzania is very new to information technology. Even now the prices are high and software is quite inaccessible. Technology and infrastructure are the basis of the process of empowerment. We felt that we ourselves would be empowered in mastering technology as a production tool, and we could in turn use it to disseminate information. As women, we saw this as particularly important, since new technology has generally been the domain of men. The technology could also generate income. We have established an effective Publishing Unit based on this fact (see Figure 14.3).

The emphasis in our publishing work has been on media images, i.e. on achieving the positive media portrayal of women and permitting the voices

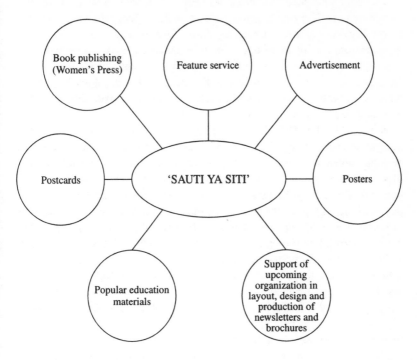

Figure 14.3 TAMWA Publishing Unit

of the voiceless to be heard. This, we feel, must be effected in a highly professional manner with aesthetically excellent programmes, whether on the air, on video, or in the print media. Professional excellence is important for ourselves, for we must and can produce quality material in spite of the so-called 'third world syndrome' (insinuating technical incompetence). One of the problems of powerlessness is the psychology of feeling inadequate which leads to sloppy work. TAMWA's experience has shown us that women generally do fear technology and have to be pushed and cajoled to master it or even try it. But once women do take it on, they are unstoppable. The fact that we can produce so-called 'first world' quality in spite of being a so-called 'third world' group has been an empowering process. Besides publications, we do popular education materials, pam- phlets, brochures, cards, reports, etc. The income generated is helping the association towards its goal of self-sustainability. We now have an e-mail system which is an aid in networking and information dissemination.

I would like to mention here that to begin with we had male consultants as our trainers. They have since gone and established their own computer technology companies. Learning from TAMWA'S experience as an organization, one of them has even established a glossy colour women's magazine with a more conventional portrayal of women! His example is another reason for us to emphasize the control of technology by women when we mobilize over issues of concern. Images portrayed through information technology are crucial.

Since 1992, TAMWA has focused particularly on the issue of violence against women. A special issue of 'Sauti Ya Siti' was produced with desktop publishing, radio programmes were transmitted, and positive images of women were produced including screen printed T-shirts and stickers. A national rally during the Day of Action included an art exhibition. On this day, we issued a call over the radio for those who felt concern over the issue to come. Some 50 per cent of those who heeded the call were men, and women came on their own initiative from up-country. Out of this initiative, a Crisis Centre was born – the only one of its kind in Tanzania. The centre promotes legal literacy, provides counselling, and fights court cases involving violence against women. It also provides paralegal training, an exposure to and training in information technology, and some training in NGO management to members of up-country women's organizations, who then return to establish community-based centres in rural Tanzania. This kind of development gives us hope and the strength to go on.

CONCLUSION: TAMWA AND INFORMATION TECHNOLOGY

As TAMWA grows as an organization, and undertakes a restructuring this year (1994), we are becoming very conscious of information technology. But we continuously ask the question, for whom and to what purpose are we using it? If expertise becomes a status symbol, it is of no use to those whom we wish to empower. If mastering these technologies raises class barriers or leads to a glossier type of publication in a foreign language, this is not progress. If, through the control of information technology, one maintains two-way communication in the language of the people, and women are portrayed in a manner which will create growth and empowerment, then it is to be encouraged.

Another important aspect is the demystification of information technology for that class which needs it the most in order to have their voices heard. To this end we produce booklets which teach, in practical terms, how to produce a newsletter using locally available materials. These booklets are used in participatory methodology workshops with gender perspectives. In these workshops women use the popular media, portraying problems with songs, drums, storytelling and sung drama. Within these popular media, which have largely been women's domain, women have the 'sociological space' to manoeuvre and resist the images of women portrayed in the conventional media. The process itself, combining the appropriation of conventional (i.e. technological) media with the revaluation of popular media, empowers. To bring about positive changes in women's lives, it is necessary to identify forms of expression and mobilization.

Recently, we did a four day workshop for NGOs, looking at the project proposals in their programmes to assess whether gender sensitization is incorporated. The last day was reserved for media heads, the decision makers in the newspapers and radio. The response was encouraging, and we hope the impact, although slow, will be a steady one. With advanced information technology, TAMWA is beginning to become a sophisticated alternative means of providing positive media images. As long as it continues its role of facilitating the voice of the voiceless, it will remain a force.

REFERENCES

Alley-Hamid, M. (1995), *Kanga – A Medium of Communication*, Dar-es-Salaam, TAMWA

Alloo, Fatma (1988), 'Women and Popular Media', paper presented at the Women's Visions and Movements Conference, University of Ibadan, Nigeria, 27–29 September

Alloo, Fatma (1991), 'A Regional Profile of Existing Women's NGOs and Networks in Southern and Eastern Africa', (mimeo), Dar es Salaam

ISIS-WICCE (1984), *Powerful Images: a Women's Guide to Audio-visual Resources*, Rome, Isis International

Mlama, P. and Lihaba, A. (1988), *Popular Theatre and Participation in Morogoro Region*, Dar-es-Salaam, TAMWA

Sheikh-Hashim, L. (1989), *Unyago: Traditional Sex Education*, Dar-es-Salaam

Sheriff, A. (1987), *Slaves, Spices and Ivory in Zanzibar*, Ohio, University of Ohio Press

TAMWA (1991), *Origin, Development, Programmes and Prospects of Tanzania Media Women's Association*, annual report

USAID (1985), *Women in the World: A Chartbook for Developing Regions*, Washington, United States Agency for International Development, Office of Women in Development

15 The fading of the collective dream?

Reflections on twenty years' research on
information technology and women's
employment

Ursula Huws

When Swasti Mitter asked me to write a paper for this collection, I found it
extraordinarily difficult to find a focus for it. It seemed important to find
something new to say, but every approach which occurred to me seemed,
somehow, to involve a repetition of things I had already said, or written
elsewhere. Even when new information could be added, or new texts
referred to, it was difficult to identify new concepts. In short, the whole
complex and contradictory subject of the relationship between information
technology and women's employment seemed to have gone stale for me.
With a shock, I realized that it was nearly twenty years since I had begun
grappling with these issues.

It then occurred to me that perhaps the most helpful contribution I could
make to this discussion would not be to assemble, yet again, a selection of
empirical evidence, nor to attempt, yet again, to develop an analytical
perspective which might contribute to the construction of a conceptual
framework for new research projects on technology and women's employment, nor yet to frame, yet again, a series of 'demands' to protect or further
women's interests in a technological society, worthy though any of these
might be. No, at the risk of seeming self-indulgent, it seemed that a more
useful task might be to chart the history of the various projects in this area
with which I had been associated over the years in Britain, many of which
could loosely be defined as 'feminist', to see what, if anything, could be
learned from these experiences.

The purpose of doing this is not simply to place things on the record, or
even to settle old scores, but to try to identify the concepts which have been
used to make sense of the relationship between technology, women and
work, and how these have changed over the years. In some cases, this
involves carrying out a sort of archaeology of the intellectual self, to
unearth the theoretical assumptions which we brought, consciously or
unconsciously, to our debates and research hypotheses. How typical my

experience in particular or the British experience in general has been, or what can be learned from them in other contexts, is for the reader to judge.

If there is such a thing as 'feminist research' (which many, self-proclaimed feminists included, doubt) it seems likely that its essential distinguishing feature is not so much a specific methodology or methodologies as an attitude, an attitude which can best be encapsulated in the well-worn, but still potent proposition that 'the personal is political'. If western feminism has done anything, it has surely put the subjective self at the centre of the research agenda. On the one hand it has insisted that the traditional 'objects' of social research – the poor, the oppressed, women, children, the old, whoever they may be – should be listened to with respect, and granted their subjectivity, and that the researcher should validate their view of the world. On the other, it has focused attention on the subjectivity of the researcher, challenging the notion that the positivist ideal of detached objectivity is obtainable, and insisting that the gender, race and class of this person and the circumstances which have formed his or her intellectual development will colour any piece of research. In television production there is a system called 'chromakey' which is used when a foreground image (usually a person or an animal) is required to be seen against a different background. The effect is achieved by photographing the foreground image against a monochrome background (usually blue) and screening out the same colour when filming the background scene. The two images can then be superimposed on each other without any apparent colour distortion. In some ways, this system provides an appropriate metaphor for this view of research. In it, it is as though the researcher's taken-for-granted assumptions create a sort of colour screen which renders whole areas of the spectrum invisible. The audience for this research, unless they are perspicacious enough to challenge these assumptions, will be required, so to speak, to look through a similar screen and will see an appearance of completeness. In the past, of course, it has often been women who have been rendered invisible in this way.

Although they have been adopted and refined by many researchers who call themselves feminists, post-1960s feminism cannot be credited with inventing these notions. The attempt to see the world through the eyes of the people who form the subject of the research has for decades been a common feature of ethnographic research. The political project of trying to build an alternative, oppositional ideology from the experiences of oppressed peoples can be traced back to the Maoist idea of 'consciousness raising', and to Gramsci, among others. Similarly a rejection of the supposed 'objectivity' of the scientist is common to many critiques of positivism which gained currency during the 1950s and 1960s. Nevertheless, it is experience in particular or the British experience in general has been, or what can be learned from them in other contexts, is for the reader to judge.

If there is such a thing as 'feminist research' (which many, self-proclaimed feminists included, doubt) it seems likely that its essential distinguishing feature is not so much a specific methodology or methodologies as an attitude, an attitude which can best be encapsulated in the well-worn, but still potent proposition that 'the personal is political'. If western feminism has done anything, it has surely put the subjective self at the centre of the research agenda. On the one hand it has insisted that the traditional 'objects' of social research – the poor, the oppressed, women, children, the old, whoever they may be – should be listened to with respect, and granted their subjectivity, and that the researcher should validate their view of the world. On the other, it has focused attention on the subjectivity of the researcher, challenging the notion that the positivist ideal of detached objectivity is obtainable, and insisting that the gender, race and class of this person and the circumstances which have formed his or her intellectual development will colour any piece of research. In television production there is a system called 'chromakey' which is used when a foreground image (usually a person or an animal) is required to be seen against a different background. The effect is achieved by photographing the foreground image against a monochrome background (usually blue) and screening out the same colour when filming the background scene. The two images can then be superimposed on each other without any apparent colour distortion. In some ways, this system provides an appropriate metaphor for this view of research. In it, it is as though the researcher's taken-for-granted assumptions create a sort of colour screen which renders whole areas of the spectrum invisible. The audience for this research, unless they are perspicacious enough to challenge these assumptions, will be required, so to speak, to look through a similar screen and will see an appearance of completeness. In the past, of course, it has often been women who have been rendered invisible in this way.

Although they have been adopted and refined by many researchers who call themselves feminists, post-1960s feminism cannot be credited with inventing these notions. The attempt to see the world through the eyes of the people who form the subject of the research has for decades been a common feature of ethnographic research. The political project of trying to build an alternative, oppositional ideology from the experiences of oppressed peoples can be traced back to the Maoist idea of 'consciousness raising', and to Gramsci, among others. Similarly a rejection of the supposed 'objectivity' of the scientist is common to many critiques of positivism which gained currency during the 1950s and 1960s. Nevertheless, it is does not fit it. Such processes are generally closely bound up with notions of professionalism. I can remember exercising similar forms of censorship myself when working as an editor twenty years ago.

As with editors, so with academics, even in oppositional fields like women's studies. The conventional structure of the academic text, with its grandiose opening placing the work in an overarching theoretical context, its 'objective' presentation of the evidence, its tidy conclusion, its scrupulous citations and carefully arranged bibliography, has little space for the untidy self of the author which is normally smuggled in only in the form of references to previous publications or, occasionally, when reporting on the methodology of some sorts of social research, an oblique reference to ways in which some of the personal characteristics of the author might have affected interviews with respondents who did, or did not, share these characteristics.

The third danger is by far the most serious. This is that in chronicling pieces of work or social movements with which I have been involved, I might appear to be taking full credit for them when in fact, in many cases, my role may have been relatively small. In a paper of this scope it is impossible to give full acknowledgement to all the people who have helped form these concepts, either directly or indirectly. In many cases it is no more possible to disentangle individual contributions from the collective effort than it is to identify which drops of water make up a wave. I hope that readers will understand that, in the pages which follow, when I write in the first person about any particular set of ideas I am not claiming ownership of them but am treating myself as an archaeologist treats a patch of soil, or a chemist a sample of material: as a test-bed whose component parts can be analysed and sorted, in order to identify the answers to questions like: how did those ideas get there?; when did they arrive?; where have they come from?; how have they changed? and how were they used? The answers to these, will, I hope, make it possible to address further questions: are they still relevant?; can they be adapted to new situations in other times or places? or are they as outmoded as the clothes we wore when we thought such things?

In this spirit, I should begin by describing the circumstances in which I first became involved in discussions about 'new technology' (as it was then called) and work.

I was at the time (the early 1970s) working in the publishing industry producing books and audio-visual materials for schools. The industry was a notoriously low-paid one then, with poor working conditions. When I started, in 1970, a new graduate editorial recruit was paid an annual salary of £750 and received two weeks holiday a year, at a time when the average annual salary of a male non-manual worker was £1,862. Annoyed by this apparent injustice, and finding it almost impossible to remain solvent, I had become actively involved in attempts to unionize the industry. This entailed not only coming to grips with the structures of the National Union of Journalists, which represented editorial staff, but also of a plethora of other trade unions, still largely organized on a craft basis, representing secretarial staff, designers, warehouse workers, typesetters and other specialist print workers.

Independently of this, influenced particularly by the writings of Sheila Rowbotham (1969, 1973a, b), I had begun to get involved with the emerging women's movement in Britain. Many of the radicals whom I met in the National Union of Journalists had, like myself, been students during 1968, and brought with them into their union activities a set of beliefs which were rooted in the libertarian and/or Marxist student politics of the time. When these beliefs are examined in retrospect, several themes stand out as particularly important. One was a faith in the spontaneous ability of rank-and-file workers (once the causes of their oppression had been pointed out to them) to organize themselves, frame appropriate demands, and fight for their own liberation. This was associated with a mistrust of full-time union officials or other bureaucrats who, because their interests as a class were not the same as those of workers, would, if given a chance, always negotiate a 'sell-out'. A second theme was the importance of unity between different groups of workers. The pursuit of sectional interests by any particular group was seen as diversionary and divisive. Appeals to unity were often used to deter groups of women workers from pursuing demands for 'special provisions', such as maternity rights which would, it was thought, alienate their male colleagues. The general atmosphere in which these themes were developed was one of heady political optimism and urgency. Although the expansionary economic conditions of the 1960s were already over, there was still a strong sense that things could only get better; indeed, in some circles it was defeatist even to mention the possibility that a socialist revolution might not be round the corner.

In this context, when rumours began to reach Britain of a new technology which would transform the nature of typesetters' work, the first response was to perceive it as a threat to workers' unity. Radical members of the journalists' union, together with a few colleagues from other print unions, decided that this issue could not safely be left in the hands of full-time officials, and formed a worker-based group to research it (Barbara Gunnell, Christina Potrykus and Jenny Vaughan are three of the people whom I remember as being particularly active in the process, perhaps because they were the only women in the group; perhaps because they really did most of the work). It was argued that, if all the print unions did not stand firmly together, journalists would be able to input copy directly, thus putting the typesetters out of work. This would weaken all the other unions, journalists included, because only the typesetters, traditionally very well-paid, had the industrial muscle to bring the newspaper proprietors instantly to the negotiating table, a strength they had frequently exercised in the past by threatening or taking immediate strike action (of a type then known in the press as 'wildcat strikes') which could completely halt production of a newspaper (Journalists' Charter).

The issues, then, were redundancies and trade union unity. Indeed, it was sometimes claimed that managers' sole reason for introducing new technology was to 'smash the print unions'. One member of the union working group, Jenny Vaughan, visited the United States to find out what had happened when the technology was introduced there, and came back with information which reinforced this view. The possibility that VDU work might entail health hazards was mentioned in passing but not made much of. The fact that the skills required to operate the new technology were those of a typist – normally seen as a woman's occupation – was not the subject of comment, perhaps because journalism was at the time virtually the only occupation in Britain in which men were required to be able to type. In keeping with this analysis, the action enjoined on workers was resistance: they should boycott all new technology in the interests not only of preserving jobs but also of preserving union strength.

Although at the time I made no connection between the two discussions, while this debate was going on in the trade union, I was also reading every feminist publication I could find. Among the socialist feminists with whom I identified, two 'demands' seemed to be the most important preconditions for women's liberation: economic independence and the socialization of housework. The former led to a focus on paid work; the latter to a focus on what was unpaid. I can remember spending a lot of time puzzling over the relationship between privatized, unpaid domestic labour and the money economy, helped by a largely Marxist feminist literature (especially Gardiner, 1975).

In 1976 I got a job with a large company in the North of England, which owned a number of factories, as well as the publishing division for which I was working. It was very hierarchically organized, with sharp contrasts between the conditions of the managers, mostly male, and the clerical staff, who were almost exclusively female. Such union organization as there was was dominated by men on managerial grades. Together with one of these men, who was sympathetic to feminism, I concluded that it would be necessary to hold women-only meetings if we were to find out what the real grievances of the majority of the workers were. It was here that I had my first direct encounter with the effects of new technology – in the ladies' lavatory. One day I met a young woman there, sitting, doubled-up, with her head clutched in both hands, rocking backwards and forwards in what appeared to be considerable pain. When I asked her what the matter was she said it was 'them machines' which gave her excruciating headaches. 'Them machines' turned out to be terminals connected to the company's mainframe computer, on which she was processing invoices. I decided to bring this up at the first women-only meeting we were organizing, and included a reference to it in the publicity material produced for the meeting. At the meeting it emerged that, although currently only a minority of the clerical staff – mainly invoice clerks – was working on computer terminals, the company was about to introduce some mysterious new machines called word processors into the customer services department.

From their description I recognized that these machines bore some family resemblance to the 'new technology' we had heard about in newspapers, and realized that this technology was not just likely to affect the jobs of a few hundred male print workers but of tens of thousands of female office workers. I started collecting all the information I could about these machines – attending office equipment trade fairs, reading the special supplements on microprocessor technology which were beginning to appear in the business press, and writing to the British Society for Social Responsibility in Science (which produced a magazine about occupational health called the *Hazards Bulletin*) to see whether anything was known about the health hazards of VDUs.

This last request elicited copies of two research papers on the subject, one American and one Swedish (Ostberg, n.d; Busch, 1976). By following up all the references in each, I was able to assemble a file of information on the subject. This contained some useful, albeit fairly technical, information on eyestrain and the ergonomics of keyboard work, together with some less informative articles dismissing 'radiation scares'. To my surprise, I discovered that the possession of this file gave me the status of an 'expert' on the subject. From other discussions with people involved in producing the *Hazards Bulletin*, especially Charlie Clutterbuck, I gained a more general introduction to the ideas in general currency in the radical science movement at the time: that science is not neutral and that the general principle to be followed in any analysis of occupational hazards is that the design of the job, rather than the individual worker, is likely to be to blame, from which it follows that the solution to the problem is to redesign the job, rather than the worker.

In the meanwhile, I was getting involved with a group of people grievances of the majority of the workers were. It was here that I had my first direct encounter with the effects of new technology – in the ladies' lavatory. One day I met a young woman there, sitting, doubled-up, with her head clutched in both hands, rocking backwards and forwards in what appeared to be considerable pain. When I asked her what the matter was she said it was 'them machines' which gave her excruciating headaches. 'Them machines' turned out to be terminals connected to the company's mainframe computer, on which she was processing invoices. I decided to bring this up at the first women-only meeting we were organizing, and included a reference to it in the publicity material produced for the meeting. At the meeting it emerged that, although currently only a minority of the clerical staff – mainly invoice clerks – was working on computer terminals, the company was about to introduce some mysterious new machines called word processors into the customer services department.

From their description I recognized that these machines bore some family resemblance to the 'new technology' we had heard about in newspapers, and realized that this technology was not just likely to affect the jobs of a few hundred male print workers but of tens of thousands of female office workers. I started collecting all the information I could about these machines – attending office equipment trade fairs, reading the special supplements on microprocessor technology which were beginning to appear in the business press, and writing to the British Society for Social Responsibility in Science (which produced a magazine about occupational health called the *Hazards Bulletin*) to see whether anything was known about the health hazards of VDUs.

This last request elicited copies of two research papers on the subject, one American and one Swedish (Ostberg, n.d; Busch, 1976). By following up all the references in each, I was able to assemble a file of information on the subject. This contained some useful, albeit fairly technical, information on eyestrain and the ergonomics of keyboard work, together with some less informative articles dismissing 'radiation scares'. To my surprise, I discovered that the possession of this file gave me the status of an 'expert' on the subject. From other discussions with people involved in producing the *Hazards Bulletin*, especially Charlie Clutterbuck, I gained a more general introduction to the ideas in general currency in the radical science movement at the time: that science is not neutral and that the general principle to be followed in any analysis of occupational hazards is that the design of the job, rather than the individual worker, is likely to be to blame, from which it follows that the solution to the problem is to redesign the job, rather than the worker.

In the meanwhile, I was getting involved with a group of people organizations. Numerous television programmes and educational films were commissioned, and reports and popular booklets published.[1] The issue was also taken up by women's groups for the first time.

On the academic left, Harry Braverman was a dominant influence. His *Labour and Monopoly Capital* (1974) had launched a whole generation of labour process analysts, virtually all of whom (quite against the spirit in which Braverman had written his book) appeared to concentrate their attention almost exclusively on car production workers. Into the discussions on technology, which had previously focused on job loss and unity, was introduced a new subject, that of skill. It was generally assumed that the Fordist tendency of capital to introduce ever simpler industrial processes in order to deskill workers was an absolute one. New technology was simply an instrument of deskilling, so far as this school of thought was concerned. Jane Barker and Hazel Downing (1980) showed that it was possible to adapt Braverman's model so that it could be applied to the introduction of new technology into typing and secretarial work. The ideas that the concept of skill might be a problematic one when applied to women, or that there might be situations when the introduction of a new process involving more difficult skills might be in an employer's interest, were not receiving attention. When I wrote a paper which attempted to analyse the changing skill content of domestic labour using Braverman's notion of deskilling, it received a very hostile reception from the men in the CSE Microelectronics Working Group.[2] As far as they were concerned, the automation of household tasks was unproblematically a 'good thing' and did not require any further analysis. Because it was occurring in the 'sphere of consumption' rather than that of production, it had no relevance whatsoever to their discussions.

There were also attempts to integrate an analysis of the effects of technological change into economic theory, both orthodox and Marxist. Kondratiev's idea of cyclical 'waves' of technological development was much discussed. The spectre of technologically-induced mass unemployment remained the dominant theme. Although it was sometimes pointed out that this may be a transitional feature of a massive restructuring of capital, most commentators were at a loss when it came to understanding the basis on which the next boom would be based. Robots don't buy cars, it was said, so where would the mass markets come from for the next wave of commodities to be produced? Again, there was enormous resistance among the male economists who dominated these debates to any suggestion that the automation of domestic labour might have anything to do with the generation of new commodities (CSE Microelectronics Group, 1981).

Meanwhile in the trade union movement some first-hand experience of the introduction of the technology was beginning to accrue. The question to which most people wanted answers, was: 'how many jobs will it destroy? In some circles any stance other than out-and-out opposition was still regarded as treachery. Sometimes negotiations on the conditions of introduction were refused, which was not in the interests of the workers (generally women) who ended up having to use the machines. In other cases, the white-collar trade union representatives responsible for representing workers' interests in the negotiations were drawn from precisely those strata of lower management, professional and technical staff who had most to benefit from new technology. They were perceived as the cause of, rather than the solution to, the problem by the secretarial and clerical women workers who had most to lose. In some cases this led to increased militancy among the women workers, many of whom, for the first time, put themselves forward for elected union positions and eagerly attended conferences on women and new technology organized by women's groups or trade unions. The technology-related issues they were most concerned with were health and safety, job design and access to training. However it was clear that in many cases these were inseparable from the other problems they faced as women in their workplaces. Meetings called to discuss technology often ended up discussing how to deal with the sexist attitudes of male trade union colleagues or the opposition of husbands or lovers to women being active in the union at all. I can remember one woman (a convenor in a factory which manufactured cosmetics) whose husband would wait impatiently outside the meeting room for her to finish, looking angrily at his watch and accosting anyone else who came out. Another (a school secretary) had been told by her husband to choose between him and the union ('Well', she told me, 'I thought about it for a while and then I decided, I'll take the union, thank you very much').

In the literature we produced at the time there is usually a silence surrounding these problems. Much was written about the burdens of the 'double shift' – the combination of paid work and unpaid housework. Little, however, was said in public about the third shift – the work for the union. In retrospect, this was often more burdensome and brought fewer rewards than either of the others. At its worst, it involved spending exhausting hours in draughty, smoky meeting rooms, in the company of abusive, argumentative men (many of whom would have been completely at a loss socially without a meeting to go to), getting home to a dirty house and an empty fridge long after the shops had closed, being attacked as a militant by the right and a reactionary by the left, never thanked, always blamed, while relationships fell apart about one's ears. As the 1970s progressed, the euphoric moments of victory became ever rarer.

Yet the tone of our publications was relentlessly optimistic. Between 1976 and 1980 I was working on the manuscript of an ambitious 'Working Women's Handbook', supposed to be published by Pluto Press in their *Workers' Handbook* series. Delayed by overwork, illnesses and bereavements in my own life and overtaken by events (the Thatcher government, once elected in 1979, immediately began to dismantle much of the legislation which I had so painstakingly anatomized), this was never quite finished and remains unpublished to this day. Its language and approach are, however, typical of the period. Each section starts with an analysis of a problem (for instance, lack of childcare facilities, or low pay), illustrated by tightly-edited quotations either taken directly from working women I had interviewed or gleaned from secondary sources. The tone then shifts to a more prescriptive one ('This is what you can do about it'), again copiously illustrated with examples of how particular groups of women workers have successfully overcome it. The collection of all this information, in which I was greatly helped by Jo Fitzpatrick and Marianne Dee, involved not only following up large numbers of personal leads, through contacts made at meetings or conferences, but also the accumulation of large files of newspaper cuttings, magazine articles, pamphlets and books. It could not have been achieved had we not been simultaneously setting up a library of such information at the resource centre. What strikes me when rereading this material now is the curious shift in emotional tone from the extreme pessimism of the way in which 'problems' are presented to the inspirational triumphalism of the 'solutions'. The combined effects of capitalism and patriarchy are presented as producing such an enormity of suffering that language can hardly contain it, yet in these accounts women organizing together, fuelled by feminist understanding and righteous anger, generate such a glow of sisterhood, such strength, that they appear to become invincible. I do not think that this was mere projection, or wishful thinking. It is so general in the socialist feminist literature (and in some films) of the time that I am convinced that it expresses something we really felt, an emotional atmosphere which we breathed, then, but which is difficult to describe now without resorting to clichés about 'the transformation of consciousness through struggle' or the like.

Trade unions were not, of course, the only arena in which women were active then. There was a proliferation of small single-issue groups many of which, by the end of the 1970s, had begun to address various aspects of the relationship between technology and women's lives. Some, either seeing the technology as inevitable, or as 'neutral' and desirable, saw women's exclusion from science and technology as a major problem, and began to agitate for more training for women and, where necessary, for that training to be carried out in women-only groups. Feminist teachers set up projects in schools and colleges, while other women set up groups to raise funds for women's technology training centres. One of the first of these, if not the very first, was the East Leeds Women's Workshop, in which Lynette Willoughby, a feminist electronics engineer, played a key role. There was some debate as to what the purpose of such training was. Were women to be trained simply to fill low-level niches in a system which exploited them? Were a favoured few to be given access to 'male' skills so that they could climb a 'career ladder' leaving most of their sisters behind? Were women to be educated *about* the technology rather than *in* it, so that they could develop a critique of an essentially male technology? Or was the technology neutral, capable of delivering good things to society if only it were controlled by women with humanitarian motives, rather than by men with destructive and profit-seeking ones? After a decade in which women have been urged to become assertive, independent and autonomous (not to say greedy). Such questions have a curiously old-fashioned ring to them.

Concern about the neutrality and control of science and technology were not exclusive to the discussion of information technology. These debates were paralleled and cross-nourished during this period by lively (and in some respects more advanced) discussions among feminists about medical technology and its impact on women's lives, and the beginnings of a public debate about the relationship between gender and military technology (which was to culminate several years later in the Greenham Common peace camp).

Another important set of concerns was the role of transnational corporations and the development of international solidarity between women. Copies of Rachel Grossman's (1979) description of conditions in the silicon chip factories of South East Asia had reached the UK by 1979, and profoundly shocked many women who had focused their attention on the impact of information technology on the work processes of the user industries, forgetting to ask how it was itself produced.

In 1979 and 1980, several feminist conferences on women and information technology were held, each very well-attended. I still have the roneoed double-sided sheet of paper which was handed out to advertise one of them, organized in the name of the Yorkshire and Humberside Regional Socialist Feminist Group. This conference gave birth to the West Yorkshire Women and New Technology Group, which later produced a special issue of the magazine *Scarlet Women* on the subject (West Yorkshire, 1982). The leaflet is reproduced as an appendix to this chapter because it gives what still seems to me one of the best summaries of 'Why New Technology Specially Affects Women' (the title of the paper) while still giving off a pungent odour of its time. The rhetorical question of the title was answered under four main headings: 'Because of the sorts of jobs we have'; 'Because we also work at home'; 'Because of how we are educated' and 'Because economic crisis hits women hardest'. Under these four headings it manages to work in a remarkably complete agenda of the issues which were of major concern at the time. These include: 'skill loss'; 'double shift'; 'mobility'; 'trade unions'; 'consumption'; 'homeworking'; 'unemployment'; 'cuts' and 'multinationals'. After an anxiety-provoking run-through of all the detrimental effects on women's lives the new technology was likely to bring, it ends with a series of open-ended questions, under the general heading: 'Could new technology bring women's liberation?' I can re-member writing it, with Jude Stoddart, after an exhausted brainstorming session, late one night, typing straight onto a stencil with a mechanical typewriter. The need to say everything on two sides of A4 paper, to keep the language simple, and to avoid saying anything which might lead to an inadvertent interpretation which was not politically correct, meant that every word had to be carefully scrutinized before it was committed to the stencil. Not much room for subjectivity here.

In 1979 the centre where I worked actually received some money (from the Equal Opportunities Commission) for research on the impact of new technology on women's working lives. This meant that, for the first time, I had to grapple with some serious methodological problems. There did not appear to be a single academic discipline which could provide the tools for any systematic analysis of the social impact of technological change. During the 1960s, as a summer job when I was a student, I had worked as a reporter on a series of interdisciplinary conferences on the 'City of the Future', and had picked up a little knowledge of forecasting techniques, but even futurology seemed to be of little help here. The relevant books I could find were scattered across library shelves: some in economics; some in sociology; some in psychology; some in medicine; some in technology; some in geography; some in the newly-emerging 'women's studies' and 'business studies' sections. Many of the most useful pieces of empirical information came from none of these, but from trade journals, newspapers, conference papers and government reports. Yet these often had a certain circularity. A tentative speculation made in one quarter would be published as a prediction in another, which would then be cited as an authoritative source in a third. The unique library classification system we had at the resource centre (devised by Marianne Dee) meant that these could all be filed together under commonsense headings related to the research in hand, and made it possible to develop some sort of overview of the literature (a resource which was frequently used, usually without acknowledgement, by visiting academics). Nevertheless, this did not necessarily produce a very coherent conceptual framework. I found myself collecting scraps of empirical information, almost randomly, and then sorting them and resorting them until I could identify headings under which they could be grouped without too much distortion.

A central difficulty was finding quantitative information which would enable me to assess the relative importance of different types of women's employment. Which sorts of jobs were likely to be automated? And how many women were employed in such jobs? All the up-to-date employment figures I could find were based on industries, rather than occupations. Research which had been done in the past on the distribution of occupations within industries (Crum and Gudgin, 1977) was useless for my purposes because it aggregated the figures for men and women, making gender segregation invisible. In order to collect this information, and establish the long-term trends in occupational change and changes in their gender composition, it was necessary to go back to the primary sources (censuses of population and employment, going back to the beginning of the century) and spend many tedious hours with a calculator (a task I could not have achieved without the unstinting help of Quentin Outram). This was my first first-hand encounter with official statistics, and a very disillusioning one.

I was aware of the work of the Radical Statistics Group, which was about to publish a book called *Demystifying Social Statistics* (Irvine *et al.*, 1979), so I was prepared to find that the statistics embodied values which might be regarded as 'establishment' ones. However up to that point I had somewhat naively believed in the comprehensiveness of official data. It came as a great shock to me to discover that, on a range of issues which one might have thought would have been important to the government for its own policy-making purposes, the relevant statistics simply did not exist. It would be several years before I became confident enough to formulate specific criticisms of government research-gathering instruments, or suggest changes to them. At the time, I simply felt lost and lonely, stranded without a map in a jungle of conflicting facts. This existential angst is, perhaps, an inescapable part of the process of becoming a researcher. As the certainties crumble, and hypotheses collapse, we discover that there is no parental god up there with the 'right' answers, and it is up to us to construct our own version of reality. I cannot say that I have got used to it yet. I still write with the expectation that somewhere a reader will be taking each sentence apart, pointing out factual errors or logical flaws in the argument, and I am not sure whether I am relieved or disappointed when, having sent the finished work out into the world, there is no reaction at all, apart from citations in other people's, equally anxious, productions.

This is not the place to describe this research in detail. It did, however, establish a pattern in my life which was to last for nearly a decade, whereby each piece of research was essentially written up twice: once in the accepted scholarly way, for the client who had funded it, and then again in a popular form, for 'ordinary people'. As the 1980s progressed, however, this became more and more difficult to do, as the organizations which were willing or able to publish the popular versions dwindled in size and number. In the absence of successful mass movements or any large-scale public culture of resistance it also became more difficult to identify who this 'ordinary person' might be for whom one was producing these materials. Nowadays, having lost any sense that I have the 'right answers', I am increasingly uncomfortable using any authorial voice which is not identi- fiably my own. But this is a digression. In 1980, despite the unmistakable signs of an impending recession and the most reactionary and anti-woman government in living memory, it still seemed vitally important to make everything one learned available, as quickly as possible (while it was still warm, so to speak) to the widest possible working-class audience. I wrote *Your Job in the Eighties* (1982c) (intended as a popular women's guide to the effects of new technology on employment) in a two-week burst (fuelled by the high blood pressure of mid-pregnancy) in 1981, but its spirit is from the 1970s. It still has the 'you too can do it; all you need is organization and courage' tone of the rallying publications of the previous decade. It still focuses exclusively on collective action, implicitly suggesting that the individual, acting as an individual, is powerless.

During the early 1980s this mood was to change. The individual members of the discussion and campaigning groups of the later 1970s went their separate ways. Some went to work for the Greater London Council or one of the other newly radical local authorities which seemed, for a time, to offer the possibility of islands of socialism within the greater sea of Thatcherism. Some became academics. Some withdrew into child-bearing and domesticity. Some went to work full-time for trade unions, charities or campaigning bodies. Some set up training projects or consultancies or other new enterprises. Some retrained so that they could practice psychotherapy or osteopathy or other, more esoteric alternative therapies. Some became professional politicians. Some died. As survival became more difficult, and the experience of political defeat more common, only a few, with excep- tional stamina, managed to sustain the rhythm of regular meetings and continue to engage in discussion for discussion's sake. Activities which had previously been carried out in people's spare time, for their own sake, without payment, were increasingly becoming the preserve of a profes- sionalized 'voluntary sector'. It was often difficult to tell whether people were speaking from their own political beliefs or regurgitating the terms of their job description.

These changes inevitably led to a shift of focus, often a narrowing, more directed to the achievement of realizable short-term goals: the setting up of a particular training course; the opening of a women's centre; a change in policy. A new and pragmatic generation was emerging, familiar with feminist and socialist ideas because they had heard them from radical teachers at school and university, but also hard-nosed about their own survival. They often made the veterans of the 1960s feel hopelessly naive and unrealistic. Many of the theoretical debates of the 1970s were left unresolved because they suddenly seemed irrelevant. The contents of the shelves of feminist book shops changed out of all recognition. When I looked, in about 1984, under the heading 'employment' in *Sisterwrite* (my local feminist book shop) expecting to find, as I would have a decade earlier, a selection of heavy works of political economy, campaigning pamphlets, autobiographical accounts and sociological studies, all I could find was one book about sexual harassment at work, three guides to setting up one's own business and an even larger number of handbooks for developing greater assertiveness. It wasn't that feminist publishing had declined. Far from it. There were shelves and shelves of poetry and fiction, books about sexuality, about race, about health, about housing, about violence, about psychology. It was just that the attention had shifted away from those previously central concerns of economic independence and the study of work, whether paid or unpaid. I tried looking under 'technology' and found a few collections of essays about women's relationship with technology, but these were heavily outnumbered by 'how to' books about computing. What seemed to have happened was a radical shift of emphasis from the collective to the individual.

This change did not happen all at once, however. During the early 1980s an immense amount of empirical work was done on employment, technology and gender, often designed to test the hypotheses we had developed in our discussions in the late 1970s. Ann Game and Rosemary Pringle, in Australia, published *Gender at Work* (1984), Cynthia Cockburn in Britain published *Brothers* (1983). It became clear that skill was a much more complex concept than Braverman had supposed, more a social construct than any acquired set of competencies which could be objectively measured for their difficulty. It also became clear that the impact of information technology on women's jobs was far more diverse than simplistic Marxist analyses had predicted. It was true that in some industries and some occupations there was a Fordist tendency to reduce tasks to their simplest components, minimizing the skills component and reducing the workforce

to a homogeneous, interchangeable mass. In others, however, the introduction of new technology obliged workers to acquire a lot of new skills.
Because they were usually fairly low-paid women, and the technology was
seen by their employers as an extension of the typewriter, they were often
not provided with adequate training. The word 'reskilling' began to be used
alongside 'deskilling', and evening classes in word processing had long
waiting lists.

Many of us were still grappling with broader theoretical and political
issues, trying to tease out the implications of what we had learned and apply
them to other debates. I can remember, for instance, writing an article in
which I attempted to apply Marx's theory of alienation to domestic labour,
by developing an analogy between the worker's relationship with the
means of production in the workplace and the housewife's relationship
with the means of reproduction (the home itself, and domestic technology).
Because workers were increasingly being required to become owners of
these means of reproduction, I argued, they could not express their hatred
of them and organize against them as factory workers could, although they
were just as surely enslaved to the cash economy by the need to pay for
them. I wanted to develop this argument to explore the question of what
sorts of self-hatred and neurosis might ensue from this relationship, but
lacked the courage to do so. I had so often been put down by academic
Marxists for arguing 'on the wrong level of abstraction' that I dared not risk
it again. Instead, I swung back to a discussion of high-tech homeworking,
the subject on which I had originally been asked to write (Huws, 1985a).

Meanwhile Rosemary Crompton was carrying out research (published
under the title *White-collar Proletariat*) which brought detailed empirical
evidence to the debate about how the working class is to be defined,
challenging Marxist orthodoxies in the process (1984).

An idea which received a good deal of attention during this period in
discussions of technological change was that of 'socially useful production'. The charismatic figure of Mike Cooley, who had been the main
architect of the Lucas Aerospace workers' 'alternative plan for Lucas' was
largely responsible for this (Wainwright and Elliott, 1982; Cooley, 1981).

When asked to produce a feminist critique of this idea I found myself
returning, yet again, to the subject of domestic labour and its relationship
with the money economy. It was, I thought, the emphasis on commodity
production (and with it, the idea of the 'real worker' as somebody exclusively engaged in commodity production) which was suspect in any
vision of alternative work which was supposed to prefigure a socialist
society. Was the socialist dislike of service sector employment simply a
consequence of its being largely identified with women's work, or were

there more complex issues at stake? I realized that the relationship between unpaid labour, service employment and commodity production was a dynamic one, whose boundaries were constantly changing, partly in association with the introduction of new technologies. The history of capitalism could be seen as the history of the gradual drawing out into the money economy of activities which had previously been carried out unpaid in the household. An essential part of this process was that of commodification and each wave of new technology generated new commodities. The introduction of these commodities brought changes in work processes (and hence in skills) both for the workers involved in their production and for the users of these commodities. To attempt to freeze a particular set of skills or work processes and apply them to the development of 'alternative' commodities seemed likely to be doomed to failure. Even if it succeeded, it would most likely be anti-woman in its effects, since it would also freeze the particular form of the division of labour (and hence of social relations) of the moment in which it was captured (Huws, 1985b). Increasingly, however, such articles seemed to produce no response. One might as well have dropped them into a void for all the debate they generated.

By 1982 I was living in London, alone with a baby, carrying out research on what later came to be known as 'teleworking' (a clumsy attempt on my part to translate the French coinage 'teletravail', used to refer to work carried out at a distance using information technology). This relative isolation may have coloured my experiences of the next few years. It was certainly the case that I felt distanced from whatever political debates were going on. Instead of being carried out voluntarily, the research which was going on in the areas I was interested in was increasingly being funded in academic, local government or voluntary sector contexts. A note of wariness and competitiveness began to creep into the discussions when researchers met each other. Although for some knowledge was still something to be shared as widely as possible, so that common learning could take place, for others it was clearly a valuable commodity, to be parted with only for money, promotion or glory. There were still some occasions, like the conferences organized by the Women and Computing network, which retained the atmosphere of the 1970s, but other, more academic ones, seemed imbued with a more guarded and self-seeking atmosphere. There was a terrible conflict between the sharing feminist ethic and the need to earn a living. Because I was now self-employed, survival was hard, and I sometimes felt exploited when my work was used by others without acknowledgement or payment. However, I also felt a great need to be part of an intellectual community where ideas could be freely shared, and realized that I could not have it both ways. It was my impression that, in

Britain at least, such a community hardly existed any more, although on the rare occasions when I could afford to go to conferences in other countries, my faith in the possibility of its existence was rekindled.

The first such occasion was a conference on women and new technology organized by ISIS in Switzerland in 1983.[3] There was a sense of excitement and urgency to communicate which made one realize how demoralized feminists had become in Britain under the Thatcher government. There was a wonderful paper from a group of women from the Japanese Committee for the Protection of Women in the Computer World (1983). Trini Leung, from Hong Kong, spoke movingly and inspiringly about the need for international solidarity among women working for multinational corporations in the electronics industry, and there were thought-provoking contributions from many other countries. I came away convinced that continuing to bang one's head against the brick wall of Thatcherism, as so much of the British left was doing, was not the best strategy. Instead, we should be concentrating on developing international links, and confronting international capital.

The work that I had been doing on teleworking had made me aware that when new technology is introduced it can change not just the nature, but also the location, of work. This does not just involve shifts from the office to the home or from the city centre to the suburb, but may involve regional or international shifts. It seemed possible that the sort of international division of labour which had grown up in manufacturing industries during the 1960s and 1970s might well be repeated in service industries in the 1980s and 1990s. Helped by some leads from the United States office-workers' organization '9 to 5', I had begun to collect information about the growing use of offshore information processing by companies based in North America, Europe and Australia. I was never able to get funding to develop this work systematically, but it undoubtedly informed the work I was doing with women's groups at the time, most notably in the setting up of the City Centre, a resource centre for office workers in the City of London (in which Sarah Stewart played a key role) and in Women Working Worldwide, a group specifically set up to develop international solidarity among working women, into whose development Gerry Reardon and Helen O'Connell put an especially impressive amount of energy. In general, there appeared to be something of a retreat from internationalism in the British left at the time, although there were some exceptions. The Greater London Council sponsored some work on multinational corporations (notably Kodak and Ford) and funded the London Transnationals Information Centre, but such initiatives often seemed to be regarded as aspects of development education, as do-gooding, rather than real politics. It was a rare surprise to meet someone – like Swasti Mitter – who combined an active interest in theoretical issues with a commitment to internationalism which took precedence over other political concerns (Mitter 1986).

As the 1980s ground on, either feminist initiatives on new technology became scarcer or I lost touch with them. Such projects as there were seemed mainly addressed to practical issues. The Women and Computing Network gave birth to Microsyster, a project set up to provide training and computing services to women's groups, as well as a lively newsletter.[4] Otherwise, my main contact with the issues was through correspondence with Ph.D. students, visits from overseas researchers and the occasional conference. Much of my paid work did not relate directly to technology, although there was a steady trickle of interest in teleworking. I have written elsewhere at length on the different meanings this concept acquired over the years and will not repeat myself here (Huws, 1991; 1993; Huws *et al.* 1989).

It is, though, perhaps worth noting two central preoccupations in relation to technology which surfaced during this period, which had been largely absent during the 1970s. The first of these was the concern, already referred to, with the spatial dimensions of technological change. Here, I found relatively little that was useful in either feminist theory or Marxism. The most creative thinking in the area seemed to be going on among radical geographers, such as Mark Hepworth and his colleagues at the Centre for Urban and Regional Development Studies in Newcastle (Hepworth, 1989), and in some work on racism and imperialism, notably that of Sivanandan at the Institute of Race Relations (Sivanandan, 1980).

The other concern was with the ways in which information technology not only changed the labour process itself but was also associated with transformations in relationships between employers and employees, in particular its role in bringing about the casualization of employment. When I had discussed the possibility of writing a book on the subject of the casualization of employment with Pluto Press in 1982 (shortly before the company folded), I was told by the editor concerned that there was no such word, and that even if we were to coin it, the concept would have no meaning for people. Over the ensuing decade it became abundantly clear that even if the word was not known, the condition was being experienced widely. Under the rubric of 'flexibility', large numbers of previously secure, permanent jobs were becoming temporary or casual, or farmed out to subcontractors and agencies, helped in no small measure by government policies which removed employment protection from large sections of the workforce, dismantled minimum wages and obliged public employers to subcontract many of their services. In the discussions about casualization, however, the role of technology became less and less important. It was clear that, while it was often a facilitator of casualization, the technology did not itself cause these social and legal changes (Huws *et al.*, 1989).

Perhaps partly because during the 1980s most of us had ourselves become direct users of information technology (I acquired my first personal computer in 1983, a modem in 1985, a fax in 1987), it was becoming harder and harder to focus on it as a separate issue in its own right, and the earnest debates of the 1970s about whether or not it was a 'good thing' seemed at best irrelevant, at worst downright silly. For most people in Britain under the age of forty, information technology was now a taken-for-granted feature of everyday life. It had become necessary to be familiar with it or risk being seriously disadvantaged in one's career. Ten years after I had written that first *Hazards Bulletin* article about VDU hazards, I suffered the supreme irony of developing repetitive strain injury while working on a book on that very subject, commissioned by the London Hazards Centre (Huws, 1987). Since then, I have discovered that many of my women friends who are writers have developed the same condition.

This brings me to what is, perhaps, the central paradox of so many feminists' lives – our complete failure to practice what we preach! We write about the dangers of stress-related illnesses while leading incredibly stressful lives ourselves. We fight for the rights of low-paid workers while often accepting pitifully low fees or working for nothing ourselves. Some of us write about the exploitation and isolation of casually-paid homeworkers, while working as home-based freelances ourselves. We encourage other women to act collectively out of self-interest and not allow themselves to be guilt-tripped into self-sacrifice while ourselves taking on the most self-punishing roles in the interests of the common good. Are all our goals mere projections of our own unexpressed needs? In puzzling over such questions I find myself returning again and again to the conflict between individualism and collectivism. In retrospect, it now seems to me that of all the changes which have taken place over the last two decades, perhaps the most important has been the erosion of any belief in the power of collective action, and the slow dawning in each of us of the depressing realization that if we don't do it for ourselves, the chances are that nobody else will do it for us.

It seems to me that this has not just led to demoralization among people with a political commitment to trying to make life better for working women, it has also led many thousands of individual working people to make choices in their lives (which they might not have made in less fearful times) which, together, have transformed the nature of employment and of other features of their working lives. Losing faith in the possibility of public organizations being able to remain good landlords, they have bought their previously rented apartments. Losing faith in the possibility of getting their children decently cared for in public childcare facilities, they have chosen to work from home and look after them themselves. Losing faith in the possibility that their trade unions can secure their future, they have chosen instead to put money into private pension schemes. The sum of all these individual decisions has been a near-complete collapse of the public infrastructure in which new collectivities can be woven. I do not know whether this British experience has been reflected elsewhere in the world, although the news stories from Eastern Europe suggest that features of it are certainly evident there. What does seem apparent to me is that any solutions which we might wish to propose, any demands which we might wish to make for the future, must take this context into account. It may be that there is still the possibility of generating some enormous, collective act of hope which will enable people to begin trusting each other again. Failing this, we must try to find demands which do not force them to make a harsh choice between self (and individual certainty) and others (and possible loss). We cannot demand altruism. The best we can do is to trust women to see where their own best interests lie, and pursue them, with or without the aid of information technology.

APPENDIX

Yorkshire and Humberside regional socialist feminist conference, 3 November, 1979, 'women and new technology'

Why does new technology specially affect women?

Because of the sorts of jobs we have

Service sector   In both public and private services, the vast majority of people doing other people's housework are women – in hospitals, nurseries, hotels, schools: cooking, cleaning and caring. Women are also the main processors of information – in shops, offices, banks, local and central government. Many of these areas are already being directly – and drastically – affected by new technology, e.g. word processing is being introduced in offices; automatic checkouts in supermarkets; 'cash-point' machines in banks; centralized, computer-controlled cooking in schools and hospitals.

Manufacturing   In manufacturing, the 'service' jobs are affected in the same way, but women are also affected by changes in the production process itself. Here, women are mainly ghettoised in the boring, repetitive, unskilled jobs which are the first targets for automation. Changes in the actual products reduce the number of components necessary – one electrical part can take the place of scores of mechanical ones – and cut the number of fiddly soldering and assembly jobs – also work mainly done by women.

Skill loss   These changes mean fewer jobs for women, and higher unemployment all round. For the minority of 'skilled' women workers, the chance to use these skills will disappear. For those classified as 'unskilled', work becomes even more stressful and machine-like.

Because we also work at home

Double shift   Our double responsibilities – for home and work – restrict the hours we can work, and how far we can travel to get there. New technology brings changes in working hours (e.g. twenty-four-hour shift systems) and location of employment.

Mobility   We are moved in and out of the workforce (because we have kids, because husbands move, etc.). This means we have little or no employment protection – and present government policies are removing what little we had. Ours are the jobs that disappear with 'voluntary redundancy' and 'non-replacement' policies.

Trade unions   Although our record of militancy is quite as good as men's when we're given a chance, we are poorly served by unions, and badly represented within them. We don't have time to go to meetings (which are held at the wrong times); are patronized or ignored by sexist union officials; and our interests put at the bottom of lists of priorities. We are also much more likely to be working for small firms or isolated in scattered workplaces such as cafés or shops – the areas where unions can't or won't recruit. All this makes it harder to fight back when our jobs are threatened.

Consumption   As the people mainly responsible for 'consumption work', women bear the brunt of the depersonalisation and extra work created by automation in services, e.g. queueing for hours in clinics, government offices or supermarket checkouts, coping with the frustration when machines go wrong, and suffering the rudeness of unsatisfied deskilled bureaucrats.

Homeworking Government reports predict that new technology will bring new jobs that can be done in the home, e.g. using terminals linked up to central computers over GPO lines. But how much of a gain will this be for women if homeworkers remain isolated, ununionized and badly paid, pressurized into working too fast because of the inadequate piece rates? Do we really want the stress of having our kids around while we work, machinery cluttering up our living rooms, and the pile of work always there, waiting to be done, twenty-four hours a day?

Because of how we are educated

Conditioning Both the schooling we get and general attitudes to women in society mean that most of us know very little about science and technology. This means that we are unlikely to get the few skilled and relatively creative jobs which new technology introduces. More importantly, it means that we are badly equipped to challenge the increasing domination and control of our lives by the technology and its applications, whether in the workplace (e.g. a machine recording every time you stop for a fag or a pee) or outside it (e.g. your social security file or medical records ending up on the police computer).

Because economic crisis hits women hardest

Unemployment No research has been done on how women's personal lives are affected by unemployment, although male unemployment is recognized as leading to increased suicide, illness (mental and physical) and other 'social problems'. A very high proportion of women are now the sole breadwinners for their families, and many who are not single parents are dependent on their wage to live above starvation level. Women form a growing proportion of the unemployed, and this will continue to rise as male workers demand that 'women's jobs should go first'. In the past, new jobs were created in the service sector for those displaced from manufacturing, but this is no longer the case, as new technology decimates the service jobs.

Cuts Cuts in public spending force women back in to the home at ever-increasing rates. Not only are womens' jobs lost from this sector, but the cuts also place a heavy burden on all women – looking after children, preparing school meals, caring for the sick, the elderly and the mentally ill.

Multinationals New technology is capitalism's answer to the crisis. It allows for a major shake-out of labour and investment in new machines which can produce huge increases in productivity with a much smaller, super-productive and super-exploited workforce. To the multinationals, women are an attractive source to draw on for this new labour force – cheap, under-organized and dispensable. Already, much of the labour-intensive work required for silicon chip production is done in South East Asia, where the electronics multinationals can employ young girls for as little as 40p a day. The production process is extremely hazardous, and the employment system is highly authoritarian. After four years in this type of work, the eyesight deteriorates to an extent that makes the women unemployable. Often, the only alternative source of income is prostitution.

Could new technology help bring women's liberation?

As the people most directly on the receiving end of all the worst effects of the new technology, in all areas of our lives, women are in the best position to develop a total picture of its likely effects. We are used to bridging the gap between the two worlds of home and outside work-place, and have learned the importance of taking action on both fronts. If new technology is not to be used to erode the gains we have made and oppress us even further, it is up to us to work out the demands we want to make.

- Could the technology be used to get rid of unpleasant jobs – paid or unpaid – and free us for creative lives – or would we need a different technology to liberate us?
- How should we organize to take action at work, in the community and with other women?
- What should our demands be in our unions, and how should we raise them?
- How can we raise these issues with other women?
- How can we combine struggles in unions with struggles elsewhere?
- What sort of technology do we want?

(J. Stoddart and U. Huws for the Planning Group)

NOTES

1 Much of this literature is reviewed in Huws, 1980; 1982a.
2 Huws, U., *New Technology and Domestic Labour*, unpublished paper, October, 1979. Parts of this paper formed the basis of Huws (1982b). Some of these ideas were further developed in Huws (1988).
3 This conference, entitled 'ISIS International Conference on New Technology and Women's Employment', was reported in *ISIS Bulletin*, Geneva, Autumn 1983.
4 The *Women and Computing Newsletter* (women only), available on subscription from Women and Computing Newsletter, c/o Microsyster, Wesley House, Wild Court, Kingsway, London WC2B 5AU.

REFERENCES

Barker, J., and Downing, H. (1980), 'Word Processing and the Transformation of Patriarchal Relations', in *Capital and Class* 10, London, pp. 64–99

Braverman, H. (1974), *Labour and Monopoly Capital: the Degradation of Work in the Twentieth Century*, New York, Monthly Review Press

Busch, G. (1976), *Ergonomic Problems with VDUs in the Banking and Insurance Industries*, report to FIET, USA

Cockburn, C. (1983), *Brothers*, London, Pluto Press

Committee for the Protection of Women in the Computer World (1983), *Women and Microelectronics in Japan*, Tokyo, CPWCW

Cooley, M. (1981), *Architect or Bee?*, Slough, Langley Technical Services

Crompton, R. and Jones, G. (1984), *White-collar Proletariat*, Basingstoke, Macmillan

Crum, R. E., and Gudgin, G. (1977), *Non-production Activities in UK Manufacturing Industry*, Commission of the European Communities, Brussels

CSE Microelectronics Group Conference of Socialist Economists Microprocessors Group (1981), *Microelectronics: Capitalist Technology and the Working Class*, London, CSE Books

Freire, P. (1970), *Pedagogy of the oppressed*, New York, Seabury Press.

Game, A. and Pringle, R. (1984), *Gender at work*, London, Pluto Press

Gardiner, J. *et al.* (1975), 'Women's Domestic Labour', *New Left Review* No 89, pp. 47–58

Grossman, R. (1979), 'Women's Place in the Integrated Circuit', *Southeast Asia Chronicle 66/ Pacific Research 9*, (joint issue), San Francisco

Hepworth, M. (1989), *Geography of the Information Economy*, London, Bellhaven Press

Huws, U. (1980), *The Impact of New Technology on the Working Lives of Women in West Yorkshire*, Leeds, Leeds Trade Union and Community Resource and Information Centre

Huws, U. (1982a), *New Technology and Women's Employment: Case Studies from West Yorkshire*, Manchester, Equal Opportunities Commission

Huws, U. (1982b), 'Domestic Technology: Liberator or Enslaver?', *Scarlet Women*, No. 14, January; reprinted in Kanter, Lefanu, Shah and Spedding (eds), (1984), *Sweeping Statements: Writings from the Women's Liberation Movement 1981-1983*, London, The Women's Press

Huws, U. (1982c), *Your Job in the Eighties*, London, Pluto Press

Huws, U. (1985a), 'Terminal Isolation: the Atomisation of Work and Leisure in the Wired Society', in *Making Waves*, *Radical Science*, 16, Winter/Spring

Huws, U. (1985b), 'Challenging Commodification', in *Very Nice Work if You Can Get it: the Socially Useful Production Debate*, Collective Design/Projects (eds), Nottingham, Spokesman

Huws, U. for the London Hazards Centre (1987), *VDU Hazards Handbook*, London, London Hazards Centre

Huws, U. (1988), 'Consuming Fashions', *New Statesman & Society*, August

Huws, U. (1991), 'Telework: Projections', in *Futures*, January

Huws, U. (1993), *Teleworking in Britain*, London, Employment Department Research Series

Huws, U., J. Hurstfield and R. Holtmaat (1989), *What Price Flexibility?: the Casualization of Women's Employment*, London, Low Pay Unit

Huws, U., W. Korte and S. Robinson (1990), *Telework: Towards the Elusive Office*, Chichester, John Wiley

Irvine, J., I. Miles and J. Evans (eds) (1979), *Demystifying Social Statistics*, London, Pluto Press

Journalists' Charter, *Journalists and New Technology*, London, Journalists Charter, undated but almost certainly 1976

Mitter, S. (1986), *Common Fate, Common Bond: Women in the Global Economy*, London, Pluto Press

Ostberg, O. (n.d.), *The Health Debate*, Department of Human Work Sciences, University of Lulea

Rowbotham, S. (1969), *Women's Liberation and the New Politics*, Mayday Manifesto, reprinted 1971, Nottingham, Bertrand Russell Peace Foundation

Rowbotham, S. (1973a), Women's Consciousness, Man's World, London, Allen Lane

Rowbotham, S. (1973b), *Hidden from History*, London, Pluto Press

Sivanandan, A. (1980), 'Imperialism in the Silicon Age', *Race and Class*, 8, London

Wainwright, H. and D. Elliott (1982), *The Lucas Plan*, London, Allison and Busby

West Yorkshire Women and New Technology Group (1982), 'Women and New Technology', *Scarlet Women*, 14, Leeds, January

Afterword

Sheila Rowbotham

The contributions in this collection chart new zones of contradiction and possibility by opening up the impact of new technology upon women as a global phenomenon. This 'second industrial revolution' is no longer confined to the old capitalisms of the richer countries; it is affecting poorer countries which have assimilated differing elements of that first industrial revolution. These new capitalisms, it is evident, can no longer compete by exploiting their resources of cheaper labour. The pressure of the international economy is pushing them towards new technology. Women, already recruited into the global assembly line, are yet again pivotal in this extraordinary process of transformation.

In differing ways these accounts pose the question: what kind of development will new technology bring for women? Gender stratification is already apparent within these very new technological processes. As Swasti Mitter observes, a reflex demand for equal opportunities is not sufficient. Although it is important that women rise through the existing structures, such an approach only accounts for the improvement in the circumstances of a minority. What is to become of the rest, concentrated in the lower echelons of information labour or indeed, of the women who vanish from view – the workers in manufacturing displaced by new technology? The material presented in this examination of new technology outlines the economic trends, but it also considers the differing social consequences for varying groups of women. Several of these essays moreover demonstrate that an exclusive focus on gender is misleading; ethnicity, race and class are just as significant. Gender in fact has no single meaning, but is affected by a whole complex of social relationships.

The questioning of how work is organized, how people relate within the structures of production and how paid work interrelates with daily life came out of the early women's groups in countries such as Britain, Italy, France and North America during the 1970s and early 1980s. There was, among socialist feminists, a concern to extend the opportunities for equality in workplaces and in society. But by the late 1980s this approach was being replaced by the preoccupation of popular media feminism with women on top. The meaning of 'feminism' narrowed. In contrast the women's movement in Asia and Latin America retained links with women workers and poor women's community groups, and presented a much broader social vision of the interconnecting changes necessary to improve women's lives. Despite the odds, these movements have been less susceptible to the fatalism which has paralysed the feminist movement in the west. The importance of internationalism is in the possibility of balancing strengths and weaknesses. Feminists in the richer countries do have institutional strengths and contact with other organizations, ranging from trade unions to churches. They also have a great deal to learn from women organizing at the grassroots in the developing countries.

These studies show how important it is to cast the questions about gender and the structuring of work in a global perspective. Workers in the North have already experienced that the body can be assailed as badly by the light 'modern' technology as it was by the steam-driven machinery of the first industrial revolution. In a few short years the hazards of new technology in conditions of intensified work and stress have wrecked many lives. Now, as the arguments for ergonomic workplaces, education about how hazards can be prevented and the necessity of changing patterns of continuous and stressful work begin to have an impact on unions, employers, legislators and – perhaps most important – insurance companies, new technology is reaching new groups of workers. It is important they too are able to communicate with groups working around the need to ensure that technology is geared to people's needs not profits.

The international character of capital is not of course entirely new, however the speed of change has accelerated. Recognition of the need for global links to exchange information about women's labour has led to the formation of several networks in the last decade, and these have interacted both with women at the grassroots, with NGOs, with trade unions and with the large international organizations. These *ad hoc* responses to vast new problems are fragile in contrast to the resources of large multinational companies, however they form a basis for comparing experiences and combining diverse skills. There is a real need for resources to strengthen exchanges which have been developed between women in the poorer countries, making sure that these involve both researchers and organizers, for direct contact enables comparisons and the interweaving of experience to occur. The structures of funding institutions and research are geared to richer countries, and there is a powerful tendency for information to be sucked towards the North and then get stuck in limited circuits of communication which move between academics. While it is important to extend intellectual enquiry and broaden the scope of study in the North, it is vital that the circuits are opened so that the information and ideas reach those directly affected. Women's studies after all had its origins not only in the desire to extend what was studied but to transform the power relationships in how knowledge was constituted and communicated.

All these accounts begin with what is happening, and there is no doubt at all that much of what they describe is a daunting picture; but as Swasti Mitter points out in her introduction they are all extremely particular, revealing considerable unevenness in the social contradictions generated by these new circumstances of labour. By gathering and comparing what has been done by women's groups and trade unionists, new technology ceases to be a Leviathan deskilling all and sundry, which was a determinism in the early 'labour process' thinking. It becomes instead a vehicle for various social possibilities. Beginning with what is does not make us accept that there is only one kind of production and that short-term gain is the only reality. But it does avoid the absolute utopianism which, being so total in its rejection of what is, fails entirely to engage with the actual happenings of the world. Instead this book takes on the transforming challenge of new technology, describing what is and suggesting what might be.

Index